A Personal Note from Ha

Do you feel frustrated when you use the Internet? Do you feel inadequate when something goes wrong and you don't know what to do? Are you confused when you want to find some information and you don't know where to start?

Let me tell you something. *Everyone* feels that way—everyone, that is, who has not yet learned how to use the Internet well.

There are many skills we need to develop in order to function well in our society. When we are young, we learn how to speak, read and write, and we spend years in school acquiring a basic education. As we get older, we learn how to drive a car, manage our money and live on our own. Although it is possible to live without these skills, few people would choose to do so.

Realistically, you can never be the total master of your fate, but if you have some understanding how things work, you *can* control your actions and, thus, have some influence over what happens to you.

With the Internet, all this takes is for you to develop a number of basic skills. Once you do — I promise you — you will feel a *lot* more comfortable and confident.

To take control of any situation, you need to understand the fundamental forces that are at work. My goal in this book is to explain how the Internet works, and how you can use it to get what *you* want.

Please read this book, and join me as we explore the various parts of the Internet. As you do, you can count on me in several important ways:

- I promise to discuss everything you need to get started: how to choose a computer, how to connect to the Net, and how to find the programs you will want to use.

- I promise to introduce you to the words and technical terms you will encounter as you learn about the Internet. I will explain each of these words to you and show you how to use them well.

- I promise to explain the important ideas you need to use the Internet, and how to use your programs well in harmony with these ideas.

- Most important, I promise to teach you how to understand what you are doing and how it fits into the Internet as a whole. I will show you the ideas be   power and beauty that

All I ask of you are two things.

First, read the entire book.

Although you can look up a particular topic and read it in isolation, I wrote this book for you to read from cover to cover — from start to finish. Please do so. You will not only enjoy yourself, you will find a lot more than you expect. (As I am sure you realize by now, this is not an ordinary computer book.)

Second, as you read, I want you to think about the following idea. As a human being, you are blessed with intelligence, creativity and curiosity. Many people never live up to their potential because they allow themselves to become lazy or discouraged. Along the way, such people lose (or never develop) self-confidence. They are afraid of new ideas, and they are scared that they will not be able to understand and master new technology.

I want to make sure this does not happen to you. I want to make sure you understand that everyone has trouble learning how to use complicated tools and understanding complicated ideas. The world is full of people who will promise to teach you quickly and simply, but don't be fooled. Learning how to use an intricate system well takes time and mental effort.

You and I are going to spend many hours together, and my job is to make sure that time is well spent. The Internet helps us communicate and learn. I wrote this book in the same spirit. As you read, I will be by your side: explaining, teaching and, at times, entertaining you.

Throughout this book, I will show you a lot more than how to use the Internet. I will show you how to work — and how to think about your work — with elegance and style. I will show you how to open doors that you may not even know exist. You and I will walk through those doors together, and, in the weeks and months that follow, you will find that our world is a lot more exciting and wonderful than you ever dreamed.

The Internet is important, and I want you to be able to use it well. I want you to understand what it does, how it works, and why it is so important to us.

Above all, I want you to enjoy using the Internet, secure in the knowledge that you know what you are doing, that you understand what is going on, and that you belong.

HARLEY HAHN

www.harley.com

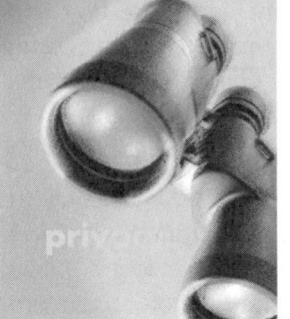

email

search

community

privacy

the web

security

HARLEY HAHN'S
internet

How to Make **Online** Life
Work for **YOU**

advisor

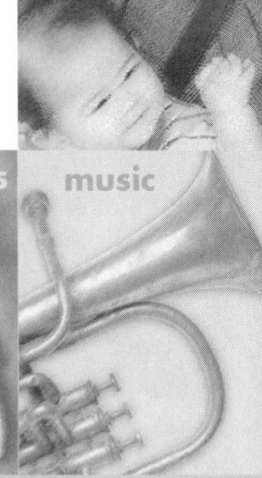

family

getting
started

relationships

music

QUE

HARLEY HAHN

About Harley

Harley Hahn is an internationally recognized writer, analyst and consultant. He is the author of 28 books on various topics, including the best-selling *Harley Hahn's Internet Insecurity*, *Harley Hahn's Internet Yellow Pages*, *Harley Hahn Teaches the Internet*, *Harley Hahn's Readme First Guide to the Internet*, *The Internet Complete Reference*, and the highly regarded *Assembler Inside & Out*. His Unix books include *Unix Unbound* and *Harley Hahn's Student Guide to Unix*.

Hahn has a degree in mathematics and computer science from the University of Waterloo, Canada, and a graduate degree in computer science from the University of California at San Diego. Before becoming a professional writer, he studied medicine at the University of Toronto Medical School, where he wrote the book *Unconventional Medicine Explained*.

Hahn enjoys writing computer books because "I get to sleep in, and I like telling people what to do."

Hahn does not live in a converted farmhouse in Connecticut with his wife, three children, and a Labrador retriever named Rolf. Nor does he commute frequently to New York.

His favorite pajamas are light blue.

email

search

community

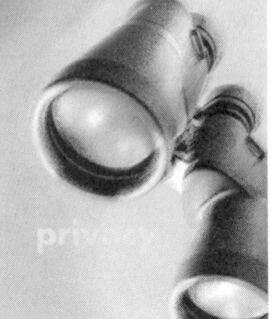
privacy

the web

security

HARLEY HAHN'S

internet

How to Make **Online** Life **Work** for **YOU**

advisor

family

getting
started

relationships   music

que®

HARLEY HAHN

Harley Hahn's Internet Advisor

International Standard Book Number: 0-7897-2697-1

Library of Congress Catalog Card Number: 2001096308

Printed in the United States of America

First Printing: November, 2001

04   03   02   01   4   3   2   1

The following are all registered trademarks of Harley Hahn: the names "Harley Hahn" and "Harley Hahn's Internet Exploration Station", the stylized Harley Hahn signature *HARLEY HAHN* and the Unisphere logo.

To Lydia Hearn, my Chief of Staff, who has never, ever had a book dedicated to her. Now she has.

List of Chapters

List of Figures

List of Internet Resources

Table of Contents

Acknowledgments

I'd like to take a few minutes to thank all the people who helped me put together this book. It may be, of course, that you don't personally care about any of these people. After all, why should you? You have never met any of them, and you probably never will. Boring, I hear you say, or, if you are French, *je m'en fiche*.

And you are right. After all, these people helped me, not you. So why should you spend your valuable time reading about a bunch of strangers? After all, you bought this book to learn about the Internet, not to find out that, say, Lydia Hearn is a remarkable copy editor, or that Cheryl Lenser is an innovative indexer.

So, to make this whole experience worth your while, I have carefully crafted these acknowledgments to provide you with valuable personal insight. Here is how it works.

Within this section, I am going to mention 8 different people. I have interviewed each of these people and asked them the following three questions:

1. When you were a child, what did you want to be when you grew up?

2. When you are not working, what is your favorite personal activity?

3. Right now, if you could do any work you wanted (not counting your current job), what would you choose to do?

After I talk about a particular person, I am going to tell you how that person answered the first two questions, regarding their childhood dream and their favorite activity. Your job, once you have finished reading, will be to guess how each of these 8 people answered question number three, about their ideal job. Later, I will show you how to use your guesses to find great insight into your own personality. (Wait and see.)

Before we start, here are the names of all the people I will be mentioning. To the right, you will see the list of the ideal jobs these people mentioned. However, the jobs are not in the correct order. Remember, your task, when you are finished reading this section, is to match up each person with his or her ideal job.

Names	Ideal Jobs
Cheryl Lenser	open public Internet clubs
Eugene Katunin	college-level philosophy teacher
Greg Wiegand	statistician for the L.A. Lakers
John Pierce	professional golfer
Lydia Hearn	lead singer in a rock band
Sandra Schroeder	Indy car race driver
Sharry Gregory	astronaut
Tom Hayes	explorer who discovers new lands

Ready? Okay, let's push on to the acknowledgments.

To start, I thank Lydia Hearn my chief of staff and copy editor, an absolute marvel. When she is not working with me, Lydia is a professor of English at De Anza College in Cupertino, California. She is also a talented singer, musician (piano), athlete (volleyball), and the most organized person I know. On a slow day, she performs only five or six miracles. On a busy day, she is a national wonder.

When Lydia was young, she wanted to be an Olympic volleyball player, sports writer and teacher (all at the same time, no doubt). When she is not working, her favorite activity is playing volleyball.

Next, I would like to thank my technical reviewer, Eugene Katunin. Eugene is an extremely intelligent, hard-working young man, who lives in Odessa, Ukraine. His job with this book, was to read everything closely, making comments on every technical point in every chapter. I first started to work with Eugene six years ago, when he was 14. At the time, he helped me with the research for the third edition of my Yellow Pages book (*Harley Hahn's Internet Yellow Pages*). Today, Eugene has a university degree in business and economics, and works as the sales and marketing manager for a freight forwarding company.

When Eugene was young, he wanted to be a captain of a large passenger ship. When he is not working, his favorite activity is driving his car to places he has never visited.

Moving on, I would like to thank various people at Que Publishing who worked with me on this book. Let's start with John Pierce, Director of Marketing for Que.

John is a visionary with a comprehensive grasp of the publishing industry and a fund of good stories. Moreover, he is one of the most highly skilled and knowledgeable people I know. I have spent a lot of time working with John, and I have to tell you, this guy knows everything. For example, I once had a lot of extra tomatoes from my garden. I told John and he sent me his personal recipes for "Marinated tomatoes stuffed with a shrimp salad" and "Tomato and okra salad". Aside from being a master chef, John understands history, psychology, literature, music — in fact, just about everything you would expect a cultured, educated man to know. He also has more insight into the publishing industry than anyone I have ever met. More than anyone, John is the person who helped me shape this book and bring life to my vision.

When John was young, he wanted to be a clinical psychologist. When he is not working, his favorite activity is playing the saxophone.

Greg Wiegand is an Associate Publisher at Que. This means that he is in charge of a particular area of publishing, in this case, consumer computer books. Greg worked with me for several months, planning this book, and organizing the production. During this time, I found Greg to be a quiet, phlegmatic, easy-going person, who is a delight to work with. Let me tell you something fascinating about Greg. In college, he was a competitive diver. In the summer between college and graduate school, Greg worked as a high-diver in an amusement park, where he would dive from an 80-foot platform into 8 feet of water. (The secret, according to Greg, is to land, feet first, in a way that your body slips into the water at an angle. This actually gives you about 15-20 feet in which to stop safely.)

When Greg was young, he wanted to be a veterinarian. When he is not working, his favorite activity is riding his bike, both mountain biking and road biking.

To conclude, I would like to thank several other people at Que Publishing who helped me create this book.

Tom Hayes is the managing editor who coordinated the production of the book. This calls for superb organizational skills, stamina and (since he is working with me, and I like to get everything perfect) lots of patience.

When Tom was young, he wanted to be a sports writer. When he is not working, his favorite activity is hiking in the mountains.

Cheryl Lenser is the indexer. In fact, she is the Best Indexer in the World. She is so good that I requested her specifically to index this book. At my request, Cheryl created a personalized style of indexing which, for historical reasons, we call "Jackson Double Post Topical Indexing". (Cheryl's maiden name was Jackson.)

When Cheryl was young, she wanted to be a mainframe computer operator. When she is not working, her favorite activity is playing with her birds.

Sandra Schroeder is the design manager and, as such, spent a lot of time creating the front and back cover of the book, as well as the interior design. She showed infinite patience, working with John Pierce and me until everything was perfect.

When Sandra was young, she wanted to be a biochemist. When she is not working, her favorite activity is gardening.

Sharry Gregory is a Team Coordinator at Que. As such, it is her job to handle all the administration, which takes a lot of skill. Sharry is a superb organizer, a highly responsible person who, single-handedly, makes sure that everything that needs doing is done right. In her spare time, Sharry has worked as a tax preparer for 13 years. In that time, she has learned a lot about people, which makes her especially pleasant to work with.

When Sharry was young, she wanted to be an elementary school teacher. When she is not working, her favorite activity is doing needlework.

So now that we have made it to the end of the acknowledgements, go back to the beginning and look at the list of people and ideal jobs. See if you can figure out which ideal job goes with which person. (If you really want to be cool, draw a line from each person to their job. That way anyone who picks up this book after you will be able to admire your skill at understanding other people.)

Once you have made your choices, check them against the correct answers below:

Names	Ideal Jobs
Cheryl Lenser	Indy car race driver
Eugene Katunin	open public Internet clubs
Greg Wiegand	astronaut
John Pierce	college-level philosophy teacher
Lydia Hearn	statistician for the L.A. Lakers
Sandra Schroeder	explorer who discovers new lands
Sharry Gregory	lead singer in a rock band
Tom Hayes	professional golfer

You can now grade yourself as follows:

If you scored 8-11 correct, congratulations. You are a shrewd student of human nature with a rare insight into other people. You are universally admired as someone who understands life and its nuances, with a degree of wisdom that is obvious to all who know you.

If you scored 4-7, you are a solid, middle of the road person, with both feet planted firmly on the ground. You have a strong appreciation for the thoughts of other people, but your intuition is tempered by experience, which keeps you from jumping into a new situation until you have analyzed it properly. Other people depend on you to keep an even keel when the going gets rough.

If you scored 0-3, you are a hard-working, creative person, not easily distracted by the actions of the people around you. You live in a world of your own, filled with enormous integrity and self-worth. For you, there is no higher calling than to set and achieve your goals based on what makes sense to you, as long as it is in harmony with your ideals.

Understanding the Internet

*Once you have access to
the Internet, the distinction
between your personal
computer and the rest of the
world begins to blur. You
will be connected.*

The INTERNET — often referred to as the NET — is a general-purpose, international communication and information system. Once you have access to the Net, there are many things you can do. You can send and receive messages, access a great deal of information, and participate in ongoing discussions with people all over the world. You can also read the news, chat with people, go shopping, search for information, play games, look at pictures, listen to music, watch videos, and find lots of free programs for your computer.

So what is the Internet? It's really not one simple thing, but rather, a complex collection of resources. To understand the Internet and what it means to us today, let's take a few moments and start at the beginning.

What Is the Internet?

The roots of the Internet go back to the late 1960s. At that time, a project called the ARPANET was funded by the U.S. Department of Defense (ARPA was the Advanced Research Projects Agency). The goal of the Arpanet was to connect a number of computing facilities around the United States.

In general, we connect computers in order to share information and resources. When we do so, it is called a computer NETWORK. The Arpanet was a long distance computer network with a special requirement, one that would later turn out to be very important to the Internet.

The late 1960s was during the Cold War, and the U.S. Department of Defense was particularly concerned with the possibility of nuclear attack. For this reason, the Arpanet was designed to keep working even if someone dropped a bomb on part of the network. If some of the communication links were destroyed, the rest of the network would still function.

The project to create such technology was successful, and throughout the 1970s and 1980s, the network expanded and became the Internet. At first, the Internet connected only military and university computers, but gradually, more and more companies and individuals joined. Today, millions of people around the world have access to the Net.

Thus, in a single generation, the Internet grew from an experimental project to a global network that has permanently changed our culture. By any standard, the Net has been fabulously successful. But why did this happen, and how did it happen so quickly? The answer is twofold.

First, the original technology developed for the U.S. Department of Defense has proven to be highly reliable. Although no one has ever dropped a bomb on the Internet, it is common for computers and communication lines to stop working temporarily. When this happens, the computers that run the Internet automatically re-route the flow of information around the broken links until they start working again. So one reason the Internet has grown so large is that it is so resilient.

When a computer or a communication line stops working, we say that the computer (or line) is DOWN. Similarly, when a computer or a line is working, we say that it is UP. The Internet is vast and at any time, there are bound to be some computers that are down. Regardless, the Internet as a whole is robust enough that it never goes down. In fact, the Internet is so large and so complex that there is really no way to turn it off.

Think about that. For the rest of your life — and for many years to follow — there will be an Internet and it will always be up. Indeed, the Internet will still be around when you and I are long gone.

The second reason the Net grew so quickly has to do with the nature of human beings. We are a species that loves to communicate. To participate in the Internet you need a computer, but it was not until the mid-1990s that personal computers became both powerful and inexpensive. However, once the average person could afford a PC, it didn't take long for tens of millions of people to buy computers and join the Net. The history of the 20th century shows us that people have always used new technologies to communicate faster and better. There is something in our biological blueprint that makes us want to talk to each other and to share information.

To be sure, everything is not perfect on the Net. There are dishonest people who will be glad to cheat you out of your money and lie to you if it will help them get what they want. And there are individuals who are willing to use the Internet for anything — legal or not — in order to make a buck.

But this is life, and any group of people is going to have its share of dishonesty and deceit. However, as you learn more about the Internet and how it works, you will come to a marvelous realization. The Internet provides a safe way for people to gather, and, when people feel safe, they have a natural tendency to share and to help one another.

The Internet is a wonderful system, and in a very real sense, it reflects our biological destiny as a species.

What Is It Like to Use the Net?

Using the Internet is a lot like using a computer for anything. You sit in front of the monitor (computer screen) and look at words and pictures; you use the keyboard to type words, commands and other information; and you use the mouse to click on particular objects and to make selections.

However, there are two important considerations when you use the Net. First, you can't use any Internet resources until your computer connects to the Internet. For home users, the most common way to access the Internet is to have your computer connect to another computer over a telephone or cable line.

The second consideration is that it takes longer to access information from the Internet than it does to access information from your own computer. For example, when you use a word processor to write a letter, the information you type is saved to a file on your computer. You can access that file whenever you want, usually within a second or two. When you access information over the Internet, you must wait for a request to be transmitted from your computer to a remote computer, and then for the information to be sent from the remote computer back to you.

Sometimes this happens so quickly, you don't even notice the delay. Other times, however, you will find yourself waiting for seconds at a time. Although this might not seem like much, your brain works quickly, and waiting even a few seconds can be boring and aggravating. For this reason, I suggest that you get yourself as fast an Internet connection as possible. (We will talk about Internet connections in more detail in Chapter 3.)

I'll tell you something interesting, though. Once you have access to the Internet, the distinction between your personal computer and the rest of the world begins to blur. Within a short time, you will become so used to accessing information from around the world that you will take your position in the global community for granted.

You will be *connected*.

The Secret of the Internet: Clients and Servers

The Internet is a vast network involving millions and millions of computers all over the world. So how is it that you can connect to the Net whenever you want and just start using it? And how can it be that you can sit in front of your computer, typing and mouse clicking, and have the Internet respond to what you are doing? The secret is an arrangement based on programs called "clients" and "servers". However, before we discuss clients and servers, I want to take a moment to talk about computers in general.

When we talk about a computer, we are really talking about three completely different systems working together. First, there is the HARDWARE, the physical parts of the computer (the machinery, so to speak). Second, there is the SOFTWARE, programs that control the operation of the computer. Finally, there is DATA, all the information that is stored in the computer.

What is a program? Most machines in our lives are designed for specific purposes. An oven heats food. A telephone lets us talk to another person. A car moves us from place to place. Computers are different in that they are designed as general-purpose machines capable of doing many, many things. A PROGRAM is a long list of instructions that, when carried out by a computer, make it act in a certain way. A computer is versatile because it can carry out many different programs, each of which makes the computer act differently.

When a computer follows the instructions in a program, we say that the computer RUNS or EXECUTES the program. For example, to make your computer act like a word processor, you tell your computer to run a word processing program.

Now let's relate this to the Internet.

Think about the telephone system for a moment. This is a system designed to be used by people. You pick up a phone and you call another person.

On the Internet, it is the computer programs — not the people — that communicate with one another. If you want something, you need to have a program do it on your behalf. Even when you send messages to another person, you need a program to carry the messages back and forth. Thus, the Internet is not really designed for human beings — it is designed for computer programs.

Just think for a second how totally cool this is. We (the human race) have created a huge, global information network in which computer programs — like trained robots — are constantly running around doing things for us.

Broadly speaking, there are two types of programs used on the Internet: those that provide a service and those that request a service. A program that provides a service is called a SERVER. A program that requests a service is called a CLIENT.

Here is an example. Say you want to use electronic mail to send a message to someone. You use a mail client program that runs on your computer. Once you have composed the message, your mail client uses the Internet to contact a mail server program on a remote computer. Your client sends the message to the server, which makes sure it is delivered. (Don't worry about the details for now.)

Similarly, you can use your mail client to check for messages that have been sent to you. Your client contacts the mail server and requests any messages that have been sent to your electronic mail address. The server sends the messages to your client, which then displays them on your computer.

Much of learning how to use the Internet involves learning how to use the various client programs. In Chapter 2, I will discuss many of the resources that are available on the Net — for example, electronic mail, the Web, and Usenet discussion groups. To use an Internet resource, all you need is an Internet connection, the appropriate client program (running on your computer), and a knowledge of how to use that program to get what you want. For example, to send and receive electronic mail, you use a mail client; to access the Web, you use a Web client; and to participate in a Usenet discussion group, you use a Usenet client.

So that is the secret of the Internet. The whole network is one large client/server system. The purpose of the Internet is to provide a reliable way to pass data between clients and servers.

To access the Internet, you use client programs that run on your computer. Your clients carry out your commands by passing data back and forth to server programs. A server program might be in the next room, across the country, or on the other side of the world. It's all the same to the client. And *that* is what makes the Internet so powerful.

How TCP/IP Makes the Internet Work

To make the Internet function, computers connect to one another in order to pass data (information) back and forth. In fact, one might characterize the Internet as millions of interconnected computers constantly passing around data. To make such communication efficient and reliable, the Internet uses a system in which data is sent in chunks. Here is how it works.

When a computer needs to send data to another computer, it divides the data into electronic PACKETS. The packets are numbered and marked with the address of the destination computer. They are then sent out over the Internet to be delivered. At the other end, the destination computer collects the packets and reassembles them into the original data.

For example, say you use electronic mail to send a picture of yourself to your mother. The actual picture is stored in a file on your computer. That file is broken into packets and sent to your mother's computer, where the packets are automatically reassembled into a copy of the original file. The beauty of the Internet is that your mother doesn't have to worry about the details. As far as she is concerned, the file was sent intact from your computer to hers. All she has to do is look at the picture and send you a message back asking when you are going to get a haircut.

This system has two important advantages. First, it is efficient. No matter how much information is sent from one computer to another, the data is always broken up into packets that are the same size, and the Internet is fine-tuned to transport such packets as quickly as possible.

Moreover, it doesn't matter how the packets are sent to the destination or in what order they arrive. The Net can route each packet using whatever connections are available at that moment. Because the packets are numbered, it is no problem to reconstruct the original data once all the packets reach the destination, even if they did not all follow the same route. This flexibility allows the Internet to operate as efficiently as possible.

The second advantage to this system is reliability. The destination computer has a way to test each packet as it arrives to see if any errors were

hint

A server is a program that offers a service, but we often use the word "server" to refer to the computer itself.

For example, say you are being given a tour of a company. As you pass a room full of computers, the tour guide points to one of the machines and says, "That's our Web server." What he really means is, "That's the computer that runs our Web server program."

introduced while the packet was in transit. If a packet has errors, the destination computer will send a message to the source computer asking it to send the packet again. In this way, all the data does not need to be resent, only those packets that arrived with errors. This system makes the Internet reliable without slowing things down unacceptably.

When computers send data back and forth, we say they TALK to one another. Of course, this is only a metaphor. Computers don't talk to each other the way people do. What is really happening is that a program running on one computer sends data to a program running on another computer. (Still, it's fun to imagine millions of computers on the Internet connecting and talking to each other, at high speed, without any help from humans.)

For this system to work, the various computer programs that run the Internet must be able to send and receive data according to standard specifications called PROTOCOLS. There are well over a hundred different protocols used on the Net, each for a specific purpose. For example, there are different protocols used to transport electronic mail, to distribute Web-based information, to copy files from one place to another, and so on. The Internet protocols are highly technical, and you certainly don't have to understand them to use the Net.

Still, some of them are used a lot, and you will see their names, so, for reference, I have listed the most important Internet protocols in Figure 1-1. Don't worry about understanding what they all mean for now. I just want you to see the list so you will recognize the various names when you see them.

hint

If you want to sound like a real pro when you talk about TCP/IP, don't pronounce the slash. Just say the five separate letters real fast.

For example, "Of course I know all about T-C-P-I-P. It's the family of protocols that is used to run the Internet."

The various Internet protocols are developed and approved by an organization called the INTERNET ENGINEERING TASK FORCE (IETF). The IETF forms working groups to study problems and create solutions. This allows the Internet to function smoothly and to evolve as conditions change.

Earlier, I explained that all data on the Internet is transported as packets. The two most important protocols are the ones that provide this basic transport. IP (Internet Protocol) is used to move data packets from one place to another. TCP (Transmission Control Protocol) manages the flow of packets and ensures that the data arrives intact without errors.

Figure 1-1: Important Internet (TCP/IP) Protocols

Name	Full Name	Purpose
DNS	Domain Name System	Translate domain names to IP numbers
FTP	File Transfer Protocol	Copy files between computers
HTTP	Hypertext Transfer Protocol	Distribute Web data (hypertext)
IMAP	Internet Message Access Protocol	Access mail and other messages
IP	Internet Protocol	Transport data packets
MIME	Multipurpose Internet Mail Extensions	Encode different types of data
NNTP	Network News Transfer Protocol	Distribute Usenet news articles
POP	Post Office Protocol	Get messages from a mail server
PPP	Point-to-Point Protocol	Connect a computer to the Internet
S/MIME	Secure MIME	Encode data securely
SMTP	Simple Mail Transfer Protocol	Send messages to a mail server
TCP	Transmission Control Protocol	Manage the flow of data packets
Telnet	Telnet	Log on to a remote computer

These two protocols are so important that the family of all the Internet protocols is called TCP/IP. Thus, what keeps the Internet running is millions of computers running millions of programs, all talking to each other using the TCP/IP set of protocols.

Talking About the Net

We all identify with our computers, much more than we like to admit. Perhaps this is because computers are brain tools: we use them to gather information, to help our thinking and to aid our creativity. You can see just how close we have become to the machines by noticing how we talk about them.

When you use a computer, it is common to talk as if you and the computer form one indivisible unit. For example, say you are in a bookstore — looking for new Harley Hahn books — and you run into a nerd (computer expert) who asks if you have any Internet problems.

"Well," you say, "I've been hearing about computer viruses. Do I need to do anything to protect myself against them?"

"Most of the time," replies the nerd, "viruses aren't much of a problem. However, if you are worried, you can always use an antivirus program."

Notice that the nerd talks as if *you* would use the program, even though programs are run by computers, not people. Notice also that you used the expression "protect myself" when you really meant "protect my computer".

This sort of talk is so common that we take it for granted, especially when we talk about the Internet. For instance, it is common to hear people say things like, "I went crazy during my vacation. I couldn't connect to the Net for a whole week."

Similarly, we use the word ON to describe being connected to the Internet. ("Shirley spent so much time on the Net, she didn't even notice her husband had run off to Venezuela with the cleaning lady.")

However, in one sense, using words in this way *is* accurate. The Internet is much more than computers and information and wires. A big part of the Internet — perhaps the major part — is the people who use it. When you use the Net, your mind connects to something a lot larger than yourself. As you will come to realize, the power of the Internet lies in its ability to connect millions of human minds into one gigantic, global organism.

Thus, you will see the word ONLINE used to describe anything that is connected to the Internet: people, computers or services. ("Shirley spent a lot of time using the Net, but her husband was rarely online, and she didn't get a chance to talk to him very often. Fortunately, she found a brand new Web site that had just come online, one where she could talk to people about relationships.")

Since people are so important to the Internet, I would like to finish this section by discussing a couple of words that are used on the Net to describe special types of people.

I have already referred to a nerd. A NERD or a GEEK is someone who spends large amounts of time engaged in an activity in which he is particularly knowledgeable.

Most of the time, these words are used to describe someone who knows a lot about computers and the Net. ("Tammy knows everything there is to know about designing Web sites. She's a real nerd." Or, "Alex is a Visual Basic geek, so ask him if you have any programming questions.")

However, a nerd or a geek can also be someone who has a particular type of esoteric knowledge. ("Eugene is the Buffy nerd around here, so he's the one to ask if you have any questions about Spike and Drusilla.")

The difference between a nerd and a geek is that nerds spend a lot of time by themselves, while geeks have better social skills. In other words, a geek is a nerd who is cool. ("I wish I had the nerve to ask out Lunaea on a date. She's such a Buffy geek.")

Words to Avoid

As you learn to use the Net, you will encounter a great deal of Internet terminology, and throughout this book I will be teaching you a lot of new words. However, there are a few words I want you to avoid, so let's talk about them now.

First, never, ever use the word SURF to refer to using the Internet. This word is so overused as to instantly mark you as a person who doesn't know what he is talking about. This is fine if you are a politician giving a speech about "Communication in the 21st Century", but for everyone else, "surfing" is out.

Similarly, never use the word CYBERSPACE (or cyber-anything for that matter) to refer to the Net. If there was ever a time when these words were cool, it passed a long time ago.

What's in a Name?

surf

cyberspace

information superhighway

Using the word "surf" in relation to the Internet comes from an article entitled *Surfing the Internet*, written for a librarian's journal by Jean Armour Polly in 1992. After the journal was published, Polly used the Internet to make the article available for free, and it soon became enormously popular. By the mid-1990s, people all over the world were using the word "surf" to refer to cruising around within a big system, for example, "surfing the Internet" or "channel surfing" (jumping from one TV channel to another).

The word "cyberspace" comes from a 1984 book called *Neuromancer*, written by William Gibson. In the book, cyberspace was a futuristic computer-mediated environment. As the Internet became popular, the word "cyberspace" — and then the prefix "cyber" — was used to refer to anything having to do with computer networks.

My advice is to never use any of these words. "Surf" and "cyberspace" haven't been cool for years.

hint

If you spend a lot of time on the Net, try to become a geek rather than a nerd.

Finally, I want to mention the word NEWBIE. A newbie is a person who is a newcomer to the Net, but the only people who use this word are newbies, so please, leave it out of your vocabulary.

The Internet is a place where how you talk and how you act is much more important than what you look like, where you live, or how much money you have. People on the Net will judge you by the words you use, and I want you to look good. You are one of my readers, and it is important to me that people see you as the intelligent, discriminating and thoughtful human being you are — not a clueless goober.

(After all, if you were a dummy you wouldn't be reading *this* book.)

Who Runs the Internet?

Nobody runs the Internet. This is because the Internet is not one big network. It is actually a collection of many, many smaller networks, computers and data communication lines. Each of these pieces is administered by some person or organization, but no one manages the Internet as a whole.

For example, say that a company has 100 computers connected into a local network. This network connects to the Net, providing Internet access to each of the 100 people who use those computers. The company is responsible for managing its part of the Net: the 100 computers, the local network, and the link to the Internet.

Here is another example. Consider a large university that has thousands of computers. These computers are organized into many small networks that connect to a larger, campuswide network. The campuswide network connects to the Net, giving everyone at the university Internet access. The university as a whole manages the campuswide network and the main Internet connection. Each individual department manages its own local computers and networks.

This sense of responsibility scales down as well. You are responsible for your own part of the Net: your computer. It is only a small part, and it is yours and you are in charge of it.

That is how the Internet is administered. Each person or organization is responsible for their own part and nothing more. So although every part of the Internet is managed by somebody, no one is in charge of the whole thing.

One important characteristic of the Net is that, because no one is in charge, you have a great deal of freedom. For example, you can say whatever you want, and you can offer whatever information you want to the world at large. Remember, though, other people have the same freedom, so you need to be careful. No one regulates the Net and if something bad happens or someone offends you, there is no one to whom you can complain. It is up to *you* to keep yourself out of trouble (but it is also up to you to have fun).

You might wonder, why is the Internet organized this way? Human beings do not generally set up organizations without putting somebody in charge. The answer is that the Internet was not developed to reflect human nature. The Internet was developed to offer reliable connections between *computers*.

Earlier in the chapter, I explained that the technology that drives the Net was originally developed by an agency of the U.S. Department of Defense. Their goal was to create a network that would keep functioning if parts of the network went down. To achieve this goal, the creators of the Internet came up with a design in which each part of the Internet has its own independent existence, and a computer can access the Net simply by connecting to any computer that is already on the Net.

As human beings started to use the Internet, they created a strange mixture of human/computer collaboration in which intelligence and power are distributed throughout the Net and not centralized. What makes this even more remarkable is that virtually all of this creation was done without conscious thought on our part. Each of us just does what comes naturally, not really thinking about what the whole thing means on a global scale.

Thus, as we begin the 21st century, we find ourselves with the Internet — a marvelous communication and information system that is large enough to span the globe and small enough to connect to a single personal computer — all without having anyone in charge.

No one runs the Net and no one owns the Net, but don't let that bother you. No one owns the sun and the stars, and no one runs the air, the water and the land, but somehow everything works just fine.

The Net is relatively new, but it is going to be here for the rest of your life —and it will be around long after you and I are gone.

Where Is the Center of the Net?

On the Internet, the lines of communication stretch out indefinitely in every direction. The reason is that TCP/IP — the family of protocols used to run the Net — was designed to transport data packets between any two specific computers. Still, there is no way to send data to everyone at the same time. This is fortunate, because if the Net did have universal broadcasting capabilities, it wouldn't be long before the entire network would become completely clogged to the point of uselessness. (Just imagine, for example, what the Internet would be like if companies could broadcast commercials.)

This gives rise to an interesting phenomenon. In theory, having Internet access allows you to reach millions of people. In practice, since there is no way to broadcast to everyone, you can't really reach people unless they want to reach you, or unless you have their electronic mail addresses.

For instance, say you put up some information on your own personal Web site. (We'll talk about the Web later.) In theory, millions of people around the world can now access that information. In practice, however, there is no way to compel anyone to look at your site, and the chances of millions of people visiting are remote.

However, the Net is a funny place. Once you put something on your Web site, people who are interested in that type of information will find it. As strange as it seems, on the Net, information has a life of its own. If you offer something that is important or useful or interesting or fun, the word will spread and the right people will find you.

Let's say, for example, you enjoy model railroads, so you create an interesting Web site devoted to your hobby. It won't be long before the model railroad enthusiasts will find you. Word will spread in various ways: by electronic mail, within various discussion groups, and on the Web itself. Pretty soon, other model railroad buffs will start to make links from their Web sites to your Web site.

There are other ways in which information spreads on the Net (including special tools we call "search engines"), and we will talk about them throughout the book. For now, all I want is for you to begin to appreciate the power of the Net and why it is so good for humanity. The Net helps people find what they want when they want it, and it brings like-minded people together to share and to collaborate.

hint

Wherever you are is the center of the Net.

Pornography, Bad People, and Other Evil Things Hastening the Downfall of Civilization

Since no one runs the Internet, there are no Net police, and people can pretty much do what they want. Of course, you still have to follow the laws where you live. For example, if you make money on the Net, you do have to pay taxes, and if you break the law, you can be arrested.

Humans do not function well in anarchy, and, through the years, a great many customs have developed to make the Net a tolerable place. The most important custom is that you are responsible for your own actions. You are not responsible for the actions of other people. If you disagree with what someone is doing, ignore it; if you don't like certain people, avoid them; and if you are bothered by the information or pictures someone has put on a Web site, don't look at them.

This isn't as harsh as it sounds. The Net is used by millions of people from many different cultures, and there is no possible way to devise laws — or even guidelines — that would be acceptable to everyone. From the beginning, the custom has been to live and let live, and, as a result, the Net has become our primary vehicle for free speech and dissemination of information.

When you first start using the Net, this may bother you. I guarantee that, with only a little effort, you will be able to find a great deal of material that will offend you. For example, no matter what beliefs you hold sacred, there are Web sites accessible to anyone in the world that ridicule and criticize your beliefs, and there's not much you can do about it.

Let's take an example. In the United States, there are many people who are offended by the fact that there is pornography on the Net. If you are such a person, I understand how you feel (although I don't agree with you). In the U.S., this issue is aggravated by the fact that Americans (as compared to, say, Europeans) are particularly troubled by displays of sexuality and naked bodies.

Thus, many people are bothered by the fact that anyone with an Internet connection can access pictures of all the naked bodies he or she wants. Will this not corrupt our youth, they ask? Do we not have an obligation to protect the moral fiber of our nation and teach enduring values to our children?

The answer is, yes, we do have those obligations, but the way to fulfill them is not by censorship — not on the Net, anyway. The Internet is important to everyone, and to restrict access to anyone because of the fear of what he or she will see or do is not only a bad idea, it is short-sighted.

The Internet is still a new part of our culture and, as such, it demands a new approach to how we think about the rest of the world. We need to teach our children — and ourselves — how to understand and use this wonderful communication and information system. In particular, we need to develop our judgment, our tolerance and our self-control.

I don't mean to preach —well... yes, I do, but I care about you, and I know what I am talking about, so listen to what I have to say.

Judgment: Just because you read something on the Net doesn't mean you should believe it. Before you accept anything as fact, ask yourself, "Does it make sense? Is it likely to be true?" Do your own research; ask tough questions and look for corroboration. On the Internet, you must be extra careful not to pay too much attention to appearances: some of the most despicable organizations have the most beautiful Web sites. You must learn to judge information on its own merits, and you must be skeptical of anything that doesn't look right.

Tolerance: No matter what you believe, there are many, many people in the world who disagree, and a lot of them are on the Net. Don't let it get to you. If you really don't want to look at something, you don't have to look; if you really don't want to hear something, you don't have to listen. However, it isn't inherently bad to read or listen to things that are antithetical to what you believe. Tolerance not only makes you easier to get along with, it can open doors you didn't even know existed. The Internet is a safe place to explore ideas that are strange to you, and to meet people with different values. If you give the Net a chance, it will bring out the best in you.

Self-control: Not everything on the Net is good for you. In fact, there is probably a lot that is bad for you. The Internet is a wonderful source of stimulation, but there are times when we all need to exercise self-control. For example, there are various games and activities that can become addictive, especially for certain types of people. This is important for children to learn as they use the Net. If you are a parent, there are computer programs you can use to limit what your kids can and cannot look at, but no program is perfect. Nothing can take the place of a parent who takes the time to teach his or her children what is right and what is wrong. I think you'll find that the best way to teach is by setting a good example.

So what about all the pornography? The Internet has shown us that looking at pictures of naked men and women has an enormous universal appeal, and that's not going to change. Moreover, pornography isn't the only thing to worry about: the Net has its share of dishonest people, misleading information, harmful activities, and ways to waste your money. Should we be concerned?

Of course we should, but on the Net, censoring the activities of other people doesn't work. What does work is to spend some time and effort developing your judgment, tolerance and self-control. In my book, anyone who tells you different is trying to sell you something. (This is my book.)

2

An Overview of the Internet

*Human beings love to
communicate. We love
to talk, argue, share
information, complain,
gossip, solve problems,
tell jokes, spread rumors,
ask questions and
help one another.*

The Internet is a global information and communication system that is used by millions of people all over the world. Once you start to use the Net, you will be astonished by the amount of imagination and creativity you will find. In this chapter, I will take you on a guided tour of the Net. Along the way, I will introduce you to some of the important words and terms we use to talk about the Internet and its resources.

If you are new to the Net, you may be wondering what everyone is talking about. Let's start by talking about what the Net has to offer to you.

What Can You Do on the Net?

I explained in Chapter 1 that the Internet is based on technology developed in the late 1960s by ARPA, an agency of the U.S. Department of Defense. The original network (which later became the Internet) offered a single service: you could use the network to run programs on a remote computer. Soon after, two more services were added: you could copy files from one computer to another, and you could send messages by electronic mail.

Over the years, the Internet has expanded enormously, and you can now use the Net for many different things. Here are some examples:

- Send and receive electronic mail
- Access information on just about any topic you can imagine
- Talk with other people
- Play games (by yourself or with other people on the Net)
- Read the daily news (and the comics, weather and sports)
- Take part in ongoing discussions
- Do research
- Get free software for your computer
- Shop for just about anything
- Buy and sell stocks
- Display maps and driving instructions
- Look up someone's address and telephone number

- Do your banking and check your credit card accounts

- Make payments

- Buy and sell using online auctions

- Listen to music, radio, concerts and other live events

- Plan a trip, make reservations, buy tickets

- Study, learn, take classes

- Watch video

- Visit imaginary environments

- Gamble

All the activities I mentioned above are built on just a few basic Internet services. In this chapter, I will explain these services and teach you the most important words and technical terms you need to know to use the Net well. My goal is to give you an overview of what you can do on the Net, so for now don't worry about the details. We will cover them later in the book.

hint

When it comes to the Net, just about anything you can think of is out there somewhere.

A Quick Overview of Email

(We will talk about email in detail in Chapters 5 and 6.)

ELECTRONIC MAIL is a facility that allows you to send messages to anyone on the Internet. In addition, once you are on the Net, anyone else can send messages to you. Electronic mail is usually referred to as EMAIL or, more simply, MAIL. Both words are also used as verbs, for example, "Would you like me to mail you an invitation to my sausage party?"

Everyone on the Internet has an email ADDRESS. In order to send mail to someone, you must have his address. Similarly, if you want someone to be able to send you mail, you must give him your address.

Standard messages consist of regular text you type using your keyboard. However, you can also ATTACH a file of data to a message, and the file will be delivered along with the message. (The file is referred to as an ATTACHMENT.) For example, you can send someone a word processing document by saving it to a file and attaching the file to a message. In general, you can attach anything that can be stored in a file: a picture, a program, a voice message, and so on.

To have mail service, you arrange for an account on a MAIL SERVER. This is a computer that acts as a local email post office for a group of people. When someone sends you a message, it is stored on the mail server until you pick it up. The company that provides you with Internet access, your INTERNET SERVICE PROVIDER or ISP, will also provide you with mail service (including an email address).

As I explained in Chapter 1, you access Internet facilities by running client programs on your computer. For email, you use a mail client, commonly referred to as a MAIL PROGRAM.

The job of your mail program is to send and receive messages on your behalf. When you send a message, your mail program looks at the address and then delivers the message to the mail server that accepts mail for that address. To accept incoming messages, your mail program contacts your mail server and checks to see if any messages are waiting for you.

On the Internet, when people use the word "mail", they always mean email. When it is necessary to talk about post office mail, people will sometimes refer to it as SNAIL MAIL (the implication being that post office mail is slow compared to email). For example, you might tell someone, "I'll mail you the marriage proposal, and if you like it, I'll send you the final copy by snail mail."

In everyday conversation, we use the word "email" (or "mail") in two different ways. First, to refer to the idea of electronic mail in general:

- "Mary uses email for everything, even accepting marriage proposals."

Second, to refer to actual messages:

- "Martin's mother wouldn't let him see the movie until he had answered all his email."

In general, it sounds better if you do not refer to messages as "emails". For example, do not say, "I received several emails yesterday," or "Please send me an email." Instead, say, "I received several messages," or "Please send me email." Here is a real-life example to show you what I mean.

Overheard in the fruit and vegetable section of a grocery store:

Mr. Wrong: Excuse me, ma'am.

Beautiful Woman: Yes?

Mr. Wrong: If you give me your Internet address, I would be glad to send you an email.

Mr. Right: Excuse me, ma'am, but I, too, would like your address, so I can send you email.

Beautiful Woman: I am sorry, Mr. Wrong, but I do not give my email address to people who obviously don't know the first thing about the Net. Mr. Right, I would be glad to give you my address, because you are such a cool dude. Also, you may carry my pomegranates.

A Quick Overview of the Web

(We will talk about the Web in detail in Chapter 7.)

The WEB is an information delivery system that can display many different types of data and allow you to access a variety of services. The Web is unlike anything that has ever existed, and is the most powerful and most popular part of the Internet — so much so that beginners sometimes think the Web *is* the Net. Actually, the Web is only one part of the Internet, but as you will come to see, the lines that separate the Web from the rest of the Net are often blurry.

The Web is based on the concept of HYPERTEXT, data that contains LINKS to other data or to resources. As you look at hypertext, you can use the links to jump from one place to another. All you have to do is use your mouse to click on a link, and the data you are looking at will be replaced by new data. When this happens, we say that you are FOLLOWING the link. Here is an example to show you how it works.

Let's say you are using the Web to read a hypertext article about gardening. Throughout the article, the author has placed links to related information, such as plant care, pest control, growing seasons, choosing new plants, and so on. Within the hypertext, the links are displayed in a special way so they will stand out (for example, they may be underlined or in a special color).

To follow a link, you click on it with your mouse. In our example, you might click on the "plant care" link. When you do, the article you are reading will be replaced on your screen by an article about plant care. If, instead, you click on the "pest control" link, you will jump to an article about pest control. And within these new articles, there will be more information containing more links.

Thus, the basic experience of using the Web is read, click, read, click, read, click. As you use the Web, you get a definite impression of jumping from one place to another.

What's in a Name?

hypertext

Web

In science fiction, spaceships need to travel vast distances in a short time. To make this possible, science fiction authors commonly have the ships travel through something called "hyperspace". Traveling in hyperspace allows a ship to jump magically from one side of the galaxy to another in a brief instant. (Actually, it's not a bad way to travel, except there's usually a 30 minute wait for luggage.)

When you use the Web, you click on links to jump from one Web page to another, similar to a spaceship jumping through hyperspace. Back in 1981, a fellow named Ted Nelson wrote a book called *Literary Machines* in which he coined the word "hypertext" to describe the type of data that might make this possible (that is, data containing links to other data).

In 1989, two scientists, Tim Berners-Lee and Robert Caillau, started work on a project to provide access to hypertext over a computer network. They conceived of their system as a large "web" of information. When the first version was ready, in May 1991, they decided to call it the WORLD WIDE WEB. Over time, as the system evolved, the name World Wide Web was shortened to the "Web".

The Parts of the Web

When we talk about computers, we use the word "data" to refer to all the various types of information. In broad terms, there are three types of data:

- TEXT consists of characters: the letters of the alphabet, numbers, punctuation, and so on.

- GRAPHICS refers to pictures, such as drawings, photographs and illustrations, as well as other visual elements.

- MULTIMEDIA refers to things that move or make sounds, such as animation, video and audio.

Information on the Web is organized into files called WEB PAGES. Web pages can contain not only data (such as text, graphics and multimedia), but programs as well. Thus, where some Web pages are simple, containing only plain text with perhaps a few pictures, other pages are sophisticated productions with graphics, sound and animation, all tied together with programs that run automatically, doing wondrous things.

Throughout the Internet, there are a vast number of computers called WEB SERVERS that store Web pages and make them available to anyone. There are literally hundreds of millions of Web pages available on the Net, with more being created all the time.

A collection of related Web pages created by a particular person or organization is called a WEB SITE (often spelled as a single word "website"). Many companies and individuals have their own Web sites, and once you get some experience, you will be able to create your own. Once you create some Web pages and put them on a Web server, anyone in the world will be able to look at them.

To access the Web, you use a program called a BROWSER to act as your Web client. Whenever you request a Web page, your browser contacts the appropriate Web server and asks for a copy of that page. Once the information arrives, your browser displays it for you. (You may have to wait a few moments, especially if you have a slow Internet connection.)

There are many browsers available for free on the Net. However, by far, the two most popular are INTERNET EXPLORER, developed by Microsoft, and NETSCAPE, developed by Netscape Communications (which used to be independent but is now owned by AOL).

What's in a Name?

Netscape

The Netscape software is actually a collection of programs called Netscape Communicator. Within this collection, the browser is named Netscape Navigator. However, informally, we generally refer to the browser as "Netscape".

Thus, if you are talking to someone about the Internet, he might ask you, "Which browser do you use, Internet Explorer or Netscape?"

Browsers are designed to perform several different jobs. The basic job of a browser is to act as a Web client. As such, your browser displays Web pages for you and follows whatever links you click on with your mouse.

hint

When you see the word "hypertext" used to describe the content of Web pages, remember that it can contain graphics and multimedia as well as plain text.

hint

On the Internet, anyone can be a publisher.

In addition, most browsers are integrated with mail clients and Usenet clients. That means you can use your browser not only to access the Web, but to send and receive mail, and participate in Usenet discussion groups (see below).

The Internet Explorer browser has a fourth function: it can also act as a file manager, allowing you to access all the information and programs on your computer. This is part of Microsoft's plan to make their browser an integral part of the overall Windows working environment.

Internet Talk Facilities

(We will discuss talk facilities in detail in Chapter 8.)

The Net is a great place to talk to people. You can keep in touch with friends, or talk to people you don't know and make new friends. There are lots of ways to talk on the Net, but before we get into the details, I want to discuss a basic idea: what do we mean by the word "talk"?

In regular life (off the Net), we talk by speaking, whether in person or on the phone. On the Net, it is possible to have voice communication, but much of the time we communicate by typing what we want to say. Thus, when we say TALK, we refer to typing messages back and forth, as well as regular speech.

There are a variety of ways in which you can talk on the Net. You can have a private conversation with one person at a time; you can have a private discussion with a group of people so that everyone in the group can see what the others are typing; or you can talk in a public area, where anyone who wants can join the conversation. Some public discussions are devoted to particular topics, others are for general conversation. You can choose whatever you feel like at the moment.

The most common talk Internet facility is known as IM or INSTANT MESSAGING. Instant messaging is easy, and it is extremely popular among teenagers, who like to spend hours and hours talking to their friends. This is especially true among AOL users, because instant messaging is built into the AOL system.

Another way to talk to people is found on the Web. There are a great many public talk areas called CHAT ROOMS. Some chat rooms are for general discussion; others are devoted to specific topics. Using a chat room is even simpler than using IM. You just visit the Web page where the chat room resides, enter the chat, and start talking.

The largest and oldest talk facility on the Net, IRC (Internet Relay Chat), is more complex. There are a variety of different IRC networks, each of which has many CHANNELS. Each channel supports a single conversation, often with many people talking at the same time. You can join any channel you want and be part of the conversation, and you can start your own channels whenever you want. If you like a lot of stimulation, you can join more than one channel at the same time and try to follow several conversations at once.

Aside from IM, Web chat rooms and IRC, there are talk facilities within imaginary environments called muds. A MUD is a text-based world in which you adopt the role of an imaginary character. Most muds are devoted to particular themes, such as fantasy, gothic or science fiction. Since muds are text-based, you don't see any pictures. Instead, you read descriptions of places, people and events, and build your own vision using your imagination (just like when you read a book). But unlike a book, muds are interactive: what you experience depends on what you do.

Muds are multiuser, which means that many people can use the mud at the same time. Whenever you are on a mud, you will be able to see and talk to anyone else who is there. Some muds are devoted mainly to conversation and are highly social places. Other muds are designed more for adventures: killing monsters, going on quests, accumulating points, and so on. Adventure muds can be complex places, and it may take you weeks or months to explore everywhere and become a master.

Like everything you do on the Net, talking requires the use of a client program. The client you use depends upon which talk facility you are using. With Web chat rooms, your client is your browser. To use IM, IRC or a mud, you need special-purpose clients — an IM client, an IRC client, or a mud client — which you can get for free on the Net.

These clients provide a variety of useful services aside from talking. For example IM and IRC clients allow you to transfer files from one person to another, share pictures, and send quick, private messages to someone during a conversation.

I mentioned earlier that most talking on the Net is by typing messages back and forth. This is true, but it is also possible to talk using speech, just like a telephone. Talking in this way can be a lot of fun because you can hear people's voices from all over the world, and you talk as long as you want without having to pay long distance bills. Of course, if you want to talk in this way, your computer will need a microphone and speakers. (Most new computers come with such hardware.)

In addition, there are systems that allow other people to look at you as you talk. Again, you need the appropriate equipment. Aside from a microphone and speakers, you also need a special video camera, called a WEBCAM.

Downloading Free Software

(We will talk about downloading software in detail in Chapter 9.)

There is an enormous amount of free software available on the Net. Most of this software is made available via a system called anonymous FTP. Although you don't hear people talk much about anonymous FTP, it is one of the most important services on the Internet because it allows reliable, worldwide distribution of software and other data. However, before I explain how it works, we need to go over some basic terminology.

Let's start with the idea of a file. On a computer, a FILE is a collection of data (information), that is stored under a particular name. Files can contain any type of data, such as word processing documents, pictures, email messages, Web pages, computer programs, and so on. Your computer has many files stored on its hard drive (a storage device inside the main box). Files are also stored on other types of media, such as CDs, floppy disks, removable disk cartridges and tapes.

One of the basic services offered by the Internet is the capability of copying files from one computer to another. This is important because it allows you to get programs from other computers to use on your own computer.

When you copy a file from a remote computer to your computer, we say you DOWNLOAD the file. When you copy a file from your computer to a remote computer, we say you UPLOAD the file.

The service that provides a lot of the file transfer on the Net is called FTP (the name stands for File Transfer Protocol). FTP can be used in two ways. First, if you have permission to use a particular computer, you can use FTP to copy files to or from that computer. In such cases, you will need a user name and a password to access the remote computer.

An example of when you might use FTP in this way is when you create your own Web site. As I explained earlier in the chapter, to make your own Web site, you create some Web pages and then copy them to a Web server. You design the Web pages on your own computer and store them in files. Once they are ready, you can use FTP to upload the files to the Web server. In other words, you "publish" your Web pages by using FTP to copy them to a Web server where they can be accessed by anyone on the Net.

What's in a Name?

FTP

FTP — File Transfer Protocol — is the name of the service that allows you to copy files from one Internet computer to another. On the Net, we also use the word "FTP" as a verb. For example:

Jack: When is the new Web site going to be ready?

Jill: Well, I've made all the final changes. All I have to do is FTP the files to the Web server.

Jack (who grew up in the Sixties): Far out!

There is a great need on the Net to be able to distribute programs and other files to the general public. All over the Net, there are many computers, called FTP SERVERS, that store files for public downloading via FTP. However, FTP requires that you have a user name and password in order to be able to access the files on a remote computer.

Clearly, it is not feasible to give each person in the world a user name and password for every FTP server. Instead, we use a system called ANONYMOUS FTP that allows anyone, anywhere, to access particular files on an FTP server. This is the second way in which FTP can be used. Here is how it works.

The people running the FTP server set aside a special area to hold files for the general public to download. To access these files, you use FTP to connect to the computer and then specify a user name of **anonymous** with any password that you want. (The custom is to use your email address as a password. This allows the people running the FTP server to see who is using it.) Once you connect to an FTP server in this way, you are allowed to download any of the files that have been placed in the public anonymous FTP area. However, you are not allowed to access files in the nonpublic areas.

The power of anonymous FTP is that it can allow anyone to download anything. In particular, anonymous FTP is used to distribute the software that runs the Net. This is one of the most important reasons why the Internet was able to grow so quickly. On a more personal level, anonymous FTP provides you and me with free access to a massive amount of software and information.

hint

There are many programs you can use to design Web pages. Some of these programs are able to upload the finished pages right to your Web server. Although you may not realize it, these programs are using FTP behind the scenes.

To use FTP, you need an FTP CLIENT program. All browsers can act as FTP clients for anonymous FTP. In fact, when you download software or other files from a Web site, you are sometimes using anonymous FTP without even knowing it. The browser will take care of all the details automatically (such as specifying the user name of **anonymous** and a password). All you will have to do is tell the browser where you want to store the downloaded file.

If you need more than anonymous FTP — for example, if you need to upload files — you need a more powerful FTP client. There are many such programs available on the Net.

A Quick Overview of Usenet

(We will talk about Usenet in detail in Chapter 13.)

Human beings love to communicate. We love to talk, argue, share information, complain, gossip, solve problems, tell jokes, spread rumors, ask questions and help one another. In my years of using computers, I have noticed an enduring principle I believe is a part of human nature. Whenever a new technology arises, people will find a way to use it to talk to one another. Nowhere is this better illustrated than with Usenet.

USENET is a system of discussion groups in which people all over the Net participate in ongoing discussion. There are thousands of different Usenet groups. Each group is devoted to a particular topic, and you can join the discussion for free. In its infancy, Usenet was originally designed for the posting of news articles, so you will often see the discussion groups referred to as NEWSGROUPS. Usenet itself is often referred to the NEWS, or sometimes NETNEWS.

Within the various Usenet newsgroups, people discuss every topic imaginable in perfect freedom with no censorship. The topics include serious discussions of science, health, computers, politics and culture; less serious chat about movies, music, sex and television; and lots of jokes, humor, complaining and debate. Literally, any topic you can think of is discussed somewhere on Usenet.

What's in a Name?

Usenet

Usenet was started in 1979. At the time, the Internet had not yet developed. The people who started Usenet used computers that ran an operating system (master control program) called Unix, which had been developed by AT&T.

At the time, there was a Unix users group called the Usenix Association (which still exists). This group had originally been called the Unix Users Group. However, the word "Unix" was a trademark of AT&T, and their lawyers were very picky about who could use the name, so the group decided to change their name to Usenix.

The inventors of Usenet chose the name "Usenet" to sound like Usenix, because they hoped that the Usenix Association would help organize the new discussion group system (they didn't). In retrospect, the name was a good one for two reasons. First, it sounds like the word "Internet", and, second, it looks like an abbreviation for "users network".

In addition to public newsgroups, Usenet can also be used for discussions within an organization or group. For example, I have a friend who is a professor of mathematics at Cornell University. His classes use local Usenet groups to discuss questions and answers for the course. Usenet is used this way in many schools.

To access Usenet, you use a client program called a NEWSREADER. Both of the popular browsers (Internet Explorer and Netscape) can act as newsreaders. So to access Usenet, you can either use your browser or get a special-purpose newsreader program. (Serious Usenet people often prefer the special-purpose newsreaders.)

People participate in Usenet by sending messages, called ARTICLES or POSTINGS, to the newsgroups. Using your newsreader, you can read the articles in any group. You can also send in articles of your own which can then be read by anyone on the Net. Articles are stored on computers called NEWS SERVERS and are saved for at least several days. Thus, at any time, you can use your newsreader to see what people are currently talking about in a particular group.

If you want to use Usenet, your newsreader must have access to a news server, and it is up to you to find such a service. However, most Internet service providers maintain a news server as a service to their customers, so Usenet access usually comes free with an Internet connection.

Although we talk a lot about the Web, it is not the only important part of the Internet. Throughout this book, I will teach you about the Web, but I also want to make sure that you appreciate Usenet and learn how to use it well. You will find Usenet to be especially useful when you have a question or when you need to find out some information. Just send a message to the appropriate discussion group, and more than likely, someone will read your request and post an answer.

People love to talk, and on the Net, people have been talking on Usenet for over two decades.

A Quick Overview of Mailing Lists

(We will talk about mailing lists in detail in Chapter 14.)

MAILING LISTS, like Usenet, are used for ongoing discussions among people all over the Net. However, with a mailing list, all the messages are sent via email. Instead of using a newsreader client to access a Usenet news server, you simply read the messages that appear in your incoming mailbox.

There are many thousands of mailing lists that cover just about any topic you can imagine. Like Usenet, mailing lists are free. However, you do need to join a list in order to participate. When you want to stop receiving mail from the list, you need to remove yourself from the distribution.

How do mailing lists compare to Usenet? Both Usenet and mailing lists are used for public and private discussions. In the same way that there are local Usenet groups, there are a great many private mailing lists that are set up for a select group of people.

However, there are some differences. Mailing lists tend to have more serious, longer lasting discussions, while Usenet newsgroups are like open forums where anybody can show up and say whatever they want. On the other hand, Usenet is better for browsing. You can check a newsgroup and see what articles happen to be there whenever you feel like it. With a mailing list, you have to join the list and wait for messages to arrive in your mailbox.

Finally, compared to Usenet newsgroups, mailing lists have much less trouble with unsolicited advertisements, called spam (see below). This can be an important consideration.

Advertising and Spam

As you use the Net, you are going to have a huge amount of in-your-face advertising forced upon you, particularly on the Web. Personally, I don't like it one bit (and I hope you don't either), but the economics that drive the Net are based in large part on advertising revenues, and there's not much anyone can do to change that. From time to time, people do come up with programs to filter out the ads, and I will discuss such programs in Chapter 7. Still, for the foreseeable future, advertising on the Web is here to stay.

However, there is another type of advertising, called spam, that people are doing something about. SPAM refers to unsolicited advertisements that are sent to people's personal email accounts and to Usenet newsgroups. The people who send such ads are called SPAMMERS.

As an Internet user, you will notice spam in two important ways. First, if your email address gets on a spammer's address list, you will begin to see advertisements in your mailbox. As time passes, this will get worse and worse, as your address is passed around and sold from one spammer to another.

Eventually, you will find that you are receiving a great deal of unsolicited advertising. Whether or not this bothers you depends on your temperament. It doesn't cost you anything to receive email, and it is simple to delete any unwanted messages. Still, no matter how genial your personality, I predict that, when the spam gets bad enough, you will start to complain. By then it will be too late. There are brokers who sell lists of addresses, and once your name is on a list your privacy is gone for good.

The second way in which you will notice spam is on Usenet. As I explained earlier, Usenet consists of a great many discussion groups (called newsgroups). Traditionally, Usenet has afforded people as much freedom as possible. In particular, anyone is allowed to send an article to any newsgroup, and some people send a lot of articles. But this is nothing compared to the spammers who use automated programs to send advertisement after advertisement to every Usenet newsgroup. This means, for example, that if you want to read the articles in a newsgroup devoted to pets, you may have to wade through a lot of advertisements offering ways to "make money fast".

Spam is bad for the Internet (and for you) in two ways. First, unsolicited messages are irritating, whether you find them in your mailbox, in a Usenet newsgroup, or on a mailing list.

Second, when the spam count gets high enough, the junk really starts to get in the way. A lot of spam is carefully crafted by experts to look like important mail (just like postal junk mail), and you may have to look at many bogus messages to make sure you don't accidentally delete a real one. However, unlike postal junk mail — which requires paper, printing, envelopes and postage — spam is electronic and costs very little per message. Thus, spammers have no economic motivation to remove you from their mailing lists or to target their advertising to only those people who want it.

This problem has choked many Usenet newsgroups to death. As part of my work, I maintain a master list of Usenet newsgroups. From time to time, I go through all the groups bringing the list up to date. I have seen many groups that have been rendered unusable by high amounts of spam. In fact, more than any single thing I can think of, spam has really hurt the Usenet community.

Fortunately, there are a lot of anti-spam nerds on the Net who have developed two types of anti-spam software. One type, used for email, filters messages as they arrive in your mailbox. Messages that look like spam are thrown away automatically. The second type of software is used on Usenet to eliminate spam before it gets into the newsgroups. The Usenet software has worked particularly well, helping to make Usenet a lot more pleasant to use.

What's in a Name?

spam

Spam is a canned meat containing pork shoulder and ham, first produced in 1937 by the George A. Hormel Food Company (now Hormel Foods). The name Spam was chosen to mean "spiced ham".

On December 15, 1970, the Monty Python's Flying Circus television show had a skit in which a woman and man in a restaurant find that every dish on the menu contains Spam, Spam, and more Spam.

Some years later — because of this skit — the word "spam" was adopted on Usenet to refer to articles that were sent to many different newsgroups. The idea is that, no matter which newsgroup you choose to read, you will have spam forced upon you, just like the people in the Monty Python skit.

Telnet

TELNET is a service that allows you to connect to a remote computer and run programs. Telnet was the first service developed for the original Arpanet (the network that grew into the Internet). In those days — the late 1960s — the only way to use a computer interactively was via a device called a TERMINAL. A terminal had a keyboard, a monitor, and not much more, and had to be connected directly to the computer, which was called the HOST. To use the computer, you would turn on the terminal and LOG IN by typing a user name and a password. You could then use your terminal to type commands which would be carried out by the host.

Telnet was developed to allow people to log in and use a remote computer over a network. Without telnet (or something like it), you could not interact with a computer unless you had a terminal that was physically connected to the host.

To use telnet, you run a TELNET CLIENT program on your computer. The telnet client connects to the remote host and then begins to act like a terminal. (In computer talk, we say that the telnet program EMULATES a terminal.) You can now log in by typing your user name and password.

What's in a Name?

telnet

The ancestor of the Internet was called the Arpanet (named for the Advanced Research Projects Agency, a part of the U.S. Department of Defense). The first goal of the Arpanet researchers was to create a way for people to access remote computers. Here is an excerpt from one of their early memos (named RFC-5), written on June 2, 1969:

"The initial ARPA network working group met at SRI [Stanford Research Institute] on October 25-26, 1968. It was generally agreed beforehand that the running of interactive programs across the network was the first problem that would be faced."

Telnet was formally proposed in a technical note (RFC-15) written by C. Carr and dated September 25, 1969, and as I mentioned, telnet became the first service offered over the new network.

The origin of the name "telnet" is unknown. My best guess is that Carr chose it to incorporate the words "teletype" (an early device that was used as a terminal) and "network".

The word "telnet" is often used as a verb, for example, "In the olden days, people would telnet to a computer in order to use it remotely."

In general, you can't use telnet unless you have an account (a user name and password) on a remote host. In years past, there were computers on the Net that would allow public telnet access for certain specific services, such as library catalogs or BBSs (bulletin board systems). Nowadays, though, most such services have moved to the Web, where you can access them by using your browser.

Making Sense of It All

There is a lot to do on the Internet, and there is a lot to learn. To make sense out of it all, just remember these three basic ideas:

- The most important services on the Net are mail, the Web and Usenet.

- The Internet is based on a client/server system. You run client programs on your computer. Your clients connect to various servers on the Net in order to carry out your requests.

- The most important program you need to learn how to use is your Web client, called a browser. The most popular browsers, Internet Explorer and Netscape, are integrated with mail and Usenet clients, so you can use one main program for almost everything.

For reference, Figure 2-1 contains a summary of the clients and servers we have discussed. The fact that you understand this summary means that you now know more about the Internet than almost everyone else in the world.

Figure 2-1: Important clients and servers used on the Internet

Internet Service	Client	Server
Mail	Mail program	Mail server
The Web	Browser	Web server
Usenet	Newsreader	News server
FTP	FTP program	FTP server
IRC	IRC client	IRC server
Mud	Mud client	Mud
Telnet	Telnet client	Host

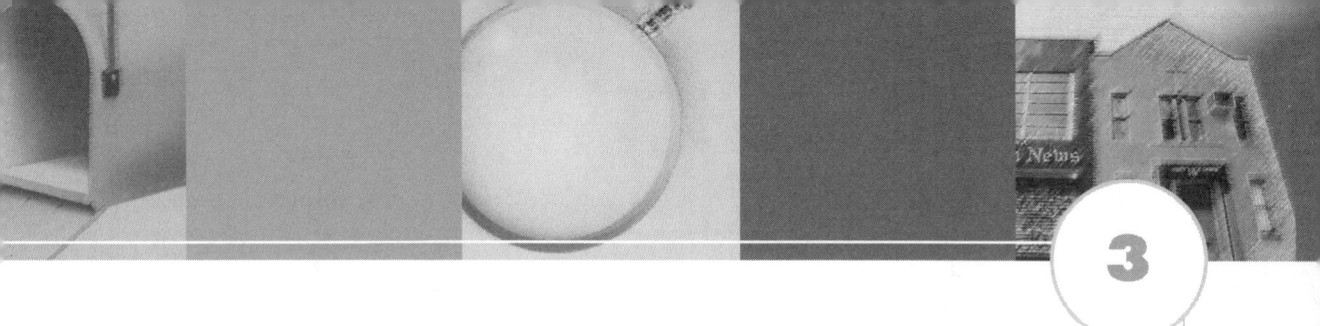

3

Everything You Need to Connect to the Net

A computer is a tool for
your mind, and you
deserve the best such tool
you can afford.

To use the Net, you need a computer, software and an Internet connection. In this chapter, I will discuss what type of computer to buy, where to get your software, and the best way for you to get connected.

Even if you are already using the Net, I would still like you to read this chapter for two reasons. First, I am going to explain a lot of basic computing terms that I want you to know, and second, you may learn about something that will help improve your current setup.

The Summary in Advance

What computer, software and Internet access do you need?

Here is the wisdom from this chapter, condensed into a short summary. Don't worry if you don't understand all the words and abbreviations, I will explain them all as we go through the chapter. I just wanted to get everything into a few paragraphs to give you a preview of what we're going to talk about. Once you have finished the chapter, you can copy this page and take it with you when you go computer shopping.

Harley Hahn's Quick Guide to What You Need to Use the Internet

Buy a computer running Windows XP, with at least 128 MB of RAM (more if possible). The computer should have a fast processor, a V.90 56K modem, speakers, a microphone, a CD-RW and a built-in Ethernet port. Don't buy a Macintosh unless you are a professional graphics designer.

For software, if you want a word processor, get Microsoft Word. For everything else, wait until you see what software comes with the computer and what you can find for free on the Net. You don't need to buy an antivirus program right away.

Get the fastest Internet connection you can afford, either DSL or cable. Do not use a regular dialup (modem) connection unless DSL and cable are not available in your area. Choose an ISP that gives you a flat rate with reasonable customer service. Don't use AOL unless you know for sure that you want the extra content.

Processors

If you were to open a computer, you would see some circuit boards, some metal boxes and various wires. On the circuit boards you would see a large number of small, flat electrical chips.

The main circuit board is called the MOTHERBOARD. The whole computer is built around this board. One of the chips on the motherboard is the PROCESSOR, the most important component of the whole computer. To the extent that a computer can be said to have a "brain", the processor is the brain. In Chapter 1, I explained that programs were actually long lists of instructions. Well, when you run a program, the processor is the part of the computer that executes the instructions. Thus, the speed and power of your computer depend on the speed and power of the processor.

Processor speed is measured in GHz (gigahertz) or MHz (megahertz), where 1 GHz = 1000 MHz. For example, a 1.8 GHz processor is faster than a 1.4 GHz processor, which is faster than a 900 MHz processor. The speed of a computer depends on a lot more than just the processor, so you can't say that a computer with a 1.8 GHz processor is going to be twice as fast as a machine with a 900 MHz processor. However, the first computer will be significantly faster.

hint

Get the fastest computer you can afford. You will not regret it.

Memory

Within a computer, data is organized into units called BYTES, each byte storing a single character. For example, it takes 11 bytes to store the name "Harley Hahn". (The space counts as one character.)

When we talk about quantities of memory, we use names based on the metric system: a KILOBYTE (abbreviated KB) is a thousand bytes, a MEGABYTE (MB) is a million bytes, a GIGABYTE (GB) is a billion bytes, and a TERABYTE (TB) is a trillion bytes. So, for example, 1 MB = 1,000 KB. (There is actually a little more to it than I explain here. See the technical hint below.)

Computers have two types of memory: working memory and long-term storage. The working memory is called RAM. The name stands for "random-access memory" and is used for historical reasons, so don't try to make sense out of it.

You will remember that I explained that the processor is the "brain" of the computer. Well, RAM is working memory, used by the processor. When you turn off your computer, all the data stored in RAM is lost. This is why, each time you turn on a computer, you have to wait for everything to reload. This is also why, when you start a new program, it sometimes takes a few moments. You are waiting for the program to be

hint

The cheapest way to make a computer faster is to buy more memory. When you buy a new computer, make sure it has at least 128 MB (megabytes) of RAM. More is better.

hint

In the metric system, kilo means a thousand (1,000), mega means a million (1,000,000), giga means a billion (1,000,000,000), and tera means a trillion (1,000,000,000,000). However, when we talk about computer memory or storage, we use slightly different values for these prefixes.

Computer scientists and programmers work with computer memory by using a mathematical system called the BINARY SYSTEM. The binary system is based on powers of 2 (such as 1, 2, 4, 8, 16, 32, and so on), and within this system, it is more convenient to have "kilo" stand for 1,024, not 1,000. This is because 1,024 is 2^{10} (2 to the power of 10), and in the binary system, 2^{10} is a round number. Similarly, "mega" stands for 2^{20}, "giga" stands for 2^{30}, and "tera" stands for 2^{40}. *(continued)*

copied from the long-term storage to RAM. (The long-term storage is the hard disk, which I will discuss below.)

Inside your computer, RAM is provided by electronic chips that plug into the motherboard. RAM is measured in MB (megabytes). The more RAM you have, the better. With most computers, you can upgrade the memory by buying more RAM chips and plugging them into the motherboard.

When we talk informally, we often refer to megabytes as "megs", and gigabytes as "gigs". Thus, if you were visiting the Queen of England, you might hear her tell one of her ladies-in-waiting, "On your way back from McDonalds, can you pick me up a new computer — something real fast, with at least 256 megs of RAM and a 40-gig hard drive."

Disk Drives

Inside a computer, long-term storage is furnished by a number of different devices called DISK DRIVES or DISKS. Every computer comes with a HARD DISK, a small box inside the computer. The name comes from the fact that, inside this box, data is stored on several hard disk-shaped plates. Unlike RAM, data on a hard disk does not disappear when you turn off the computer. The data is stored permanently, until you (or one of your programs) erase it. In fact, when you turn on the computer, the system will spend a minute or so copying data from your hard disk (long-term storage) to RAM (working memory).

The capacity of a hard disk is measured in GB (gigabytes). Typically, a new computer will have a hard disk with a capacity of 10 to 40 GB or even more, but you don't have to worry about the exact size. Modern computers come with enough long-term storage.

A second long-term storage device is a FLOPPY DISK DRIVE, sometimes called a DISKETTE DRIVE. This is a small box inside your computer with an opening into which you can insert a FLOPPY DISK (often called a FLOPPY). A standard floppy disk can hold up to 1.44 MB (megabytes) of data.

Some computers have an extra disk drive that uses special removable hard disk cartridges. If you have such a disk drive, you can keep large amounts of data on separate cartridges. In particular, removable hard disk cartridges are excellent for holding copies of large files and for making backups. (A BACKUP is a copy of important data, maintained as a safeguard in case the original data is lost. It is a good idea to keep backups in a safe place away from your computer.)

You will often hear people refer to these types of disk drives as ZIP DRIVES. That name comes from a particular brand of removable hard disk made by the Iomega company. (Actually, even better than zip drives are CD-RW drives, which I will discuss in the next section.)

What's in a Name?

floppy disk

The outside of a floppy disk is hard plastic. However, in the olden days, floppy disks were larger and thinner, and really were floppy. Even today, if you open one up, you will find a flexible, wafer-thin disc. So inside, floppies are still floppy.

CD Drives

Most new computers come with a CD drive. This drive is able to work with several different types of CDs:

- **CD-ROMs:** These are the standard computer CDs. CD-ROMs can hold 650 MB of data and are generally used to distribute software.

- **Music CDs:** The CD drive in your computer can read regular music CDs as well as CD-ROMs. Thus, your computer can double as a stereo, and you can listen to music as you work.

- **DVDs:** A DVD is a special type of CD that can store computer data, sound and video. In particular, DVDs are used to distribute movies, so if your CD drive can read DVDs, you can use your computer to watch movies.

Some computers have CD-RW (rewritable) drives that can both read and write. If you have a rewritable drive, you can put your own data on blank CDs. In particular, you can make your own music CDs that can be used with standard CD players. I will discuss these drives in Chapter 10, at which time I will show you how to access music from the Internet and create your own custom music CDs.

A CD-RW drive is also useful for making backups. In fact, CD-RW drives are better backup devices than the zip drives I mentioned in the

The following table shows these prefixes and their values when used to measure computer memory:

Kilo	2^{10}	1,024
Mega	2^{20}	1,048,576
Giga	2^{30}	1,073,741, 824
Tera	2^{40}	1,099,511, 627,776

I won't go into the details except to say that, unless you are a computer scientist or a programmer, none of this really matters. For normal people, 1 KB of memory is about a thousand bytes, and 1 MB of memory is about a million bytes, and that's all that counts. When you compare memory sizes, 2 MB is twice as much as 1 MB no matter how you measure it.

hint

Get yourself an extra floppy disk and open it up for fun. (Just pull it apart.) The disk will become unusable, but floppies are cheap and it's interesting to see what is inside.

For extra fun: If you are going to perform this demonstration in front of other people, stick a label that says "Master Tax Files" on the disk before you pull it apart.

previous section. Rewritable CDs hold more data than zip drive cartridges, and are much less expensive. If you are thinking of buying a CD-RW drive for your computer, read the discussion in Chapter 10, where you will find some important hints.

The speed of CD drives is expressed as a number followed by the letter "x" — for example, 8x, 24x, 48x. These numbers are relative and indicate the speed of the drive compared to the original CD drives. In other words, a 4x drive is 4 times as fast as one of the original CD drives; a 24x drive is 24 times as fast; a 48x drive is 48 times as fast. (In this sense, the "x" means "times", as in multiplication.)

When you buy a computer, don't worry about the exact speed of the CD drive, just compare the numbers. For example, a 48x drive is faster than a 24x drive, which is much faster than a 8x drive. As with most computer-related equipment, faster is better. However, having a fast CD drive is not nearly as important as having a fast processor and lots of memory.

What's in a Name?

disk

disc

When we talk about CDs, we use the word "disc" (as in compact disc), but when we refer to hard disks and floppies, we use the word "disk". This dates back to the original IBM PC (1981), in which floppy disks were called "diskettes".

What's in a Name?

CD

CD-ROM

DVD

A CD is a "compact disc".

The name CD-ROM stands for "compact disc, read-only memory", which indicates that the data on the disc can be read, but not changed.

Originally, the name DVD meant "Digital Video Disc". However, for marketing reasons, the DVD industry has changed the meaning to "Digital Versatile Disc".

Operating Systems (Windows)

An OPERATING SYSTEM is a master control program that runs a computer. Almost all computers use an operating system called WIN-DOWS. Windows is made by Microsoft, and every now and then, they come out with a new version. The latest version is Windows XP. (According to Microsoft, XP stands for "experience".)

What's in a Name?

Windows

Windows 2000

Windows NT

Windows CE

WINDOWS is a general marketing term, used by Microsoft to describe a variety of different operating systems. Informally, when people refer to "Windows", they are usually talking about the most common PC operating systems, Windows XP/Me/98/95. However, there are other Windows operating systems you may hear about.

WINDOWS 2000 is the name for a family of operating systems used to run some commercial computers, especially servers. The ancestor of Windows 2000 was Windows NT, which was released in July 1993. In October 1998, Microsoft announced that all new versions of Windows NT would be named Windows 2000. Thus, WINDOWS 2000 is just a newer version of Windows NT.

WINDOWS CE, released in September 1996, is an operating system used with small portable computers, such as handheld and palmtop computers, as well as some video game systems. Windows CE can also be used with small specialized computers called EMBEDDED SYSTEMS, that are used within larger machines, such as cars, microwave ovens and VCRs.

You are probably wondering, what do NT and CE mean? At one time, NT meant "new technology", and CE meant "consumer electronics". Today, the official Microsoft dogma is that these are simple designations that never had a particular meaning.

This might be a good time to recall one of the slogans of the totalitarian government in George Orwell's novel *1984*:

Who controls the past controls the future; who controls the present controls the past.

hint

What if your current computer uses an older version of Windows? Should you upgrade to a new operating system? Unless you are a real nerd, don't bother.

If your computer is working fine, stick with the operating system you have, and get the new operating system when you buy your next computer.

The first Windows was version 1.0 (released in November 1985). It wasn't until version 3.0 (May 1990) that Windows became widely used, and even today, there are many computers that still run a version of this older system, Windows 3.0, 3.1 or 3.11. For convenience, these versions are referred to collectively as 3.x.

In August 1995, Microsoft came out with a new version of Windows that was totally different from the old ones, so for marketing reasons, they made a big change in the name. Instead of calling the new operating system version 4.0, they called it Windows 95. Since then, Windows 95 has undergone a variety of updates, under the names Windows 98 (June 1998) and Windows Me (September 2000). The newest version, Windows XP (October 2001), is a big upgrade from the older versions.

What does this mean to you? When you buy a computer, make sure it comes with the newest version of Windows already installed. Do not accept a computer with an old version of Windows.

Software

When you buy a new computer, it will come with a lot of free software. Not only will you get the current version of Windows, you will get a lot of programs that Microsoft includes with Windows. In addition, most computers come with a variety of other software. When something is given away as part of the overall purchase price, we say that it is BUNDLED with the main product. In this case, we can say that Windows, as well as other software, is bundled with the computer.

Having so many programs included with a new computer is convenient, as the software will already be installed and working. This is particularly important with respect to Windows, because installing an operating system is a time-consuming process with many potential pitfalls. Microsoft saves everyone (including themselves) a lot of trouble by having Windows already working on the computer when you buy it.

When you buy a new computer, the question may arise as to whether or not you should buy extra software at the same time. (If the question doesn't arise by itself, the salesman will probably offer some "suggestions".) Actually, you don't really need to buy any other software right away. A new PC comes with everything you need to use the computer and to connect to the Internet. You may want some extra programs to use various Internet facilities, but you can download these from the Net for free. In fact, there is so much software on the Net —in any category you could want — that I would suggest not buying anything extra until you have learned how to download software and explored the many software archives. (We'll talk about how to download software from the Net in Chapter 9.)

So, with one exception, I would suggest not buying anything right away. The exception is, if you know you will be doing a lot of word processing, buy the newest version of Microsoft Word. This product is pretty much the standard in its category, and can be bought as part of a collection of programs called Microsoft Office.

Such collections are called software SUITES. Other companies besides Microsoft offer suites, and they provide good value. Some computers come bundled with a suite of programs, so you may get what you want for free anyway.

One last question: it is common for salesmen to suggest you buy an antivirus program to protect your computer. Should you do so? I won't talk about computer viruses now (we'll do that in Chapter 12). However, I will say that the dangers posed by viruses, even on the Internet, are highly exaggerated by the companies that sell antivirus software, and by people who like to scare other people.

It is not necessary to pay extra for an antivirus program when you buy a new computer. Once you get connected to the Net, you will find a variety of free and inexpensive antivirus software to choose from. In addition, many new computers already have such software installed on the machine.

As far as Internet software goes, I explained in Chapter 2 that you access the Internet by using client programs. The most important client program is a browser, which you use for the Web and other services.

All the Internet clients you need are available on the Net. To get started, you need only (1) the software that makes the actual connection to the Net (this software is included as part of Windows), and (2) a browser. Once you are on the Net, you can use your browser to get whatever you need.

When you buy a new computer, chances are it already has a browser, probably Microsoft's Internet Explorer. If not, you should be able to get one from the company that provides your Internet connection. Don't worry about getting the newest version of the browser. Any browser will

hint

I will discuss computer viruses in Chapter 12. If you are worried, the following three precautions will provide the protection you need until you learn more.

- Never open a file that someone has sent to you by email.
- Never use a floppy disk to transfer a program from someone else's computer.
- Never allow your children to bring home floppy disks from school.

do to start. Once you get on the Net, you can download the newest versions of Internet Explorer or Netscape. (These are the two major browsers.) We will talk about browsers in more detail in Chapter 7.

What Type of Computer Should You Buy?

What type of computer should you buy to use the Internet? You have two basic choices: a regular computer or a special-purpose Internet computer. Most people use regular computers, so let's talk about those first. In this section, I'll summarize the points we have discussed so far and tell you what to buy.

When it comes to computers, you can get a PC or a Macintosh. Get a PC. Virtually all software and all new development, especially on the Internet, is for PCs running Windows. If you get a Macintosh, you will be left out of the mainstream.

Your computer should come with Windows XP already installed. As I explained earlier, the computer should have at least 128 MB of RAM (memory) — more if possible. In addition, make sure the computer has a CD-RW drive and speakers. I suggest that you also get a microphone (often included). This will allow you to talk to other people over the Net, and to record voice messages which you can send by email.

Make sure the computer's processor is fast. As I explained earlier in the chapter, processor speeds are measured in GHz, MHz (gigahertz) and MHz (megahertz). Within the same family of processors, all you need to do is compare the numbers. For example, a processor running at 1.8 GHz is faster (and better) than one running at 1.1 GHz. When it comes to processing power, you get what you pay for, so if you can afford it, pay more for a faster processor.

Most PCs use processors made by the Intel company. Although other companies make processors, Intel spends a lot of money trying to convince people they should only buy computers with Intel processors. Forget the advertisements. Although most PCs do have an Intel processor, it's okay to buy a computer with another brand. Just make sure you get a fast processor, and you will be okay.

Finally, make sure that any computer you buy has the facilities you need to connect to the Net. For fast connections such as DSL and cable (discussed later in the chapter), you will need an Ethernet port. For slow connections, you will need a modem (also discussed later).

ETHERNET is a technology used to connect computers into a local network. For example, if you have more than one computer in your home, you can connect them into an Ethernet and share resources, such as files and printers. Many businesses and schools have Ethernets.

An ETHERNET PORT is a socket you can use to connect your computer to a network. When you use DSL or cable for Internet access (discussed later), you actually connect to a network, so you need Ethernet capability. Even if you don't plan on using DSL or cable right now, you probably will later, so make sure your computer has a built-in Ethernet port. Otherwise, when you need it, you will have to install a special Ethernet adapter in the machine. (You will sometimes see such an adapter called an Ethernet NIC or network interface card.)

With respect to modems (discussed later), make sure the computer has a 56K V.90 modem.

What about the other parts of the computer? For example, do you need to worry about the size of the hard disk? If you follow the advice I have given in this section, you don't have to worry about anything else. The size of the hard disk is important (as are other considerations), but if you get the type of computer I recommend, it will include everything you need.

How Much Should You Pay for a Computer?

How much you should pay for a computer is an important question. The best answer is that it's cheaper in the long run to make sure you don't pay too little. Here is why.

Computer technology changes quickly, and every few months, new, more powerful computers come on the market. Moreover, computer software changes just as fast, and the new programs will not work well on the old hardware. For example, the current versions of Windows (XP and Me) will not run on the machines that were suitable for the older versions. As a general rule, new programs don't run well on old machines, because the programmers who design the programs depend on the power, speed and increased memory of the newer computers. However, software is being improved all the time, and you certainly don't want to be stuck with old programs.

This is why computers become obsolete so quickly: it's because software becomes obsolete, and you need a new computer to run the new software.

This consideration is important when you buy a new computer, especially when you plan to use it to access the Internet. No matter what machine you buy, I guarantee that two years from now it will look old, and three years from now it will be screaming to be replaced.

Thus, instead of buying the most inexpensive computer, I want you to spend a little more now and buy one with a faster processor and more memory. My goal is for your machine to last three years, rather than two.

Of course, nobody will make you buy a new computer in two to three years. If you want, you can use one for five years or more. There are no Internet police who will arrest you for trying to run new programs on old machines. However, the programs won't run well, and maybe they won't run at all.

For this reason, I suggest that — in the U.S.— you spend at least $1,000 for a new computer (including the monitor). The number, of course, is a guideline, but if you follow my advice I know you will be pleased with your computer, and it will serve you well for as long as possible. In today's marketplace, computers are commodities, which means that brand names aren't all that important. What's important is to recognize that the more you pay, the more you get; and the more you get, the longer it will last without becoming obsolete.

I want you to remember that a computer is a tool for your mind, and you deserve the best such tool you can afford. A friend called me recently and said, "I went computer shopping, and I can't decide whether I should buy my son a $500 computer or a $1,000 computer. What do you think?"

"That depends," I told him. "Does your son have a $500 mind or a $1,000 mind?"

Types of Internet Connections

Once you have a computer and software, you need to arrange two things in order to use the Internet.

You need to buy Internet access from an INTERNET SERVICE PROVIDER or ISP. (We will discuss how to choose an ISP later in the chapter.) For this service, you will pay a monthly fee. Some ISPs also charge a one-time setup fee.

You will also need to arrange a way to connect your computer to the ISP.

hint

Computer technology changes rapidly, and the price of a new computer decreases every few months. However, computer monitor technology does not change as quickly, and the prices are more stable.

For this reason, it makes sense to spend extra money to get yourself a large, high-quality monitor. If you do, you will be able to use it for years, no matter what computer you may buy in the future.

For a home computer, there are three choices:

- DSL
- Cable
- Dialup connection

DSL and dialup use a telephone line, while cable uses the same line that brings your TV service. There are various details you need to know, so I will discuss each of these choices later in the chapter.

The table in Figure 3-1 shows the various ways to connect to an ISP. Dialup connections are available everywhere. For the other services, you will have to check what is available is your area. If you have a choice, go with the fastest service you can get.

Figure 3-1: Various ways to connect to an ISP

Name	Speed	Connect via
DSL	Fast	Regular telephone line
Cable	Fast	TV cable
Dialup	Slow	Regular telephone line

The Speed of an Internet Connection

When you connect to the Net, the most important consideration is the speed of your connection. Faster is better, and a lot faster is a lot better. In fact, you can't get a connection that is too fast.

Why? Your mind works quickly, and no matter how fast you connect to the Net, the information will never appear fast enough for your brain. Waiting is irritating and interferes with your thought processes.

The main communication links inside the Internet are very fast. However, what you see on your computer is considerably slower. This is because, no matter how fast data travels within the Net, it must pass through one last link — the one to your computer — and that link is always the slowest. For this reason, when you arrange for your Internet connection, you should get one that is as fast as possible.

To measure speed on the Internet, we describe how much data is transmitted per second. However, before I can explain the terminology, we need to talk about how data is organized within a computer. Earlier in the chapter, I explained that data is measured in bytes, where each byte holds one character. Inside a computer, a byte is actually stored as a series of smaller entities called BITS. There are 8 bits in each byte, so that it takes 8 bits to store a single character.

Consider the name "Harley Hahn", for example. This name consists of 11 characters (counting the space) and hence, within a computer, would be stored as 11 bytes, which is the same as 88 bits.

What's in a Name?

bit

byte

Within a computer, data is stored as bits (8 to a byte). Mathematically, it is possible to work with bits by representing them as numbers using the binary system. Within the binary system, each bit is represented by a single digit, either a 0 or a 1. The word "bit" stands for "binary digit".

The word "byte" doesn't stand for anything in particular. It's just a cute word that was chosen to represent something that was bigger than a bit. Since it could be confusing to have both bits and bites, we spell it with a "y" (byte).

By the way, just for fun, here is the word "Harley" encoded as bits:

```
    H        a        r        l        e        y
01001000 01100001 01110010 01101100 01100101 01111001
```

On the Internet, we measure speed in BITS PER SECOND, usually abbreviated as BPS. For example, if I tell you that a particular connection to the Internet has a maximum operating speed of 56,000 bps, it would be the same as saying you can transmit up to 7,000 bytes per second through that connection. In practice, we mostly use such numbers to compare relative speeds. For instance, I might say that 56,000 bps is significantly faster than 33,600 bps, but not nearly as fast as 128,000 bps.

To make the numbers easier to manage, we use the abbreviation K to mean 1,000. For example, instead of saying 56,000 bps, we would write 56K bps. Similarly, we would say 33.6K bps or 128K bps. We also use M to mean 1,000,000. For example, you might read about a 1.5M bps connection.

A related term, BANDWIDTH, means the capacity to transmit data. For example, a 128K bps (128,000 bits per second) connection has about four times the bandwidth of a 33.6K bps connection; a 1.5M bps connection has a great deal more bandwidth.

On the Net, we sometimes use this word more generally. For instance, you may see people complain that spam (unsolicited advertising) wastes a lot of bandwidth.

Analog and Digital

Before we continue, I want to digress for a moment to discuss an important topic: the difference between analog and digital. (If you live in the U.K., you can pretend we are talking about analogue and digital.)

We use the word ANALOG to describe quantities that can vary continuously from one value to another. We use the word DIGITAL to describe quantities that can take on only specific, discrete values.

The most common way to appreciate these differences is to think about analog and digital clocks. An analog clock is an old-style one, with hour and minute hands. A digital clock shows you exact numbers. If you look at an analog clock, you might say the time is "a quarter to six" or "just past eleven". With a digital clock, you would see an exact time, 5:45 or 11:02.

Here is another example. In a car, an analog speedometer has a needle that moves back and forth. You might look at such a speedometer and say, "We are traveling somewhere between 50 and 55 miles per hour." If your car has a digital speedometer, you would see an exact number, say, 52 miles per hour.

Within a computer, all data is stored in a digital format as exact values (the bytes and bits we talked about earlier). This makes the data easy to manipulate (for a computer). Moreover, as this short example will illustrate, digital data is less susceptible to error than analog data.

Singing is an analog experience, so imagine yourself singing a tune that you just made up. You sing the tune to a person, who then sings it to another person, who then repeats it to another person, and so on. After several such transmissions, the tune probably wouldn't sound much like the original.

Now try a digital experience. You write down a list of ten numbers on a piece of paper. You then give the list to another person who copies the numbers onto another piece of paper and passes it to a third person. This

hint

When it is clear that we are talking about the speed of an Internet connection, we often leave out the "bps".

For instance, you might hear someone say, "I used to have a 56K dialup connection, but I recently changed to a 768K DSL connection."

person copies the numbers once again and passes them to a fourth person. As long as you can all read and write, you can transfer the digital data (in this case, numbers) as many times as you want without introducing mistakes.

And this is how it works on the Internet. All the computers and communication links (with one important exception) are digital, and data is passed from one computer to another with a minimum of errors. This is not to say that there are never mistakes in a digital system — after all, it is perfectly possible to write down a set of numbers so that one or two of them are illegible — but the Internet has ways to find such errors and correct them. (This is done by TCP, which I discussed in Chapter 1.)

Modems

Everything on the Net is digital, with one important exception: the link between you and the Net. The signal that goes over the telephone line or cable is actually analog, so you need a way to convert outgoing digital data (inside your computer) to analog data (for the phone line or cable). Similarly, incoming data (from the phone line or cable) has to be converted to digital data (for your computer). All of this is done automatically by a device called a MODEM.

Each type of connection requires its own type of modem. For a dialup connection, you can use the regular modem that came with your computer. For a DSL or cable connection, you will need a special DSL or cable modem. Telephone and cable companies usually make it easy for you to buy or rent the type of modem you need when you use one of these services.

What's in a Name?

modem

In technical terms, the process used to convert digital data to analog data is called MODULATION. The process used to convert analog data to digital data is called DEMODULATION. Thus, the device that performs these jobs is called a modem: a modulator/demodulator.

Dialup Connections

A DIALUP CONNECTION uses a modem and a regular telephone line. To access the Net, you run a program that causes the modem to dial the phone number of your ISP (Internet service provider). At the other end, another modem answers the phone and connects to your modem. Your program then sends your user name and password to log you in. You are now on the Net.

Before there were faster alternatives, virtually all Internet access from home computers was via a dialup connection. Even today, many people still connect to the Net in this manner.

There are three main advantages of a dialup connection: it is available everywhere, it is convenient if you travel with a computer, and it is cheap. Moreover, virtually all new computers come with a modem, and a dialup account with an ISP is economical. (In the U.S., it only costs about $25/month.)

There are two disadvantages. Most importantly, dialup connections are slow. Even the fastest such connection can be irritatingly slow compared to DSL or cable.

The second disadvantage is that a dialup connection ties up the telephone line, so you can't use the Net and talk at the same time. For this reason, many people install an extra line just for Internet access. This is convenient, but it will pretty much double your monthly cost.

Modern modems are advertised as running at 56K bps. However, this number is misleading in two ways.

First, the number is a theoretical maximum. Analog phone lines are susceptible to electrical noise, and this noise decreases the speed at which your modem can make a connection. A 56K modem, even with a good telephone line, will often connect at somewhere between 30K and 45K. Moreover, in the United States, the FCC limits the maximum speed to 53K.

Second, 56K modems work at this speed only with incoming data (downloading). With outgoing data (uploading), 56K modems behave like the older 33.6K modems. The reason is that, for outgoing data, the change from digital (your computer) to analog (the phone line) causes problems that restrict the modem's speed. This discrepancy isn't as bad as it sounds, though, because most of the time you are downloading data to your computer, not uploading data to the Net.

Once you have some experience, you will notice that modem advertisements (and computer salesmen) never volunteer the knowledge that your modem will not give you the advertised speed. You might ask, don't

hint

Everyone who sells computer connection hardware *always* misrepresents the speed.

the modem manufacturers and the salesmen know about this? The answer is, of course they do. However, before you judge them too harshly, consider the following real-life observation:

Traditionally, modems have been advertised with speeds that are theoretical maximums, never to be seen in real life. Today, this tradition is honorably continued with the newer forms of connectivity. For example, the people who sell DSL and cable access (which we will discuss later in the chapter) exaggerate horribly about the speed you will get. (In fact, if this were not a family book, I would say that the cable modem people lie through their teeth.)

Upstream and Downstream

In Chapter 2, I explained that receiving data from the Net is called downloading, and sending data to the Net is called uploading. We use similar terminology to describe the direction of data transmission: DOWNSTREAM and UPSTREAM.

When you use the Internet, you tend to receive a lot more data than you send. For example, with the Web, you click your mouse and type a little, and in return, you receive huge amounts of data: text, pictures, sounds, animation, even video. For this reason, the technologies used for high-speed consumer Internet connections are designed to devote more of the available bandwidth for downstream transmission than upstream transmission. When the bandwidth is distributed unevenly, we say that it is ASYMMETRIC.

The reason I mention this is that both DSL and cable are asymmetric services. For example, you might see an advertisement for a DSL service that offers 256K downstream, but only 64K upstream.

DSL

DSL (Digital Subscriber Line) is a technology that allows high-speed Internet connections over telephone lines. DSL is fast, and if it is available in your area for a reasonable price, it should be one of your top choices for an Internet connection.

DSL uses a regular phone line without interfering with the voice service. Thus, a single line can support both voice and a high-speed Internet connection at the same time. DSL is much faster than a dialup connection. I can't tell you an exact speed, because phone companies offer various services, but, at a minimum, you should be able to get several hundred thousand bps (bits per second), and perhaps, much faster.

A DSL connection is always turned on. With a dialup connection, you are not on the Net until your modem dials the phone and makes the connection. However, with DSL, you are connected permanently, until you either stop the service or die (whichever comes first).

To use DSL, you need three things: DSL service from your phone company, an account with a DSL Internet service provider (ISP), and a DSL modem. The DSL modem connects to your computer via an Ethernet port, so if your computer does not have such a port, you will have to install an Ethernet adapter.

Cable

Cable Internet connections are provided by cable TV companies. Such connections use the same wire — called COAXIAL CABLE — that is used for television. However, the Internet signal is separate from the television signals, so you can use the Internet and watch TV at the same time (although I don't recommend it, as you run the risk of having your brain explode).

Like DSL, cable connections are fast. Also like DSL, cable connections are asymmetric, with more downstream than upstream bandwidth.

Cable connections are usually easy to arrange. Your cable company will supply you with everything you need, including a cable modem and an Ethernet adapter for your computer (if your computer does not have an Ethernet port). In addition, the cable company may also be your ISP, providing Internet access as well as the connection.

When you check out prices, you will have to factor in all this information. There will be a significant startup fee, which will include installation and the Ethernet adapter. But the monthly fee will cover the use of the cable modem as well as Internet access. Remember, also, you do not need to pay for an extra phone line.

Compared to dialup connections, cable Internet connections are great, but there are some caveats. First, you should realize that you are sharing the cable with everyone in your neighborhood. As more people use the cable, there will be less bandwidth for you, and the speed of your connection will decrease, especially during times of heavy use. This is not the case with DSL.

Second, the speed you get will be fast, but not as fast as the cable company's advertisements will lead you to believe. One common number you will see is 10M bps. This is because cable modems connect to your computer via an Ethernet port, and the theoretical maximum for Ethernet is 10M bps. Don't believe it. The speed they provide won't be anywhere near this number.

Let me tell you about a real-life example. I have a friend who shall remain nameless (Josh Addison) who uses a cable Internet connection. As an experiment, Josh and I decided to test the speed of his connection. According to the cable company, Josh's connection can support 10M bps (which we know isn't true), and he should get at least about 4M bps downstream. Upstream, Josh should get 768K bps.

To run the test, Josh downloaded a large file from one of Microsoft's Web sites. (The file was the then-current version of Internet Explorer, which measured 10.631 MB.) As a control, I downloaded the same file to my computer. I have a very fast, dependable connection called a T1. A T1 connection (which is very expensive) has a maximum speed of 1.544M bps. We ran the test on a Sunday afternoon, a typical time for a home user to be accessing the Internet.

The results were as follows. Josh's cable connection downloaded the file in 8 minutes and 2 seconds, an average speed of 176K bps. My T1 line downloaded the file in 1 minute 22 seconds, which works out to 966K bps.

Compared to the large bandwidth the cable company promised, 176K looks small, and some people might be disappointed. However, 176K — a real 176K — is not all that bad. Realistically, 176K is more than five times the actual speed you get with a 56K modem, and cable is a lot more convenient. There's no need for an extra phone line, and you don't have to wait for a modem to dial a number and connect each time you start a new work session.

Josh loves his cable connection and is completely satisfied, especially when he compares it to his old dialup connection. For me, 966K is like greased lightning (to coin a phrase), and I wouldn't want to live without it. However, my T1 costs a *lot* of money, and Josh pays only $40/month.

What Type of Internet Services Are Available?

In order to use the Internet, you will need to pay money to someone. This is not a usage fee, as the Internet itself is open to everyone. Rather, you are paying for a connection to the Net. There are a variety of Internet services you can purchase, so it's a good idea to understand what is available. I'll explain each one in turn, but let's start with the full list just to get an overview:

- Basic access
- Mail
- Usenet news
- Web site hosting
- DNS service (custom address)

The basic service you need is access to the Net. To get Internet access, you arrange an account with an Internet service provider (ISP). You pay a monthly fee, and in return, they arrange for you to connect to the Internet through their system.

Just having a connection provides you with access to a lot of the Net, including all of the Web. However, you do need at least two other services: the use of a mail server and an email address (so you can send and receive email), and access to a Usenet news server (so you can participate in Usenet discussion groups). ISPs generally provide email and Usenet news for no extra cost when you pay for basic Internet access.

In addition, there are two other services you may want: Web site hosting (so you can have your own Web site) and DNS service (which allows you to have a personalized address, like `harley.com`). We'll talk about these topics later in the book.

Although your ISP will probably offer all these services, you do have choices. It is possible to buy your basic access from one ISP, and get mail, Usenet, Web site hosting and DNS from other providers. In fact, mail service and Web site hosting are widely available for free. The catch is, you will have to look at advertisements when you read your mail, and your users will have to look at advertisements when they look at your Web page. We will discuss all of these issues later in the book.

The important point is that basic Internet access can be unbundled from anything else. Just because you use one ISP for basic access doesn't mean you have to depend on the ISP for everything.

Why You Might Want Two Internet Accounts

Most people have only one Internet account, but in some circumstances you may want an extra one.

Let's say that your home Internet connection is a fast one (DSL or cable), but when you travel, you like to carry a notebook computer so you can check your mail no matter where you are. Unfortunately, your portable computer will not be able to access your home connection. The only way to use the Net when you travel is via a modem and a dialup connection.

For this reason, you may want to maintain two accounts: one for fast access at home, another for dialup access whenever you travel. The two accounts do not need to be with the same ISP.

Finding Internet Service Providers (ISPs)

One of the two most common questions people ask me is, "How do I find an Internet service provider?" (The other question is, "How many copies of your books should I buy?") In this section, I will discuss how to find and select an ISP, so you can understand the choices and make a wise decision. (The answer to the second question, by the way, is, "One copy for everyone you know.")

Do not begin to look for an ISP until you have chosen the type of Internet connection you want. Start by checking to see if DSL or cable is available where you live. If DSL or cable is available, it should be your first choice. If neither of these services is available in your area, you will have to use a dialup connection.

Once you have decided how to connect to the Net, you can choose your Internet service provider. This is the company that will provide you with Internet access. If you use a cable connection, you probably won't have a choice — the cable company will be your ISP (or will arrange for an ISP). With other types of connections, you do have a choice. The widest choice will be with dialup connections.

hint

When you buy a new computer, there will be a lot of software already installed, including Windows from Microsoft. It is common to find that your computer is set up to make it easy to connect to one or more ISPs. This is because Microsoft or the computer company has made marketing deals with the ISPs.

Ignore what is already on your computer. Follow the advice I give in this chapter and find the ISP that is best for you. If it happens to be one of the ISPs whose software is on your computer, so much the better, but don't choose blindly.

When it comes to ISPs, you have two broad choices. You can choose a local/regional provider, or you can choose a large national company. If you plan on moving, a national provider is convenient as you will not have to change your email address. Aside from that, the main considerations should be the ones I mention below.

How do you find ISPs that serve your area? First, if your local telephone company offers DSL, they may know which ISPs in your area offer Internet access using those services. If the customer service person at the phone company has no clue about ISPs (not uncommon), try their Web site.

Second, talk to people who already have Internet access. This is a good way to find out the names of some ISPs, and at the same time get an opinion as to the quality of the service.

Third, use the Web. There are a number of Web sites that maintain directories of ISPs organized by area code. In my experience, it is a good idea to check more than one directory, because none of them is complete. (If you don't have Web access, ask a friend who is already on the Net to find the information for you. Alternatively, many public libraries have computers with an Internet connection that can be used for free.)

Choosing an ISP

How do you evaluate an ISP? There are two ways. First, ask people in your area what ISP they use and what they think of the service. Asking around in this way is important, as it will allow you to avoid those ISPs that are not providing good service. Second, do a bit of research. Call each ISP and inquire about their services. If you have Web access (say, at work or at school), check their Web sites. As you do your research, consider the following:

Price: Make sure you get a flat monthly rate, not an hourly rate. (You will use the Net more than you think.) If you have a dialup connection, you will probably want a second telephone line, so you can talk on the phone while you are using the Net. Be sure to consider the price of this line when you figure your overall costs. However, when you compare prices, don't worry about small differences in the monthly fee. Go for the fastest connection you can afford.

Mail: Are you going to share your Internet connection (say, with your family, your spouse or a roommate)? Some ISPs will give you several different mail addresses with a single Internet account. Mail works better when each person has his or her own email address. This is especially true for husbands and wives. Even if you are the only person using an account, it can be handy to have more than one address. For example, if you run your own business, you can use one email address for business and another address for personal correspondence.

Usenet news: Does the ISP offer Usenet news service? If so, make sure they use filters to reduce the spam (junk advertising). This will make your Usenet experience a lot more pleasant.

Technical support: The profit margins in the ISP industry are small, and it is unrealistic to expect a lot of technical support. For example, no ISP can afford to spend time teaching you how to design your own Web page, or even how to use the Web. What you can expect is enough help to get started. If you can't figure out how to make your connection work, an ISP should help you until it works. Moreover, if you need special software to get connected, an ISP should provide it. At the very least, there should be a telephone number you can call for assistance. (Be prepared, however, to wait a long time.) When you investigate an ISP, see if they provide support on their Web site. Once you are connected, such support can be a great help.

The points we have covered so far are important, no matter how you connect to the Net. However, if you are going to use a dialup connection, there are a few extra considerations:

Local phone number: If you use a dial-up connection, your modem is going to have to dial the phone number of the ISP each time you want to connect to the Net. To keep your costs down, make sure that you choose an ISP you can access with a local phone call.

The larger ISPs have local numbers for various parts of the country. Each of these access points is called a POP (Point of Presence). So in nerd language, we can say that you should look for an ISP that has a POP in your area.

Adequate phone lines: Among people who use a dial-up connection, one of the biggest complaints about ISPs is that many of them do not have enough phone lines. When you use such an ISP, you will spend a lot of time being frustrated because you can't get through. This is especially true during times of peak usage (evenings and weekends).

Fortunately, checking if an ISP has an adequate number of lines is easy. Find out the local access number, the one your modem would call to

hint

If you use a dialup connection, check that the number your computer is dialing is not a toll call.

I know of someone in a small town in the U.S. who signed up with AOL as part of an offer to try the Internet for free. At the end of the first month, he got an unpleasant surprise when he found out that the "local access number" he was using was actually a toll call from where he lived. Every time he connected to the Internet, the phone company was charging him a per-minute long distance fee.

connect you to the Net. (This number will be different from the customer service number.) Then use the phone yourself to call the number and see what happens. Call the local access number at various times on different days. If you get through each time, that is a good sign. If you get a busy signal a lot of the time, you have found an ISP to avoid.

Internet Resources **Lists of ISPs (Internet Service Providers)**

```
http://www.ispfinder.com/
http://thelist.internet.com/
http://www.cnet.com/internet/
http://www.herbison.com/herbison/iap_meta_list.html
```

Does It Matter if Your Dialup ISP Has Lots of POPs?

If you travel with a notebook computer, you will want to be able to use the Net wherever you are. For example, it's handy to be able to check your mail. At home, you dial a local number to connect to your ISP, so there is no long distance charge. When you are traveling, however, you would have to pay extra for a phone call to your ISP at home.

All the large, national ISPs have local access numbers (POPs) all over the country, so if you use such an ISP, there will probably be a local number for you to dial when you travel. "Wow," you say, "I can check my mail wherever I go and not have to pay for a long distance call."

But wait — does it really cost that much to call long distance for a few minutes? Compared to your other travel costs, calling long distance to check your mail isn't expensive at all. For some reason, it seems cool to dial a local number when you travel, but realistically, it's just as easy, and not that expensive, to dial anywhere in the country. Here is a real-life example that illustrates what I mean.

Jack and Jill both work for the same large company. Occasionally, the company sends them on a business trip, and when they travel, they each take a notebook computer to check their email so they can stay in touch with the home office. Recently, Jack and Jill both went to New York. During the trip, their expenses were pretty much the same. Both Jack and Jill flew on the same airline, ate at the same restaurants, and stayed at the same hotel (in separate rooms, of course; this *is* a family book).

However, there was one difference. Jack has a dialup account with a national ISP, so while he was in New York, he was able to access the Net via a local phone number. Jill uses a local ISP, so every time she wanted to check her mail, she had to pay for a long distance telephone call.

At the end of the trip, both Jack and Jill added up all their expenses. Jack's trip cost $1241. Jill had to pay the long distance bill, so her trip cost more: $1256 (but that also included $5 for a chocolate bar she bought at the New York airport on her way home).

The moral of the story? When you travel, if all you do on the Net is check your mail, choose the ISP you want, because saving a few bucks on long distance charges won't make much of a difference. (However, you may want to bring your own snacks. Chocolate can be expensive at the New York airport.)

What About AOL?

AOL is, by far, the largest ISP in the world, and they offer something that the other ISPs do not have: extra services just for AOL users. One of the most popular services are the many chat rooms, where people gather to talk 24 hours a day. In addition, AOL offers many types of information as well as regular presentations. For example, there are events where famous people answer questions and talk to a live audience (by typing, of course, not voice). Overall, AOL tries to maintain the feeling of a large community, a feeling that many of their users share.

However, to access the Internet, you can use any ISP you want, and there are a number of good reasons why you should avoid AOL. First, they have a huge number of customers, and they have real trouble keeping up with the demand. AOL users often have trouble connecting over phone lines at peak periods (evenings and weekends). Moreover, AOL can be slow. Accessing the Web through a another ISP is often a faster, more enjoyable experience.

Second, in general, the Internet is free and uncensored. People can do whatever they want. AOL is a private environment. Although there is a lot of freedom, there is definitely Someone-in-Charge. This may or may not bother you.

Third, AOL does not offer anything important that is not available elsewhere on the Internet. (However, AOL does make their services especially easy to use.)

Finally, AOL is not primarily an Internet service provider. *AOL is a marketing company that sells Internet access in order to attract customers.* The distinction is an important one. AOL makes the bulk of their money from advertising revenues, by selling merchandise to their customers, and by making sales deals with other companies.

My recommendation is to forget AOL, get yourself a regular ISP, and enjoy the Net. However, I do recognize that many people want the special AOL features, so if you think you would enjoy being an AOL customer, I have a suggestion.

You do not have to use them as an ISP in order to be a customer. For a smaller monthly fee, AOL allows you to connect to their services through any ISP. Of course, you still have to pay that ISP, so overall it costs you a little more, but you will be getting the best of both worlds: faster and better Internet service, and full access to everything at AOL.

The Summary Once Again

At the very beginning of this chapter, I showed you a summary of what you were going to learn. We have covered a lot of ground since then, and I want you to appreciate how much you've learned, so take a moment and read the summary one more time. By now, you should understand it all.

Harley Hahn's Quick Guide to What You Need to Use the Internet

Buy a computer running Windows XP, with at least 128 MB of RAM (more if possible). The computer should have a fast processor, a V.90 56K modem, speakers, a microphone, a CD-RW and a built-in Ethernet port. Don't buy a Macintosh unless you are a professional graphics designer.

For software, if you want a word processor, get Microsoft Word. For everything else, wait until you see what software comes with the computer and what you can find for free on the Net. You don't need to buy an antivirus program right away.

Get the fastest Internet connection you can afford, either DSL or cable. Do not use a regular dialup (modem) connection unless DSL and cable are not available in your area. Choose an ISP that gives you a flat rate with reasonable customer service. Don't use AOL unless you know for sure that you want the extra content.

4

Internet Addresses

*The real work on the
Internet is done by
computer programs, not by
human beings.*

On the Internet, every computer, every person and every resource has its own address. One of the basic skills I want to teach you is how to understand and use these addresses. For example, here is the address of a particular Web page:

```
http://www.harley.com/25-things/index.html
```

By the time you finish this chapter, you will understand each part of this address, as well as the most important ideas related to Internet addresses.

Hostnames and Top-Level Domains

Every computer on the Internet has its own, unique name. Because Internet computers are sometimes referred to as HOSTS, these unique names are called HOSTNAMES. Here are some typical examples:

```
www.harley.com
ftp.microsoft.com
architecture.mit.edu
ucsd.edu
www.senate.gov
eff.org
mail.pacbell.net
www.dofa.gov.au
www.austemb.org.cn
www.culture.fr
www.royal.gov.uk
www.rcmp-grc.gc.ca
www.cs.ait.ac.th
```

Notice that each hostname has two or more parts separated by periods. When you say such a name out loud, you pronounce the period as "dot". For example, `www.harley.com` is pronounced "w-w-w dot Harley dot com".

Hostnames are part of a system called DNS, the domain name system (which we will discuss later in the chapter). DNS is the system that allows us to give a unique name to every computer on the Internet.

The rightmost part of the name is called the top-level domain (for a reason I will explain later), and tells us general information about the host. For instance, within the name **architecture.mit.edu**, the top-level domain (**edu**) tells us that this computer is managed by an educational institution (in this case, MIT).

When you type on a computer keyboard, small letters are called LOWERCASE and capital letters are called UPPERCASE.

With hostnames, you can use either lower- or uppercase letters or a mixture. For example, the following hostnames are all equivalent:

```
www.harley.com
WWW.HARLEY.COM
Www.Harley.Com
```

There are two types of top-level domains: ORGANIZATIONAL DOMAINS and GEOGRAPHICAL DOMAINS. Organizational domains describe a category, while geographical domains indicate a particular country. For example, the organizational domain **edu** is for educational institutions, while the geographical domain **au** indicates the country of Australia.

Figure 4-1 shows the organizational domains. Figure 4-2 shows some of the geographical domains. There are actually a great many such top-level domains — one for every country on the Net — and for reference I have put the complete list in Appendix A.

As a general rule, organizational domains are used inside the U.S., while the geographical domains are used in other countries. You will, however, see many exceptions.

hint

On the Internet, the custom is to use lowercase — especially among people who know what they are doing — and that is what you will see almost all the time. Although you can use uppercase when you type a hostname, I personally think lowercase looks a lot nicer, once you get used to it. (As always, I encourage you to think like me.)

Figure 4-1: Organizational top-level domains

Domain	Description
biz	Businesses
com	Miscellaneous [commercial]
edu	United States universities [educational]
gov	United States federal government
info	miscellaneous [information]
int	international organizations
mil	United States military
net	miscellaneous [network providers]
org	miscellaneous [organizations]

hint

When you see a host-name, look at the top-level domain (the rightmost part of the name). If the name has three or more letters, it is an organizational domain, and you can look up the meaning in Figure 4-1.

If the name has two letters, it is a geographical domain, probably representing a country. If you don't recognize the abbreviation, look it up in Figure 4-2 or in the master list in Appendix A.

Figure 4-2: Examples of geographical top-level domains

Domain	Description
at	Austria
au	Australia
be	Belgium
ca	Canada
ch	Switzerland (Confoederatio Helvetica)
cn	China
de	Germany (Deutschland)
dk	Denmark
es	Spain (España)
fr	France
gr	Greece
ie	Republic of Ireland
it	Italy
jp	Japan
nz	New Zealand
th	Thailand
uk	United Kingdom
us	United States

Why Are There Two Types of Top-Level Domains?

In its formative years, the Internet was confined to the United States, and there were only a handful of top-level domains: edu, com, gov, mil, org, net and int. When the Internet expanded to other countries, the geographical domains were added so each country could have its own top-level domain.

The original intention was that, eventually, all Internet hostnames would use geographical domains, and indeed, the United States does have a us domain. However, by the time this domain was introduced, the organizational domains had been used for so long that few people in the U.S. were willing to change.

For this reason, you will see two main types of top-level domains: the organizational domains, used mostly in the U.S., and the geographical domains, used everywhere else. (This should not surprise you. After all, the United States is the only country in the world that does not use the metric system.)

The U.S. geographical domain (`us`) is used by many schools and local governments. For example, the address of the Web site for Austin Community College in Texas is `www.austin.cc.tx.us`, and the address of the Web site for the city of San Francisco, California, is `www.ci.sf.ca.us`.

hint

Many people prefer to avoid the us top-level domain because the names are too complicated.

Exceptions to the Rules

How nice (but how boring) life would be if everyone always cooperated. Although the guidelines for using top-level domains are clear, not everybody follows the rules.

To be sure, some of the top-level domains are used consistently. Within the United States, for instance, `gov` is used only by the federal government, `mil` is used only by the military, and `edu` (educational) is used only by universities. Similarly, outside the U.S., the two-letter geographical top-level domains (`au`, `ca`, `jp`, `uk`, and so on) are almost always used appropriately.

However, `com`, `net` and `org` are a different story. The `com` designation was supposed to be for commercial organizations, `net` was supposed to be for network providers, and `org` was supposed to be for organizations that do not fit into any other category, such as nonprofit organizations. Nevertheless, there are many hostnames that use `com`, `net` or `org` that do not meet the criteria. The reasons are threefold.

First, in the mid-1990s, the Internet expanded so fast as to surprise almost everyone. Many people and organizations in the U.S. wanted their own unique hostnames, but there were not enough good names to go around. At the same time, the organization that administered the `com`, `net` and `org` top-level domains did not enforce the guidelines, so people pretty much did as they pleased.

So what do you think happened when the network administrator at the Acme Company tried to register the name `acme.com`, and he found that the name was already taken? He simply registered `acme.net` or `acme.org` instead. (I explain how to register a name in Chapter 16.)

Moreover, as the organizational top-level domain names became popular, many people wanted their own personalized hostnames, so they registered names like `alan.com` and `harley.com`. Other people who found these names already taken registered variations like `alan.net`, `alan.org`, `harley.net`, `harley.org`, and so on.

Finally, to make matters even more confusing, people and organizations outside the U.S. started to use these same top-level domains as well (even though they should have used their own geographical top-level domains).

Through it all, the registrations for `com`, `net` and `org` were accepted without anyone checking whether they were being used according to the guidelines. As a result, there are many hostnames that end in `com` that are not used by commercial entities, and there are hostnames that end in `net` or `org` that are not used by network providers or organizations.

Is this bad? Maybe yes and maybe no. How you feel about the situation depends on how much you like things to be orderly and well organized. One thing, however, that everyone can agree on is that the Internet needs more names, especially in the United States. As I explained earlier, there is a `us` top-level domain, but few people want to use it because the hostnames are so complicated.

The problem with the `com`, `net` and `org` domains arose because of the huge demand for top-level domains. To help alleviate the problem, two new domains were added in 2001: `info`, for anyone who wants to use it, and `biz`, which is reserved for businesses.

Countries That Sell Access to Their Top-Level Domains

The two-letter geographical domains were set up so that each country would have its own top-level domain: `ca` for Canada, `fr` for France, `us` for the United States, and so on. As a result, every country in the world has a code. (See Appendix A for the complete list.)

Most of the time, a computer using a geographical domain is actually in that particular country. However, this is not always the case. Strictly speaking, a geographical domain is controlled by the country, and they can use it for any computers they want. For example, the French embassy for Canada is in Ottawa. However, the embassy's Web site uses an address with the `fr` top-level domain:

```
http://www.amba-ottawa.fr/
```

(The French word for "embassy" is *ambassade* .)

As I explained above, many of the preferred domain names have already been taken. As a result, some countries use their geographical domains to sell customized names in the global marketplace.

For example, the geographical domain for the country of Tonga is `to`. Some time ago, someone noticed that this domain (which wasn't being used) looks the same as the English word "to". With the cooperation of the government of Tonga, a business was set up to sell personalized domain names, ending in `to`, to people all over the world. Thus, you will see Web addresses (which are perfectly legitimate), such as:

`http://come.to/`*something-or-other*

`http://listen.to/`*something-or-other*

`http://welcome.to/`*something-or-other*

The Kingdom of Tonga, by the way, is a country of 270 square miles (700 square kilometers), comprising 170 volcanic and coral islands in the South Pacific. Tonga has about 100,000 people, very few of whom actually use the Internet. The `to` domain business is actually run by a company in the U.S.

When the geographical domain name system was originally set up, the idea was that the top-level domain would identify a particular country. Clearly, when a country licenses the use of their top-level domain to anyone in the world, it runs counter to the spirit of the rules. Moreover, it is confusing, as the top-level domain loses its meaning.

Still, it is being done, and you should be aware of the practice. I have used the `to` domain as an example, but it is not the only one. Other countries, especially small countries, are licensing the use of their domains. For example, the country of Moldova (a small Eastern European country, northeast of Romania) happens to have the top-level domain `md`. The government of Moldova has entered into a business arrangement to license `md` domain names to doctors.

Understanding Hostnames

The secret to understanding hostnames is to look at each part of the name, reading *from right to left*. In general, the rightmost two parts of the name will tell you which organization manages that particular computer. If a name has more than two parts, the extra parts may provide even more information.

hint

If you see a two-letter top-level domain you don't recognize, look it up in the master list in Appendix A.

For example, I received an advertisement asking me to pay money for a name in the cc domain. Would this be a wise thing to do? The advertisement intimated that cc was a brand new Internet domain, and I better reserve a name before all the good ones were gone.

However, by checking the list, I was able to confirm that the cc domain is actually supposed to be used by the Cocos Islands (a group of islands, southwest of Sumatra, in the eastern Indian Ocean).

Consider the name `ucsd.edu`. Reading from right to left, we see that this name represents a computer at a university (`edu`) which is the University of California at San Diego (`ucsd`).

Now look at the name `architecture.mit.edu`. The `edu` tells us this is also a computer at a university; the `mit` designation tells us that the university is MIT; and the third part, `architecture`, shows us that the computer is managed by the architecture department.

Let's take a look at one last example, `www.royal.gov.uk`. The rightmost part of the name (`uk`) tells us that this computer is in the United Kingdom. The next part of the name (`gov`) shows us that the computer is a government computer. The third part (`royal`) indicates that this computer has something to do with the British royal family.

But what about the leftmost part of the name, the `www`?

When the Web was first developed, it was called the World Wide Web. As the World Wide Web evolved, the name was shortened, but the old name left a legacy: it has become customary to use the designation `www` to indicate a computer that acts as a Web server. Thus, `www.royal.gov.uk` is the name of the computer that hosts the Web site of the British royal family.

As you use the Net, you will see many other hostnames that begin with `www`. All of these are names of computers that host Web sites. Informally, we often refer to such addresses as if they were the actual Web sites. For example, we might say that `www.ibm.com` is IBM's Web site, `www.microsoft.com` is Microsoft's Web site, and `www.harley.com` is my Web site.

You will also see similar patterns with other types of resources. For instance, there are many anonymous ftp servers whose hostnames begin with `ftp`. (Anonymous ftp is a system that allows people to download programs and other files for free.) In addition, there are also many mail servers (which provide email services) that have names beginning with `mail`.

Here are two examples: the computer named `ftp.microsoft.com` is Microsoft's ftp server; while the computer `mail.pacbell.net` is the mail server for an Internet service provider named Pacific Bell Internet.

There are no rules forcing people to use special hostnames, and there are some Web sites whose names do not begin with `www`. However, when you do see `www` (or `ftp` or `mail`) at the beginning of a hostname, you will know what it means.

Before we leave this section, let's look at one last hostname, `www.cs.ait.ac.th`. Reading from right to left, we start with the top-level domain `th`. This is the geographical top-level domain for Thailand.

The next part of the name is `ac`, a designation commonly used to indicate a university (`ac` stands for "academic community"). We then see `ait`, an abbreviation for the Asian Institute of Technology; `cs`, an abbreviation for "computer science"; and `www`, which indicates the computer hosts a Web site.

Thus, the hostname `www.cs.ait.ac.th` represents the Web site of the computer science department at the Asian Institute of Technology in Thailand.

Now, do I expect you to be able to figure out such names instantly? No, of course not. Unless you are already familiar with a country, you probably won't recognize its top-level domain or the names of its national organizations. However, I do want you to appreciate that many hostnames are constructed to make sense, at least to the people who make up the names.

The organizational top-level domains —particularly `edu`, `com` and `gov` — are used widely within the U.S. In other countries, you will see a number of variations. In particular, you will see `ac` (academic community), `co` (commercial) and `gov` (government), followed by a two-letter geographical top-level domain.

For example, in Thailand, the Asian Institute of Technology uses `ait.ac.th`, while in England, Oxford University uses `ox.ac.uk`. Similarly, the *Times* newspaper in England uses `the-times.co.uk`, while the Bank of Tokyo-Mitsubishi in Japan uses `btm.co.jp`, and in Australia, the Department of the Treasury uses the name `treasury.gov.au`.

hint

In general, each country can use any pattern of domain names within its own top-level domain. However, as you gain experience on the Net, you will learn to recognize a number of common patterns that are followed around the world.

Domains

So far, we have talked about hostnames — the names used for computers on the Internet. I now want to discuss the more subtle concept of domains and how all the hostnames on the Internet are organized.

A DOMAIN is a set of hostnames that have the rightmost part of their names in common. For instance, all the hostnames that end in `edu` belong to the `edu` domain. Some examples are:

`architecture.mit.edu`

`www.ucsd.edu`

`www.med.harvard.edu`

Similarly, all the hostnames that end in `uk` belong to the `uk` domain. For example:

`www.royal.gov.uk`

`ox.ac.uk`

`the-times.co.uk`

(Notice, by the way, that a hyphen is a legitimate character within a hostname.)

The most general domains, such as `edu` and `uk`, are called TOP-LEVEL DOMAINS, because if you draw a diagram of hostnames, showing the most general names above all the others, these domains would be at the top.

As I explained earlier, there are two types of top-level domains: organizational domains and geographical domains (see Figures 4-1 and 4-2).

When hostnames have the two rightmost parts of their names in common, we say that they belong to the same SECOND-LEVEL DOMAIN. For instance, the following four hostnames all belong to the second-level domain `pacbell.net`:

`pacbell.net`

`news.pacbell.net`

`mail.pacbell.net`

`www.pacbell.net`

Similarly, these hostnames all belong to the second-level domain `gov.au`:

`treasury.gov.au`

`hcourt.gov.au`

`health.gov.au`

In such cases, we say that the more specific domain is a SUB-DOMAIN of the more general domain. Thus, `pacbell.net` is a sub-domain of `net`, and `gov.au` is a sub-domain of `au`.

In thes same way, the hostname `www.royal.gov.uk` belongs to the `royal.gov.uk` domain, which is a sub-domain of `gov.uk`, which is itself a sub-domain of `uk`.

Thus, all the hostnames in the Internet are organized into one large hierarchical system based on domain names. This system is called DNS, the DOMAIN NAME SYSTEM.

IP Addresses

In a minute, we'll talk about DNS in more detail, but first I want to introduce you to the idea of IP addresses.

As you know, hostnames are the unique names we use to identify computers on the Internet. Hostnames are convenient because they are simple to use, and (once you get used to them) they are easy for human beings to remember.

However, the real work on the Internet is done by computer programs, not by human beings, and it is easier for programs to deal with numbers, not names. For this reason, every computer on the Internet is given a unique number, and, internally, the Net uses these numbers, not hostnames, to identify specific computers. (These numbers are similar, in spirit anyway, to the personal identification numbers — such as the U.S. Social Security number — that most countries issue to their citizens.)

In Chapter 1, I explained that the glue that holds the Internet together is a family of protocols (technical specifications) called TCP/IP. The most important protocol is IP (Internet Protocol). For this reason, the numbers used to identify Internet computers are called IP ADDRESSES or IP NUMBERS.

As we discussed in Chapter 1, we make use of the Internet by using client programs to request information from servers. For instance, to access the Web, we use a Web client, called a browser, to contact various Web servers on our behalf. What you need to understand is that, the way the Internet is set up, your browser must have an IP address in order to contact a server.

Of course, when we tell a client program the name of a computer, we use a hostname. This means that, before the client can carry out our request, it must translate that hostname into the corresponding IP address.

Let's say, for example, you want to visit my Web site. The address is `www.harley.com`. In order to contact my Web server, your browser must find out the IP address that corresponds to this address. To do so, the browser calls upon DNS to translate the hostname into an IP address. In this case, the IP address happens to be `209.221.204.136`, and once the browser has this information, it is a simple matter to connect to computer number `209.221.204.136` and request data from the Web site.

All IP addresses have the same structure: four numbers separated by periods. The numbers can range from 0 to 255, but the actual details need not concern us, because, after all, IP addresses are for programs and computers, not for people.

For fun, however, here are some of the hostnames I mentioned earlier in the chapter, along with their IP addresses:

Hostname	IP Number
`www.harley.com`	`209.221.204.136`
`ftp.microsoft.com`	`207.46.133.140`
`architecture.mit.edu`	`18.113.0.177`
`ucsd.edu`	`132.239.1.1`
`www.senate.gov`	`156.33.195.33`
`eff.org`	`204.253.162.2`
`mail.pacbell.net`	`64.164.98.8`
`www.dofa.gov.au`	`147.211.50.107`
`www.austemb.org.cn`	`211.99.187.99`
`www.culture.fr`	`143.126.211.220`
`www.royal.gov.uk`	`193.32.29.66`
`www.cs.ait.ac.th`	`192.41.170.129`

DNS

The main job of DNS — the domain name system — is to translate hostnames into IP addresses. Everything is done behind the scenes, but I do want to take a moment to explain a bit about how it works, because it is so cool I know you will appreciate it.

Suppose someone gave you the task of keeping track of all the hostnames in the world and their corresponding IP addresses. How would you do it? One way would be to maintain a master table of all the hostnames and IP addresses. Whenever you had a specific inquiry, you could look up the hostname in the table and read off the appropriate IP address.

This is more or less the scheme that was used in the early days of the Internet, but as the years passed and the Net grew large, the hostname table grew as well and eventually became much too big. Moreover, new hostnames were being added continually, and it became very difficult to keep the table up to date. The solution was to distribute the responsibility around the Net.

As I explained in Chapter 1, the Internet is constructed such that every organization manages its own part of the Net. For this reason, it makes sense for each organization to manage its own hostnames as well. In particular, specific domains are used by organizations, who are then responsible for maintaining all the hostnames and IP addresses within those domains. For example, IBM has `ibm.com`, Harvard University has `harvard.edu`, the Australian government has `gov.au`, and so on. Each organization must arrange for at least two computers, called NAME SERVERS, to provide addressing information for all the hostnames in its domain. (Two servers are used in case one of them goes down temporarily.)

Because DNS distributes the management of the various domains, there is no need for anyone to maintain a gigantic master list of every computer on the Net. Whenever a program needs to translate a hostname into an IP address, all the program has to do is find the name server that handles that particular domain.

But out of all the name servers on the Net, how can a program find the one it needs? The solution is to start with the top-level domain and work its way down.

At various places around the Net, there are a 13 special computers called ROOT NAME SERVERS. Each root name server maintains a list of the name servers that handle top-level domains (such as `com`, `edu`, `au` and `uk`). Each of these name servers maintains a list of other name servers that handle the second-level domains, and so on.

When a program needs the IP address for a hostname, the program starts at a root name server and works its way from one server to the next until it finds the one that has the required IP address.

Here is an example. Say that a program needs to find the IP address of the hostname `www.ibm.com`. The program starts by contacting a root name server to get the IP address of the `com` name server. The program then contacts the `com` name server to get the IP address of the `ibm.com` name server. Finally, the program contacts the `ibm.com` name server to get the IP address of `www.ibm.com`.

In this way, using DNS, it is simple for any program to find out the IP address of any computer on the Net, even though no one maintains a master list. DNS works well because, as the Internet grows, DNS grows as well. For example, when the IBM network administrators create new hostnames (using new IP addresses), all they need to do is update the information in the `ibm.com` name servers.

Is DNS cool, or what?

How DNS Works for You

Your access to DNS is provided by your ISP (Internet service provider). All ISPs maintain DNS SERVERS for the use of their customers. When one of your client programs needs to find the IP address of a particular computer, the program sends a request to your ISP's DNS server. The DNS server does whatever is necessary to find the IP address, which it then sends back to your program.

Let's take an example.

You decide to visit my Web site, so you tell your Web browser to go to `www.harley.com` (the hostname for my site). In order to get the appropriate IP address, your browser sends the hostname to your ISP's DNS server.

The DNS server contacts the root name server and gets the IP address of the `com` name server. The DNS server then contacts the `com` name server and gets the IP address of the `harley.com` name server. Finally, the DNS server contacts the `harley.com` name server and gets the IP address of `www.harley.com`. In this case, the IP address happens to be `209.221.204.136`. This information is then sent to your browser which can now use the IP address to contact the Web server directly.

DNS is a good system, but it does involve a certain amount of overhead. To save time, each server at every level keeps a list of the most recently requested names and addresses. If a subsequent request comes in for the same information, the server is able to respond right away.

For example, once your DNS server has gone to the trouble of finding the IP address for **www.harley.com**, the information is kept for a certain period of time (usually somewhere between a half hour and a day), in case another program requests the same address.

As you use the Web, you will sometimes notice a delay after you type the address of a Web site. There are several reasons for this delay.

First, your browser must send the hostname to the DNS server and wait for a reply. Once the IP address is sent back, your browser then uses that address to contact the Web server. You then have to wait for data to be sent from the Web server to your computer.

During these delays, you will see informative messages, showing the progress. With the Internet Explorer browser, you will see a series of messages like:

```
Connecting to site 209.221.204.136
Web site found. Waiting for reply.
```

Now when you see these messages, you will know what they mean.

Mail Addresses

The most important service on the Internet is electronic mail. To send someone mail, you need to know his MAIL ADDRESS. Similarly, if someone knows your mail address, he can send you mail.

Once you understand hostnames, mail addresses are easy. They all follow the same pattern: a name, followed by an **@** character (the "at" sign), followed by a hostname:

name@hostname

Here are some examples:

```
billg@microsoft.com
charles@royal.gov.uk
pope@vatican.va
president@whitehouse.gov
abuse@aol.com
```

When you say a mail address out loud, the **@** character is pronounced "at". For example, the address **billg@microsoft.com** is pronounced

"Bill G at Microsoft dot com". The address `charles@royal.gov.uk` is pronounced "Charles at royal dot gov dot U.K.".

Mail addresses are not case sensitive. Thus, the following three addresses are equivalent. However, we generally use all lowercase letters (as in the first address) because it looks nicer:

`president@whitehouse.gov`

`President@Whitehouse.Gov`

`PRESIDENT@WHITEHOUSE.GOV`

Today, electronic mail is used widely, and mail addresses are ubiquitous. (For instance, some phone companies list email addresses in their telephone books.) For this reason, it is common to hear people use the word ADDRESS to refer to an email address.

If you are talking to someone on the Net, and he uses the word "address", you can assume he means an email address. If the person wants to refer to a regular street address, he will usually make it clear by context. This idea is illustrated in the following real-life example:

(A conversation that might take place in a Web chat room.)

Unknown Person: Excuse me, do you use Windows on your computer?

You: Yes, I do. Why do you ask?

Unknown Person: Well, I am Bill Gates, and I am interested in what you think of Windows and other fine Microsoft products. If I give you my personal address, would you mind sending me email with your comments?

You: Not at all, Bill, I would be glad to help.

Unknown Person: Thank you, that would be great. To show my appreciation, if you give me your postal address, I would be pleased to send you a box of money.

You: Sorry, Bill, but I make it a point to never give out personal information on the Net. I hope you understand.

Unknown Person: Of course I do, and I admire your good judgment. Well, bye for now.

Where does your personal email address come from? In most cases, you get your address from the company that supplies you with mail service.

If you use an ISP for mail service, they will assign you a name to use. For example, if your name is Benjamin Dover and your ISP is the Undependable Internet Company, your email address might be `bendover@undependable.com`.

Sometimes you can get your ISP to assign you a special name if it is not being used by someone else. So if everyone calls you Benjy, you might ask for the address `benjy@undependable.com`. The main rule everyone has to follow is that no two people can have the exact same address.

Most addresses are used by a person. However, there are some addresses that are used for special services. Companies often use names like `sales`, `support` or `feedback` to provide mailboxes for the general public. You might, for example, see the Undependable Internet Company set up the address `support@undependable.com` for customers who need a place to send a message when they have a problem.

Almost all mail systems have a standard address called `postmaster` to which you can send messages pertaining to the mail service. If you are having trouble sending mail to someone at, say, IBM, you can send a message to `postmaster@ibm.com`.

URLs

At the beginning of this chapter, I said that every computer, every person and every resource on the Internet has its own address. We have already talked about two types of addresses: hostnames (for computers) and mail addresses (for people). We will now talk about the addresses we use to identify the vast number of resources available on the Net.

The most popular resources on the Net are the many millions of Web pages stored on Web servers all over the world. Anyone with an Internet connection and a browser (Web client program) can access these pages. Of course, in order to fetch a Web page for you, your browser needs to know where to find the page. To describe the location of Web pages, we use a special type of address called a URL or UNIFORM RESOURCE LOCATOR. The name URL is pronounced as three separate letters, "U-R-L".

When we use a URL to specify the address of a particular resource, we say that the URL POINTS to that resource. For example, here is the URL that points to the main page of my Web site (don't worry about the details just yet):

hint

Many ISPs (Internet service providers) set up a mailbox with the name `abuse` to field complaints about problems caused by the ISP's customers. For instance, AOL uses the address `abuse@aol.com`.

If someone sends you threatening messages or bothers you with unsolicited advertising (spam), send a note to the `abuse` mailbox at that person's ISP. If the ISP does not have an `abuse` mailbox (and your mail comes back with an error message), send the complaint to `postmaster`.

Most ISPs take such complaints seriously.

```
http://www.harley.com/
```

Web sites can consist of many separate Web pages, and, strictly speaking, a URL points only to a single page. However, when a URL points to the main page of a Web site, we often say, informally, that the URL points to the site as a whole. Thus, I might say that the URL above points to the Harley Hahn Web site.

URLs can be used to point to all types of resources, not just Web pages. For this reason, URLs were designed to be as general as possible. As you use the Net, you will see two slightly different formats:

scheme **://***hostname***/***description*
scheme **:***description*

Here are some examples:

```
http://www.harley.com/
```

```
http://www.harley.com/25-things/index.html
```

```
http://www.ibm.com/
```

```
mailto:billg@microsoft.com
```

```
news:rec.pets.cats.anecdotes
```

```
ftp://ftp.microsoft.com/Products/msmq/demos.zip
```

The SCHEME (short for "addressing scheme") identifies the type of resource. Figure 4-3 shows the most commonly used schemes. As you use the Web, most of the URLs you will encounter will point to Web pages and, hence, will use the **http** scheme. (The name stands for Hypertext Transfer Protocol, the protocol used to transfer Web page data.) However, you will also see mail addresses (**mailto**), Usenet newsgroups (**news**) and anonymous ftp files (**ftp**).

Figure 4–3:   The most common schemes used within URLs

Scheme	Meaning
http	Web page (hypertext)
mailto	Mail address
news	Usenet newsgroup
ftp	File accessed via ftp
file	File on your computer

Although there are many other schemes, the ones I talked about are the most common. The only other scheme you are likely to see is `file`, and you will only see it if you use your browser to display a file that is stored on your own computer.

After the scheme, the next part of a URL is the hostname. This is the name of the computer on which the resource resides. For instance, the following URL points to a Web page on the computer named `www.harley.com`:

`http://www.harley.com/25-things/index.html`

Here is another example. This URL points to a file that is available via anonymous ftp from the computer named `ftp.microsoft.com`:

`ftp://ftp.microsoft.com/Products/msmq/demos.zip`

If you look at the list of examples above, you will notice that some types of URLs do not need hostnames. These URLs point to resources that, by their nature, do not reside on a specific computer.

An example of this format is `mailto`, the type of URL that specifies a mail address. If you see a Web page with a `mailto` URL, and you click on it, your browser will start your mail program and send it the specified address. This makes it easy for you to send a message to that particular address. For example, the following URL will set up a message to be sent to the person whose email address is `billg@microsoft.com`:

`mailto:billg@microsoft.com`

Aside from `mailto`, there is another common type of URL that does not require a hostname. This type of URL specifies the name of a Usenet newsgroup (discussion group). For instance:

`news:rec.pets.cats.anecdotes`

(By the way, this newsgroup is the one to which people send stories about cats.)

To read the articles in a newsgroup, you use a client program called a newsreader to access a news server. There are many news servers on the Net.

Before you can access Usenet, you need to tell your newsreader the hostname of the news server you will be using. Then, whenever you encounter a URL with a newsgroup name, your newsreader knows which computer to contact. Most people use a news server maintained by their ISP (Internet service provider) as a service to their customers.

For this reason, a URL that points to a newsgroup cannot contain a specific hostname. The URL contains the name of the group, but it is up to your browser to know the location of your news server.

So let's summarize what we have discussed so far.

URLs are designed to describe a variety of resources. There are two common variations of URLs:

*scheme***://***hostname***/***description*
*scheme***:***description*

The *scheme* identifies the type of resource described by the URL. The *hostname*, if it is included, specifies the location of the computer that contains the resource. The last part of the URL, the *description*, contains whatever other information is needed to find the exact resource.

With a **mail** URL, the *description* is a mail address; with a **news** URL, the *description* is the name of a Usenet newsgroup. However, with an **http** or **ftp** URL, the *description* must show exactly where a particular file resides. Such descriptions can be complicated, so we will discuss them in more detail, one step at a time.

File Names and Extensions

A computer FILE is a collection of data stored under a specific name. Files can hold any type of data that can be stored on a computer: text, numbers, pictures, sounds, video, and so on. In particular, the Web pages we view with our browsers are all stored in files on some computer or another. Thus, when we use a URL to point to a Web page, we need to specify not only the hostname of the computer, but the name of the exact file we want to look at.

Different computer systems have different rules for how files can be named. I won't go into all the variations, but I do want to mention one common characteristic: file names usually have two parts. The first part is chosen to describe the contents of the file in some way, the second part indicates the type of data stored in the file, and the two parts are separated by a period. Here are two examples:

```
invoice.doc

sales-order.doc
```

By looking at the first part of these file names, we can guess that the first file holds an invoice and the second file holds a sales order. The second part of a file name is called an EXTENSION. In this case, both files have the same extension, **doc**, which indicates that the files are documents. (It is common for word processor programs, such as Microsoft Word, to save files with an extension of **doc**.)

On the Internet, there are a number of extensions that you will see a lot. The most common is **html**. This indicates a file that contains hypertext — that is, a Web page. Now take a look at the following URL:

```
http://www.harley.com/25-things/index.html
```

Notice it ends with the name of a file, **index.html**. This tells you that the URL points to a Web page (although I still haven't explained all the details).

There are many different file extensions, and Figure 4-4 shows the ones you are most likely to see on the Internet. For now, don't worry about each type of file and what it means. We will discuss the various types of files as we encounter them throughout the book. I just want you to see a list of the most common extensions all in one place.

Figure 4-4: The most common file extensions used on the Internet

Extension	Pronunciation	Meaning
html	"h-t-m-l"	Web page
htm	"h-t-m"	Web page
asp	"a-s-p"	Web page generated in a special way
gif	"giff" or "jiff"	Picture stored in GIF format
jpg	"jay-peg"	Picture stored in JPEG format
txt	"t-x-t" or "text"	Plain text
zip	"zip"	Compressed collection of files
exe	"e-x-e" or "exy"	Executable program
wav	"wave"	Sound/music file
mp3	"m-p-3" or "em-peg"	Music file
mov	"move"	Video (movie) file

When we talk about a file name, we pronounce the period as "dot". The pronunciations of the extensions vary and are shown in Figure 4-4. As an example, the name **index.html** is pronounced "index dot h-t-m-l", while the name **cat.jpg** is pronounced "cat dot jay-peg".

What's in a Name?

html

htm

asp

Web pages are written using a set of specifications called Hypertext Markup Language or HTML (which we will discuss in Chapter 15). For this reason, Web pages are commonly stored in files with the extension of html.

Some computer systems do not allow more than three characters in a file extension, and, on such systems, Web pages are given the extension htm.

Files with an asp extension contain hypertext, just like html files, but are generated by a special system called Active Server Pages. (Hence the extension asp.) However, when you use your browser to look at an asp page, it works the same as a regular html page.

Directories and Subdirectories

Computers have so many files that we need a way to organize them. We do so by grouping files into DIRECTORIES. Each directory is given a name and can hold any number of files. For example, you might use a directory called **documents** to hold your word processing documents. It is easy to create and delete directories, so, on your own computer, you can modify the storage arrangement as you see fit.

Directories can contain not only files, but other directories. When a directory contains another directory, we call the first one a PARENT DIRECTORY and the second one a SUBDIRECTORY. A directory can have as many subdirectories as you need. The power of this system is that it allows you to create a hierarchy of directories to reflect a particular way of organizing files. Moreover, as your needs change, it is a simple matter to modify the directory structure and to move files from one directory to another.

Here is an example. You create a directory named **documents** to hold your word processing documents. This works fine for a few weeks, but then you notice that you have too many files in one directory, so you decide to reorganize. Within the **documents** directory, you create three subdirectories: **letters**, **writing** and **miscellaneous**. You then move each file in the **documents** directory to one of the three new subdirectories.

On some computer systems, it is customary to refer to directories as FOLDERS. This idea arose in the early days of PCs, when it was thought that personal computers were too intimidating for many people and everything should be "user friendly". The idea was that, by referring to directories as "folders", people would see the analogy between directories that contain computer files and folders in a filing cabinet.

Personally, I think the whole idea was pretty lame, and, to this day, computer companies (especially Microsoft and Apple) still continue to underestimate the intelligence of the average consumer. Thus, you will see both terms being used. When you do, just remember that a folder is the same thing as a directory, and a subfolder is the same as a subdirectory.

In general, people who like and understand computers use the word "directory", not the word "folder".

Pathnames

Now that we have discussed file names and directories, we can fill in the last part of the URL puzzle. You will remember that one type of URL uses the following general format:

*scheme***://***hostname***/***description*

The *description* is nothing more than a list of directories and a file name. Take a look at one of our previous examples:

http://www.harley.com/25-things/index.html

In this case, **25-things** is the name of a directory. Thus, the *description* refers to a file named **index.html** within a directory named **25-things**.

Here is another example:

ftp://ftp.microsoft.com/Products/msmq/demos.zip

In this URL, there are two directory names, **Products** and **msmq**. Thus, the *description* refers to a directory named **Products**. Within this directory lies a subdirectory named **msmq**, and within this subdirectory is a file named **demos.zip**. Or, to say it another way, the **demos.zip** file is in a directory named **msmq** that itself is in a directory named **Products**.

hint

With Windows, the program you use to work with files and directories is called WINDOWS EXPLORER.

hint

If you are a "directory" person, do not marry a "folder" person.

hint

When you write URLs, you use / (slash) characters to separate the directory names. For example:

`http://www.harley.com/ 25-things/index.html`

When you are working within Windows, however, you use \ (backslash) characters in pathnames. For instance, here is a typical Windows pathname that points to a file named `quikview.exe`:

`C:\Windows\System\ Viewers\quikview.exe`

In this example, the file resides in the `Viewers` directory, which is a subdirectory of the `System` directory, which is a subdirectory of the `Windows` directory on the `C:` disk.

Don't be confused. Within Windows, we use backslashes in a pathname, but in a URL we always use slashes.

As you use the Web, you will see a lot of URLs that have a series of directories ending with the name of a file. Such specifications are called PATHNAMES or, more simply, PATHS. Within a pathname, we use a / (slash) character to separate the various directory and file names.

Once you understand pathnames, it's easy to make sense out of most URLs if you remember the format:

scheme **://** *hostname* / *description*

The *scheme* shows you the type of resource, the *hostname* tells you the name of the computer, and the *description* contains a pathname.

What's in a Name?

/ (slash) for URL pathnames

\ (backslash) for Windows pathnames

Why do we use \ (backslash) characters in Windows pathnames, when using a / (slash) would be so much easier? It is a historical accident.

Windows is based on a old operating system called DOS, which uses commands that are typed by hand. The first DOS, version 1.0, was released in August 1981 along with the first IBM PC. Within DOS 1.0, the / character was used to indicate an option when you typed a command. For example, the `dir` command displays the names of all the files in a directory. The `dir /w` command displays the names using a "wide" format (more than one name per line).

At that time, PCs did not have hard disks, only floppy disks, and the amount of storage available on a floppy disk was small (just 160K). Since such a disk could not hold many files, DOS 1.0 did not support subdirectories, which meant there was no need for pathnames. Thus, it didn't matter that the / character was not available for pathnames.

In March 1983, IBM released the PC XT computer, the first PC to have a hard disk. The hard disk stored 10MB of data, which meant it was possible to store literally hundreds of files on a single disk. Thus, for the first time, there was a need for directories on a PC. A brand new DOS, version 2.0, which supported directories, was released along with the PC XT. Now there were pathnames.

Since the / character was used for command options, the designers of DOS 2.0 were reluctant to make PC users change their habits. For this reason, the \ character was used for pathnames. Through the years, DOS was improved and expanded, and at every step of the way, IBM and Microsoft opted for backward compatibility.

You might ask, why do we use a / character within Web addresses (URLs)? The answer is simple. The Web was originally designed on computers that used the Unix operating system, and from the very beginning, Unix has always used a / character for pathnames.

URL Abbreviations

Since URLs often contain a pathname, they can be quite long, and it's nice to be able to abbreviate whenever possible. To meet this need, there are conventions followed by Web servers that allow us to shorten URLs under certain conditions.

First, most Web servers follow a rule that says if the URL specifies a directory but no file name, the server will automatically look for a file with a specific name. Some servers look for a file named `index.html`, while others look for a file named `default.html` or `default.asp`. That means that, if you see a URL that ends in `index.html`, `default.html` or `default.asp`, you can usually leave off the file name and the URL will still work. Consider this URL from my own Web site:

`http://www.harley.com/25-things/index.html`

When you see a URL like this, you can guess that it might be okay to leave out the `index.html`, and most of the time (but not always) you will be right. With our example, it will work just fine if you use:

`http://www.harley.com/25-things/`

Similarly, either of the following URLs will point to the main Web page at my Web site:

`http://www.harley.com/`

`http://www.harley.com/index.html`

Another convention that lets us abbreviate has to do with the browser. If you ever type a URL that does not have a scheme at the beginning, your browser will assume the URL points to a Web page and insert `http://` for you.

In addition, if you leave out a final slash (/) character, the browser will usually insert the slash for you. For example, if you want to visit my Web site, either of these URLs will work:

`www.harley.com`

`http://www.harley.com/`

How does a Web server know if a pathname ends with a directory or a file name?

The Web server assumes that if the pathname ends with a slash (/), it indicates a directory. Thus, if you type a URL that does not have a file name at the end, you should be sure to include the slash. For example, use:

```
http://www.harley.com/
```

```
http://www.kingfeatures.com/comics/
```

not:

```
http://www.harley.com
```

```
http://www.kingfeatures.com/comics
```

Most of the time such URLs will work, even without the slash, but it is proper to include it, and, as one of my readers, I know you take pride in being proper at all times.

Case Sensitive Pathnames

There are just a few more ideas I want to explain before we finish our discussion of pathnames. However, in order to do so, I need to talk about operating systems for a moment.

An operating system is the master control program that runs a computer. Most PCs use a version of the Windows operating system: Windows XP, Windows Me, Windows 98 or Windows 95. For more powerful computers — especially those providing database and networking services — there are special versions: Windows 2000, as well as the older Windows NT.

Aside from Windows, there is a completely different family of operating systems called Unix. There are many types of Unix — with different names — that run on all types of computers, not just PCs.

The reason I mention this is that most of the Web servers on the Net run either Windows 2000/NT or Unix, and the two systems use slightly different rules for pathnames.

First, with Windows, you can write pathnames using either lower- or uppercase letters. For example, within a URL, the following pathnames are all equivalent (as long as the server is running some type of Windows):

```
products/msmq/demos.zip
```

```
Products/msmq/demos.zip
```

```
Products/Msmq/Demos.Zip
```

```
PRODUCTS/MSMQ/DEMOS.ZIP
```

Unix *always* distinguishes between lower- and uppercase. For instance, in Unix, the name `demos.zip` is considered completely different from the name `Demos.zip`. The term we use to describe such names is CASE SENSITIVE.

Recall our example:

```
ftp://ftp.microsoft.com/Products/msmq/demos.zip
```

If the computer to which this URL points is a Windows computer, you could use a lowercase `p` and the URL would still work. However, if the server is a Unix machine, the URL would not work.

In this case, the server does run Windows (which you might guess from looking at the hostname), so the following URL will work just fine:

```
ftp://ftp.microsoft.com/products/msmq/demos.zip
```

On the other hand, consider this URL from my Web site:

```
http://www.harley.com/get-rich/
```

This Web page resides on a Unix server where pathnames are case sensitive, and the last part of the pathname, `get-rich`, must be in all lowercase letters. If you change these letters to uppercase, the URL will not work:

```
http://www.harley.com/GET-RICH/
```

What a ~ (Tilde) Means in a Pathname

You will sometimes see a ~ character within a pathname. For instance:

```
http://www.psych.ucsb.edu/~kopeikin/
```

This character is called a TILDE (pronounced "til-duh"). In the United States, the standard PC keyboard has the tilde in the top left-hand corner, above the **Tab** key. To type a tilde, you need to hold down the **Shift** key. (By the way, the character you get if you don't hold down the **Shift** key is called a backquote [`]. The backquote is rarely used.) In other countries, the location of the tilde will vary. In the U.K., for example, the tilde is just to the left of the **Enter** key.

The tilde character is used primarily in Unix systems. Unix is designed to support many users at the same time, and each user is given a HOME

DIRECTORY in which to store his files. A Unix user can create whatever files and subdirectories he wants in his home directory.

Within Unix, a tilde combined with a name refers to the home directory of a particular person. For example, if you had an account on a Unix computer under the name `harley`, your home directory would be known as `~harley`.

Thus, when you see a URL that has a directory name beginning with a tilde, it means the Web site resides on a Unix system, and the directory is someone's home directory. In the example above, the URL points to the Web site of Hal Kopeikin, a member of the Department of Psychology at the University of California at Santa Barbara.

Putting It All Together

At the beginning of the chapter, I promised that by the time you finished this chapter, you would be able to understand addresses like this one:

`http://www.harley.com/25-things/index.html`

Notice how easy it is to understand such addresses once you understand the pattern. Just look for the general format:

*scheme***://***hostname/description*

Then identify the various parts. In this case:

- The scheme, `http`, tells you the URL points to a Web page.
- The hostname, `www.harley.com`, is the address of the Web server.
- The description, `25-things/index.html`, is the pathname of the Web page.

In other words, this URL is the address of a Web page named `index.html` in the `25-things` directory on the `www.harley.com` Web server.

If only all of life were so easy.

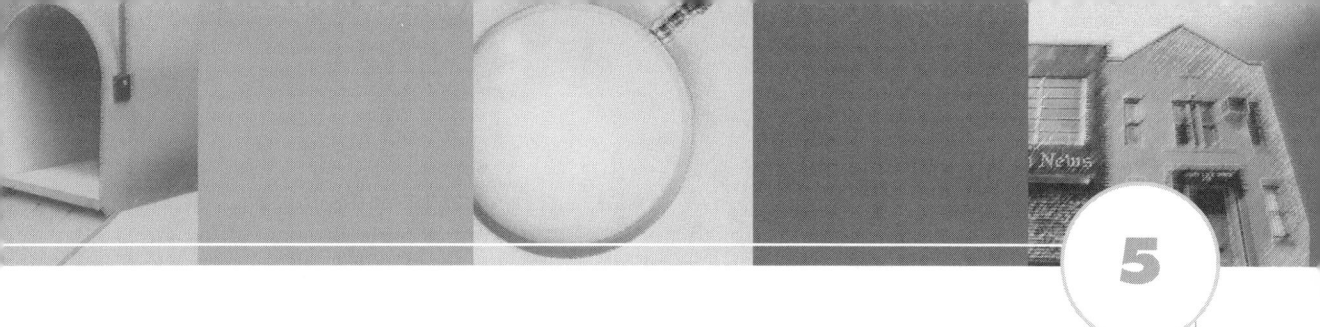

5

Mail

*My job is to ensure that
your usage of the Internet is
elegant and skillful enough
to carry you head and
shoulders above the pressing
crush of humanity.*

When I was a kid, I had to walk three miles in the freezing snow every time I wanted to check my electronic mail. Then, after checking my mail, I had to walk three miles back (and it was uphill both ways) just to get a peanut butter and jelly sandwich.

Today, life is a lot easier. Once you have Internet access, you can send and receive all the mail you want from the privacy (and warmth) of your own home.

In this chapter, I'll explain the basics: what you need to get you going and keep you going. In Chapter 6, I will give you some extra help and teach you how to use email well. After all, you are one of my readers, and it is my job to ensure that your usage of the Internet is elegant and skillful enough to carry you head and shoulders above the pressing crush of humanity.

So read on. By the time you finish these two chapters, mothers will hold up their children as you walk by and say, "Look at that person. Now, there's someone who *really* knows how to use email."

The Basic Ideas

In Chapter 2, we talked a bit about how mail works. Let's take a moment to have a quick review and add a few more details.

On the Internet, we commonly use the word MAIL to refer to EMAIL (electronic mail). Anyone who has your mail ADDRESS can send you mail. Similarly, you can send mail to anyone whose address you have. Mail addresses are in the form:

name@hostname

For instance:

`billg@microsoft.com`

Like all Internet services, mail uses a client/server system. You run a client, called a MAIL PROGRAM, on your computer. Whenever necessary, your mail program contacts a MAIL SERVER to request services on your behalf. Most people use the mail server provided by their ISP (Internet service provider). However, there are other options, which we will discuss later in the chapter.

To send mail, you use your mail program to compose a message. When you are finished, you tell your program to send the message. Your program contacts the server, and sends it the message. The server then delivers the message to the recipient's mail server.

Similarly, when someone sends a message to your mail address, it is received and stored by your mail server. From time to time, your mail program contacts the server to see if there are any messages waiting for you. If so, your program receives the messages and shows them to you.

Whenever you start your mail program, it will check for messages. After that, it will check at regular intervals (say, every 10 minutes). So although it is possible to tell your program to check for new mail, you usually won't need to. Incoming messages will arrive automatically.

SMTP Servers and POP Servers

In Chapter 1, I explained that clients and servers communicate with one another by using various protocols. There are three different protocols you will encounter within the Internet mail system. Although you don't need to concern yourself with the details, it is important to at least know the names of these protocols and what they do.

The three protocols are SMTP (Simple Mail Transfer Protocol), POP (Post Office Protocol) and IMAP (Internet Message Access Protocol). SMTP is used to send messages to a mail server, while POP and IMAP are used to receive messages from a mail server. To explain how this all works, let's take a look at when these protocols are used when you send a message.

Using your mail program , you compose a message and address it to a friend. Once the message is ready for delivery, your program uses the SMTP protocol and transfers the message to your ISP's mail server. The mail server then uses SMTP to transfer the message to the mail server used by your friend. When the message arrives at the destination mail server, it is stored until your friend picks it up.

Now consider what happens when you receive a message. When it is time to check for messages, your mail program uses the POP protocol to connect to your ISP's mail server (where all your incoming mail is stored). If there are messages waiting for you, your program uses POP to download them to your computer. Your program then shows you a summary of the incoming messages, which you can read whenever you want.

Thus, SMTP is used to send messages to a mail server, while POP is used to receive messages from a mail server. (We'll talk about IMAP in a moment.)

Thus, it follows that, before your mail program can send and receive mail, it must know the hostname (computer name) of your SMTP server

hint

Some ISPs give you a special installation program to run to set up your service. (For example, they may send you a CD to use to get started.) When you run this program, it will install a lot of software, such as a browser and a mail program. You may also find that the program configures your mail program for you. In such cases, you will not have to type in the hostnames of your SMTP and POP servers by hand. However, it is interesting to look and see what they are.

and the hostname of your POP server. In principle, the SMTP server and the POP server can be completely different computers. However, in practice, both servers usually run on the same computer.

Here is an example. A fellow named Benjamin Dover signs up for Internet service with the Undependable Internet Company, and is assigned an address of `bendover@undependable.com`. At the time he signs up, Benjamin is told that his SMTP and POP servers both have the same hostname: `mail.undependable.com`. So, before he uses his mail program for the first time, Benjamin must configure the program by specifying this information. If Benjamin ever changes ISPs, he must reconfigure his program by specifying a new address for himself, his SMTP server, and his POP server.

By the way, notice that the hostname of the mail server begins with `mail`. This is a common convention used by many ISPs.

IMAP Servers

The system I have described so far uses SMTP to send messages and POP to receive messages. IMAP (Internet Message Access Protocol) is sometimes used as an alternative to POP.

When you use POP, messages must be downloaded to your computer before you can access them. This is fine when you always check your mail from the same computer. However, if you routinely use POP to check mail from different computers, you may have a problem, because your messages can end up in different places.

For example, let's say you work for a company that provides you with a computer in your office as well as a notebook computer to use when you travel. In addition, you sometimes do office work at home using your own computer. All your work-related mail is sent to only one mail server — the one at the office — but you need to be able to check for mail from all three computers.

With IMAP, your mail client can manipulate messages on the server without having to download them. Thus, your messages stay on the server and are accessible from any computer you may use. (Of course, you can delete the messages from the server whenever you want.)

Most ISPs would not want their customers to use IMAP, because the tendency would be for people to leave all their messages on the ISP's server.

Eventually, the IMAP server would fill up, and there is no graceful way for an ISP to delete their customers' messages. However, within a well-managed private environment, IMAP can work well, as it allows people to check their mail from any computer they want and still keep all their messages in one place.

To use this system, you need both a mail server and a mail client that support IMAP.

Web-Based Mail Services

The systems I have described so far involve mail client programs using SMTP and POP (or IMAP) to communicate with mail servers. This is the way most people send and receive email. However, there is an alternative system you should know about.

Many companies offer Web-based mail services that allow you to send and receive mail using only your Web browser. With such systems, your browser acts as a simple mail client, while a special Web server at the other end acts as a mail server. Since browsers are not designed to handle mail, virtually all of the work is done by the server. All your browser does is show information and let you make choices.

There are advantages and disadvantages to Web-based mail services. The first big advantage is that, in most cases, they are free: the companies make their money by selling advertising. Free services are nice, but while you are composing, reading or sending mail, you will have to look at advertisements. Personally, this bugs me a lot, although you may not mind it as much as I do. In addition, some services also put a short advertisement at the end of each message you send out. Moreover, you may find yourself the recipient of unsolicited advertising messages. Again, this is all something you may be glad to put up with in return for free mail.

Another advantage to Web-based email is that you can use it from any computer in the world that has an Internet connection. This means that, when you are traveling, you can check your mail from anywhere you can find access to a browser. With the regular mail system, you need to be at your own computer, running your own mail program. (Even with IMAP, you still need a mail client configured for your account.)

Web-based mail makes it possible for people without computers to use mail. For example, many libraries have public Internet access, and many schools provide access for their students. If you don't have your own computer, you can use a browser at the library or at school to establish and maintain a Web-based mail account.

Finally, Web-based services provide a large measure of anonymity. When you register for such a service, you can specify any name and password you want. This is handy, for instance, when your only Internet access is at the office, and you don't want to use your work address for personal correspondence. You can get yourself a Web-based mail account, give out that address to your friends, and then use your browser at work to check your personal mail. (Although, if anyone asks, you didn't get this idea from me.)

One of the great things about such mail accounts is that you create a new one for free whenever you want. In other words, they are disposable. Disposable address are useful in a number of ways. For example, many Web sites make you register before you can use the site. As part of the registration process, you will be required to specify an email address (so the company running the Web site can send you advertising, or sell your address for money). The solution? Just use a disposable address, one that you created for free and don't mind abandoning later.

As you might imagine, the convenience and anonymity of such systems has not escaped the notice of the troublemakers of the world, and there are a lot of dishonest and shady characters hiding behind free, Web-based mail addresses.

A more immediate concern, if you have children, is that any kid with Internet access can register for a free mail address and then use a browser to access the mail when no one is looking. This is something you should be aware of, especially if you are a teacher whose students seem too well-behaved when they are using the computer lab.

Perhaps the biggest disadvantage to Web-based mail services is that they are slow to use. With regular mail service, your mail client runs on your own computer, and all your messages reside locally on your own hard disk (with POP) or on a special server (with IMAP). With a Web-based service, everything is stored at the Web site, and working with individual messages one at a time over the Web can be a frustrating experience.

So do you need a Web-based mail account? For your day-to-day mail, you are better off using the regular mail account with your ISP. But if you have a special need (such as checking your messages when you travel or hiding your mail from prying eyes), you might want to try a Web-based service.

Internet Resources   **Web-Based Mail Services**

```
http://www.fepg.net/
http://www.mail.com/
http://www.iname.com/
http://mail.excite.com/
http://www.hotmail.com/
http://www.eudoramail.com/
http://www.mail.yahoo.com/
http://www.emailaddresses.com/
http://www.internetmaillist.com/
```

hint

The distinctions between regular and Web-based mail services occasionally blur. Some Web-based services offer a POP server, so you can use a regular mail client instead of a browser to check your mail (although you may have to pay for this service).

Conversely, some ISPs offer Web access to their mail server, so you can check your mail away from your own computer.

Which Mail Program Should You Use?

The two most popular browsers, Microsoft Internet Explorer and Netscape, are bundled with a free mail program. (The Microsoft program is called OUTLOOK EXPRESS.) Both Microsoft and AOL (which owns Netscape) would like to control the browser market, and one way to do so is to provide lots of other software that is tightly integrated with the browser. In that sense, the strategy works, because most people use the mail program that comes with their browser.

Since the mail protocols (SMTP, POP and IMAP) are standardized, you can use any mail program you want. The Internet Explorer and Netscape mail programs will both work fine. However, you can use a completely different program, one that has nothing to do with your browser. For example, my favorite mail program is Eudora.

Regardless of which mail program you use, you will find it has more features than you need and more options than you will ever understand. Do not get frustrated. In this chapter and in Chapter 6, I will explain the basic features of all mail programs. I suggest that, after you read these chapters, you take a good amount of time — at least a few hours —and experiment with your particular program. Investigate all the menu items, and take a look at all the options. (They may be called "preferences".) Eventually, you will figure out what features you need and what you can ignore.

hint

Some software compa-
nies offer both free and
commercial versions of
the same program. In
such cases, the programs
that cost money have
extra features. However,
in my experience, the
free programs are usu-
ally adequate, and there
is no need to pay for a
commercial product
unless you really want
the extra features.

In this book, I have cho-
sen free resources when-
ever possible.

If you use the Internet at work, you may be forced to use the same mail program as everyone else. In my experience, people who work for large companies often do not like the standard corporate mail program. If you do work in such a company, take advantage of your freedom at home, and choose a program that suits you.

If you are new to the Net, don't worry about making a choice right away. Use whichever mail program is installed on your computer and, once you get some experience, you can download other programs and experiment. If you find a mail program you like better than the one you are using, there is no problem making a switch whenever you want.

Internet Resources   **Mail Programs**

`http://www.eudora.com/`

`http://www.microsoft.com/ie/`

`http://www.netscape.com/browsers/`

To get Microsoft's Outlook Express, you need to install Internet Explorer. To get Netscape's mail program, you need to install Communicator. Eudora is a standalone program that is installed on its own.

The Parts of a Message

Conceptually, mail is simple: you type a message and then send it to someone else. Through the years, however, electronic mail has evolved, and the nature of a message has become complex to the point where it can have up to four separate parts. These parts are: the header, the body, attachments and a signature. In this section, I will give you a quick overview. We will then discuss each part in more detail.

At the beginning of every message is a HEADER consisting of a number of specific HEADER LINES. These header lines contain technical information needed by the mail system: the name and address of the sender, the time and date the message was sent, the subject of the message, the name and address of the recipient, and so on.

After the header comes the BODY, the main content of the message. Most of the time, the body will be simple text that you have typed, but, if you wish, you can also include other elements, such as pictures or links to Web pages.

Along with the body of a message, you can also send a file. When you do, we say you ATTACH the file to the message, and the file itself is referred to as an ATTACHMENT. For example, you might send a message to a friend to which you have attached a sound file containing a song. When your friend receives the message, he can save the file to his hard disk and then listen to the song.

A SIGNATURE is a small amount of information (which you create) that your mail program puts at the end of every message you send. Having a signature is optional, though many people use one. A typical signature might contain your name, mail address, and a link to your Web site (if you have one).

The Most Important Header Lines

Each time you send a message, your mail program automatically generates a header with technical information and places it at the beginning of the message. Similarly, when you receive a message, it will have a header which you can look at if you want.

All headers more or less have the same format, but what you see on your system depends greatly on which mail program you use. Some programs attempt to dumb down everything that looks the least bit technical and hide most of the header from you. Other programs show you all or some of the header. Regardless, there is always a way to look at the full header if you really want to, although how to do so may not be obvious. You may have to use the help facility that comes with your program, or just experiment and figure it out by trial and error.

A few of the header lines are crucial, and you must be able to understand them. Others are less important and can be safely ignored. Let's start with a typical message, shown in Figure 5-1. This message shows the most important parts of the header: the `From`, `To`, `Subject`, `Cc` and `Date` lines. All mail programs show these lines, or at least the information they contain.

`From:` This line tells you the address and name of the person who sent the mail. In most cases, you can simply take the information at face value. However, if the mail seems strange in any way, you should be suspicious. It is simple for someone to configure your mail program to specify any name and address you want. Moreover, if you know what you are doing, you can forge mail so that it looks as though it comes from another computer. This is a common trick of spammers (people who send unsolicited advertising by email). So when in doubt, be careful. If you get a message with an invitation to meet the President of the United States, you might want to check carefully before you make your plane reservation.

Learn how to...

Display the Full Header of a Mail Message

When you first start to use a mail program, take a moment and find out how to look at the full header of a message.

See Chapter 17, *How to Do Stuff*, page 377 (Outlook Express).

Figure 5-1: A typical mail message

```
From: Arthur Irwin Choke <artichoke@whitehouse.gov>
To: Harley Hahn <harley@little-nipper.com>
Date: Mon, 30 Jul 2001 22:34:01 -0400
Subject: pres wants to meet with you
Cc: Charles Wagon <chuckwagon@whitehouse.gov>

To Harley Hahn:


The President of the United States has
asked me to see if you are free to meet with
him next week. He hopes you will be able to
listen to music on his computer.

Arthur Irwin Choke


Special Assistant, Computer Stuff,
Office of the President
```

hint

When you compose a message, take a moment to create a good `Subject` line. The description you write should be short, no more than a few words, but as meaningful as possible. Remember, your subject line is the only description the recipient is going to see to identify your message among the many others in his mailbox.

This is especially important when you send mail to a Very Busy Person. Some people receive so much mail that they literally do not have time to read it all. A VBP is more likely to read a message with the subject `Need a free ticket to the game?` than one with the subject `Question for you.`

`To`: This line shows the mail address to which the message was sent. Most of the time, you will see your own address. However, this is not always the case. For instance, a message can be sent to more than one person simply by putting more than one address in the `To` line. So if you see other addresses besides yours, it means that each of the other people received a copy of the message. If you belong to a mailing list (see Chapter 14), the messages from the list are addressed to a special list address, not to you personally. Thus, if you see a mailing list address in the `To` line, it means the message went to everyone on the list.

`Subject`: The information on the `Subject` line is specified by the person who sent the message. The purpose of this line, as you can guess from its name, is to provide a short summary of the contents of the message. When incoming mail arrives, your mail program shows you the subject line of each message. You won't actually see the contents of the message (the body) until you open it. Thus, whenever you look at the list of incoming mail, you are really looking at the `Subject` lines created by the senders of those messages.

`Cc`: When you compose a message, it is possible to send it to more than one person by putting more than one address in the `To` line.

Alternatively, you can send a copy to someone by putting his address in the **Cc** line. (I will show you how this works later in the chapter.) The important thing I want you to remember is that, when you receive a message, look at both the **To** line and the **Cc** line. Everyone whose address is in one of these lines has received a copy of the message.

Date: This line shows the date and time that the message was sent. The date portion is straightforward, but when you read the time you must be careful. The Internet is used around the world, and local time is not meaningful unless you know the time zone. For this reason, the time zone is always specified in some way. In our example, the time is shown as:

```
22:34:01 -0400
```

The first part of the time tells you the message was sent at 10:34 PM local time. (The Internet uses a 24-hour clock, so **22:34** means 10:34 PM.) However, how do you know what time zone this refers to? The **-0400** shows you. It indicates the number of hours difference between the local time where the message originated, and GMT (Greenwich Mean Time). In this case, the local time zone is 4 hours behind GMT. (This happens to be Eastern Daylight Time.)

Such calculations can be a bit confusing. Moreover, you may see other time zone formats than the one I have shown above.

For more information, see Appendix B, where I discuss these topics in more detail.

A Few More Header Lines

Aside from the **Date**, **From**, **To** and **Subject** lines, there are a number of other header lines. In this section, I will describe those lines that are important enough for you to care about. As an example, Figure 5-2 shows a typical message containing these extra lines.

Received: Each time a message passes through a computer, the mail program on that computer inserts a **Received** line into the header. Thus, the header always contains at least one such line. You can look at these lines to trace the path followed by the message to your mail server. In the example in Figure 5-2, we see one **Received** line. (Although it is so long as to be physically broken into two parts, it still counts as one line.)

Learn how to...

Set the Time and Date on Your Computer

Whenever you send a message, your mail program uses the date, time, and time zone settings from your computer. These three settings are maintained by Windows, and it is up to you to make sure they are correct.

See Chapter 17, *How to Do Stuff*, page 366 (Windows).

```
From: Harley Hahn <harley@little-nipper.com>
Received: from mail.little-nipper.com ([198.68.156.50])
   by mail.whitehouse.gov
Message-Id: <200107302240.WRM012367@little-nipper.com>
Reply-To: Harley Hahn <harley@little-nipper.com>
Date: Mon, 30 Jul 2001 19:40:17 -0700
Organization: The Little Nipper Foundation
To: Arthur Irwin Choke <artichoke@whitehouse.gov>
Subject: re: pres wants to meet with you
X-Mailer: Microsoft Outlook Express 5.50.4133.2400
Cc: Charles Wagon <chuckwagon@whitehouse.gov>

> To Harley Hahn:
>
> The President of the United States has
> asked me to see if you are free to meet with
> him next week. He hopes you will be able to
> listen to music on his computer.
>
> Arthur Irwin Choke
> Special Assistant, Computer Stuff
> Office of the President

Art:

I am sorry, but I will not be able to accept
your invitation to meet with the President
next week. Please tell him I will be busy
selecting Freddy the Pig pictures for my new
book.

I'm sure he will understand.

-- Harley Hahn

==================================================
Harley Hahn            http://www.harley.com/
(202) 456-1414         harley@little-nipper.com
==================================================
```

```
Received: from mail.little-nipper.com ([198.68.156.50])
  by mail.whitehouse.gov
```

From this line, we can see that the message was sent from a computer named `mail.little-nipper.com` with an IP address of `198.68.156.50`, and was received by a computer named `mail.whitehouse.gov`. Both of these computers, of course, are mail servers. When you look at `Received` lines, you will often see other types of information. Such information is usually highly technical and can almost always be ignored.

`Message-Id:` Every time a message is mailed on the Internet, the originating mail server assigns the message a unique identification code. In our example, we see:

```
Message-Id: <200107302240.WRM012367@little-nipper.com>
```

This information in itself is not all that useful to a human being. However, what *is* useful is that part of the code is always the domain name of the mail server that sent the message. Thus, if someone mails you a message with a forged address, the best way to track down the person is to look at the `Message-Id` line. It is very difficult to forge this line unless you have control over the mail server. Some spammers are sophisticated enough to do so, but most troublemakers — such as mischievous college students — are not.

If someone sends you a bothersome or harassing message from a forged address, look at the full header and find the `Message-Id` line. This will show you the name of the mail server from which the message was sent. You can then send a message to `postmaster` at that address and ask for help. When you do, be sure to include the entire original message, including the full header. This will help the postmaster track down the miscreant.

Here is an example. You receive a threatening letter with the following header line:

```
Message-ID: <3529D136.5B6B6CCC@shsu.edu>
```

Send the message, along with the full header, to `postmaster@shsu.edu` and ask for help.

`Reply-To:` When you reply to a message, your mail program will usually send the reply to the address in the `From` line. For example, if someone named Eloise Q. Abernathy sends you a message, you want the reply to go to Eloise Q. Abernathy. However, there are times when this is not appropriate. In such cases, you will see a **Reply-To** line along with an address. When this line is present, your mail program will send the reply to this address, rather than to the address in the **From** line. You will often see this with mailing lists (see Chapter 14) in which each message is sent to everyone on the list. Every time a message is sent to the list, the mailing list program will insert a **Reply-To** line to ensure that all replies go back to the list, and not to the person whose address is in the **From** line.

Organization: You will sometimes see this header line. The intention is to tell you the name of the organization to which the sender of the message belongs. Such information can be useful, but is easy to falsify, so do not depend on it.

X-Mailer: When the original technical specification for Internet mail headers was developed, a certain number of standard header lines were described. However, it was recognized that there would be a need for other, nonstandard lines, so the rules say that anyone can put extra lines in a header as long as they begin with the characters **x-**. When you look at the full header for a message, you will often see several **x-** lines, usually inserted by the sender's mail program. One common line is **X-Mailer**, used to show the name of the mail program used to compose the message. Such information may or may not be significant in your life, but if you need it, it is there. I find the **X-Mailer** line useful when I am helping someone who is having trouble with mail, and I want to know what program he is using.

The Body of a Message

The body is the main part of the message, and is usually plain text, so when you compose a message, you just type whatever you want.

Some mail programs allow you to include more than plain text by using HTML (hypertext markup language), the same system that is used to specify the appearance of Web pages. With HTML, a message can contain different typefaces, as well as italics and boldface. It can also contain pictures, links to Web sites, and various other elements that might appear on a Web page.

HTML is complex, but you don't have to understand it to use it in a mail message. You just compose the message the way you want, and your mail program automatically builds the required HTML specifications for you. Not all mail programs support HTML, but the most popular ones do, and they make it easy to insert special features into your messages.

Using HTML in a mail message might seem like a good idea, and when used judiciously it can be cool. Mostly, though, people who use HTML tend to go overboard at first and use it to excess. In addition, some mail programs do not support HTML, and when you send such a message, there is a chance the person receiving it will not be able to read it properly. I will talk more about these problems in Chapter 6.

Attachments

Along with the body of a message (either plain text or rich text), you can send one or more files. These files are called attachments and can hold anything you want: a picture, a word processing document, a program, and so on.

I have a friend named Terry who talks to people in Greece using a chat facility. Before they start the conversation, Terry and her friends use attachments to send one another sound files containing Greek music. Then, as they are talking, they use their computers to listen to the music at the same time.

Before you send someone a file, make sure the person has the proper software to use that file. For example, there is no use sending someone a file that contains a Microsoft Excel spreadsheet if he or she doesn't have a program to read that type of file. Before you send the file, you should check to see if the person will be able to use it. Don't assume that everyone has the same software as you. ("I need to send you a spreadsheet. Do you have Excel?")

Before you send someone a file, make sure the file name is something that will be meaningful to the person. Here is an example to show you what I mean.

Say that you and I are planning to host a big dinner for the Maharajah of Gaipajama. We have a phone conversation, during which you write down some notes. You use your word processor to type the notes into a file, and you save the file under the name **harley.doc**. You now want to send the file to me.

On your computer, the name **harley.doc** makes perfect sense, because it holds information you have collected during a conversation with me. However, when the file arrives on *my* computer, the same name will not be meaningful.

Learn how to...

Turn Off HTML in Mail Messages

HTML in mail messages is unnecessary and mostly useless. Moreover, it can cause problems when you send messages to people who use a mail program that is different from yours. Take a moment, right now, and make sure your mail program is set to use plain text, not HTML.

See Chapter 17, *How to Do Stuff*, page 377 (Outlook Express).

What should you do? Before you send the file, make a copy under a better name, and attach the copy to a message. In this case, you might copy `harley.doc` to `dinner-notes.doc`. After the message has been sent, you can delete the copy.

By taking an extra moment to be thoughtful, you have made it easier for me to recognize the file when it arrives.

Although this might not seem like such a big deal, it really is. I frequently get attachments with file names that make no sense to me whatsoever. Later, when I go back to look at the file, I have no idea what it contains.

In general, whenever you send mail, you should always ask yourself, "What can I do to make the message easy for the other person to understand?"

Signatures

If you find yourself typing certain routine information in all your letters, think about putting that information into a signature: a small amount of personalized information that your mail program automatically inserts at the end of each outgoing message. Once you have created a signature, it will appear at the end of all your outgoing messages.

Traditionally, signatures are used for information such as a phone number, Web page address and street address. An example of this is the signature from the message in Figure 5-2:

```
==================================================
Harley Hahn                 http://www.harley.com/
(202) 456-1414              harley@little-nipper.com
==================================================
```

Some people like to include a witty or pithy saying within their signature. This is fine: after all, we all like wit, and the person does not live who can't use a bit more pith in his life. Just make sure that your signature does not get too long. Over the years, experienced Internet users have determined, by trial and error, that signatures should be no more than four lines. Anything longer is irritating to other people.

Remember, your signature is going to be read by everyone to whom you send mail, every time they receive a message from you. For example, in the course of a month, if you send your girlfriend 100 messages, she is going to have to read your signature 100 times.

(The same advice, of course, goes for messages to a boyfriend. However, in my experience, it is almost always the men who are chronic large-signature-offenders.)

When you put a URL (Web address) in your signature, be sure to specify the full address. For example:

`http://www.harley.com/`

When you use a full address, the mail program at the other end will recognize the address as a URL and display it as a live link. That way, when someone reads your message, he will be able to click on your URL without leaving his mail program. The mail program will then send the URL to his browser automatically. Thus, when you specify a full address, you make it easy for the person to visit your Web site.

Do not use an abbreviated address, such as:

`www.harley.com`

The mail program will not recognize it as a URL, which means that if the person wants to look at your Web site, he will have to manually retype (or copy and paste) the URL into his browser.

How Mail Is Stored (Folders)

In this section, I will explain how mail is stored when you use a mail program like Outlook Express (Internet Explorer). If you use Web-based mail, discussed earlier in the chapter, the ideas will be the same, although the details will be a little different.

As the days pass, you are going to accumulate a lot of messages. To help you store them conveniently in an organized fashion, your mail program creates a set of FOLDERS, each of which can hold as many messages as necessary. If you want, you can create extra folders and move messages between them, but you will probably find that the standard folders will work just fine.

The names of the folders will vary from one program to another, but their use should be obvious. Here are the folders used by Outlook Express:

- Inbox
- Outbox
- Sent Items
- Deleted Items
- Drafts

Learn how to...

Create a Signature

When you send mail, using a signature allows you to insert a few lines of personalized information at the end of each message.

See Chapter 17, *How to Do Stuff*, page 378 (Outlook Express).

The Inbox holds all your incoming mail. The Outbox holds messages you have composed that are ready for delivery, but have not yet been sent. Once messages are sent, they are moved to the Sent Items folder.

The Drafts folder is a temporary storage area for messages that are partially typed, but not yet ready to send. For instance, if you are typing a message and you have to quit the program before the message is finished, you can save it in the Drafts folder. Some mail programs will automatically save unfinished messages to this folder when you quit the program. Other programs will not do so automatically; you must save the message yourself before you quit. (I suggest you take a minute right now and run a test to see exactly how your program works.)

As you read your incoming messages, you will want to delete them. Similarly, you will want to delete messages from your Sent folder. When you delete messages, they are not really deleted, they are simply moved to your Deleted Items folder. This gives you a chance to look at your old messages should the need arise. Eventually, you should delete the messages in your Deleted Items folder. Once you do, however, they are gone forever.

For reference, Figure 5-3 shows the life cycle of a mail message.

Figure 5-3: The life cycle of a mail message

Outbox
↓
Sent Items folder
↓
your mail server
↓
recipient's mail server
↓
Inbox
↓
Deleted Items
↓
oblivion

Address Lines Within the Header (To, Cc, Bcc)

When you compose a message, there are three lines in the header on which you can specify addresses: the To line, the Cc (copy) line, and the Bcc (blind copy) line. Each of these lines can hold one or more addresses, and *every address* you specify will be sent a copy of the message.

The To line and the Cc line are similar. The main difference is one of interpretation by the people who receive the message. When you put someone's address in the To line, it shows you consider the message to be of direct importance to that person. When you put someone's address in the Cc line, it shows you want the person to see the message, but only for his own information; you don't expect him to act upon it.

For example, say you live in the U.S., and you think your taxes should be lower. You decide to mail a message explaining your situation to the Commissioner of the Internal Revenue Service. You also decide to send copies to the President of the United States, the Vice President of the United States, the Chief Justice of the Supreme Court, and your mother. The proper etiquette is to put the address of the Internal Revenue Commissioner on the To line and all the other addresses on the Cc line:

```
To: commissioner@irs.ustreas.gov
Subject: Please lower my taxes
Cc: president@whitehouse.gov, vice-president@whitehouse.gov,
    chief@supreme-court.gov, mom@happy-family.com
```

Aside from the To and Cc lines, you can also put addresses on the Bcc line. The addresses on this line will receive an identical copy of the message, but no one else will know about it. Thus, you can use the Bcc line to send secret copies of a message. When you do, the copies are called BLIND COPIES.

In our example, you might decide it would intimidate the IRS commissioner too much if he found out that other powerful people were sent a copy of your message. So you decide to send a blind copy to the most intimidating people, and a regular copy to the other, less powerful people:

```
To: commissioner@irs.ustreas.gov
Subject: Please lower my taxes
Cc: president@whitehouse.gov, vice-president@whitehouse.gov,
    chief@supreme-court.gov
Bcc: mom@happy-family.com
```

What's in a Name?

Cc, Bcc

In the olden days, before computers and copiers, people used typewriters to write letters, and once a letter was written, there was no easy way to make a copy.

The solution was to use carbon paper. You would put a piece of carbon paper between two pieces of regular paper and insert all three pieces into the typewriter. As you typed, the keys striking the top paper would press on the carbon paper underneath and cause a copy to be made on the bottom paper. When you were finished, the bottom paper would be a duplicate of the top paper. This duplicate was called a CARBON COPY and would normally be filed in your records. (If you are not sure what carbon paper is, ask an old person.)

If you needed to send an extra copy of a letter to someone, you would have to use a second piece of carbon paper with an extra piece of regular paper, and make two copies instead of one. This extra copy could then be sent to a second recipient. To indicate that a copy was sent, you would type "`Cc:`" followed by that person's name at the bottom of the letter.

For example, say you were typing a business letter to Rick Shaw, with a copy to Mary Q. Contrary. At the bottom of the letter, you would type:

`Cc: Mary Q. Contrary`

When Rick saw this line, he would know that Mary was sent a carbon copy of the letter.

That is why, to this day, we use a `Cc` header line within an email message to indicate who is to receive a copy of that message. The `Bcc` (blind copy) designation is simply a variation of `Cc`.

Using an Address Book

If you send many messages, it is convenient to have a permanent list of names and addresses. All mail programs let you do this by maintaining a personalized ADDRESS BOOK. The address book contains a number of entries, each of which has room for a name, a mail address, and miscellaneous notes. The actual details depend on your program. Some store only this basic information; others allow you to put in other types of information, such as a company name, a postal address, phone numbers (work, home, fax), and so on.

To use an address book, you create one entry for each person to whom you send mail. Then, whenever you want to send a message, you can select a name from the address book and the program will fill in the details (such as the address). Some programs will automatically look in your address book whenever you start to type a name in the **To** line of a new message. If the program can guess which name you are starting to type, it will do its best to fill in the rest of the name for you.

Most mail programs make it easy to create an address book. In particular, as you read a message, there will be a way to tell your program to extract the name and address of the person who sent the message and automatically create a new entry in your address book. Thus, it is easy to build a personal address book one entry at a time as you receive messages from various people.

Replying

After you have read a message, you can REPLY to the person who sent it to you. The details vary depending on which mail program you use, but they should be simple.

If the message was sent to more than one person, your mail program will give you two choices: you can reply only to the person who sent the message, or you can reply to everyone who received a copy (that is, to everyone whose address appears on the **To** and **Cc** lines). Before you choose, take a moment and ask yourself: Do I really want everyone to see my reply?

When you reply to a message, your program creates a new message, all ready to send. The old message will be included as part of the new message, so you can use all or part of it within the reply, and will be marked in some way to make it stand out. The most common convention is to preface each line of the old message with a **>** (greater-than) character.

When you include part of the original message within a reply, we say that you QUOTE the original message. For an example of what this looks like, take a look at the message in Figure 5-2.

It is important to make your replies as readable as possible. Do not always quote the entire original message. Instead, quote only what you need and delete the parts that are irrelevant. Sometimes a message will go back and forth several times, with new text added each time, and, if you don't edit and prune the message as it develops, it will grow excessively long and become difficult to understand.

hint

Take a moment now and find out how to create an entry in your address book using your mail program. In particular, find out how to save the name and address from a message directly to your address book.

For Outlook Express, right-click on the message and select **Add Sender to Address Book**.

Here is an example to illustrate how to write a good reply. A person named Rick sends the following message to a person named Ilsa:

```
Ilsa:

Would you like to meet me this evening after the club-
closes?

We could talk over old times and have a drink. We haven't
seen each other in years, and I would love to spend some
time with you again.

If you come, please wear a pink carnation so I will be
sure to recognize you.

-- Rick
```

When Ilsa replies to Rick, she quotes only the parts of the original message that are relevant to her reply. She also makes sure to put Rick's name at the top of the message and her name at the bottom.

```
Rick:

> Would you like to meet me this evening after the club
> closes?

Yes, that would be great.

> If you come, please wear a pink carnation so I will be
> sure to recognize you.

I don't know if I can get a carnation on such short
notice. Would a ranunculus be okay?

-- Ilsa
```

Rick now replies to Ilsa's reply. Notice that parts of the very first message are now marked by >> (two greater-than characters). This is because a single > character is inserted into the old text each time you reply. Notice as well that Rick, like Ilsa, has deleted all but the relevant parts of the message to which he is replying.

```
Ilsa:

>> If you come, please wear a pink carnation so I will be
>> sure to recognize you.

> I don't know if I can get a carnation on such short
> notice. Would a ranunculus be okay?

That would be fine. See you tonight.

-- Rick
```

When you reply to a message, your mail program will change the `Subject` line slightly by inserting the characters `Re:` at the beginning of the subject. This lets the recipient know he is looking at a reply. For example, say you send a message to your friend Vladimir with the following `Subject` line:

`Subject: Do you need a banana?`

When Vladimir replies, the `Subject` line will look like this:

`Subject: Re: Do you need a banana?`

If you would like to see another example of how this works, take a look at the messages in Figures 5-1 and 5-2 earlier in the chapter. The message in 5-2 is a reply to the message in 5-1.

People often use mail to have a discussion of some topic in which each message is a reply to the previous one. In such cases, we refer to the sequence of messages as a THREAD. Within a thread, the `Subject` lines of the messages will all be the same.

When looking back over old messages, it can be convenient to view them arranged in threads. To do so, just tell your mail program to sort the messages by subject. (All programs have a way to do this.)

Forwarding

From time to time, someone will mail you a message you want to send to a third person. When you do, we say that you FORWARD the message. Like replying, forwarding is easy (though the details vary from one mail program to another).

When you forward a message, some (but not all) mail programs insert a few characters at the beginning of the `Subject` line to let the recipient know he is looking at a forwarded message. Microsoft Outlook Express uses `Fw:`. For example, say you receive a message with the following `Subject` line:

`Subject: I am having a party on Friday`

You use Outlook Express to forward the message to your friend Alan. When Alan receives the message, it will have the `Subject` line:

`Subject: Fw: I am having a party on Friday`

hint

When you reply to a reply, your mail program will *not* insert a second `Re:` at the beginning of the `Subject` line.

Thus, when you see `Re:` at the beginning of the subject, you won't be able to tell if you are looking at the first reply or a subsequent reply until you open the message.

hint

When someone forwards you a message alerting you to something bad or outrageous, do not forward the message unless you are sure it is true.

Forwarding mail is so easy that people do it a lot, and it is common to receive a message that contains information that has been forwarded many times, from one person to another. Sometimes this is okay, such as when a collection of jokes is being sent around the Net.

Other times, forwarding is not so benign. For example, it is all too common for people to receive a message with false, but alarming, information, and to immediately forward a copy to thirty of their closest friends. An enormous amount of misinformation is circulated throughout the Net in just this manner.

Whenever you receive a forwarded message, never believe what it says unless you can independently verify the facts. Be especially suspicious of messages that purport to alert you to something bad or outrageous. Such messages are almost always wrong.

hint

Never, ever send a message that would cause you problems or embarrassment if it were to be made public. When you have something delicate to say, do so over the phone, where you will not leave a permanent record that can be saved and forwarded to the world at large.

Although this guideline may seem awkward, it can save you more trouble than you would ever believe (until it happens to you).

Here is a common example. If you ever receive a forwarded message telling you about a dangerous new computer virus, don't worry. Unless the message was sent by a computer expert whom you know personally, you can ignore it. Such messages are almost always wrong, and are forwarded around the Net by misinformed people who think they are doing their friends a favor.

For more information, see Chapter 12.

Misinformation not withstanding, the worst forwarding problems come from people who pass on messages that were meant to be confidential. Some people are incorrigible forwarders, and they love to send messages all over the place. The only way you can stop such people is to not send them confidential mail in the first place.

Once you mail a message, there is no way to get it back, and there is no way to keep someone from forwarding it. Moreover, there are probably copies of the message stored on various computers, so nothing you send is ever completely private. If it seems like a lot of trouble to be careful about sending mail, take a few moments and imagine what fun a jealous co-worker or a disgruntled girlfriend/boyfriend might have with your old messages.

Understanding Mail Error Messages

Occasionally, you will mail a message that cannot be delivered. In such cases, the message will be returned to you. We describe this by saying that the message BOUNCED. For example, a friend might tell you, "I got a message from Tom Cruise last week. He didn't know your email address, and he wanted to know if you would like to spend the weekend at his ranch. I sent you mail, but it bounced, so I had to go instead."

There are various reasons why a message might bounce. Usually, either your mail server could not send the message, or the recipient's mail server could not accept the message. In either case, one or both of the servers insert some lines into the header of the message before sending it back. Thus, when you receive bounced mail, the first thing to do is look at the full header. Some of the header lines will be highly technical and hard to understand, but if you look carefully, there will be a clue as to what went wrong.

When you look at the header of a bounced message, you will sometimes see a notation of a "permanent fatal error". Don't panic, no one died. This is just nerd talk for "the mail server gave up because it encountered a problem that didn't go away".

To help you figure out why a message bounced, here are some of the more common terms you may encounter:

User unknown or **Invalid recipient:** The recipient's mail server did not recognize the name at the beginning of the address. Check the address. You may have used an incorrect name, or you may have spelled it wrong.

Host unknown or **Host not found:** Your mail server could not find the computer to which you tried to send the message. Check the address. The hostname may be incorrect, or you may have spelled it wrong.

Time out: Your mail server gave up waiting for the recipient's mail server to respond. Try again later. The recipient's mail server may be down temporarily. If mail keeps bouncing, make sure you are using the correct address.

Mailbox full: The system to which you are sending a message has limits on the amount of storage space for each individual user. The person to whom you are sending a message has so much unread mail that his mail server will not accept any more messages on his behalf. Try again later.

Connection refused: For some reason, the recipient's mail server would not accept a connection from your mail server. Try again. If the message keeps bouncing, check the address.

No route to host: Your mail server could not find a way to contact the recipient's mail server. Try again. If the message keeps bouncing, check the address.

Message size exceeds maximum message size: You tried to send a mail message that was larger than the recipient's mail server will accept. This may be because you sent a very large attachment. Many mail servers will not accept messages that are larger than a particular size.

6

Using Mail Well

*Every time you send a
message, it does more than
convey words from one
place to another. The
messages you send also
represent you to
another person.*

Mail is important, and I want you to be able to use it well. Every time you send a message, it does more than convey words from one place to another. The messages you send also represent you to another person.

With what you learned in Chapter 5, and with a little practice, you will be able to send and receive mail quickly and easily. However, you must make sure you are not misunderstood and that you do not accidentally offend someone. You must also learn how to safeguard your privacy, follow the accepted conventions, and use the mail system to your advantage.

In this chapter, I will teach you the nuances and give you an understanding of a few advanced tools. You already know how to use mail. By the time you finish this chapter, you will know how to use it well.

Email Conventions

When you talk in person or on the telephone, there is more to the conversation than your words. Your voice has certain tones and rhythms that help you communicate. In person, your gestures and body language also have meaning. Even more important, as you talk with someone, you can interact with him or her in such a way as to avoid serious misconceptions.

hint

When you start to use a system that millions of people are already using, it is not a good idea to try to redefine the rules.

Sending mail on the Internet is a lot different. You can send a message whenever you want and read incoming messages at your convenience. What you can't do, however, is be with the other person when he or she reads your mail.

Electronic mail has been used for years, and in that time people have found it all too easy to send a message that is misunderstood. To avoid such problems, a number of conventions and practices have been worked out over the years. At first, you may decide that some of these conventions don't make sense and don't apply to you. Remember, though, what I am telling you in this chapter is based on the experience of many people. If you don't understand why something is necessary, all I can say is you will. If you follow the guidelines in this chapter, you will be doing the right thing.

Have a Mail Address of Your Own

Electronic mail works best when each person has his or her own mail address. One mistake I see many beginners make is to share a single mail address. The most common case is a couple who decides it would be cute for the husband and wife to have the same address.

For example, let's say Marlene and David Tugbottom use the Undependable Internet Company for their ISP. When they create their account, they might ask for one of the addresses:

`marlene-david@undependable.com`

`tugbottoms@undependable.com`

When you receive a message from Marlene or David, the `From` line might read:

`From: Marlene and David Tugbottom <tugbottoms@undependable.com>`

This is a bad idea for several reasons. First, when you see a message in your Inbox from either Marlene or David, you can't tell who really sent the message. Second, when you send mail to one of these people, you don't know which one will be reading it.

However, the most important reason to have your own mail address is more philosophical. On the Internet, people are individuals. Although you may be a part of a family, other people on the Net will treat you as a separate person with your own individual interests and characteristics. That is the way the Net works.

Does this mean your Internet experiences should be completely separate from those of your family? Not at all. Many husbands and wives routinely share interesting mail. Moreover, if you have children, they should understand that you have the right to look at their mail messages. (See the section entitled *Children and the Internet* in Chapter 12.)

Many ISPs will give their customers multiple mail addresses, one for each member of the family. Alternatively, you can use a free Web-based mail service (see Chapter 5), and establish as many mail accounts as you need.

Some mail programs make it easy for people who share a computer to use separate mail addresses and keep their messages separate. This is the case with Outlook Express:

- To create a new mail account, pull down the **File** menu, click on **Identities** and select **Add New Identity**.

- To change from one account to another, pull down the **File** menu, click on **Switch Identity**.

hint

Every person who uses the Internet should have his or her own mail address.

Make Your Messages Easy to Read

There is one idea about sending mail that I want everyone in the world to learn:

Make sure your messages look good and are easy to read.

It is so easy to type a message that many people do so without remembering that, at the other end, someone actually has to read what they type. All too often, email messages are poorly formatted and difficult to read.

Whenever you send mail, please take an extra moment and make the body of the message neat, orderly and easy to read. Start each message with the name of the recipient and end with your name. If you choose, you can have a signature appended to the end of the message (see Chapter 5).

Take care to divide your message into paragraphs, fix spelling mistakes, and edit any problem areas. In other words, take the same care with an email message as you would with a regular letter.

As an example, compare the message in Figure 6-1 with the one in Figure 6-2. You might think that Figure 6-2 is an exaggeration, but it is not. I get mail like this all the time.

Figure 6-1:   An example of a good mail message

```
Harley:

Your books have changed my life. I didn't realize how much
the Internet had to offer, and how much I could do on the
Net until I read your Yellow Pages book.

I like the name Harley because I think motorcycles are
cool. I used to have one of my own, but I had to sell it
when I went to college.

My father and mother are just starting to use the Net and
I gave them your book. I told them your Web site is cool
and they should be sure to check it out.

Ever since my mom got a computer, she has been sending me
email notes about life.

Thanks again for writing such cool books.

-- Fester Bestertester
```

Figure 6-2: An example of a bad mail message

```
Your bOoks have changed my life. I DIDn't realize how much
the Internet had to offer, and how much i could the Net
until i read your Yellow Pages bOOK. i like the name
Harley because I think motorcycles are cool""!! I used to
have one of my own but I had to sell it when I went to
colege.My fathr and mothr are   just starting to use the
Net and i gave them your bookI told them your Web site is
cool and they should be sure to check it out. eVER SINCE
MY MOM GOT A COMPUTER, SHe has been sending me email notes
about life. Thanks again for writing such cool books.
Fester BEstertester
```

Figure 6-2 has a lot of obvious mistakes (including spelling), but there is one particular problem that is not so obvious: the person has written the message as one long paragraph, which is not as easy as reading a letter on paper. Thus, it behooves you to use short, well-constructed paragraphs.

I have a friend who is a highly educated professional and a master at writing business letters. However, he has little experience with email and the Internet, and when he composes a message, he tends to write one huge paragraph that is very difficult to read. Like a lot of people, he doesn't treat email as if it were as important as "real mail". This is a mistake.

As a general rule, your message will be easier to read if you use small, well-structured paragraphs. Remember, the person who receives your message will be looking at a computer screen, and he will be reading a lot faster than you did when you typed the message.

How to Make Sure Your Messages Look Good

The biggest reason people send confusing mail is they never read their own messages. If you are a beginner, I have a great trick to help you learn how to write messages that look good. Before you send someone a message, send it to yourself so you can see what it looks like.

When you send a regular printed letter, you always read it before you send it. As you do, it is easy to make sure the letter looks good and is easy to read. Here is how to do the same thing with email.

hint

Before you send a message, re-read it in its entirety. As you re-read, check your spelling and take a moment to fix any writing mistakes. With Outlook Express:

- Pull down the **Tools** menu and select **Spelling**.
- Or, you can press the **F7** key.

Type the message in the regular manner, but address it to *yourself*. When you are finished typing the message, send it and it will be delivered to you. Once the message arrives, take a look at it. I bet you will find all kinds of small things that need fixing. If the message is especially important, print it and see what it looks like on paper. This will allow you to catch mistakes that would otherwise be hard to find.

Now resend the message (see the information below). This time, change the address to the person you want to receive the message. However, before you send it, make whatever corrections are necessary.

This is a particularly good technique to use when you are sending an important message, such as a job application or business proposal.

Learn how to...

Resend a Mail Message

There are times when it is a good idea to send a message to yourself before you send it to someone else.

See Chapter 17, *How to Do Stuff*, page 379 (Outlook Express).

One thing many people have trouble with is writing replies that are easy to read. I strongly suggest you look at several of your longer replies before you send them out. Once you do, you will realize how important it is to take a few extra moments to delete extraneous material and format your replies nicely.

I get many replies from people who do not realize how difficult their messages are to understand. In particular, they either mix up the original text with their response in such a way that it is all a muddle, or they do not quote the original text properly. For some reason, this is especially common among people who work in large companies. (For help in learning how to reply well to an email message, see the section entitled *Replying* in Chapter 5.)

Thank-You Notes

Whenever someone gives you a present, you are obligated to send that person a thank-you note. This is not optional. No matter what other people may do in such situations and no matter what your friends may think, thank-you notes are required, and you must send them. (If you don't believe me, ask your grandmother.)

The reason I mention this topic is because I have noticed a distressing tendency for people to use mail on the Internet to fulfill certain social obligations in a highly inappropriate manner. Electronic mail is great for just about anything: planning a meeting, talking to a friend, asking a question, passing around information, debating an issue, or discussing the meaning of existence. However, there are a few important times in life when you must not use email, no matter how convenient it may be. In such situations, you must either send a letter on paper or talk in person.

So, for future reference, I now declare that you may not use electronic mail to:

- Send a thank-you note

- Ask someone to marry you

- Break off a relationship

- Inform a loved one of a death

- Fire someone

Internet Resources   **The Importance of Thank-You Notes**

`http://www.harley.com/success/`

Smileys and Other Communication Conventions

Reading a textual message on the Internet does not convey the same nuances and subtleties as a face-to-face conversation or even a telephone conversation. For this reason, people on the Internet have developed a number of important conventions that are used to ensure good relations. These conventions are used not only in mail, but anywhere people on the Net communicate via the written word: in Usenet discussion groups, on IRC (Internet Relay Chat), in chat rooms, and on Web pages.

Perhaps the most important convention is the SMILEY, a series of characters that looks like a sideways face. There are many variations of a smiley, but the basic one looks like this:

:-)

You will also see:

:)

(To see the smiling faces, tilt your head sideways to the left.)

The role of the smiley is to tell the reader that what you are saying should be taken as inoffensive. In spoken conversation, you can use a certain tone of voice, a facial expression, or a wink. In a mail message, you use a smiley. For example, say you are replying to a message in which a friend has asked you to have lunch with him. You might write:

```
I'll be glad to have lunch with you on Friday. I can use
a free meal :-)
```

In this case, the smiley says, "I am making a joke, so don't be offended." Smileys are also useful when you are demonstrating a devastating wit that a lesser mind might erroneously interpret as sarcasm:

```
Of course, I think your new dress is lovely. I used to
have one just like it when I was a kid. :-)
```

Sometimes you will see the word <grin> or, more simply, <g> used instead of a smiley. When you do, it means the same thing:

```
Of course, I think your new dress is lovely. I used to
have one just like it when I was a kid. <grin>
```

```
Of course, I think your new dress is lovely. I used to
have one just like it when I was a kid. <g>
```

Another important convention is that writing in all uppercase letters means (figuratively) that you are shouting. For example, compare the following two sentences:

```
I NEED YOU TO SEND ME THAT REPORT BY TOMORROW. I need you
to send me that report by tomorrow.
```

We sometimes refer to words that are entirely in uppercase as being in ALL CAPS (all capital letters). On the Net, typing in all caps is considered to be highly emphatic and rarely appropriate, so don't do it unless you really mean to.

On a more personal level, there is a convention regarding how you refer to yourself. The Internet is an informal place, where people are judged mainly by the quality of their ideas. Thus, it is customary for people to refer to themselves by their name only, omitting titles such as Doctor, Professor, Mrs., Mr., Ph.D., and so on.

For example, say your name is Laura Schlessinger, and you have a Ph.D. in physiology. In your personal life, you might puff yourself up by swanking around, demanding that people call you Dr. Schlessinger or even Dr.

Laura. However, on the Net, you are better off signing your messages as "Laura" or "Laura Schlessinger". Using the title "Dr." would give people the impression that you are insecure and pretentious.

The final convention I want to mention has to do with abbreviations and acronyms. Because all mail messages must be typed, many people use abbreviations to save time. Figure 6-3 shows some of the more common abbreviations used in mail messages.

Figure 6-3: Common abbreviations used in mail messages

Abbreviation	Meaning
AFAIK	as far as I know
BTW	by the way
F2F	face to face (in person)
FAQ	frequently asked question list
FWIW	for what it's worth
FYI	for your information
IMHO	in my humble opinion
IMO	in my opinion
LOL	laughing out loud

Such abbreviations are used wherever people type messages, not only in mail, but in Usenet discussion groups, IRC (Internet Relay Chat), chat rooms, and so on. For reference, I have put a more comprehensive list of common abbreviations in Appendix C. Take a moment now and give the list a quick glance.

Be Careful What You Write

Once a message is sent, you can't get it back. For this reason, I want you to get into the habit of using your very best judgment when it comes to sending mail. For example, it is common for someone to receive a message that makes him angry and, without thinking, fire off an angry reply. A few hours later, the person is less angry, but it is too late, the message has been sent. Even if you change your mind ten seconds after a message has been sent, it is too late to stop it from being delivered.

Moreover, electronic mail can be stored indefinitely. The message you send today will exist as long as the person who receives it decides to keep

hint

When you configure your mail program, you will need to specify your full name. This is the name that is used in your return address.

On the Net, it is customary to use your name only. Do not use an honorific, such as Dr. or Prof., or a designation, such as M.D. or Ph.D. It will only make you look pretentious.

it, and a year from now, it is just as easy to forward a message to someone else as it is today. Furthermore, it doesn't take much effort to put the text of a mail message on a Web page, where it is accessible to the general public.

I have a friend who sent a private message to someone and was later astonished to find that a third person had seen the message. My friend was astonished because that person doesn't even have email access. How could this be? Simple. The person who received the message printed it out and delivered a copy to the third person.

hint

Whenever you receive a mail message that makes you angry, *always* force yourself to wait 24 hours before answering the message.

No exceptions.

The following hint may seem over-cautious, but I promise you, it is one of the most valuable pieces of advice you will ever read. If you follow this advice, you will thank me over and over.

Aside from anger, you also need to be careful when it comes to romance. Although you may be tempted to use email to send romantic missives to the adorable object of your affections, you must remember that messages are easy to save and easy to forward. It doesn't take much imagination to see how an ex-boyfriend or ex-girlfriend, armed with a collection of your email love letters, could wreak havoc with your life. This is especially true if your messages were even the least bit suggestive. My advice is, if you want to get romantic or sexy, forget email and confine yourself to the more traditional methods of sending special notes back and forth (like using your employer's FedEx account).

To be completely safe, you should never write anything in a mail message you would not want to be made public. I know this sounds extreme and unrealistic: rules that guarantee complete safety are always extreme and unrealistic. However, I do want you to remember that mail on the Internet is *not* always private, and a wise person uses judgment and discretion.

This guideline is important when you use the mail system at work. From day to day, you may feel you have complete freedom to send whatever mail you want, but that is an illusion. You and I need to be very clear here: if you send and receive mail at work, your employer has every right to look at it and, if it serves his interest to do so, he *will* look at it.

I know someone who once used the mail system at work to send a message to a friend in which she described a co-worker as a "psycho bitch from hell". No doubt there was some truth in this assessment, but I can only imagine that such a revealing description would be difficult for that person to explain during her next performance evaluation.

My suggestion is to never, ever use your employer's mail system for personal messages. Save your social correspondence for your leisure hours at home. If you really do find it necessary to send personal mail at work, get yourself a disposable Web-based mail account (see Chapter 5) and use your browser. And, for goodness sakes, don't get caught.

hint

Every message you send is only a few keystrokes away from being forwarded to anyone on the Net.

Mail is not private.

Is It Okay to Use HTML in a Mail Message?

Most messages are composed of plain text (letters, numbers, punctuation, and so on). In Chapter 5, we talked about using HTML in a mail message. (HTML is the same stuff out of which Web pages are made.) With HTML, you can use the same types of elements you might see on a Web page: various typefaces, pictures, graphics, links to Web sites, and so on. Some mail programs (like Outlook Express) allow you to go even further, by making it easy to use backgrounds that give your messages the look of real stationery.

HTML is wonderful when you really need to dress up a message. The thing is, how often do you really need to dress up a message? In my experience, people who know what they are doing never use HTML in their messages. Those who do are mostly newcomers, and they tend to get carried away with totally unnecessary typefaces, backgrounds and pictures.

The ultimate effect of HTML depends a great deal on what mail program the recipient uses to read your messages. If you send an HTML message to someone who is using the same mail program as you, what he sees will be pretty much what you want him to see. However, if he is using a different program, the results may not be what you intended. For example, I have received many messages that were next to unreadable, because they were composed with a type of HTML that my mail program couldn't handle well.

There is also another potential problem with HTML. It is common for people to reply to a message, and, when they do, the text of the original message is usually quoted within the reply (see Chapter 5). If you use HTML and send a message to someone with a different mail program, there is a good chance the quoted part of the reply will be messed up. (I have seen this happen a lot.)

Learn how to...

Turn Off HTML for Mail Messages

Configure your mail program so the default is plain text, not HTML. HTML is best used for Web pages. In mail messages, HTML is unnecessary and troublesome. This is especially true when you use email at work.

See Chapter 17, *How to Do Stuff*, page 377 (Outlook Express).

Thus, my advice is to use HTML only when you know for sure that your recipient is using a mail program that can handle the type of HTML your program produces. If you both use the same program, HTML is a safe bet. Otherwise, the two of you should send a few test messages back and forth to see if HTML will work well with your programs.

Even if you can get HTML to work perfectly for you, use it sparingly. It is often better to spend a few extra moments looking for better words than to use HTML to enhance a mediocre message. Although there will be times when you think you need boldface or italics, what you really need is a better verb.

Putting URLs in Messages

There will be many times when you will want to send someone the address of a particular Web site. To do so, all you need to do is include the URL (Web address) in a message. When the recipient reads your message, his mail program will recognize the address as a URL and turn it into a live link. This makes it easy to go to that Web site. All the person has to do is click on the URL. When he does, his mail program will send the URL to his browser.

Although some mail programs allow you to copy a Web page into a mail message, do not do so. Send the URL instead. Doing so will make your message smaller and easier to read. Moreover, it ensures that the recipient will view the page within his or her own browser. This works a lot better than using a mail program to look at a copy of the Web page.

Almost all mail programs will recognize URLs within a message. However, they may not be able to do so unless you specify the entire URL. In Chapter 4, I explained that you can abbreviate URLs when you type them into your browser. In particular, you can omit the `http://` at the beginning of the address.

For example, a browser considers the following URLs to be equivalent:

```
http://www.harley.com/
www.harley.com
```

A mail program, however, may not. Most mail programs will recognize the first URL, but some will not recognize the second one without the `http://`. Since you don't know which mail program your recipient is using, you should always be sure to specify the entire URL, including the `http://`.

Whenever you put a URL into a mail message, be sure to use the entire URL, including the `http://` at the beginning. The best, most reliable way to do so is as follows:

1. Use your browser to navigate to the Web page you want.

2. Click once on the URL within the address bar. This will select the entire URL.

3. Copy the URL to the clipboard. (Pull down the **Edit** menu and select **Copy**. As a shortcut, you can press **Ctrl-C**.)

4. Change to your mail program.

5. Paste the URL right into your message. (Pull down the **Edit** menu and select **Paste**. As a shortcut, you can press **Ctrl-V**.)

My advice is to always copy and paste URLs. Never re-type them — it is too easy to make a mistake.

Sending Mail to a Group of People

You can send a message to more than one person simply by putting more than one address in the `To`, `Cc` or `Bcc` lines in the header (see Chapter 5). People commonly do this when they want to share information. For example, someone mails you a collection of grapefruit jokes, and you decide to forward a copy to all your friends. In such cases, I want you to be sure to do two important things.

First, edit the message and remove all the junk. Delete everything from the message except the basic information you want to send. I often see people forward messages that have been forwarded that have been forwarded, and at the top of the final message, there are tens of lines of junk (usually old message headers) that should have been deleted. This practice is to be deplored, so don't do it.

Second, do *not* send a message with a whole bunch of addresses in the `To` line. Put the addresses in the `Bcc` line. Here is why:

Each person who receives the message will see all the addresses on the `To` line and the `Cc` line. Some of your friends, however, may want their email addresses kept private. Moreover, some of the people who receive the message are going to forward it to friends of their own, and (unless they have read this book) they will not bother to edit out the header of the original message. If the information in the message is interesting, it

Learn how to...

Use the Windows Clipboard

Using the clipboard to copy and paste information is one of the fundamental skills you need as a Windows user.

See Chapter 17, *How to Do Stuff*, page 366 (Windows).

will be forwarded again and again, and in a short amount of time, the names and addresses in the original message will be spread around the Net.

In such cases, the best thing to do is to address the message to yourself, and send blind copies to all your friends. (A blind copy is one in which the recipient's address does not appear. See Chapter 5 for the details.) In other words, put your address in the `To` line and put your friends' addresses in the `Bcc` line.

Here is an example. Let's say I wanted to send a message to several friends. The right way to do it would be as follows:

```
From: Harley Hahn
To: Harley Hahn
Subject: Grapefruit jokes
Bcc: Charles Wagon, Arthur Irwin Choke, Ben Dover,
 Al Abaster, Ellie Fant, Mel Norman Collie, mom
```

The wrong way would be to put all these names in the `To` line:

```
From: Harley Hahn
To: Charles Wagon, Arthur Irwin Choke, Ben Dover,
 Al Abaster, Ellie Fant, Mel Norman Collie, mom
Subject: Grapefruit jokes
```

hint

When you send a message or reply to a message, be careful of any addresses that do not look familiar. If you are suspicious, send a test message.

I have a friend who unknowingly sent highly sensitive mail to an address that was an alias for a large, public mailing list. As a result, many people who were complete strangers to him saw the message.

If you have a group of people to whom you send mail regularly, you can put an entry in your address book to represent a group of addresses. For example, if I were to create an entry in my address book called `friends` that contained this list of addresses, I could simply mail a message to `friends` and a copy would be sent to everyone on the list:

```
From: Harley Hahn
To: Harley Hahn
Subject: Grapefruit jokes
Bcc: friends
```

(For a general discussion of address books, see Chapter 5.)

When you use an entry in an address book in this way, to represent more than one address, the name of the entry is called an ALIAS. In this case, the name `friends` is an alias for a list of seven different addresses.

Finding Someone's Mail Address

There are millions of people on the Internet, but as we discussed in Chapter 1, the Net itself is not run by any particular organization. For this reason, there is no central directory in which you can look up someone's address. Nor is there an easy way to see if a particular person is even on the Internet.

So what do you do when you want to send mail to someone, but you don't know his address? There are several things to try.

First, although this may sound obvious, the very best way to find out someone's address is to ask him. Although it is possible to search for an address on the Net (as I will explain in a minute), nothing is faster than calling a person on the telephone and asking him, "What is your email address?" If you have trouble reaching the person you want, a good bet is to ask someone who knows that person.

For example, say you want the email address of someone who works at a company, but you can't reach him by phone. Call the company and ask the receptionist for that person's email address. Similarly, if you want to get in touch with an old friend you haven't seen in years, and you don't have his phone number, you can often get better results by calling his mother than by searching the Net.

If you do need to search for an address, there are mail address directories on the Net you can use. These directories use a standard protocol called LDAP (Lightweight Directory Access Protocol). Using LDAP, your mail program can query such a directory on your behalf and display the results. All you need to do is specify a name, and, if that person is listed, you will be given their address. When you find an address you want, it is easy to add it to your address book.

Mail programs that support LDAP usually come with a built-in list of directories that are available for searching. You can add to this list whenever you want, when you find an LDAP directory that is not on the list. In addition, the public LDAP directories all have their own Web sites, which you can access directly by using your browser.

What's in a Name?

LDAP

Most of the mail address directories on the Net support a protocol called LDAP (Lightweight Directory Access Protocol). By using this protocol, a client such as your mail program can query a directory (LDAP server) on your behalf and display the results.

LDAP was developed as an alternative to other, more complex protocols. The word "Lightweight" was chosen to indicate that LDAP is simpler and easier to use than these other protocols. (It's a nerd joke.)

hint

Occasionally, you may find yourself talking to someone who wants to give you his mail address, but who doesn't know what it is. This is especially common with people who are brand new to the Net and don't yet understand how such things work.

In such a case, give the person your address, and tell him to send you a message. When the message arrives, you can look at the header and see the person's address in the From line. Even easier, you can tell your mail program to look at the message, extract the return address, and put it in your address book automatically. (See Chapter 5.)

The LDAP directories contain a great many names, so there is some chance you will find the person you want. However, there are many millions of people on the Net, and most of them are not in such a directory, so you may have to search further.

When all else fails, the final way to find an address is to search the Net for some trace of the person. For example, if you can find a person's Web site, you will often find his or her mail address on one of the Web pages. Or, if you can find an article the person has posted to a Usenet discussion group, there will be a mail address in the header of the article.

To search the Web, you use one of the Web search engines, which we will discuss in Chapter 11. To search Usenet, you use a Usenet search engine, also discussed in Chapter 13.

Internet Resources   **Mail Address Directories**

```
http://www.bigfoot.com/
http://www.infospace.com/
http://www.people.yahoo.com/
http://www.switchboard.com/
http://www.whowhere.lycos.com/
```

Spam and Privacy

There are various reasons why you might want to keep your mail address private. The most important reason is spam (which I discuss in Chapter 2).

SPAM is advertising that is sent to your mail address without your permission. A person or company that sends spam is called a SPAMMER. Receiving spam is similar to receiving junk mail from the regular post office system. However, there is a major difference. With postal mail, it costs significant money to send a letter. There are printing costs, handling costs and postage. For this reason, junk mailers do not want to send mail to people who have no interest in their products. Although this may seem hard to believe (especially if you get a lot of irrelevant junk mail), it is true. If you call a junk mailer and ask to be taken off their list, they will do so, because spending good money to reach the wrong people only raises their overhead.

Spam is different, because it costs nothing to send an email message. If a spammer sends 90 percent of his mail to people who are not interested

Learn how to...

Search for a Mail Address

The Internet has no central administration, and there is no such thing as a master list of names and addresses. However, there are a number of directories, and some mail programs have built-in facilities to help you search for mail addresses.

See Chapter 17, *How to Do Stuff*, page 380 (Outlook Express).

in the product, what does he care? Thus, unlike the postal junk mailers, email spammers have no economic motivation to make an effort to send their mail only to those people who might be interested. More important, they have no economic motivation to take you off their lists once they have your address.

If you don't mind spam (and some people don't), that's fine. However, if you dislike unsolicited messages in your mailbox, you need to learn how to keep your address private.

The first thing to realize is that many spammers are basically dishonest people. Here is why:

Every ISP (Internet service provider) has a strong policy against spamming. When an ISP sees a customer using their system to spam people, they cut off that customer immediately. In addition, there are many technically adept people on the Net who hate to receive spam, and if they find the email address of a spammer, they will retaliate in some way (say, by spamming *his* system).

For these reasons, virtually all spammers structure their mail messages to have a fake return address and to hide the origin of the spam. Otherwise, they would lose the services of their ISP and incur the wrath of tens of thousands of people. In other words, just to be in the spam business requires a person to be dishonest.

There is only one sure way to keep yourself out of the spam lists: do not allow your address to get on a list in the first place. So, to understand how to keep your mail address private, you need to understand how spammers get such addresses.

First, they sell and trade them in *huge* lists. In fact, you may get advertisements inviting you to pay money to send a message to millions of people.

Second, spammers use automated programs to scan vast numbers of Web pages looking for email addresses. This is called TROLLING.

Third, spammers use programs to scan all the articles from all the Usenet newsgroups looking for return addresses in the headers. (We will talk about Usenet articles in Chapter 13, but basically, they have headers similar to mail headers.)

In other words, spammers will do everything they can to get as many addresses as they can. Once they do, they will sell the addresses repeatedly. (After all, it doesn't cost anything to copy a file of data.)

The following hints will help you protect the privacy of your address. Some hints are more extreme than others, so you will need to decide for yourself how much it is worth to you to keep your address private.

Harley Hahn's List of 7 Ways to Keep Your Email Address Private

1. Be selective about giving out your address.

Give your address only to people whom you want to have it. Tell those people not to give out your address without your permission.

2. Lie about your address.

There are many Web sites that demand that you "register" before you can access the site. As part of this registration, you are asked for your address. Why do you think they want it? Even if you are dealing with a legitimate company that promises not to sell your address, they still want to send you their own spam. The best solution is to specify something that looks like an address, but is fake, for example `z@z.gov`.

You might ask yourself, is this a moral thing to do? The answer is yes. No one on the Net has a right to demand your mail address for any reason.

In some cases, you may have to give a real address to access the site. (For example, they may want to send you a personal password by mail.) In such situations, think carefully and decide if giving out your address is worth access to that site.

3. Get a disposable address for non-private mail.

An alternative to using a fake address is to get a free, disposable address from a Web-based mail service (see Chapter 5). You can treat such addresses as temporary, throwing them away whenever you want. This gives you an address to use when you register at Web sites, while allowing you to keep your personal address completely private.

4. Don't register your software.

Many software programs ask you to "register" (there is that word again) your software as part of the installation process. Of course, as part of the registration, they want your address. Don't register. Your software will still work. All they want is your email address.

5. Use a disguised address when you post to Usenet.

Unfortunately, Usenet has suffered greatly from spammers in two ways. First, they send a great many advertisements to the Usenet newsgroups, and, second, they steal legitimate addresses from the headers of messages for their mailing lists. To protect yourself, use a disguised return address when you post Usenet articles. To do this, modify your address in a way that a person would recognize the change, but an automated spam program would not. For example, say your real address is:

`bendover@undependable.com`

When you post a Usenet article, you might use a return address of:

`bendover@undependableREMOVE.com`

If someone wants to reply to your article, he will know to delete the characters **REMOVE** from the address. However, an automated program trolling for addresses will be fooled.

6. Don't put your address on your Web page.

Either omit your email address entirely from your Web page, or use a disguised address as I discussed above. Remember, spammers use automated programs that troll Web pages, looking for mail addresses.

7. Don't put your address in your Web browser.

When you configure your browser, there is a place to specify your mail address. For complete privacy, do not do so. As you navigate the Web, it is possible for a Web site you happen to be visiting to run a program on your computer that, without your permission, sends back your address as well as all the other personal information your browser knows about. Omitting this information from your browser's configuration data protects your privacy.

Filters

Some mail programs have a facility called FILTERS that allow you to process incoming mail automatically in various ways. For example, you can arrange that all mail from a particular address should be deleted before you even see it. (This is an easy way to eliminate some types of unwanted mail.) Or you might want all messages that have a specific **Subject** line to be moved to a special folder.

hint

To use filters within Outlook Express, pull down the **Tools** menu, select **Message Rules**, then **Mail**.

You can create as many filters as you need, each one having its own name and its own characteristics. To create a filter, you specify one or more criteria and choose what you want to happen whenever an incoming message meets those criteria. As incoming messages arrive, your mail program will check each message and perform the appropriate actions automatically.

As you gain experience with mail, you will probably come up with useful ways to use filters to preprocess your messages and to help you organize your incoming mail. One nice thing is that you can create as many filters as you want, and turn them on or off to suit your needs.

The details of creating a filter differ from one mail program to another, so it is best to spend some time experimenting with your particular program.

7

The Web

*Everything you see on the
Web was created by
a person, not a mysterious
force of nature. There
is nothing you can't
understand if you are
willing to take the
time to learn about it.*

As you read the next few chapters and as you explore the Web on your own, you will find many new things to investigate and many new technical terms. At times, you may feel that the Web is overwhelming and the features of your browser are incoherent. If so, I want you to remember a secret that will make your life a lot easier:

You don't need to understand everything.

Ever since the Web became popular, it has been the focus of intense, sustained marketing wars. At first, Microsoft and Netscape (now owned by AOL) competed ruthlessly, each one trying to gain market shore for their browsers. Later, in order to dominate the marketplace, Microsoft began to integrate its browser, Internet Explorer, with Windows (the operating system) and with other Microsoft software.

Because market share was seen as being more important than quality, browsers were planned, implemented and rushed to market without extensive long-term testing. Thus, even today, many of your browser's features are there for marketing reasons, not because the designers made a careful, deliberate study of the needs of the users (you and me). As a result, your browser is a large, impenetrable hodgepodge of self-serving commercialism.

For this reason, you encounter an interesting paradox when you learn how to use the Web. At first, it will only take you a few minutes to learn how to look at a Web page and click on the links, and much of the time that's all you really need to know. You will say to yourself, "Boy, using a browser is easy. This hardly takes any time at all to learn." However, to use the Web *well*, you need to understand various details, including the idiosyncrasies of your browser, and *that* takes a lot more time than it should.

As you use your browser, there will be occasions when things happen that you don't understand. At such times, remember that everything you see was created by a person, not a mysterious force of nature, and there is nothing on the Web that you cannot understand, at least in general terms, if you are willing to take the time to learn about it.

On the other hand, it is not necessary to know everything. Believe me, you could walk into any conference of Internet experts, close your eyes and throw a brick, and not have to worry about hitting anyone who completely understands the Web (or even his browser).

The Web is the medium for much of the innovation in the Internet, and as a result, you will find a huge number of resources. However, many of these resources and many of the new ideas are experimental and have not yet stood the test of time; what is here today may not be here tomorrow.

Beginning with this chapter, I will help you understand the most important, most useful, and most enduring parts of the Web. However, the Web contains far more than any one person needs to understand, so let us start by recalling our most important observation: You don't need to understand everything.

The Basic Ideas

In Chapter 2, I discussed the basic ideas related to using the Web. Before we move on, let's take a moment to go over those ideas.

The WEB is an information delivery system. You can use the Web to look at many different types of information and to access a variety of services. Like all Internet resources, the Web is based on a client/server system. You use a client program, called a BROWSER, to access the information on WEB SERVERS (of which there are millions around the world). The two most widely used browsers are INTERNET EXPLORER (from Microsoft) and NETSCAPE (from AOL).

Information on the Web is organized into files called WEB PAGES, although they are not real pages like in a book. A WEB SITE (sometimes spelled "website") is a collection of related Web pages. Many organizations and people have their own Web sites. For example, IBM has a Web site, the U.S. Senate has a Web site, and I have a Harley Hahn Web site. If you are so inclined, you can create your own Web site and make it available to everyone on the Net. (We will talk about how to do this in Chapter 15.)

Web pages can contain all types of information, including TEXT (characters), GRAPHICS (pictures and photographs), and MULTIMEDIA (animation, video and sounds). The defining characteristic of Web pages is that they can contain links to other pages or resources. This type of information is called HYPERTEXT (for a reason I will explain in a minute).

As you read a Web page, you will see the LINKS. If you click on a link (using your mouse), your browser will fetch and display the Web page to which that link points. When this happens, we say you are FOLLOWING the link. From your point of view, it looks as if you are jumping from one Web page to another, just by clicking on a link.

If you are a science fiction fan, you may be familiar with the idea of rocket ships that jump from one part of space to another via "hyperspace". On the Web, information that contains links allows you to jump from one Web page to another. Hence, the name hypertext.

Now that you know about hypertext, you can understand two of the common technical terms you will see on the Web: HTML and HTTP.

HTML (Hypertext Markup Language) is the system of specifications used to define the appearance and structure of Web pages. That is why the files that contain Web pages have names that end with `html` or `htm`, for example, `index.html`. (The `html` part of the name is called an extension.) We will talk more about HTML in Chapter 15.

HTTP (Hypertext Transfer Protocol) is the protocol used to transfer data between Web servers and Web clients (browsers). In Chapter 4, we talked about URLs (uniform resource locators), the types of addresses that point to Web resources. Now you see why so many URLs start with the letters `http`. For example, the URL for my Web site is:

`http://www.harley.com/`

The `http` designation tells your browser that the resource in question contains hypertext and must be accessed via the `http` protocol.

The best way to learn how to use your browser is to take some time to explore its features and to experiment. In the following sections, I will explain how to use your browser to perform the most important tasks. There will be slight differences depending on whether you are using Internet Explorer or Netscape. Where the differences are important, I will point them out along the way.

I do want to tell you that I find using a mouse slow and awkward, and I would rather use the keyboard. So, whenever I can, I will show you keyboard shortcuts that can make using your browser faster and easier.

If you would like to experiment with different browsers to see which you like best, I encourage you to do so. After all, when you choose a browser you are also choosing a mail program and a Usenet newsreader. However, remember that you do not have to use the mail program and

hint

Even if you already have a browser, check to make sure you have the latest version. The browser companies release new versions every now and then, and it is a good idea to keep your software current.

If some of the instructions in this chapter don't match exactly what you see in your browser, it may be because you are using an old version.

newsreader that come with your browser. There are a variety of such programs, and they will work with any browser.

The following Internet Resources show the URLs where you can find the latest versions of Internet Explorer and Netscape.

Internet Resources   **Browsers**

```
http://www.netscape.com/download/
http://www.microsoft.com/windows/ie/
```

Before we move on, take a look at Figures 7-1 and 7-2. They show what Internet Explorer looks like while viewing a typical Web page. From time to time, I will refer to the particular parts of the browser window, and, if necessary, you can refer to these figures.

By the way, don't worry if your browser looks a bit different. The appearance sometimes changes from one version to another, but the changes are usually minor. Moreover, you can control whether or not various parts of your browser window are hidden or showing. For example, Figure 7-2 shows what Internet Explorer looks like when the Links toolbar, Radio toolbar, and the Favorites list are visible. (We will discuss these toolbars later in the chapter.)

Learn how to...

Control the Appearance of Your Browser

You can customize your browser by hiding or showing some of the toolbars and buttons.

See Chapter 17, *How to Do Stuff*, page 370 (Internet Explorer).

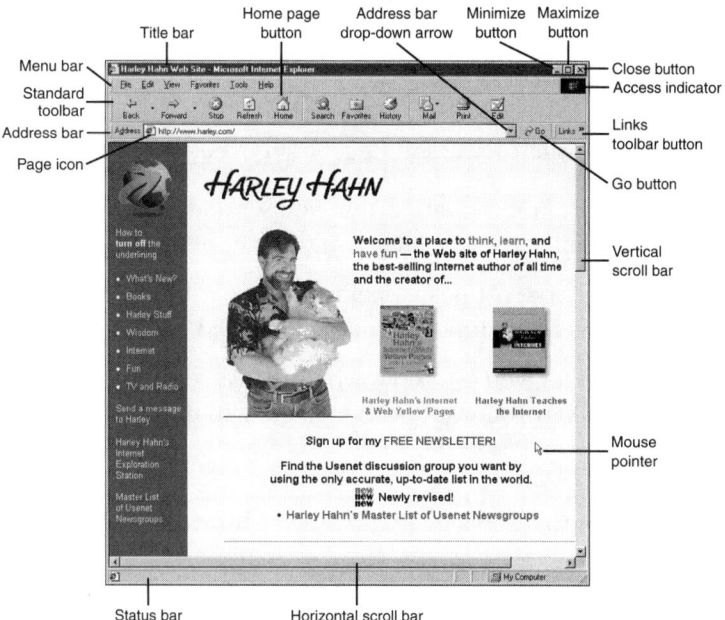

FIGURE 7-1

A typical Web page within Internet Explorer

FIGURE 7-2

Variations in the appearance of Internet Explorer

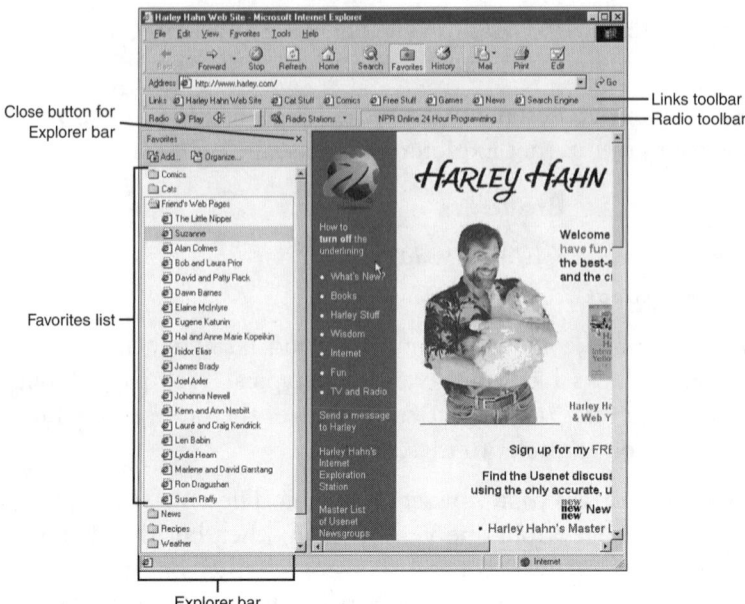

Close button for Explorer bar

Links toolbar

Radio toolbar

Favorites list

Explorer bar

Options and Preferences

Browsers are complex programs and, as such, have a variety of settings you can change. These settings give you some measure of control over the operation of your browser (although, if you are like me, not as much control as you would like). Within Internet Explorer, the settings are called OPTIONS.

There are many such settings, but generally, there are two types:

- Configuration information that you set once: for example, your name, email address, mail server, Usenet news server, and so on

- Settings that control the operation of your browser: for example, control over how links should be displayed

It is important for you to know where these settings are and how to change them when you want, so here is how to find them:

Internet Explorer

- Pull down the **Tools** menu and select **Internet Options**.

- Or, you can get at the same settings via the Control Panel. Click on the **Start** button, select **Settings**. Click on **Control Panel**. Double-click on **Internet Options**.

Once you find the settings for your browser, you may want to experiment, and I encourage you to do so. The only warning I would give you, however, is not to change settings that look crucial unless you are sure you understand what they do. As a precaution, you might want to write down the current settings before you make any changes, so you can restore the original values if you want.

Aside from changing the settings, you can also modify the appearance of your browser. Pull down the **View** menu and test the various choices. By doing so, you can add and remove the various buttons and bars, as well as change their size.

Blocking Advertisements

If you hate to look at advertisements, there are two ways to avoid most of them. The first technique is based on the fact that most advertisements are graphics (pictures).

Within your Options, there is a setting that tells your browser not to load graphics automatically. The setting was intended for people with slow Internet connections, because it takes a lot longer to load graphics than text. People with slow connections can turn off the graphics to decrease the time spent waiting for Web pages to load.

However, regardless of your type of Internet connection, turning off graphics effectively cuts out the ads. Instead of seeing irritating pictures, you will see only outlines of boxes, showing where the pictures would go if you had loaded them. Here is how to tell your browser not to load graphics automatically:

Internet Explorer

- Pull down the **Tools** menu and select **Internet Options**.
- Click on the **Advanced** tab.
- Go down to the **Multimedia** section, and uncheck the box next to **Show pictures**.

From time to time, you may see a page in which you want to see one of the pictures. In such cases, there is an easy way to override the default setting and tell your browser to load a picture on the current page. All you need to do is use your mouse to point to the picture, click the right button, and select **Show Picture**.

So, if you hate the ads, you don't have to look at them. You can block all the graphics (and virtually all the ads) as a default, and look at only those pictures *you* want to see. This method isn't foolproof, because you have to block all the graphics, and some of them are not ads. However, at least you have some measure of control over your own computer.

The second way to avoid advertisements is to use software that is designed to block the ads. Such software acts as a barrier between your browser and the outside world, by filtering out the ads before they even get to your browser. Some of these programs cost money, but they work well, and if you hate ads the money is well spent.

I strongly advise you to try one of these programs. It makes a huge difference when you look at the Web without ads. Once you try it, I bet you won't want to switch back. According to my ad blocking program, which keeps statistics, in the last 3 months (as I write this), the program has blocked 95,597 ads. That's 95,597 ads that I didn't have to look at; 95,597 times that someone tried to sell me something that I didn't even notice.

If your children use the Internet, the best favor you can do for them is to find a way for them not to have to look at so many advertisements. There are two reasons I say this.

hint

If your children use the Web, get an ad blocking program. This will remove the worst of the Internet from their environment. Realistically, when it comes to influencing children, the ads are much more troublesome than anything else on the Net.

First, children are exposed to far too many ads of all types and, on general principles, I think it is best if children's Internet experiences are as non-commercial as possible.

Second, Web-based ads only work if they get your attention. Thus, they are designed to emit the type of visual stimulation that will draw your eye away from the main content of the page.

However, children already have far too much rapid, transitory visual stimulation in their lives. Just ask any teacher how difficult it is to control hyperactive children whose patterns of behavior have been influenced by television and video games. It is much better for your children if their time on the Internet is more like a classroom experience (slow, thoughtful and rewarding) than like a video game (fast, superficial and meaningless).

Internet Resources   **Ad Blocking Software**

http://www.zapada.com/
http://www.webwasher.com/
http://www.adsubtract.com/

```
http://www.guidescope.com/
http://www.savethefreeweb.com/
http://www.junkbusters.com/ijb.html
```

The Junkbusters site is for advanced users, especially those who maintain a Unix system or a network.

Where to Get Help

A moment ago, I told you not to change a crucial setting unless you understand it. But where do you go for assistance if you have trouble understanding something? There are two important sources of help.

First, your browser has a built-in help facility. There are two ways to access it: you can either pull down the **Help** menu or you can press the **F1** key.

The second way to get assistance is to ask other people for help. This is important because the built-in help facility often will not answer your questions, or will answer them in a way that you can't understand. (Don't feel bad. It's not your fault. Most help systems aren't that good.)

When all else fails, the best place to get help is from someone who knows more than you. For this reason, I strongly suggest you cultivate the friendship of one or two computer nerds.

Entering a URL

The basic function of a browser is to let you look at Web pages, so the first thing you need to learn is how to tell your browser to go to a particular URL.

There are several ways to do this. First, near the top of your browser window is an area called the ADDRESS BAR. In Internet Explorer (Figure 7-1), the address bar is just to the right of the word **Address**. To enter a URL, use your mouse and click anywhere in the address bar. Then type a URL and press the **Enter** key. If you want, you can click on the **Go** button instead of pressing **Enter**.

If you want to try an example, use the following URL. (This is the address of my Web site.)

```
http://www.harley.com/
```

As a convenience, you do not have to type the `http://`. If you leave it out, your browser will insert it for you automatically. In addition, with

hint

Press the **F1** key whenever you need help.

This is worth remembering because, as a general rule, **F1** is the standard help key in almost all programs, not just browsers.

hint

During times of total confusion, the phone number of a nerd is worth more than all the built-in help facilities in the world.

simple URLs like the one above, you can also leave out the / character at the end of the URL. Thus, your browser considers the following abbreviated URL to be the same as the one above:

`www.harley.com`

(I discuss this and other URL abbreviations in Chapter 4.)

Once you press **Enter**, your browser will contact the appropriate Web server, download the information from that site, and display it for you.

Although it is easy to type a URL into the address bar, there are two alternatives that you may prefer. First, use your mouse to pull down the **File** menu and select **Open**. Your browser will display a small window in which you can type a URL. Type the URL and press **Enter**.

An easier way to do this is to press **Ctrl-O**. This is a shortcut that will display the small window immediately. I often use **Ctrl-O**, as I find it a lot faster than using the mouse.

What's in a Name?

Dialog box

From time to time, a program you are using may require you to enter a bit of information or make a choice of some type. The program will display a window with a place for you to type something, some buttons to press, or both. This window is called a DIALOG BOX.

As an example, when you are using a browser and you press **Ctrl-O**, you get a dialog box into which you can enter a URL.

The Fastest Way to Enter a URL with Internet Explorer

What I am about to show you is the single most useful hint you can learn about using Internet Explorer.

As you know, there are many URLs of the form:

`http://www.`*something*`.com/`

Within Internet Explorer, there is a fast way to type such URLs into the address bar. All you need to do is type the *something* and then press **Ctrl-Enter**. (That is, hold down the **Ctrl** key and press **Enter**.) The browser will immediately fill in the rest of the URL and go to that address.

For example, to visit my Web page, click on the address bar, type `harley`, and then press **Ctrl-Enter**. The browser will automatically change `harley` to:

`http://www.harley.com/`

Now, in order to type an address in this manner, you first need to jump to the address bar. There are two ways to do so. You can either click on it with your mouse, or you can press **Alt-D** (that is, hold down the **Alt** key and press **D**).

Putting all this together, here is the big hint:

With Internet Explorer, there is a fast way to enter a URL of the form:

> `http://www.`*something*`.com/`

Press **alt-D**.

Type the *something*.

Press **Ctrl-Enter**.

To try this hint, type:

`Alt-D   harley   Ctrl-Enter.`

This should take you to my Web site. Now try it with your own name and see what happens.

This technique is valuable because there will be many times when you will want to guess at the name of a Web site, and using these shortcuts makes guessing quick and easy. For example, say you want to visit the IBM Web site. You have never been there before, but you guess that the URL is:

`http://www.ibm.com/`

All you have to do is press **Alt-D**, type `ibm`, and press **Ctrl-Enter**.

Using AutoComplete with Internet Explorer

To make it easy to enter a URL, Internet Explorer offers a facility called AUTOCOMPLETE. As you are entering a URL, your browser tries to guess what you are typing, based on the addresses of the Web pages you have already visited and the contents of your Favorites list. (I explain the Favorites list later in the chapter.) As soon as you have typed enough letters for AutoComplete to make a guess, it will fill in the rest of the letters for you. In addition, it will also show you a list of other similar addresses.

You now have three choices:

- You can ignore the suggestion and keep typing.
- If you like the suggestion, you can stop typing and press **Enter**.
- You can select an address from the list. (Press the **Down** key to move to the address you want. Then press **Enter**.)

AutoComplete is handy when you want to revisit a Web site and you don't want to retype the entire URL. Just type a few letters, select the URL from the list, and press **Enter**.

If you want to re-use a URL you have typed recently, there is another shortcut. Use your mouse and click on the small down arrow at the right end of the address bar. This will pull down a list of the URLs you have typed. Just click on the one you want.

Navigating

hint

The Web seems like a place, but it is really a thing.

As you use the Web, a lot of your time will be spent changing from one Web page to another. We call this activity NAVIGATING. The metaphor is a convenient one, and I will use it myself, because it is handy to talk as if you are actually moving from one place to another. However, as you use the Web (and as you read this book), don't lose track of the fact that you are not really moving through some mysterious universe. What is really happening is that your browser is presenting one page after another for your perusal.

In other words, there is no "cyberspace". (See Chapter 1.)

Learn how to...

Tell Your Browser Not to Underline Links

I suggest that you tell your browser not to underline links. Web pages will look less cluttered and be easier to read.

See Chapter 17, *How to Do Stuff*, page 371 (Internet Explorer).

Most Web pages contain links to other pages, and the simplest way to move from one page to another is to follow a link. To do so, move your mouse pointer to the link and click on it. Your browser will then do whatever is necessary to get you the information to which the link points. Typically, your browser will contact the appropriate Web server, request the new Web page, wait for it to arrive, and then display it on your screen. How long you have to wait depends on several factors, the most important of which is the speed of your Internet connection.

After awhile, using the Web takes on a peculiar rhythm to which your mind will begin to synchronize:

Click... *wait*... read... Click... *wait*... read... Click... *wait*... read...

When you are reading a Web page, how do you know where the links are? There are several ways. First, most links are attached to words, and these words will be displayed in a special way. For example, they may be a different color than the rest of the text, or they may be underlined, or both. Most browsers have settings that give you some control over how links are displayed. Experiment with your browser and see what you prefer.

There are two other ways to tell if something is a link. When you point to a link with your mouse, the pointer will change to a picture of a hand, and the browser will display the address (URL) of that link in a special box at the bottom of the browser window. (This area is called the STATUS BAR.)

Aside from words, links can also be attached to pictures. Usually, the pictures are small ones, referred to as icons. (Within Windows, an ICON is a small picture that represents a resource.) If you point to such a picture, you will see the address of its link in the status bar. To follow the link, just click on the picture.

One special type of picture is an IMAGE MAP. With an image map, various parts of the picture correspond to different links. Here is a typical example. You are visiting a Web site that has travel information about the United States. The main Web page has a picture of the U.S. showing all the states. To see information about a specific state, you simply click on that state. In this case, you are looking at an image map in which each state points to a different Web page.

As you jump from one Web page to another, you will often want to go back to a previous page, and once you do, you may want to move forward again. This is easy: your browser has **Back** and **Forward** buttons. Just click on the one you want.

For a more elaborate way to move forward into the past, you can use the HISTORY LIST, a record your browser maintains of your recent Web page visits. To see the History list, click on the **History** button.

Reading a Web Page

Reading a Web page is mostly straightforward: you read it. However, I do have a few hints to help you have more control over your Internet

hint

To find out if something is a link, move your mouse pointer over the item, and see if the pointer changes to a hand. If so, you are pointing to a link.

If you are not sure what the link does, click on it and find out. (Nothing bad will happen.)

hint

Although it is possible to move back and forth within your recently visited Web pages by clicking on the **Back** and **Forward** buttons, that way is for weenies.

The fast, cool way to move around is by using the keyboard and pressing **Alt-Left** or **Alt-Right**. (That is, hold down the **Alt** key and press the key with the left arrow, or hold down the **Alt** key and press the key with the right arrow.)

Alt-Left moves back, and **Alt-Right** moves forward. Most people don't know about these shortcuts, but they are so cool I want you to memorize them right now.

experience. Some of these hints, by the way, are general Windows tech-niques that apply to any program you may be using, not just to browsers.

Many Web pages are so long that the complete page will not fit within the browser window. In order to read the parts of the page that are not visible, you need to move the page up and down (or left and right) within the window. This action is called SCROLLING, and you can do it with either your mouse or with the keyboard. Let's start with the mouse.

When a Web page does not fit into the browser window, your browser will show you as much as will fit and will place SCROLL BARS along-side the border of the window. (You can see scroll bars labeled in Figure 7-1.) There are two ways to use a scroll bar. You can either click on one of the arrows at the end of a bar, or you can use your mouse to drag the slider within the bar. (To DRAG an object, move the mouse pointer over it, press the left mouse button, and move the mouse while holding down the button.)

In addition, some mice have a built-in scroll wheel. If your mouse has this feature, you can move up and down a Web page simply by moving the wheel.

The scroll bar on the right is called a VERTICAL SCROLL BAR because it moves the Web page up and down. The scroll bar on the bot-tom is called a HORIZONTAL SCROLL BAR because it moves the Web page left and right.

Aside from using the mouse to scroll, you can also use the keyboard. The **Up** and **Down** keys move the Web page up and down by a small amount. The **PageUp** and **PageDown** keys move the Web page up and down in larger jumps. (Experiment and you will see what I mean.) As an alter-native, you can press the **Space** bar to page down, and (in Internet Explorer only) **Shift-Space** to page up.

If the page is too wide to fit in the window, you can use the **Left** and **Right** keys to move it horizontally. Finally, for large movements, you can use **Ctrl-Home** to jump to the very top of the Web page and **Ctrl-End** to jump all the way to the bottom.

Within Windows, you can only control one window at a time. The win-dow that is currently under your control is said to have the FOCUS. To move the focus to a particular window, all you need to do is use your mouse and left-click anywhere in that window.

hint

Your browser will only show scroll bars when necessary. If the entire page fits in your browser window, you won't see any scroll bars at all.

If the Web page is nar-row enough to fit hori-zontally, but too long to fit vertically, you will only see a vertical scroll-bar (because that is all that is necessary).

The reason I am telling you this is because, on occasion, you will press a key (say, the **PageUp** or **PageDown** key) and nothing will happen. Usually this means that the window you want to control—the one containing the Web page —does not have the focus.

In such cases, just click on the Web page. Once the window has the focus, you will be able to control the Web page by using your keyboard.

Most Web pages are displayed using the entire window. Some Web pages, however, are divided into sections, each of which lies within a small window of its own. These sections are called FRAMES.

Frames are used when the Web page creator wants to have more than one independent window within a single page. This is useful when the sections of a page may need to be manipulated individually. For example, one frame might contain a table of contents that is always available, while a second frame contains information that changes. When you click on a link in the first frame, the results are shown in the second frame.

Figure 7-3 shows a Web page that has three frames. The first frame, near the top, contains a navigation banner. The second frame, on the left, contains links. The third frame, on the right, contains text.

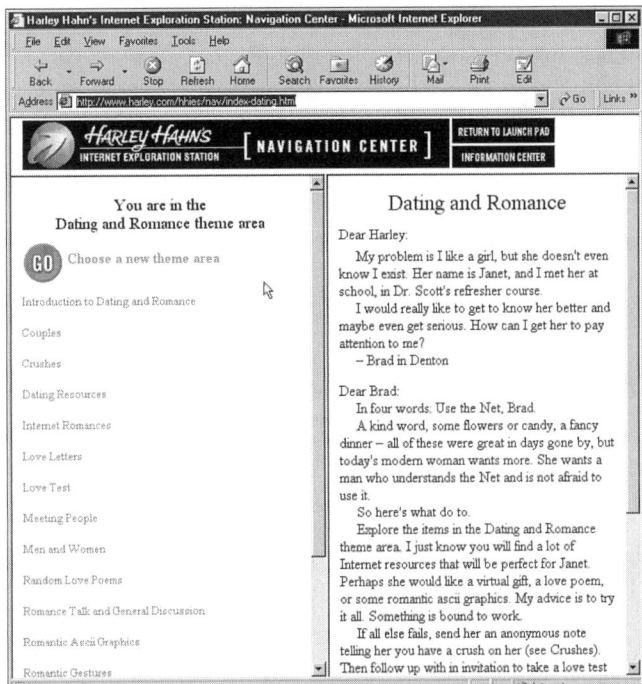

FIGURE 7-3

A Web page with frames

When you read such a page with frames, you can control the scrolling of each frame independently, either with the mouse or with the keyboard. With the mouse, each frame will have its own scroll bars as necessary. With a keyboard, you can use the same keys within the frame as you do for a full-sized window (**Up, Down, PageUp, PageDown, Ctrl-Home** and **Ctrl-End**). However, before you can control a specific frame, you will have to click inside the frame in order to give it the focus.

Right-Clicking

When it comes to using your mouse, you usually press the left button. Indeed, throughout this book, when I say to CLICK on something, I mean to point to it with your mouse and press the left button. When I say DOUBLE-CLICK, I mean to press the left button twice in a row. However, you will sometimes need to press the right button, and when you do, we say that you RIGHT-CLICK.

Although you use the left mouse button most of the time, the right button is important. As a general rule within Windows, right-clicking on an object displays a CONTEXT MENU containing selections relevant to that object. For example, if you right-click on an icon, you will see a context menu with selections relating to icons.

Right-clicking is important because, typically, the context menus allow you to manipulate an object and look at its properties. Thus, if you become familiar with the various context menus, you will be able to use your programs (and Windows) more efficiently.

The reason I mention all this is because I want you to right-click on the various parts of your browser window just to see what happens. In particular, load a Web page and right-click on the page, away from a link. Now right-click on a link. Notice that you get different context menus depending on where you right-click.

What to Do When a URL Doesn't Work

From time to time, you will have a problem with a URL that doesn't work properly. For instance, you may try to connect to a Web page and, instead, you get an error message.

There are two types of error messages. First, you may see a message like "File not found", or "The requested URL was not found on this server".

hint

Although most people don't know it, there is a way to use the keyboard to simulate a right-click on your mouse: just press **Shift-F10**.

hint

Whenever you feel like a quick break, take a moment and right-click on something, just to see the context menu.

You can't do any harm by right-clicking.

Learn how to...

Change Your Mouse to be Left-Handed

If you are left-handed, you can reverse the function of the left and right mouse buttons by changing a setting.

See Chapter 17, *How to Do Stuff*, page 369 (Windows).

This means your browser was able to connect to the Web server, but the server could not find the file you wanted. (Remember, each Web page is stored in a file.) Sometimes, you will see a "File not found" message along with error code 404. This is the standard error code sent by a Web server when a file cannot be found. (There is nothing cosmic about the number 404.)

A second type of error occurs when your browser cannot even connect to the Web server. In such cases you will see a message like "Cannot open the Internet site", "There was no response", "The page cannot be displayed", "Cannot locate the server", and so on.

There are several things that might be wrong. First, if you typed the URL yourself, you may have made a spelling mistake. Check the spelling carefully. Many URLs are complex and it is easy to make a typing mistake.

If you click on a link and get an error message, it may still indicate a spelling problem, because the person who created the Web page may have made a spelling mistake when he typed the address. Such mistakes are more common than you might think.

If you think the address is correct, the next thing to do is make sure your Internet connection is working. An easy way to do so is to try an address that should always work, such as:

`www.ibm.com`

`www.microsoft.com`

`www.netscape.com`

If URLs like these do not connect, you are probably having a problem with your Internet connection.

If your Internet connection is working, and you are sure the URL is spelled correctly, the address itself may be bad. This can happen when a Web site is reorganized and some of the addresses that used to work stop working.

In such cases, I have a trick for you: chop off the right-most part of the URL and try again. For example, let's say you try to connect to the following URL, but it doesn't work:

`www.harley.com/freestuff/valuables/money/news.html`

In this case, the right-most part of the URL is **news.html**. Chop it off and try again:

```
www.harley.com/freestuff/valuables/money/
```

If that doesn't work, repeat the process:

```
www.harley.com/freestuff/valuables/
```

```
www.harley.com/freestuff/
```

```
www.harley.com
```

Eventually, either something will connect, or you will have proven that the Web site itself is not working.

Managing Your Browser Window

In this section, I am going to show you a number of ways in which you can control your browser window. I am mentioning these procedures here because they are useful while you are using the Web. However, most of what I am about to show you are general techniques that will work for any program running under Microsoft Windows. In particular, I am going to show you how to move, resize, minimize, maximize and close your browser window.

Now, I have to mention that whenever I run up against stuff like this, I'm never quite sure how much detail to explain. After all, there are lots of new users who don't know much about Windows, and if I simply assumed they know all the basics, the conversation might go like this:

Me: If you have trouble reading a Web page, you can always resize the browser window.

New User: What's a resize?

Me: Or you can maximize the window to get more room.

New User: What's a maximize?

Me: And if you want to put away the window temporarily, you can always minimize it to the taskbar.

New User: What's a ...?

Well, you get the idea.

On the other hand, if you are an experienced user, you may already know how to manipulate windows, and I certainly don't want to bore you while I attend to the newcomers. "Old hat," I hear you say (or, if you are French, "*Vieux chapeau.*") So, if you already know how to use Windows, it's okay if you let your attention wander for a few minutes. After all, there are plenty of other things you might be doing: feeding the cat, putting away those old magazines in the garage, or maybe just catching up on your stamp collection.

All set now? Okay, let's push on.

The Web browser and everything it displays is contained within a window. You can control that window in various ways. First, you can change its size by making it as large as possible. To do this, use your mouse and click on the MAXIMIZE BUTTON in the top right-hand corner of the window. The maximize button is the one with the picture of a small square (see Figure 7-1).

When you click on this button, your window will expand to fit the entire screen. (We say that you have MAXIMIZED the window.) When a window is maximized, the single square on the button is replaced with a small picture of two overlapping rectangles. If you now click on the button again, the window will shrink back to its original size.

An alternative way to maximize a window is to use your mouse to double-click on the TITLE BAR (the bar at the very top of the window). Once the window is maximized, you can restore its original size by double-clicking on the title bar once again. In other words, double-clicking on the title bar alternates the window from maximized to non-maximized.

Another way to change the size of a window is to use your mouse to drag a corner or an edge. When you drag any of the corners, you make the entire window larger or smaller. When you drag an edge, you make the window larger or smaller in one direction only. For example, to make a window wider, you would drag either the left or right edge outward.

When you change the size of a window in this way, we say that you RESIZE or SIZE it. Whenever you resize a browser window, the browser automatically redisplays the contents to fit the new size, creating or removing scroll bars as necessary.

When you have finished with a browser window, you can close it by clicking on the CLOSE BUTTON. This is the button with an **X** on it, in the top right-hand corner of the window, just to the right of the maximize button. (See Figures 7-1.) Alternatively, you can use the keyboard to close a window by pressing **Alt-F4**.

hint

When you close a window, the program inside it is terminated automatically.

If you are working with a data file, be sure to save the file before you close the window.

hint

When you minimize a window, the program inside it does not stop running.

Thus, if you are waiting for a program to finish a long operation, you can minimize its window and move on to something else. This is convenient when you are downloading a large file, and you want to do something else while you are waiting.

If you want to put away a window temporarily without losing the contents, you can click on the MINIMIZE BUTTON. This is the button with a single small line, just to the left of the maximize button. When you click on the minimize button, the window will disappear and we say that you have MINIMIZED it.

A minimized window is not closed. You can restore it to its original size whenever you want by clicking on the appropriate button on the taskbar. (The TASKBAR is the long bar that contains the **Start** button, as well as buttons for the various programs that are running).

An alternative way to restore a minimized window is to press **Alt-Tab** repeatedly and select the program you want. (A lot of this will make sense when you try it.)

The last basic operation you need to know is how to move a window. Just drag the title bar, and the entire window will move. In other words, move the mouse pointer to the title bar, hold down the left mouse button, and then move the mouse while holding down the button. When the window is where you want it, release the mouse button.

Opening a New Browser Window

There will be times when you will want to look at more than one Web page at a time. You can do so by opening a new browser window. In fact, you can open as many browser windows as you want. You can then switch from window to window, using each one as you see fit.

If you accumulate extra windows you don't need, you can get rid of them by closing them. When you close the last browser window, it stops the browser program itself.

Opening a new window is easy.

Internet Explorer

- Pull down the **File** menu, select **New**, then **Window.**
- Or, you can simply press **Ctrl-N.**

I get bored easily, so I tend to open a new browser window whenever I have to wait for anything.

For example, let's say I am reading the daily comics. I connect to a Web site to read *Doonesbury*, but it takes too long to load. I immediately press **Ctrl-N** to create a new window, and use that window to start loading *Cathy*. Then I switch back to the original window and read *Doonesbury* (which has loaded by now).

After reading *Doonesbury*, I press **Alt-F4** to close the window and switch back to the other window to read *Cathy*.

(Although this scenario sounds complicated, it's actually fast and easy. Try it.)

Internet Resources **Daily Comics**

```
http://www.comics.com/
http://www.creators.com/comics.html
http://www0.mercurycenter.com/comics/
http://www.washingtonpost.com/wp-dyn/style/comics/
http://www.kingfeatures.com/features/comics/comics.htm
```

So far, I have described how you can create a new browser window intentionally. It is possible, however, for a new window to be created automatically.

Sometimes this is useful. For instance, a Web page might be designed to serve as a table of contents for various resources. When you click on a link, the resource you choose can be automatically displayed in a second window so as to keep the original window available (so you can choose one resource after another).

Most of the time, however, automatic window creation is used for a more aggravating reason: to make an advertisement pop up in your face. If you use an ad blocking program (see earlier in the chapter), it can be configured to block the creation of pop-up windows. Otherwise, there is not much you can do about this except to avoid the Web sites that do this. In my experience, some of the worst offenders are the sites that offer free Web site hosting services. They seem to be "free", but only because they make the people who visit the pages look at lots of ads.

(Actually, I have seen worse: Web pages designed to create a whole cluster of new browser windows, each of which contains an ad, and each of which must be closed separately.)

hint

When a Web site creates an unwanted pop-up window on your screen, remember the two ways to close a window:

You can either click on the close button in the top right-hand corner of the window, or move to the window and press **Alt-F4**.

Reloading a Web Page (the Cache)

It can take a long time to download all the information for a Web page, and while it is downloading, you have to wait. For this reason, your browser uses a temporary storage area, called the CACHE, to save the information from recently viewed Web pages. Whenever you want to load a page, your browser looks in the cache to see if the page is already there. If so, there is no need to reload the page from the Internet. Thus, the second time you look at a Web page, it should load much faster (because it is in the cache).

Using a cache is great, because it can really speed things up. However, there is a problem. The content of Web pages changes from time to time, and if you always load a particular page from the cache, you will never know if the page has changed.

To obviate this problem, your browser will only keep information in the cache for a limited amount of time. After that, if you request the same Web page, your browser will go to the Net and load it again, just to make sure you get an up-to-date copy. You can control how often your browser reloads a page by changing the cache settings (see below).

At any time, you can force your browser to ignore the cache and reload the current Web page from the Internet.

Internet Explorer

- Click on the **Refresh** button.
- Or, press **Ctrl-R**.

Creating a Shortcut to a Web Page

In your adventures on the Internet, you will find lots of Web pages you want to visit again. For example, you may have a news source you like to check each day for the latest scoops, or you may find an interesting site you want to revisit when you have more time.

There are two ways you can save such URLs: you can either create a shortcut to the Web page, or you can save the address on a special list. In this section, we will talk about shortcuts. In the next section, I will show you how to create a list of URLs for your favorite Web pages.

A SHORTCUT is an icon that represents a resource (such as a URL). Normally, a shortcut resides on your desktop, the area represented by the background of your display area. (The DESKTOP is what you see when you have no open windows.) Once a shortcut is on your desktop, it is a

Learn how to...

Change the Cache Settings

You can control how your browser uses the cache by changing its settings.

See Chapter 17, *How to Do Stuff*, page 371 (Internet Explorer).

simple matter to access the Web page. All you have to do is double-click on the icon. This action sends the URL right to your browser. (If your browser is not already running, it will be started automatically.)

A typical way in which you might use a shortcut is to point to your favorite news site. Then, whenever you want to check the news, all you have to do is double-click on the icon or drag it over to your browser window.

So how do you create an icon? There are several ways. As you are reading a Web page, use your mouse and right-click anywhere on the page. When the context menu pops up, select **Create Shortcut**. A shortcut to the current page will be created and placed on your desktop.

Another, more interesting way to create a shortcut is to use the small icon just to the left of the address bar. This icon represents the URL of the current page. In Internet Explorer, the icon is called a PAGE ICON. Take a moment and look at Figure 7-1. I have labeled this special icon, so you can see exactly where it is.

Once you know where the page icon is, creating a shortcut to the current page is easy. All you need to do is use your mouse to drag the page icon to the desktop. A shortcut will appear automagically. Try it.

So far, we have talked about creating a shortcut to the current Web page (the one you are reading). As a convenience, it is possible to create a shortcut to a specific link on the current page without having to click on the link and wait for the page to download. Just use your mouse and drag the link to the desktop. This creates a shortcut to the link, rather than to the current page.

For example, say you are looking at a Web page that has weather information. The page contains links to information about particular cities, and you want to create a shortcut to the Web page for your city. Just drag the appropriate link over to the desktop.

Once you create a shortcut, there are several ways to customize it:

- **To rename an icon**: Click on it and press the **F2** key, or right-click on the icon and select **Rename**. Then type the new name and press **Enter.**

- To move an icon: Use your mouse and drag the icon to a new location.

- **To delete an icon**: Click on it and press the **Delete** key; or you can right-click on the icon and select **Delete**.

Saving URLs in Your Favorites List

In the previous section, I mentioned there are two ways to save URLs. The first way is to create a shortcut stored as an icon on your desktop. Shortcuts work fine for a small number of URLs, but as you use the Web over a period of weeks and months, you are bound to encounter more than a few Web pages whose URLs you want to save, and the best way to do so is by making a list.

All browsers allow you to create and maintain such a list, however, the name of the list and the details of how it works differ from one browser to another. With Internet Explorer, the list is called the FAVORITES LIST.

A Favorites list consists of a number of ITEMS. Each item has a name and represents a specific Web page. (Within the item is the URL for that page.) The various items are stored in FOLDERS, which you can organize as you see fit. Thus, you can customize your list to be exactly the way you want it.

When you first use your browser, the Favorites list may already have some folders and items. These are set up for you by Microsoft or the company that made your computer, and you do not have to keep them. You can delete anything you want and create your own, brand new list.

The items in the preset list did not get there by accident. They were put there to help promote their products and marketing programs. (Don't feel bad about deleting the entire list if you feel like it and building your own from scratch. As one of my readers, you are a thoughtful, imaginative individual with important human needs—not a mindless pawn to be manipulated by big companies and their advertisers.)

It is worth your while to spend some time learning how to use and organize your Favorites list, and to get you started, I am going to explain the most important things you need to know: how to use the list, how to create a new item, how to edit your list, and how to make a backup copy to guard against accidental loss.

Before we start, though, I want to give you a hint:

Internet Explorer: Using the Favorites List

There are two ways to display your Favorites list. You can either click on the **Favorites** button, or you can pull down the **Favorites** menu. Try both methods and see which one you like better.

hint

In my experience, if you don't save a URL the first time you see a Web page, you will probably never see that page again. Although you may think you will remember how to find it, you won't. So, if you are looking at a Web page and you feel like you may want to return, don't hesitate to save the URL to your Favorites list.

Don't worry about saving too many URLs. From time to time, you can edit your list and get rid of the junk.

You will notice that the list has a number of folders. You can navigate in and out of the folders just by moving your mouse. (Try it.) When you see an item that looks interesting, click on it. The URL for that item will be sent to your browser, which will fetch the appropriate Web page and display it for you.

As an example of what an open Favorites list looks like, take a look at Figure 7-4. It shows a typical Favorites list with a number of folders open. Notice that I have used my mouse to navigate to a particular item (the one that contains the URL for Suzanne's Web page). If I were to click on that item, my browser would fetch that Web page for me.

FIGURE 7-4

A typical Favorites list within Internet Explorer

The first time you use your browser, there may already be various folders. As I mentioned, these folders contain items chosen by Microsoft or the company that made your computer in order to advance their own marketing goals. I created my own folder to hold my own personal items. I then went through the other folders and items, and saw if there was anything I wanted to keep.

hint

When you start to orga-
nize your own Favorites
list, feel free to remove
any of the preset items
and folders. Nothing bad
will happen.

hint

Whenever you see a Web
page you might like to
save on your Favorites
list, just add it to the bottom of the list.

Later, when you get a
spare moment, you can
edit the list and process
all the new items that
have accumulated, delet-
ing them or putting
them into folders as you
see fit.

hint

Whatever items you place
in the Links folder will
automatically appear as
buttons on the LINKS
BAR (see Figure 7-2).
Thus, you can create your
own convenient, custom
buttons simply by orga-
nizing the Links folder.

Creating a new item is easy. Whenever you find a Web page worth
remembering, use your mouse to pull down the **Favorites** menu and click
on **Add to Favorites**. You will then be shown a dialog box.

If you click on **OK**, the item will be saved to the bottom of the Favorites
list.

If you want to put the item in a particular folder, click on the **Create in**
button, and you will be shown a diagram of all the folders in your
Favorites list. To indicate where you want to place the new item, just
click the folder of your choice. (If you see a folder with a plus sign [**+**]
next to it, it means there are subfolders. To look at the subfolders, click
on the plus sign.)

To edit your Favorites list, pull down the **Favorites** menu and select
Organize Favorites. Your browser will create a new window containing
the entire list.

Once you see the new window, you can make any changes you want. For
example, if you don't like the name of an item, you can rename it. The
details are straightforward, so I won't go into them here. Just experiment
for awhile, and it won't be long before you will be able to do whatever
you want.

The last thing I want to teach you about your Favorites list is how to
make an extra copy of it, just in case something goes wrong and you lose
the original. (Such a copy is called a BACKUP.)

Internet Explorer stores your Favorites list as a folder in the Windows
directory on your hard disk. The best way to make a backup is to use
Windows Explorer (the Windows file management program) to make a
copy of the entire Favorites folder. My suggestion is to save the backup
folder in a completely different location, away from the Windows folder.

If you do not know how to use Windows Explorer to copy folders, ask
someone to help you. Don't muck around with your Favorites folder
unless you are sure you know what you are doing.

Sending a URL or a Web Page to Someone

There will be lots of times when you see a cool Web page that you want to share with a friend (and one of the best things about the Internet is that sharing is easy). At such times, you have two choices: you can send the URL or you can send a copy of the actual page.

My preference is to send the URL. This is because a URL is only a single line of text—much smaller than an actual Web page—and it is more efficient to send the address of a page than the page itself. When someone receives a message that contains a URL, his mail program will recognize the URL as a Web address and will display it as a link. All the person has to do is click on the link and the URL will be sent to his browser automatically. Moreover, if he wants to share the Web page with another person, he can forward the message.

There are several ways to send a URL to someone. The basic idea is simple: get the URL into a message and mail it. One way is to copy the URL to the clipboard and paste it into a message. My advice is to always copy and paste URLs. Never retype them, because it is too easy to make mistakes.

Internet Explorer makes it easy to create a mail message containing the URL of the current Web page.

Internet Explorer

- Click on the **Mail** button and then select **Send a Link.**

- Or, pull down the **File** menu, then select **Send** and **Link By E-mail**.

The second way to share a Web page is to send a copy of the actual page. Doing so is the same as mailing a message that contains HTML. In Chapter 6, I discuss the problems involved when you mail HTML. The biggest problem is that you can't count on your recipient being able to view the HTML properly unless he or she uses the same mail program as you. Thus, I encourage you to send URLs rather than the actual Web Pages.

Having said this, I will now tell you how to do it.

Learn how to...

Use the Windows Clipboard

Using the clipboard to copy and paste information is one of the fundamental skills you need as a Windows user.

See Chapter 17, *How to Do Stuff*, page 366 (Windows).

Internet Explorer

- Click on the **Mail** button and then select **Send Page**.

- Or, pull down the **File** menu, then select **Send** and **Page By E-mail**.

Setting Your Home Page

Each time you start your browser, it automatically loads a specific Web page. We call this your HOME PAGE. The first time you use a browser, it will have the address of a default home page. However, you can change it to whatever you want. All you have to do is change the home page setting. Here is how to find it:

Internet Explorer

- Pull down the **Tools** menu and select **Internet Options**.

- Then click on the **General** tab (if it is not already showing).

Once you know how to find the home page setting, you can change it as you see fit, so experiment and see what you like best. If you find a home page you really like, there is an easy way to jump to it whenever you want: just click on the **Home** button near the top of your browser window.

What's in a Name?

home page

The term "home page" is used in two different ways.

First, your home page is the Web page your browser displays automatically whenever it starts. In this sense, "home" refers to the place from which you begin your Internet explorations.

Second, we use the term to refer to the main page of a Web site: the place from which you start to explore that site. It is common for Web sites, especially the larger ones, to have one main page to act as a starting place. Typically, this page—the home page—contains an introduction to the site, navigation aids, news about the site, and so on.

With respect to your default home page, I am going to tell you something interesting that many people don't realize. The location of this page is an extremely valuable commodity. Most people don't bother to change their home page, so each time they start their browser, they see the default home page. Overall, this creates a vast amount of traffic to this page, making for a huge captive audience.

For this reason, both Microsoft and Netscape have created elaborate home pages which they set as the default for their respective browsers. These home pages provide a variety of links to useful information, as well as a great deal of self-promotion and advertising.

For this reason, the browser companies use their default home pages to create a huge captive audience to whom they can show massive amounts of advertising. My feeling is you should change your home page just on general principles.

If you are not sure what to use as your home page, you may want to use my Web site:

`http://www.harley.com/`

This is the easiest way I know to show your friends and family that you are a person of great distinction and excellent taste.

hint

Regardless of what you choose to use as your home page, my advice is: *Take control.*

Talking on the Net

People all over the world are talking on the Net, and in a short time, you will be one of them.

Why do so many of us have computers, and why do we spend so much time using the Internet?

I don't know that we can ever answer these questions entirely, but I do know that all the time and effort we spend on the Internet has more to do with our nature than with making money and selling advertising. Human beings need to connect to one another, and that is why we have built so many tools to communicate using the Net.

In previous chapters, we have discussed electronic mail, Web sites, Usenet discussion groups and mailing lists. All of these are important, but they do not allow you to carry on a real conversation. In this chapter, I will explain how to use the Internet to talk to other people. People all over the world are already talking on the Net, and in a short time, you will be one of them.

The Basic Ideas

The term REAL-TIME refers to a process in which you sense and respond to something as it is happening. For example, talking on the telephone is a real-time experience, because you hear the other person's words as he says them. On the other hand, sending email is not real-time communication, because you do not see the messages as they are typed. Instead, you have to wait until a message is delivered before you can read it.

On the Internet, the word TALK refers to all types of real-time communication. For instance, let's say you and a friend are having a conversation by using a program that allows you to type messages back and forth. Even though you are typing (and not speaking), we say that you are talking. We often refer to this type of talking as CHATTING.

Most of the talking on the Internet is done by typing. However, there are other ways: you can talk by voice (as you do on a telephone), and you can also use real-time video (like people in the future). We will discuss all of these facilities — chatting, voice and video — in this chapter.

Talking on the Internet can be a lot different than talking in regular life. For example, it is common to talk with people on the Net whom you have never met face to face and probably never will. In addition, it is perfectly acceptable to start a conversation with someone you don't know. As a matter of fact, most people use anonymous nicknames, and much of the time, there is no way to know who you are talking to.

This makes for an interesting type of communication in which your mind communicates directly with another person's mind, with no voice, physical cues or other knowledge to distract you. As you might imagine, this type of talking has its own nuances and considerations (which we will discuss later in the chapter).

When you talk in person or over the telephone, you hear the other person's voice instantly. On the Net, however, there is sometimes a delay. As you type back and forth, it may take a few moments for the messages to be transmitted. Similarly, when you are talking via voice, there may be a short delay between the time you say something and when the other person hears it. This delay is referred to as LAG.

When the lag is small — as is often the case — the conversation flows smoothly and easily. If the lag becomes significant, however, it can make the conversation disjointed. Still, a bit of lag now and then is a normal phenomenon, and after a while, you will find yourself adjusting to subtle changes without even noticing. Indeed, some people are so used to the lag that they routinely carry on several conversations at the same time, using the brief waiting periods to jump from one conversation to another.

To access a talk facility, you use a program called a TALK CLIENT. There are many different talk facilities available on the Internet for free. The particular client you use depends on which talk facility you want to access.

When you use the Web to talk, your browser can act as your talk client. Most of the non-Web talk facilities use a proprietary design which requires you to use a specific talk client. A few talk facilities allow you a choice of clients. In particular, this is the case for IRC, muds and most voice systems (all of which I will discuss later in the chapter).

In broad terms, there are two kinds of talk facilities.

The first kind uses a TALK SERVER as a central way station. When you use such a system, everything you type first goes to the server. The server then sends the information to all the other people taking part in the conversation.

The second kind of system uses a direct connection. Your talk client connects to the other person's talk client, and as you type, your words are sent from your computer to the other person's computer without going through a central server.

Each of these systems has advantages. With a central server, it is possible to support a large number of people and a large number of simultaneous conversations. An example of this is IRC (Internet Relay Chat). When you connect to an IRC server, you will usually find hundreds of different conversations involving thousands of people from all over the world. Such systems are great places to hang out, because there is always someone to talk to.

hint

On the Internet, people care about your ideas and what you have to say. Who you are and where you live are less important.

Direct connections do not offer the same type of access. Since you are connected to, at most, a few people, you do not get the feeling of being in an international gathering place. However, you do have more privacy and control over your environment. Moreover, since your messages do not go through a central server, there is usually less lag, which makes it easier to carry on a more focused conversation.

Some talk clients will ask you to register before you can use the client. To register, you will have to give your name and mail address. My advice is to protect your privacy. Do not use your real name. Using a nickname is not only common, but perfectly acceptable. For advice on how to protect your mail address, see Chapter 6.

When you register with a particular talk facility, the information you specify is sent to a central server that acts as a public repository of names and addresses. The job of this server is to act as a directory for all the people who use the system. This is true even for systems that use direct connections, because you may still need a way to look up someone's name and address.

As you will see, the Internet offers a wide variety of ways to talk to other people. Throughout this chapter, I will discuss the various types of systems, and give you the information you need to get started. You can then experiment with the different talk facilities and see which ones you like best.

To start, let's talk about the simplest type of talk facility, Instant Messaging.

Instant Messaging

The most popular talk facility on the Internet is known as INSTANT MESSAGING or IM. Instant messaging allows you to have a private conversation with another person, or with several people.

The term IM is often used as a verb. For example, "Clarisse told me that she tried to IM you last night, but you weren't available".

There are a number of different IM systems, all of which are free. The most popular systems are:

- AOL Instant Messenger or AIM
- MSN Messenger (Microsoft)
- ICQ
- Yahoo Messenger

AIM and ICQ are both owned by AOL, although they are completely different systems. The name ICQ, by the way, is a pun. It means "I seek you."

To use an IM system, you need to download and install the appropriate IM client program for that system. For example, to use MSN Messenger, you need the MSN Messenger client. To use ICQ, you need the ICQ client. All of these clients are available for free. I have put the Web addresses for each system at the end of this section. If you need help with downloading, see Chapter 9.

If you are an AOL user, the AOL Instant Messenger program is included with your AOL software. If you are not an AOL user, you can download the AIM client free, which will allow you to talk to other AIM users.

Each IM system has its own central IM server. MSN has its own server, AIM has its own server, ICQ has its own server, and so on. The server keeps track of all the people who are registered with the system and which ones are currently online.

How does this work? Each time your IM client starts up, it contacts its server and tells it that you are online. This ensures that, whenever your computer is on and you are connected to the Net, your IM server knows that you are available to talk.

To help you keep track of other people, your personal IM client maintains a list of names of everyone you talk with. During the times you are connected to the Net, your IM client stays in contact with the server. This allows your client to show you, at any time, which people on your list are online and which ones are not available.

All of this makes it simple and easy to talk with someone. Just select a name from your personal list, and if the person is available, your IM client will immediately establish a connection. (This is why it is called instant messaging.) Figure 8-1 shows an example of an IM conversation.

FIGURE 8-1

An instant messaging conversation

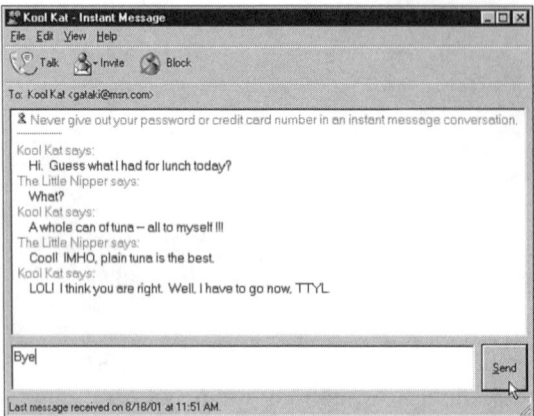

Each IM system has a different term for your personal list of names. The most common terms are shown in Figure 8-2.

Figure 8-2: Instant Messaging systems: lists of names

IM System	List of Names
AOL Instant Messenger	Buddy List
MSN Messenger	Contact List
ICQ	Contact List
Yahoo Messenger	Friend List

When you IM with people, your conversations are completely private. No one can eavesdrop unless you invite them into the conversation.

You can also have privacy in other ways. For example, you can block specific people from contacting you. This is handy if someone is bothering you. In addition, some IM systems allow you to be "invisible". This means that you are connected to the system, but not visible to anyone.

All IM systems let you talk with people whose names you have added to your list. Some systems also have organized chat groups that are devoted to different interests. You can join and leave such conversations whenever you want. This allows you to talk to people all over the world, about all kinds of things.

The various IM clients are sophisticated programs, which offer a variety of different services. Although each program has its own features, here are some of the most common ones:

- **Talking**: Send and receive messages.

- **File transfer**: Send files from your computer to another person's computer. You may find it easier to transfer a file this way than to attach it to a mail message.

- **Voice chat**: Talk to another person by voice. (This requires a microphone.)

- **Phone calls**: Make phone calls from your computer to a telephone. (Also requires a microphone.)

- **Paging**: Send a message to someone's cell phone or pager

- **Web browsing**: Allows one person to control another person's browser. This is handy when you want to show someone specific Web sites while you talk.

Here are a list of Web sites where you can get the client programs for various IM systems. In order to use any of these systems, you will need to register. If you are concerned about your privacy, do not use your real name or mail address. Either use fake information or a disposable, Web-based email address. (For a discussion on how to keep your mail address private and how to set up a free Web-based email account, see Chapter 5.)

Internet Resources **Instant Messaging Systems**

```
http://aim.aol.com/
http://www.icq.com/
http://www.odigo.com/
http://www.jabber.org/
http://www.paltalk.com/
http://messenger.msn.com/
http://messenger.yahoo.com/
http://messenger.excite.com/
```

Chat Rooms

A CHAT ROOM is a talk facility that works over the Web. Each chat room supports one multiperson conversation. There are many Web sites that offer public chat rooms.

When you visit such a Web site, think of yourself as being at a party in a large house with many different rooms. In each room there are a number of people talking. You can move from room to room. As you do, you can participate in the various conversations or just listen.

hint

There are several ways to manually reload a Web page:

Internet Explorer

● Click the **Refresh** button
● Press **Ctrl-R**
● Press the **F5** key

Some chat rooms are set up for general conversation. Others are devoted to particular topics or particular groups of people. For example, you might find a chat room where people talk about a popular television show, or a chat room just for teenagers.

Using a chat room is easy, because you do not need to install a special client program. All you need is a browser. There are two different ways in which this might work.

First, the chat room Web site may send your browser a Java applet to act as your talk client. (See Chapter 12 for a discussion of Java.) If so, your browser will run the applet automatically. You can see such a program in Figure 8-3.

FIGURE 8-3

A chat room using a Java talk client

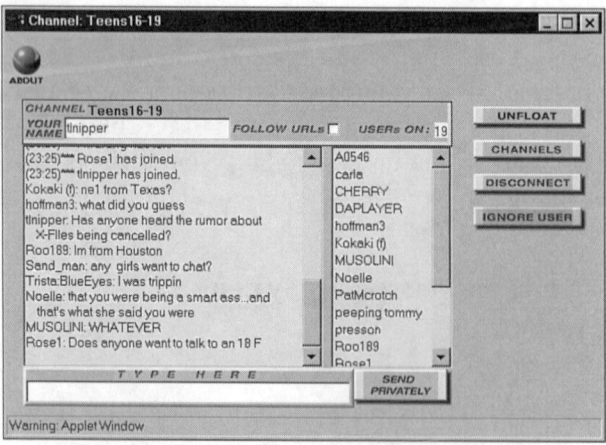

The other possibility is that you will use your browser as a talk client. You can see this in Figure 8-4. When you use a browser as a talk client, you are displaying regular Web pages that do not change. Thus, you must reload the Web page in order to see any new messages. For convenience, most chat rooms tell your browser to reload the Web page automatically at regular intervals.

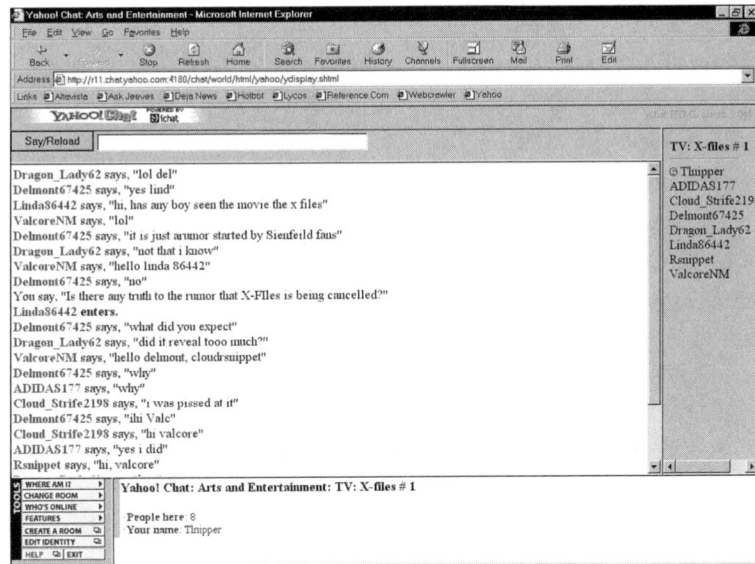

FIGURE 8-4

A chat room using a browser as a talk client

A chat room works by having a central server that acts as a way station. Everything you type is sent to the server, which then relays the information to the various client programs. Thus, all messages must pass through a server; they do not go directly from one person to another.

Chat rooms are popular because they are readily available and do not require special software. If you have a browser running, you are ready to join a chat room. However, much of the conversation in chat rooms is transient and superficial. This is not the place for deep conversation or meaningful relationships.

Most chat rooms use only plain text. A few chat rooms enable you to display a picture along with your messages. This allows you to choose an image that illustrates your personality and makes it easy for people to recognize you. Other Web sites offer chat rooms with a specific visual environment. For example, while you are talking, it may look as if you are in a cave, or a forest, or a palace.

A few chat rooms are even more elaborate: they create imaginary 3D environments that you visit as you talk. You can move around from one place to another, and talk to the people you encounter. Some of these environments are simple, while others are very complex. Within a 3D chat room, each person is represented by an AVATAR: a small picture or figure that moves and talks on your behalf. You control the appearance and actions of your avatar, which allows you to exhibit some of your own personality.

Internet Resources   **Chat Rooms**

```
http://chat.yahoo.com/
http://communities.msn.com/
http://www.chatlist.com/
http://www.chatropolis.com/
http://www.excite.com/communities/
http://www.talkcity.com/
http://www.webarrow.net/chatindex/
```

Internet Resources   **Avatar-based Chat Rooms**

```
http://www.activeworlds.com/
http://www.chatpop.com/english/eindex.htm
http://www.cybertown.com/
http://www.moove.com/
http://www.penguinchat.com/
```

Abbreviations Used While Talking

When you first start to talk on the Net, it is easy to feel a bit confused. If you are visiting a chat room or an IRC channel (discussed later in the chapter) where a number of people are talking at the same time, it may take a while to learn how to make sense out of what is happening. However, it won't be long before you start to feel the rhythm, and everything falls into place.

People who talk on the Net use a lot of abbreviations. This is because talking involves typing, and typing is slow compared to regular conversation. To help you get started, Figure 8-5 shows the most important abbreviations used while talking on the Net. You will find a more extensive list in Appendix C.

For the most part, the abbreviations are straightforward. However, there is one I want to discuss for a moment: the smiley. A SMILEY is a tiny representation of a smiling face:

`:-)`

(To see the smiling face, tilt your head sideways to the left.)

Figure 8-5:	Abbreviations used while talking on the Net
Abbreviation	**Meaning**
:-)	smiley
;-)	winking smiley
<G>	grin (same as a smiley)
AFAIK	as far as I know
AFAIR	as far as I remember
ADDY	address
AFK	away from keyboard
A/S/L	what is your age, sex, and location?
BBL	be back later
BF	boyfriend
BRB	be right back
BTW	by the way
CUL8R	see you later
CYA	see ya (good-bye)
F2F	face to face (in person)
FYI	for your information
GF	girlfriend
IC	I see
IMHO	in my humble opinion
J/K	just kidding
L8R	(see you) later
LDR	long distance relationship
LOL	laughing out loud
OIC	oh, I see
PUTER	computer
PAW	parents are watching
PDA	public display of affection
RL	real life
ROFL	rolling on the floor laughing
SO	significant other
TTYL	talk to you later

From time to time, you will find yourself typing something you mean as a joke, but which could be taken as being offensive. When this happens, you use a smiley to tell the other person not to be offended. The smiley means "just kidding".

For example, say you are talking about UFOs, and someone is describing how he was kidnapped the other night by a bunch of aliens dressed as Supreme Court justices. You might say:

```
I do find that hard to believe, but the next time
I see the Tooth Fairy, I'll ask her what she thinks :-)
```

Sometimes, you will see `<G>` or `<g>` ("grin") used instead of a smiley.

Voice Chatting and Video Chatting

Most people talk on the Internet by typing messages back and forth. This is the case with instant messaging and chat rooms, as well as with IRC and muds (which we will talk about later in the chapter). However, it is also possible to use VOICE CHAT to communicate over the Net using voice. To use voice chat, you must have the appropriate equipment on your computer: either a microphone and speakers, or a headset with a built-in microphone.

The biggest advantage of using a voice chat system is the cost. There is no special fee for talking to people over the Internet, no matter how far away they may be, so you can talk as long as you want for free.

One particular type of voice chat is an INTERNET PHONE SYSTEM. Such systems are integrated with the telephone system in a way that allows you to use your computer to call someone's telephone directly. When the other person answers, you talk to him using your microphone and speakers (or headset) on your computer, and he uses his phone.

So why doesn't everyone use the Internet for talking instead of the telephone system, at least for long distance? There are several reasons.

First, the regular telephone system is reliable and offers a high quality connection. With voice chat or an Internet phone system, you can't always connect perfectly whenever you want and the quality of the connection can vary significantly, even from minute to minute. Most of the time the connection is adequate, but there is sometimes a noticeable lag or an echo, which can quickly take the fun out of talking.

Second, the regular telephone system is extremely convenient. When you want to talk with someone, you pick up a phone and make the call. You can call from any telephone you want, including a portable phone or a cell phone. With an Internet phone system, you can only make a call if you are at your computer. Moreover, if you want to use regular voice chat, the other person will also have to be at his computer, running the same voice program as you.

Finally, although voice chatting is free, Internet phone systems cost money to use. Since Internet phone companies need to be competitive, they will typically charge a bit less than the regular phone system. However, the regular phone system is more reliable, easier to use, and offers better quality.

My feeling is that, when you need to make a phone call, you are better off using the regular telephone system, especially if you live in a country like the United States, where long distance rates are low. However, there is one situation in which it makes sense to use voice chat or an Internet phone system.

If you have a need to make many expensive long distance calls to the same number, you can save a lot of money by talking over the Net. For example, if you live in the U.S., an Internet phone system is an ideal way to spend several hours a night talking to your boyfriend in Australia. Or, if you work at a company in New York and you need to talk to your branch office in Paris for an hour every day, you might be willing to put up with the lower quality connection in order to save money.

Some voice chat systems have video capabilities as well as voice. To receive video, you do not need special hardware. The video client program will display images for you on your monitor. To send video, however, you need a WEBCAM, a video camera that is designed to connect to your computer.

Video over the Internet can be fun to play with, but you should realize that it is not the high resolution, full motion video you see on your television. Although you see images, they are updated intermittently, not continuously.

hint

One of the big advantages to talking to someone without video, is that you do not have to look at each other while you are having a conversation.

To tell you the truth, although the idea of free video conferencing over the Net sounds cool, it's really not that big a deal, unless you have some friends that you like to talk with regularly.

Most voice/video chat programs offer other features besides the basic connection. While you are talking, you may be able to:

- Type messages back and forth (instant messaging)
- Play sounds on the other person's computer
- Transfer files
- Control the other person's browser
- Collaborate by drawing within a shared window (called a WHITEBOARD)
- Control a program running on the other person's computer. This is called APPLICATION SHARING.

Internet Resources   **Voice and Video Chatting**

```
http://aim.aol.com/
http://www.eyeball.com/
http://www.paltalk.com/
http://messenger.msn.com/
http://messenger.yahoo.com/
http://www.microsoft.com/netmeeting/
http://www.netscape.com/communicator/conference/
http://messenger.yahoo.com/messenger/help/voicechat.html
```

IRC: Internet Relay Chat

IRC (Internet Relay Chat) is the largest of the Internet talk systems. The first version of IRC was created in 1988 by a Finnish programmer named Jarkko Oikarinen. Since then, IRC has grown enormously.

To use IRC, you must first download and install an IRC CLIENT on your computer. Once you have an IRC client, you use it to connect to one of the IRC NETWORKS. You can then talk to anyone else who is connected to the same network. IRC is so popular that, no matter when you connect, there will be many people for you to talk with.

There are more than 50 different IRC networks, each one using its own group of IRC SERVERS. The larger networks have dozens of servers around the world; the smaller networks have only a few servers. To use a particular IRC network, all you need to do is tell your IRC client to connect to any server on the network. Once you are connected, you have access to the entire network.

What's in a Name?

EFnet

Undernet

DALnet

IRCnet

Through the years, many IRC networks have been formed with varying degrees of success. Today, there are more than 50 different networks, the largest of which are EFnet, Undernet, DALnet and IRCnet.

IRC was started in 1988. By 1990, the original network had grown to encompass a number of servers around the world. The people in charge had intense philosophical disagreements over the design of the network. As a result, one group of people and the server they ran were banished from the network. The server was a computer named `eris.berkeley.edu`. This group formed their own network, but eventually it died out. In the meantime, what was left of the original network became known as the "Eris-free Network" or EFnet. Since then, EFnet has grown enormously, and to this day, it is still the largest of the IRC networks.

By 1993, EFnet was becoming large and cumbersome, and another group of people decided to start an alternative network, which they named Undernet. The name was chosen as a whimsical description of an "underground network", hidden from the main network.

In 1995, another group of EFnet people created a network called DALnet as an alternative to EFnet and Undernet . The name comes from one of the members of this group, Sven Nielsen. Sven's nickname was "Dalvenjah FoxFire".

In 1996, the last of the large IRC networks, IRCnet, was started by yet another group of people who broke away from EFnet.

IRC is a mature, complex system, and there is a lot for you to learn. To get you started, I will explain the basic terminology, and show you where to get the software and the information you need. Once you have read this section, you can start by downloading and installing your own IRC client. You will then be able to connect to a server and start talking.

Each IRC network has a number of CHANNELS, each of which supports a different conversation. Once you have connected to an IRC server, you can JOIN one of the channels. This allows you to participate in that particular conversation. When you are tired of that conversation, you can LEAVE the channel.

All networks have a variety of channels; a large network may have thousands. Channels are dynamic: anyone can create a channel at any time. Once the last person leaves, the channel is automatically deleted. Some channels have an automated program, called a "bot", that stays on the channel permanently to keep it open. (We will talk about bots later in the chapter.)

When someone creates a channel, he specifies a name for it. He can also specify an optional short description called a TOPIC. The purpose of the topic is to let people know what the channel is being used for. Some channels are created to discuss a specific subject, while others are used for more general conversation. As you use IRC, you can join and leave channels whenever you want, and you can be in more than one at the same time.

Channel names start with the # (number sign) character. Here are some examples:

```
#hottub
#beginner
#help
#IRCaddicts
#Wasteland
```

When you type a channel name, you can use either upper- or lowercase letters. Although some names are created with uppercase letters, it is easier to use all lowercase when you type.

The person who creates a channel is the CHANNEL OPERATOR or OP. The op has special control over that particular channel. He or she decides whether the channel will be open to the public, or whether it will be private (in which case, people may join by invitation only or by entering a password). If someone in the channel is a troublemaker, the op can kick him off the channel or even ban him permanently. The op can share power by allowing someone else to also become an op (for that channel).

People on IRC do not use their real names. Instead, each person uses a NICKNAME or NICK. You can use any nick you want (and you can change it whenever you want), as long as no one else on the network is already using the same name.

Most IRC clients put each channel in a separate window to help you keep the various conversations separate. You can then follow the conversation just by looking at the window. Every time anyone sends a message, it will be broadcast to everyone who has joined that channel. As you watch a channel, you will see messages appear near the bottom of the window and scroll up. At the very bottom of the window, there is an area that you use to type your own messages. When you do, they will be sent to the server which will broadcast them to everyone in the channel.

Figure 8-6 shows a typical IRC session. Within this session, I am participating in three different channels, each of which has its own conversation in its own window. In addition, there is a fourth window (on the bottom right) that shows various status messages.

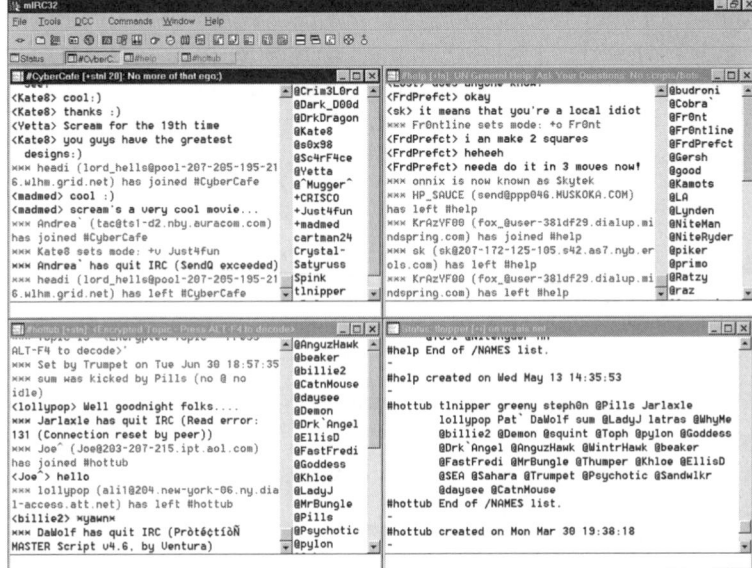

FIGURE 8-6
A typical IRC session

As you watch the window for a particular channel, you will see two types of messages in the window. First, you will see the regular messages that people type back and forth. These messages will have the form:

<*nickname*> *message*

For example, here are two messages sent by a person using the nickname `carrie`:

```
<carrie> It takes a lot of energy to be so cute...
<carrie> But I manage :-)
```

Aside from conversation, you will also see system messages, generated by the IRC server. These messages give you information about the channel itself. For instance, every time someone joins or leaves a channel, you will see such a system message. All system messages start with the characters `***`. For example:

`*** carrie (amish@cascade.net) has joined #hottub`

In a busy channel, the messages will fly by quickly and you may be confused. Don't worry. Once you get used to IRC, your mind will notice what it needs to notice and will ignore everything else. In no time at all, you will be able to keep track of several different channels, while carrying on several conversations at the same time.

To control your IRC session, you use IRC commands. All of the commands start with a / (slash) character, in order to distinguish them from regular messages. For example, the command to join a channel is `/join` followed by the name of the channel. Thus, to join the `#hottub` channel, you would type:

`/join #hottub`

To leave a channel, you use the `/leave` command:

`/leave #hottub`

Figure 8-7 contains a summary of the most important IRC commands.

In order to get used to IRC, take some time to experiment with the various commands. As you do, don't forget to type a / character at the beginning of each command. Otherwise, your command will be interpreted as a message, and it will be broadcast to everyone in the channel. Consider this example.

The command to send a private message is:

`/msg` *nickname message*

To send a private message to the person using the nick `carrie`, you would type:

`/msg carrie Did you get the secret letter I sent you?`

What happens if you inadvertently leave out the / character?

`msg carrie Did you get the secret letter I sent you?`

Figure 8–7: Important IRC commands

Command	Description
`/dcc chat` *nickname*	Start or accept a direct talk connection
`/dcc send` *nickname files*	Send files to the specified person
`/help`	Display help information
`/help` command	Display help about the specified command
`/join` #*channel*	Join the specified channel
`/leave` #*channel*	Leave the specified channel (same as `/part`)
`/list`	Display a list of all channels
`/list` #*channel*	Display information about the specified channel
`/list -max` *n*	Display channels that have no more than *n* people
`/list -min` *n*	Display channels that have at least *n* people
`/me` *action*	Emote (show) the specified action to current channel
`/mode` #*channel* `+pi`	Make the specified channel completely private
`/msg` *nicknames text*	Send a private message to specified people
`/nick` *nickname*	Change your nickname to specified name
`/part` #*channel*	Leave the specified channel (same as `/leave`)
`/ping` nickname	See how long it takes to get to specified person and back
`/query` *nicknames*	Open private message window to talk to specified people
`/quit`	Disconnect from the server
`/who *`	Show basic information about everyone in current channel
`/who` *nickname*	Show basic information about the specified person
`/whois` *nickname*	Show all available information about the specified person

The IRC server will interpret what you typed as a regular message and show it to everyone in the channel.

Want to have some fun? Try this. Join a crowded channel, and after waiting a few minutes, enter the following commands:

```
msg hotlips I would love to meet you in person
msg hotlips don't forget the whipped cream
```

(Be sure you do *not* type a / character at the beginning of the command.)

Aside from channels, IRC also supports a facility called DCC (which stands for "Direct Client to Client connection"). DCC allows you to establish a direct connection with another person. Once you establish

hint

For security reasons, never accept a program or a script via DCC to run on your computer. It is not uncommon for people to offer programs that can cause harm to your system. One of my friends, who shall remain nameless (Martin Rivers), once got into trouble in just that way.

He was talking to someone via DCC, and the person offered him a batch file (a type of script). Martin accepted the file and ran it. The batch file then proceeded to delete some important Windows files from his computer. As a result, Martin had to reformat his hard disk, which caused him to lose all his files.

such a connection, you can talk in private, as well as transfer files back and forth. The basic DCC commands are listed in Figure 8-7. DCC is useful to know, so when you get a chance, see if you can find someone to help you practice the commands.

The next idea I want to mention is that of a BOT. A bot is a program that performs actions automatically in a specific IRC channel. (The name stands for "robot".) A bot can be programmed to respond to different types of input, to generate output, and to carry out various tasks. For example, a bot can be used to keep a channel open permanently, even when there are no people in it. Although bots can be helpful, many people have used them to cause trouble and abuse the system. For this reason, some IRC networks ban bots altogether. Other networks allow them, but impose restrictions to make sure that the bots are not disruptive.

To finish this section, I would like to leave you with some resources to help you get started. First, you need to download and install an IRC client. The clients I have suggested here are particularly good ones. If you need more help, you can either look at the help system within your client program or check with the help resources on the Web. Once you have an IRC client, connect to a server and join a channel. If you need more information, check with some of the resources listed below.

Internet Resources   **IRC Clients**
_____

http://www.dircchat.com/

http://www.jpilot.com/

http://www.leafdigital.com/software/leafchat/

http://www.mirc.com/

http://www.xircon.com/

Internet Resources   **IRC Help Information**
_____

http://www.irchelp.org/

http://www.newircusers.com/

http://www.mirc.org/links.htm

Muds

Real life is fine when it's time to balance your checkbook or go to the dentist, but once in awhile we can all use a break. When the time comes to escape reality, there are many imaginary environments on the Net where you can go to explore, have adventures, meet people, or indulge in good, old-fashioned make-believe.

A MUD is an elaborate, text-based imaginary environment. Although muds are used for talking, they offer a lot more: you can have adventures, explore exotic places, and solve puzzles. You can also take part in group events, such as going on a quest or attending a wedding.

Muds are fantasy role-playing environments in which each person becomes a character. For example, you might be a magician, a druid, a thief, a warrior, a pirate or an assassin. As you use the mud, your character interacts with other characters and with the mud itself. You move around from place to place, and as you do, things happen. For instance, you may be exploring a cave and happen upon an evil magician who tries to kill you. Or you may encounter a young warrior who asks you to join her on a quest to save a city from a hungry dragon.

Participating in a mud is a long-term experience. Every mud has regular users who form a large, extended family. Once you join a mud (which is free), you can create your own character and use it every time you visit that mud. It is common for people to return to a mud over and over, for months or even years. Each time you return, you will meet some of the same people, and over time, you will develop long-term friendships.

Muds provide a rich experience, because they offer a detailed environment that changes as you move from one place to another. Since muds are text-based, there are no pictures, only words to describe what you see. However, words are more compelling than pictures, and the imaginary world of a mud will, over time, become as real to you as the setting of a novel.

Each mud has a geography that is created by the people who administer the mud. Every mud is different, with its own villages and towns, and with a large number of rooms to explore. Figure 8-8 shows a typical description of a setting within a mud.

Figure 8-8:   An imaginary setting within a mud

```
You are in the Heart's Haven Square.
This is the central gathering place for people
traveling in and out of the city. Heart's Haven
is a coastal city, with the ocean located to the
southeast. To the northeast, the city rises up a
gentle-sloping hillside, and to the northwest you
see a massive rock face. In any direction you look,
you can see interesting shops and beautiful places
to wander. You feel very welcome here. A tall,
black obelisk decorates the center of the town
square. The bustle and commotion of a thriving town
surround you.

There are four obvious exits:
    east, north, south and west.
```

What's in a Name?

mud

The first mud dates back to a role-playing program developed in 1978 by Richard Bartle and Roy Trubshaw. At the time, they used the acronym MUD to stand for "Multi-User Dungeons" (as in Dungeons and Dragons). Later, people started to use "Multi-User Dimension", but eventually the name "mud" became a full-fledged word on its own (which is why I write it in lowercase letters).

The word "mud" can also be used as a verb. For example, "I have to finish my homework, so I can go mud" or "Monica fell asleep during the President's speech, because she was tired from mudding all night."

Broadly speaking, there are two types of muds: social muds and adventure muds.

Social muds are used primarily for chatting and socializing. They do have an imaginary geography, and people do adopt character roles, but mostly, these muds are for talking. Unlike chat rooms and IRC, muds provide an enduring social setting. People tend to stay longer, return more often, and take time to learn how things work. Once you start to spend time on a mud, you will make friends who will become an important part of your life. In fact, it is common for people on muds to have friendships that last for years.

Note: You will see social muds referred to by a variety of names: TinyMUDs, MUSHs, MUCKs, MUSEs and MOOs. The distinction between the various subcategories is not important. Just remember that all muds of these types are for talking.

Adventure muds have two purposes. They are for talking and for role-playing adventures. The examples I described above, including the one in Figure 8-8, are taken from adventure muds. Every adventure mud has a complex environment based on a particular theme. For example, there are adventure muds based on medieval fantasy, gothic horror, science fiction settings, and futuristic techno-cultures. I myself sponsor an adventure mud named Zhing. To give you an idea of what these muds are like, here is a brief description of Zhing.

Zhing was planned and developed by a group of people who have years of mudding experience. These people have created a rich and engaging environment based on a medieval fantasy theme. Like all adventure muds, you can spend time talking with other people, but there are also a great many places to explore. Zhing has five continents, one of which is an archipelago. There are coastlines, mountains, forests, streams, caves, cliffs (which you can climb), castles, beaches, docks (where you can catch fish to eat), parks, an underground cavern, a maze, roads, and cities that have restaurants, pubs, hospitals, armories and various types of shops. Within Zhing, there are a lot of activities to keep you busy, either alone or in the company of other people, so there is always something to do.

hint

Muds are magical places. There is nothing else like them, on or off the Net.

So how do you access a mud? Muds use a client/server system, so to start, you must download and install a mud client. Once your client is up and running, you can have it connect to any mud you want.

In order to connect to a mud, you need to know two pieces of information. First, you need to know the address of the mud. This is a regular Internet address that identifies the host (that is, the computer) on which the mud resides. For example, the host for Zhing is `zhing.com`.

The second thing you need to know is the PORT NUMBER used by the mud. Port numbers work as follows.

Because Internet computers can provide a variety of services, a client must be able to tell a server exactly what type of service is being requested. To do this, the client uses a port number. All Internet client/server systems use port numbers, but in most cases, you don't have to worry about them, because your client takes care of the details automatically. For example, the basic Internet services, such as mail and Usenet and the Web, all use standard port numbers. When you access one of these services, your client automatically sends the appropriate port number to the server.

Muds, however, do not use standard port numbers. For this reason, in order to access a mud, you must specify a port number as well as an address. In general, people who design muds choose port numbers that are easy to remember. For example, the port number for Zhing is `4000`.

In case you were wondering about other port numbers, Figure 8-9 shows some of the standard numbers used on the Internet. Most of the time, you don't really need to know any of this, so don't worry if you don't recognize some of the technical terms. Your client programs know what to do.

Figure 8-9: Standard port numbers used on the Internet

Service	Port Number
DNS	53
FTP	20, 21
IRC	194
Mail	25 (SMTP), 110 (POP), 143 (IMAP)
Telnet	23
Usenet	119 (NNTP)
Web	80 (HTTP), 443 (HTTPS), 8080 (HTTP, sometimes)

To start mudding, begin by downloading and installing a mud client on your computer. Then take a few minutes and read some of the basic information to make sure you get started properly. To help you, I have put an introduction to muds on my Web site. The address is:

`http://www.harley.com/muds/`

When you need more information, you can take a look at the FAQs (frequently asked question lists) and tutorials listed below. Once you are

ready to start mudding, check out the lists of muds for one that looks
intriguing. (Your mud client will also come with its own list of muds.)
Most muds have their own FAQ, which you should read if you are a newcomer.

If you would like to visit the Zhing mud, you can connect by using the
following information:

```
Zhing mud
```
host = `zhing.com`

port = `4000`

Internet Resources   **Mud Clients**

```
http://www.mud-master.com/
http://www.game.org/clients.html
http://www.gammon.com.au/mushclient/
http://www.nanvaent.org/help/clients.shtml
http://www.zuggsoft.com/zmud/zmudinfo.htm
http://www.interlog.com/~sofa/client/madclient2.html
```

Internet Resources   **Mud FAQs and Tutorials**

```
http://www.harley.com/muds/
http://www.moo.mud.org/moo-faq/
http://www.lysator.liu.se/mud/faq/
http://www.faqs.org/faqs/games/mud-faq/
http://www.imaginary.com/LPMud/lpmud_faq.html
```

Internet Resources   **Lists of Muds**

```
http://moolist.yeehaw.com/
http://mudlist.eorbit.net/
http://www.topmudsites.com/
http://www.radeleff.de/swmudlist/
http://www.mudconnector.com/mud_category.html
```

Expectations and Reality

Isn't it amazing that you can sit in front of your computer and, just by
clicking your mouse and typing on your keyboard, talk to people all over
the world?

Talking on the Net is a pleasant way to pass the time, but it can be much more. The Internet is a part of our mainstream culture, and meeting people on the Net is considered a normal, legitimate way to make friends. Many people use the Net every day to meet with their friends and to develop relationships. Some relationships are brief; others last for months and years. Some relationships are casual; others are deeply passionate and enduring.

You may hear someone talk about the Internet as if it were different from "real life", but for a great many people, the Net *is* part of real life. The friends they have on the Net are just as real as their job, their home and their family.

And why not? When you talk on the Net, you are communicating directly with other people's minds. By bypassing the limitations of appearance and physical presence, you learn to judge people by their ideas and by how they express themselves. All this makes for a culture in which *what* you are matters a whole lot more than *who* you are. However, the Internet is different from other parts of life. To be successful, you need to develop new skills and new ways of looking at other people.

To start, you need to be persistent. When you begin to talk on the Net, it is easy to feel confused and overwhelmed. As you watch the conversation in a chat room or an IRC channel or a mud, you will see people coming and going. Moreover, the messages move fast, and it can be hard to understand what is happening.

Don't worry. All the people who look as if they are so confident were, at one time, beginners just like you. Human beings are flexible and adaptable, and it won't be long before you know what you are doing and you will feel right at home. Whatever happens, don't allow yourself to be intimidated by other people. Not everyone on the Net is polite, and a few people take particular delight in being mean to newcomers. All they are doing is demonstrating their own insecurities, so don't let such people hurt your feelings.

To help you get off to a good start, I have two suggestions. First, recognize that the Internet talk facilities have been around for some time and have all developed their own cultures. (This is especially true of IRC and the muds.) Your first steps should be to learn how things are done, just as you would if you moved to a foreign country.

At the beginning, it is a good idea to listen more than you talk. Do your best to learn the new words and to understand the behaviors that are expected of you. Each type of talk facility has a rhythm of its own, which you will absorb. After all, there are many thousands of people using the Internet to talk right now, and most of them aren't nearly as smart as you.

My second suggestion is to put some effort into improving your typing. The better you type, the faster you will communicate, and the more likely people will respond to what you have to say. Remember, people judge you by what they see, and on the Net, all they can see is your words. In my experience, the easiest way to learn to type quickly is to spend lots of time talking on the Net.

hint

When your mind wants to say something, your fingers will figure out what to do.

As a rule, people who talk on the Net use nicknames to remain anonymous. As a result, the Internet has developed a wonderful freedom of expression in which people are comfortable saying whatever they want. There are a lot of advantages to such an environment. After all, the Internet is the largest open forum in the world and people should feel free to express themselves however they want. As you talk on the Net, you are in an environment where people's ideas and personalities matter more than who they are or where they live.

For this reason, you must realize that many people are not who they seem to be. People can present themselves in any way they want: they can tell the truth, they can lie, and they can exaggerate. For example, it is common for people to misrepresent their age, their weight and even their sex. This does not mean that you always need to be distrustful and suspicious. Rather, you must learn to accept people based on their ideas. Do not depend on what anyone says about himself, unless you have a way to verify it independently.

If you are talking with someone and your intuition tells you that something is not right, be prudent and break off the conversation. Be polite, but don't worry about hurting someone else's feelings. There are plenty of other people to talk to.

Just as important, be sure to protect your own privacy. As a general rule, do not tell anyone your real name, your phone number or your street address. If you get to know someone well, you may want to give some personal information, but please make sure you really do know him or her well, and use your discretion.

Hint for parents

Before you let your children talk on the Net, teach them that they must never give out any type of personal information without your permission.

If your children are young, you can find places for them where they will be talking with other children. To make sure you feel comfortable, you may want to watch as they talk.

Once you start to make friends, the time may come when you want to meet someone in person. Such meetings can work out well, and many satisfying relationships have started on the Internet. However, you should realize that it is possible to develop a deep bond with people, even to the point of intimacy, and still not really understand who they are.

On the Internet, people can present themselves in any way they want, and it is human nature for all of us to dwell on our strengths and downplay our weaknesses. When you talk to someone in person, you can see what he looks like, his body language, and his mannerisms. You can also see how he reacts to you, and how you feel being with him.

All this is missing when you talk over the Net. So, when you are going to meet somebody in person for the first time, do not take anything for granted. Arrange to meet the person in a public place and if possible, take a friend with you. The friend will be more than a chaperone. Although you may have talked to someone for hundreds of hours, meeting him or her in person is bound to generate a lot of pressure and some awkwardness. Having a friend with you will make the meeting more relaxed and a lot more comfortable.

If you participate in the "adult community" on the Net—where people are primarily interested in sexual and fetish activities—you must be especially careful when you arrange to meet someone in person. Here are three important suggestions.

First, do *not* engage in any sexual or fetish activity during the first meeting. Make the other person agree to this ahead of time, and don't let him or her change your mind.

Second, before you meet, you and the other person should exchange photocopies of your driver's licenses.

Third, make sure that at least one friend knows all the details: where you are going, the name of the person you are meeting, that person's description, what you plan to be doing, and so on. Tell the friend that you will call him or her several times: when you meet the new person, a few hours later, and when you arrive home. This is known as making a SAFE CALL. If you have a cell phone, you can also have your friend call you at prearranged items. If you do not make a safe call on time, your friend can do something to help you (such as calling the police or your mother).

The last point I want to make has to do with developing a sense of perspective. Talking on the Net is fun and making friends is certainly rewarding, but you must never forget that there is more to life than the Internet. Many people get so wrapped up with their Internet friends that they neglect other aspects of life. (I discuss these issues at length in my book *Harley Hahn's Internet Insecurity*.)

Another common problem is that many people are drawn into unwholesome sexual/fetish activities. (There are a huge number of people engaged in such activities on the Internet, and a great many well-established communities.) This often happens to adventurous people, who think they are in full control of their lives, and who don't realize that their thinking is being changed, a tiny bit at a time.

I have seen some sad things happen to otherwise smart, well-adjusted people. Unfortunately, when you get used to something a bit at a time, strange new activities can seem normal, and it is all too easy to lose your perspective. To use an old-fashioned idea, people do get corrupted.

It is important for your health and your sense of well-being to maintain a balance in your life. You are a human being, and you need fresh air, exercise, and healthy, face-to-face relationships that involve normal responsibilities and obligations. Moreover, common sense should tell you that, if you start participating in an area of life in which safe calls are necessary, you might want to rethink your priorities.

hint

Go outside. The Net will be there when you get back.

Net Sex

warning

The following section contains material for mature audiences only, so do not read it unless you are an adult or your parents are not in the room.

NET SEX refers to an activity in which two people type erotic messages back and forth in order to achieve a state of sexual arousal leading to physical resolution. The word CYBER is sometimes used as a verb to indicate participating in net sex. For example, "Janice had not been in the chat room more than 2 minutes before a stranger asked her if she wanted to cyber."

For the most part, net sex takes place between two consenting people in a private place within some type of talk facility. Frequently, the people having net sex are masturbating at the same time. There is nothing wrong with this; after all, it is a private activity. However, if you choose to engage in net sex, I do want you to understand what is probably happening at the other end. Net sex is safe in a physical way, because there is no actual contact. However, there are a few important considerations.

Net sex involves real feelings and real sensations. Within the anonymity of the Internet, it may be easy to forget your inhibitions, but you must remember that you are interacting with another person. People have feelings, so don't forget to be nice.

If you ever meet a net sex partner in person, do not have any expectations. Do not assume that, just because someone had net sex with you, he or she will want to have real sex. Nor should you assume that you have a deep relationship with someone just because you have had net sex. For many people, net sex is a way to experiment or to release sexual tension. Chances are, there is not much meaning beyond the obvious.

You should be aware that most talk programs have a way to save the transcript of a conversation. Although you may think your encounter is completely private, your partner may be recording everything. For this reason, some people will only have net sex with people they know well.

Finally, you must remember that the Internet is based on anonymity and voluntary standards of behavior. When you meet someone on the Internet, there is no way to know who they really are or if they are telling the truth, so please use discretion and judgment. (But don't forget to have fun.)

hint

Net sex requires you to use your imagination, and there is no doubt that experiences that fulfill your fantasies can be highly satisfying.

However, imagine your disappointment if you were to find out that the blonde, 21-year-old college girl who likes to be tied up and ravished is really a balding, 55-year-old accountant named Marvin from Fargo, North Dakota.

9

Downloading and Installing Software

The Internet is the largest
library of software in the
world, and there are a vast
number of programs
available to you for free.

The Internet is the largest library of software in the world, and there are a vast number of programs available to you for free: programs to use for fun, to help you with your work, and to increase the utility of your computer. In this chapter, I will show you how to locate and obtain free programs from the Internet. These skills are important, as you will always have a need for new software.

Before we can cover these topics, however, we need to lay some groundwork. To start, let's take a few moments to discuss the various type of files you are likely to encounter on the Internet, and how your browser recognizes them. From there, we will discuss certain types of programs, called plug-ins and controls, that can be used to expand the capabilities of your browser. Then we will discuss free software: how to find it, and how to install it on your computer.

File Types and Extensions

Web pages can contain different types of data: HTML, pictures, sounds, video, and so on. For this reason, it is important that, when a file arrives from a Web server, your browser be able to tell what type of data is contained within that file.

In Chapter 4, I explained that every file name has a suffix called an extension that indicates the type of data contained in that file. For example, if you see a file named **harley.html**, you know it contains HTML (that is, a Web page), because you see the **html** extension. If you see the file **harley.jpg**, you know it contains a picture, because of the **jpg** extension.

The table in Figure 9-1 (copied from Chapter 4) shows a list of file extensions and what they mean. There are many more extensions in use than you see in this table, but these are the most common ones on the Web.

File extensions are used by every program, not just by browsers. In fact, file extensions are so important that Windows keeps a master list. Each item in the list describes a particular type of data, its file extension, and the name of the program that handles that type of data.

To see the master list of file types:

1. Start Windows Explorer. (Click on the **Start** button, point to **Programs**, then click on **Windows Explorer**.)

2. Display the Folder Options. How you do this depends on your version of Windows:

- Pull down the **Tools** menu, select **Folder Options**.
- Pull down the **View** menu, select **Folder Options**.
- Pull down the **View** menu, select **Options**.

3. Click on the **File Types** tab.

4. Within the box named **Registered file types** you will see a long list. Take a minute and use the scroll bar to look through the list just to see what's there. Don't change anything.

5. To close the window, click on the **Cancel** button.

hint

Within a file name, the . (period) character is pronounced "dot".

Thus, the name `harley.html` is pronounced "harley dot h-t-m-l". The name `harley.jpg` is pronounced "harley dot jay-peg".

Figure 9-1: The most common file extensions used on the Web

Extension	Pronunciation	Meaning
html	"h-t-m-l"	Web page
htm	"h-t-m"	Web page
asp	"a-s-p"	Web page generated in a special way
gif	"giff" or "jiff"	Picture stored in GIF format
jpg	"jay-peg"	Picture stored in JPEG format
txt	"t-x-t" or "text"	Plain text
zip	"zip"	Compressed collection of files
exe	"e-x-e" or "exy"	Executable program
wav	"wave"	Sound/music file
mp3	"m-p-3" or "mpeg"	Music file
mid	"midi"	Music file
mov	"move"	Video (movie) file

This list is important because whenever you need to do something with a particular file, Windows must be able to know which program handles the type of data contained in that file.

For example, say you are using Windows Explorer and you double-click on a file named `harley.html`. This tells Windows you want to process the file. In technical terms, we say that you are asking Windows to "open" the file.

To do so, Windows looks at the extension, `html`, and then checks the master list of file types to see which program processes `html` files. In this case, it would be your browser, so Windows launches the browser program (if it is not already running) and sends it the file `harley.html`. In other words, by looking at a file's extension, Windows can tell which program should be used to open the file.

Can you see how powerful this system is? Windows can figure out what to do with any type of data simply by looking up the file extension in the master table and launching the appropriate program.

As you use the Web, your browser has similar responsibilities. Every time a file arrives from a Web server, your browser must figure out how to process that file. First, your browser looks at the extension to see what type of data is in the file. Certain types of data can be handled internally by the browser itself, for example, `html`, `gif` and `jpg` files. Other types of data (and there are many other types) require the use of a separate program.

Thus, your browser needs its own master list of file types, in order to be able to look up an extension to find out which program should be used to process the data in a particular file.

For example, files with an extension of `mov` contain Quicktime movies (short movies that use the "Quicktime" format developed by Apple Corporation). On its own, a browser cannot display `mov` files, so whenever such a file is encountered, the browser must call upon another program to process the data.

Opening a File

Within Windows, the expression "opening a file" has a specific technical meaning that is not at all intuitive, so I want to make sure you understand it.

To OPEN a file means to process the file in an appropriate manner. Most of the time, Windows opens a file by sending it to a program. For example, if you tell Windows to open a file named `harley.html`, Windows will send the file to your browser. The browser will then do whatever is appropriate for `html` files. If you were to open a file named, say, `notes.doc`, Windows would recognize it as a document and send it to your word processor program. As I explained in the previous section, Windows knows what program to use by looking at the extension of the file.

In one important case, however, Windows opens a file differently. When a file has a name with the extension `exe`, it indicates that a file contains a program (`exe` stands for "executable program"). Windows opens such a file by starting the program within the file. We say that Windows RUNS or EXECUTES the program.

So how do you tell Windows to open a file? There are several ways. First, within Windows Explorer, you can open any file by double-clicking on its name. You can also right-click on the file name (which will pop up a menu) and select **Open** from the list of choices.

For example, if you double-click on the name of a file that contains a program, Windows will run that program. If you double-click on the name of an `html` file, Windows will send that file to your browser. If you double-click on the name of a `doc` file, Windows will send that file to your work processor.

You can also open a file by double-clicking on an icon. For example, the icons on your desktop all represent files. When you double-click on an icon, Windows opens the file "behind" the icon.

You can also start various programs by clicking on the **Start** button and making a selection. Most of the choices you see are actually icons that represent files. Thus, when you select an item from the **Start** menu, you are really telling Windows to open the file associated with that icon.

Thus, there are several ways to open a file. You can double-click on the name of the file within Windows Explorer; you can right-click on the name of a file and select **Open**; you can double-click on an icon on your desktop; and you can select an icon from the **Start** menu.

What's in a Name?

open

The word "open" actually has two meanings. In a formal sense, "open" refers to the action of Windows processing a file. Thus, we can say that Windows opens a file either by running it or by sending it to another program to be processed.

Informally, we also use the word "open" to refer to what we do when we tell Windows to open a file. For example, I might tell you, "You can open a file by double-clicking on its icon." Of course, you don't really open the file yourself, Windows opens it.

The distinction between these two meanings of the word "open" is subtle, but real, and it serves to illustrate one of the reasons why computer systems seem confusing to beginners.

Many of the technical words we use (such as "open", "file" and "folder") look like everyday words, but are not. Within the world of computers, such words have exact, technical meanings that are anything but intuitive. Moreover, we often talk in such a way as to blur the distinction between ourselves and the computer.

ActiveX Controls

All browsers need auxiliary programs to process the various types of data the browser cannot handle by itself. With Internet Explorer, this job is done by what is called a CONTROL.

In the world of Microsoft, a control is a type of tool used by programmers. Each control is designed to perform a specific function. When a programmer builds a program, he or she can use controls as building blocks.

For example, say a programmer is creating a program that must display a dialog box to ask the user a question. Instead of programming this himself, the programmer simply uses a standard dialog-box control. Conceptually, he just plugs the control into the program wherever he needs to display a dialog box.

In Chapter 12, I will discuss ActiveX, a programming system based on Microsoft's family of programming tools. ActiveX is an elaborate system that can be used to create all types of programs. In particular, the controls are used to enhance the capabilities of Internet Explorer within the ActiveX system. For this reason, they are sometimes referred to as "ActiveX controls".

Whenever Internet Explorer encounters a Web page that requires a control you don't already have, you will see a message like the one in Figure 9-2. All you need to do is click on the **Yes** button, and the control will be downloaded and installed on your computer automatically.

If you would like to see all your Web-related ActiveX controls, look in the following directory:

`C:\Windows\Downloaded Program Files`

You can do this directly, by using Windows Explorer to look at the directory. Alternatively, you can use Internet Explorer as follows:

Internet Explorer

1. Pull down the **Tools** menu and select **Internet Options**.
2. Within the **Temporary Internet files** section, click on the **Settings** button.
3. Click on **View Objects**. You will now see a window showing you the various controls.

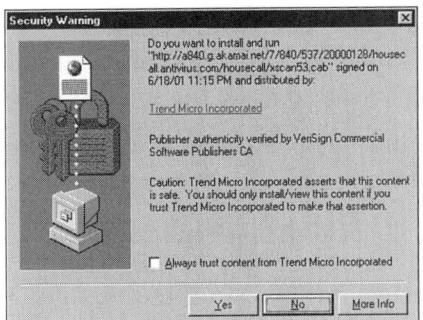

FIGURE 9-2

Dialog box asking to download an ActiveX control

Programs and Downloading

DOWNLOADING means copying a file from a remote computer to your computer. Once you know how to find and download software from the Internet, you will have access to virtually all the programs you will ever need.

The programs we have discussed so far — the ActiveX controls — are used to augment the capabilities of your browser. These programs are relatively simple in that they more or less install themselves. Most programs, however, are more elaborate, and before you can use them, you will have to carry out a sequence of specific actions. We will discuss the details in a moment, but before we do, I want to talk about how programs are distributed on the Net.

Almost all programs consist of multiple files, and to use a program, you need all of its files. For example, a program might require 15 different files in order to perform its job.

It would be a lot of bother to have to download 15 files, one at a time. You would have to initiate 15 separate download operations, and make sure that all 15 files ended up in the right place.

To solve this problem, all the files needed for a particular program are gathered together into a single large file called an ARCHIVE. It is the archive that is stored on the Internet and made available for downloading. Thus, no matter how many files a program may require, you need only download a single file, the archive.

Within an archive, files are compressed so as to take up less room. Thus, the size of an archive is less than the size of all the files together, which means it is faster to download the archive than it would be to download all the separate files. Once you have downloaded an archive, you need to uncompress and restore the original files. We call this UNPACKING the archive. (We will talk about the details later in the chapter.)

Within the collection of unpacked files there is an INSTALLATION PROGRAM. The job of the installation program is to do everything necessary to make the software ready to run on your computer.

Thus, to download and install a program from the Internet, you follow these steps:

1. Find the program you want.
2. Download the archive for that program.
3. Unpack the archive.
4. Install the program.
5. Delete the archive and the unpacked files

Once you get used to it, this 5-step procedure is simple. Since this is such an important procedure, modern browsers have built-in capabilities that make it easy to download and unpack an archive, and then run the installation program with a minimum of fuss.

There are a number of large Web sites that act as software repositories, and these are the best places to get free software. Most of the programs will be either FREEWARE (completely free) or SHAREWARE (try the program for free and pay money only if you decide to keep using it). I use these Web sites a lot, either when I am looking for a particular program, or when I have a few spare moments and I would like to try something new just for fun.

Many companies that offer freeware or shareware versions of their programs also offer commercial versions that cost money. These versions will have more features, but in my experience, you usually don't need them, so always try the free version first.

What about safety? When you get software from one of these sites, is there a danger of downloading a program with a virus? The answer is no, so don't worry about it. (See Chapter 12 for the details.)

Internet Resources   **Windows Software Sites**

```
http://www.nonags.com/
http://www.tucows.com/
http://www.winsite.com/
http://cws.internet.com/
http://download.cnet.com/
http://www.thefreesite.com/Free_Software/
http://www.zdnet.com/downloads/win95.html
```

hint

Be aware: some companies that offer shareware and commercial versions of their programs purposely design their Web sites to trick you. You go to the site looking for the free version, and it looks as if you have no choice but to pay for the commercial version. (I have a friend, a beginner, who was tricked in just this manner.)

My advice is never to pay money for a program you have not tried. On the Internet, just about every type of program you might want is available as freeware or shareware.

Downloading a Program

Once you find a program to download, you will reach a point where you click on a link and the downloading will start. The first step in the process varies slightly depending on your browser. Some browsers (such as Internet Explorer) show a dialog box similar to the one in Figure 9-3. You are offered a choice to either run the program or save it to disk. For now, make sure **Save this program** is selected, and then click on the **OK** button. (We will discuss the other option later.)

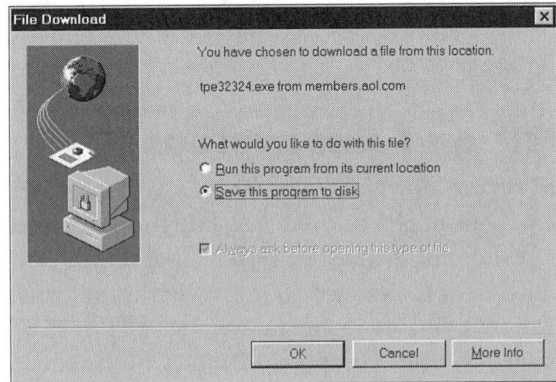

FIGURE 9-3
Beginning a download with Internet Explorer

Ultimately, you will end up with a dialog box similar to the one in Figure 9-4. You are being asked to specify where to save the downloaded file. Just specify the directory (folder) where you want to save the file, click on the **Save** button, and your browser will start the downloading process. Once it finishes, you are ready to install the program.

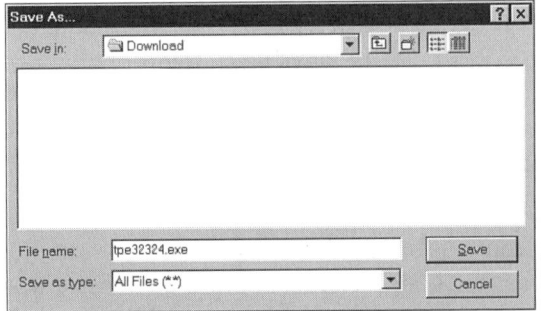

FIGURE 9-4
Specifying where to save a downloaded file

Before we continue, let's talk for a moment about where you should save the file. I have a friend who has often had a problem installing new software. She would download the archive and then not be able to find it. (This is easier to do than you might think.) You can avoid this problem by putting all your downloaded files where they are easy to find.

hint

In Windows, the names you choose for directories and files are not case sensitive: you can mix upper- and lowercase letters. My suggestion is to use the following conventions.

For directory (folder) names, use a single uppercase letter followed by lowercase letters, for example, `Download`.

For file names, use all lowercase letters, for example, `tpe32324.exe`.

My suggestion is to use Windows Explorer to create a directory called `Download`, and to use this directory for all your downloaded files. (If you are not sure what a directory is, take a moment to review the discussion in Chapter 4.) In Figure 9-4, you can see I am about to save a file called `tpe32324.exe` into my `Download` directory.

I want you to think of this directory as providing temporary storage only. Once you have finished installing a program, you can delete all the files in the download directory. There is no point keeping an old archive. If, for some reason, you ever want to reinstall the program, you can download the archive again. In fact, you will sometimes find a newer version of the program.

FTP and Anonymous FTP

When you download a file from a Web page, there are two different systems that might be used: HTTP (the same as is used to download Web pages) or anonymous FTP (see Chapter 2). Either way, it doesn't matter much to you, because your browser knows what to do. In fact, the only clue that you are using anonymous FTP might be the letters `ftp` in the name of the computer from which you are downloading (say, `ftp.microsoft.com`).

FTP (File Transfer Protocol) is used throughout the Internet to copy files from one computer to another, both uploading and downloading. When you use FTP, the remote server requires you to identify yourself by specifying a user name and password. Anonymous FTP is a variation of this system that provides public access, for example, to download programs.

With ANONYMOUS FTP, the user name is always `anonymous`, and the password can be anything. Traditionally, people would use their mail address as a password, to allow whoever was maintaining the FTP server to know who is using the service. For privacy, however, your browser does not give out your mail address in this way.

As I have described, when you download files from a Web site, the procedure is mostly automatic. I only mention anonymous FTP here, because it's interesting to know a bit about what is happening behind the scenes . For more details about FTP, see the discussion in Chapter 2.

Installing a Program

Once you have downloaded an archive, you are ready to install the program. However, before you do, you should take a minute and look at the Web site where you got the archive to see if there are any installation instructions. If so, you should read the instructions *before* you install the program.

A moment spent reading the instructions can sometimes save you a lot of bother. For example, I have a friend who went through the entire process of downloading and installing a particular program. It was only after the program was installed that she read the instructions and found that the program would not work on her system.

Most programs come with a README FILE, usually named `readme.txt`. This file contains information that you should read before you use the program. You will often find that most of the information in the readme file is highly technical and not relevant to you. Still, you should spend a moment skimming this file. If, during the installation process, you are asked if you want to look at the readme file, always say yes. With some programs, the readme file is available on the Web site where you got the program. If so, read the file before you start the download. With other programs, the readme file will not be available until after the program is installed.

Generally speaking, there are two types of archives. The first type is, in itself, an executable program. You can tell because the file name has an extension of `exe`, as with the file named `tpe32324.exe` in our example above. With such archives, it is easy to start the installation process. Just use Windows Explorer to navigate to your download directory, and double-click on the archive file. Windows will start the program for you.

In most cases, once the program starts, everything is automatic. It will unpack itself and run the installation program. All you have to do is follow the instructions. When it is finished, you can clean up by deleting the archive.

The second type of archive is a ZIP FILE, so called because the file name ends in `zip`, for example, `harley.zip`. Zip files are not executable: you must unpack them yourself. This process is called UNZIPPING the file.

When you unzip an archive (that is, a zip file), you end up with a collection of files. Within these files will be an installation program (usually called `setup.exe` or `install.exe`). Run this program to carry

hint

Many programs will put an icon on your desktop as part of the installation process. This is only for your convenience. If you don't want the icon, you can delete it so as to reduce the clutter.

There are three ways to delete an icon on your desktop:

- Click on it and press the **Delete** key
- Right-click on it and select **Delete**.
- Drag the icon to the **Recycle Bin** icon.

out the installation procedure. After the installation program is finished, you can delete it, along with the rest of the unpacked files and the archive.

To unzip an archive, you need a ZIP FILE PROGRAM. (Sometimes such programs are called COMPRESSION UTILITIES, because the zip format is used to compress files.) There are many zip file programs available, some freeware, some shareware, and some commercial. I suggest you take some time now to select and install a zip file program. Once you start downloading software from the Net, I guarantee you will run into zip files, and it is best to have your zip file program ready.

When you install a zip file program, it registers itself with the Windows master list of file types as being the program to handle all files with the `zip` extension. From then on, whenever you tell Windows to open a zip file, it will automatically start your zip file program.

Thus, to install a program that comes in the form of a zip file, follow these steps:

hint

Some zip file programs come with special features to automate the installation process. For example, a zip program can look inside the zip file archive for files named `setup.exe` or `install.exe`. If the zip program finds such a file, it will display an **Install** button. Just click on this button, and the installation will start automatically.

1. Download the zip file.
2. Use Windows Explorer to navigate to your download directory.
3. Double-click on the zip file to start your zip file program.
4. Use the zip file program to unzip the file into the download directory. (Your program may refer to this process by another name, such as "extract".)
5. Once the file is unzipped, look for and read the readme file.
6. Run the installation program. (If you don't see an installation program, look for instructions in the readme file.)
7. After the installation is complete, delete the files in the download directory, including the zip file.

Internet Resources **Zip File Programs**

```
http://www.edisys.com/
http://www.zipitfast.com/
http://www.powerarchiver.com/
http://www.pkware.com/shareware/
http://www.tucows.com/comp95.html
http://www.handybits.com/zipngo.htm
```
You will be able to find a freeware or shareware zip program. There is no need to pay for a commercial version.

Installing a Program Automatically

I mentioned earlier that some browsers offer you a choice when you download a file. Take a look at Figure 9-3. Notice that you can either run the program or save it to disk. If you select "run", your browser will download the program to a temporary location on your hard disk, start the program, and wait for it to finish. Once the program is finished, it will be deleted automatically.

Using this option can make the installation process a lot simpler. If the archive is in the form of an executable program (an **exe** file), you will not have to worry about saving it, running it, and deleting it. Everything will be automatic.

If the program is in the form of a zip file, the "run" option will cause Windows to start your zip file program, which you can then use in the regular manner.

Some people prefer to save a program or zip file to their download directory, and then run the program themselves. This gives them more control over the installation process. Try it both ways and see which option you prefer. Personally, I like to save the zip file.

hint

With large programs that take a long time to download, it is better to save the file before you run it. That way, if something goes wrong, and you need to rerun the program, you won't have to wait for it to download all over again.

Uninstalling a Program

If you have a program you don't want to use any longer, you can get rid of it by UNINSTALLING it. To do so, you must follow a specific procedure — do not simply delete the directory in which the program resides. Most installation programs make changes to your system that are hidden from you. These changes must be reversed when you uninstall the program.

The best way to uninstall a program is by using the Windows Add/Remove facility. The steps are as follows:

1. Click on the **Start** button. Select **Settings** and then **Control Panel**.

2. Double-click on **Add/Remove Programs**. This will start the Windows install/uninstall facility.

3. Scroll down the list of installed programs and find the name of the program you want to uninstall. Click on the name and then click on the **Add/Remove** button. This will start the uninstall process.

hint

Before you uninstall a
program, make sure it is
not running.

4. When the uninstall is complete, click on the **OK** button to close
   the window.

If the program you want to uninstall is not in the Add/Remove list, look
at the directory in which the program is installed. If there is a readme
file, look in it for uninstall directions. (To read the file, double-click on
it.) If there are no uninstall directions, look for a special uninstall program (such as `uninstall.exe`). If you find one, run it.

Sometimes an uninstall program will not remove all the program files. If
so, you will have to finish the job yourself.

When the uninstall program is finished, use Windows Explorer and
check if the directory that held the program still exists. If so, it is safe to
delete the directory and its contents.

Similarly, if the uninstall program did not remove the program's entries
from the **Programs** folder on your **Start** menu, you can do so yourself.
The **Programs** folder resides at:

`C:\Windows\Start Menu\Programs`

10

Music on the Net

*Imagine finding a radio
station that plays your
favorite type of music
24 hours a day. You'll
find it, and a lot more,
on the Internet.*

Imagine finding a radio station that plays your favorite type of music 24 hours a day. You'll find it, and a lot more, on the Internet.

The Internet is the largest source of music in the world, and much of it is free. Rock, jazz, oldies, classical, hip-hop, blues, country music — just about anything you might want to listen to is available, whenever you want it. Aside from recorded music, you can also listen to many types of broadcasting, including radio stations from around the world, live concerts, and small Internet-only stations that cater to esoteric audiences. You'll also find interesting curiosities such as live police broadcasts and air traffic controller communications.

In this chapter, I'll show you how to find the music you want, and I'll explain what you need to do to listen to it once you find it. I'll also explain what is involved in downloading music from the Net and making your own CDs.

Music is important to all of us in ways that we can't really understand, but that we recognize. There is something deep within all of us that responds to rhythm, melody, harmony and counterpoint, as well as the poetry of a well-written lyric.

As long as there have been people, people have been making some kind of music — and because of the time period in which we are living, we have access to tools that allow us to use music in ways that are brand new to human culture.

After you read this chapter and spend a few hours experimenting, you will come to an amazing realization: that once you learn how to use your hardware, your software and your Internet connection, your computer will become nothing less than an incredibly powerful and versatile music machine.

What You Need to Listen to Music on Your Computer

To listen to music you need a computer with speakers and a sound card. You can use the speakers that came with your computer, or if you want better sound, you can substitute your own speakers. The SOUND CARD is a special circuit board inside the computer that provides sound-related capabilities. Virtually all new computers come with both of these features.

The CD that came with your computer can read not only computer CDs (CD-ROMs), but music CDs as well, so you can use your computer as a stereo and listen to music from CDs while you work. If you want to create your own CDs, you will need a special type of CD drive, called a CD-RW. We'll talk about this later in the chapter.

What if you have an older computer? Is it worth upgrading it by adding a sound card, speakers and a CD-RW drive? My advice is don't bother —you will just be wasting your money. Putting new parts in an old computer is generally not a good idea. No matter what you do, the system will never work as well as a new computer. Moreover, trying to get all the components working properly can use up a lot of your time and start you on a voyage of major frustration. Save your money and put it toward a new computer with everything already built in.

Music File Types

On the Internet, there are three file types that are commonly used to store music and other types of audio data: wav, mp3 and mid. The most common file type is mp3.

WAV files: These are the basic sound files used by Windows. As you use Windows, you hear sounds from time to time (for example, the sound Windows makes when it starts). All of these sounds are stored in wav files, each sound in its own file. On the Internet, wav files are used to hold sounds for Web pages. If you ever click on a link and hear a short sound, that sound was probably stored as a wav file. Later in the chapter, when we talk about making your own CDs, you will see that wav files have another use. They are used to hold music that is going to be written to a CD.

MP3 files: The mp3 file format was developed to store audio data in a compressed format. For example, I have the Beach Boys song "Surfing USA" stored as a wav file on my computer. This song is only 2 minutes, 29 seconds long, and yet the wav file is 13.8 MB (megabytes). The mp3 version of the same song takes up only 2.0 MB. Here is another example. The Billy Joel song "Piano Man" is 5 minutes, 35 seconds long. As an mp3 file, it is 5.3 MB; as a wav file, it is massive: 57.9 MB. So, on the Internet, music is most commonly stored as mp3 files, and as a rule of thumb, 1 minute of music in mp3 format requires 1 MB of data.

MID files: The mid file format is used to store music in MIDI format. MIDI was originally developed in 1982 to allow musicians to connect one synthesizer to another. Today, a modern version of the MIDI format is used to store and manipulate music on computers, synthesizers, keyboards, and other electronic music devices. On the Internet, mid files are commonly used by people who compose music, and who use computer programs to work with the music. You will find a lot of original music on the Net in mid format.

What's in a Name?

wav

mp3

mid

The wav format for storing sound was developed by Microsoft. The name stands for "waveform data". (As you may know, sound travels in the form of waves.)

The term mp3 stands for "MPEG 1 audio layer 3". MPEG 1 (pro-nounced "em-peg-1") is one member of a family of formats used to store video and audio data. Within the MPEG 1 system, there are three ways to compress audio data. They are referred to as layer 1, layer 2 and layer 3. Files using the mp3 format store audio data using the MPEG 1 layer 3 method. Thus the name mp3.

The MPEG standards were developed by an organization called the Moving Picture Experts Group. For this reason, mp3 files are often referred to as MPEG files.

The term mid is an abbreviation for MIDI, "Musical Instrument Digital Interface".

Streaming

As I explained in the last section, audio files are large. An mp3 file uses about 1 MB of data to store a minute of music, and a wav file requires much more data than that. Thus, downloading an entire song from the Internet can take a long time, especially if you have a slow connection.

However, there is a system called STREAMING that allows you to listen to music without having to wait a long time for an entire file to be downloaded. With streaming, your computer starts playing the music as soon as the first part of the data arrives. While the music is playing, your computer downloads the rest of the data in the background. As long as the downloading process stays ahead of what is being played, what you hear is a continuous stream of music.

Streaming is used on the Internet with a variety of different types of audio, such as music, live radio, concerts, talk, and so on. Without streaming, for example, you would not be able to listen to radio broadcasts on the Net. Streaming works so well with audio data that, if your computer has a fast Internet connection and good speakers, you may not be able to tell the difference between music from the Internet and music from a regular stereo.

Streaming is also used to broadcast video over the Internet. However, the picture usually looks somewhat rough and uneven —not nearly as good as television. This is because high-quality video requires much more data than can be broadcast over the Internet in real time. For this reason, video on the Internet, especially through a slow connection, is often of poor quality.

Streaming is different from regular downloading in two important ways. First, as the streaming process starts, you won't hear anything for the first few moments. This is because your streaming program (which we will discuss in the next section) must first build up a reservoir of data. Only then will the program start to play the audio or video.

While this is happening, you will see a message saying that the program is BUFFERING data. (Within a computer program, a BUFFER is a temporary storage area used for input or output.) Thus, you will not hear anything until your streaming program has downloaded enough data to fill its buffer. If it happens that, while you are listening, your Internet connection is interrupted, the sound will stop as soon the buffer is empty. You will then have to wait for your streaming program to refill the buffer. (This is called REBUFFERING.) For this reason, if your connection to the broadcast source is not a good one, the sound may stop and start intermittently.

The second way in which streaming is different from regular downloading is that the audio data is not saved. Once you have listened to something, the data is thrown away. This only makes sense. After all, even a few minutes of music would require megabytes of storage (and video would require even more), so there is no point in saving streaming data to a permanent file.

On the Internet, there are a number of systems used to provide streaming audio. Two of the most widely used are REALAUDIO and STREAMING MP3.

The RealAudio system was originally developed by the RealNetworks company. RealAudio data is identified by various file extensions, the most common of which are `ra`, `rm` and `ram`.

Streaming mp3 is based on the mp3 file format, and is identified by the file extensions `pls` and `m3u`.

You probably won't have a need to manipulate such data directly, but when you encounter it, I want you to be able to recognize it. For example, let's say you are using your browser, and you notice a link that points to `filename.ra`. The `ra` tells you that this link represents a stream of RealAudio data. Similarly, if a link points to a file named `filename.pls` or `filename.m3u`, the link represents streaming mp3 data. When you click on such a link, your browser will automatically start your streaming program, which will then begin the initial download.

Music Software

In order to listen to music over the Internet, you need a program to decode audio files and turn the data into sound. Such programs are known by a variety of names: AUDIO PLAYERS, MULTIMEDIA PLAYERS and MP3 PLAYERS.

Most audio players are capable of playing a variety of audio formats, such as music CDs, mp3 files, wav files, mid files, streaming RealAudio, and streaming mp3. Some are also able to play streaming video. The most widely used audio player is the Windows Media Player, because Microsoft gives it away for free. In fact, Windows comes with the Windows Media Player already installed.

There are a variety of audio players available on the Net, and if you listen to a lot of music, I encourage you to try different programs and find the one you like best. I have included some Internet resources below to help you locate a variety of programs.

I have also included some resources to help you search for all types of music software. If you like music, and you are at all technically inclined, the Internet has enough software to keep you occupied from now to St. Swithin's Day.

Some audio players have an interesting capability. They allow you to change the appearance of the program by installing what is known as a SKIN. When you use a skin, the program looks different, although the functionality is not changed. (It's just for fun.) You will sometimes see skins referred to by other names, such as FACEPLATES or TEXTURES.

The more popular audio players have many different skins you can download for free (donated by artistic people who want to share their efforts).

Internet Resources   **Audio Players**

```
http://www.winamp.com/
http://www.freeamp.org/
http://sonique.lycos.com/
http://www.musicmatch.com/
http://www.hitsquad.com/smm/
http://www.cowon.com/engdefault.htm
http://www.microsoft.com/windows/windowsmedia/
http://www.sonicspot.com/multimediaplayers.html
```
You will be able to find a freeware or shareware audio player. There is no need to pay for a commercial version.

Internet Resources   **Music Software**

```
http://www.sonicspot.com/
http://www.audiomelody.com/
http://www.hitsquad.com/smm/
```
In addition to these Web sites, you can find lots of music, audio and multimedia software by looking in the software archives mentioned in Chapter 9.

Radio and Broadcasting on the Net

There is a huge amount of broadcasting on the Internet. In order to listen, you need one of the streaming multimedia players I discussed in the previous section. Let me take you on a quick tour of what is available on the Net. At the end of this section, I will show you some Internet broadcasting resources.

- **Radio**: You can listen to many different radio stations from all over the world. Whatever format you prefer —music, talk, sports, news, public radio, and so on —it is all available, and you can listen whenever you want.

Learn how to...

Control the Appearance of Your Browser

You can customize your browser by hiding or showing some of the toolbars and buttons. In particular, you can tell Internet Explorer to display the Radio toolbar automatically each time you start the browser.

See Chapter 17, *How to Do Stuff*, page 370 (Internet Explorer).

If you use Internet Explorer version 6, there is a more elaborate multimedia facility. To access it, just click on the **Media** button.

If you use Internet Explorer version 5, there is a less elaborate built-in tool, the Radio toolbar. If the Radio toolbar is not visible, you can display it as follows:

1. Pull down the **View** menu.
2. Point to **Toolbars**, and click on **Radio**.

Using the Radio toolbar is simple, so I won't give you detailed instructions. Just experiment and you'll figure it out. When you find stations you like, you can add them to your Favorites list (see Chapter 7).

- **Internet-only stations**: In addition to regular radio stations, there are also a great many stations that broadcast only over the Internet. These stations tend to be commercial-free and cater to a distinct audience. You can use the Net to listen to your favorite type of music all day long, with no interruptions. Many of these stations are run, literally, by one or two people. I once had a great time listening to a guy do live prank phone calls.

- **Television**: There are a variety of television stations and networks that broadcast over the Internet. As I mentioned earlier, the quality is not as good as you would see on your television set, especially if you don't have a fast Internet connection. Still, video on the Net is available for free, and it can be interesting. (One time I watched television from Croatia.)

- **Live events**: There are a great many live broadcast events, many of which are arranged specifically for the Internet. You can listen to (and watch) live concerts, speeches, sporting events, and much more.

- **Strange things**: If you get bored, there are some unusual broadcasts you may want to try. Look around, and you'll find all manner of strange things to listen to. For example, you can listen to air traffic controllers, police and railway workers communicating over the radio. (Actually, this sort of stuff gets boring fast, but it is interesting to listen to once.)

The following Internet resources are good places to start looking for things to listen to and watch. When you get a few spare moments, these are good places to browse.

Internet Resources   **Internet Broadcasting Guides**

```
http://radio.yack.com/
http://yp.icecast.org/
http://radio.yahoo.com/
http://www.live-at.com/
http://www.broadcast.com/
http://www.shoutcast.com/
http://windowsmedia.microsoft.com/
```

Internet Resources   **Official Radio Transmissions**

```
http://www.thebravest.com/
http://www.policescanner.com/
http://www.broadcast.com/simuflite/
http://www.netnowonline.com/scanner/
http://mediaframe.yahoo.com/radio/embedded/scanner_signals
```

Learning to Work with Mp3 Files and CDs

In the next few sections, I will discuss how to get mp3 files, how to manipulate them, and how to create your own CDs.

Before I start, I want you to appreciate that all of these operations require special software, and it is going to take time for you to find, download and install the programs you need. Moreover, it is going to take more time for you to become familiar with these programs, and to learn how to use them well. Be prepared to spend at least a few hours learning how all of this works.

Once you figure out the system and understand how to use your programs, you will be able to work with mp3 files smoothly and easily. However, between here and there, it's going to take a while, so don't be discouraged, and don't be in a hurry.

hint

Some broadcasting sites force you to listen to a short commercial before the actual audio or video starts. If you would like to skip the commercial, try this trick.

The moment the commercial starts, press the **PageDown** key or click on the **Next** button. In some cases, doing this jumps to the next segment, effectively bypassing the commercial.

hint

Working with mp3 files
is more fun when you do
it with a friend. This is
especially true at first,
when you are trying to
figure out how every-
thing works.

If you can find someone who is knowledgeable about mp3 files and CDs, ask that person to walk you through the basic operations. Doing so will save you a lot of time.

Creating Mp3 Files from CDs

The two most common ways to get mp3 files are to:

- Create them from your own CDs

- Download them from the Internet

Copying songs raises some tricky copyright questions, but for now let's ignore them. I will discuss these issues later in the chapter.

To create mp3 files from a CD, you need a CD drive and a program called a RIPPER. A ripper reads data from a music CD and converts it to mp3 format. You will often see the word RIP used as a verb. ("Where did you get all those cool mp3 files?" "Oh, I ripped them from a bunch of CDs I had lying around the house.")

To use a ripper, you tell it which songs you want to copy from the CD. The ripper will then read the audio data from the CD, convert it to mp3 format, and save the songs you want as files on your hard disk.

Each song is stored in its own mp3 file, which requires about 1 MB of disk space per minute of music. Once you have such files, you can listen to them, share them with other people, and (if you have the right type of CD drive) create your own customized CDs.

Some rippers are simple, straightforward and easy to use. They copy songs from a CD to mp3 files and store the files in the directory of your choice. Other rippers are complex, sophisticated tools that take a while to master, but can perform a large variety of tasks. You will have to decide which type of ripper you like best.

It is possible that you received a ripper for free with your CD-RW drive. If not, or if you want to try a different one, check out the Internet Resources below.

Internet Resources **CD Rippers**

http://www.cdex.n3.net/

http://www.musicmatch.com/

http://www.sonicspot.com/cdextractors.html

http://www.mpegx.com/audio.asp?dcat=audiocdripper

Downloading Mp3 Files from the Internet

The Internet has a huge number of mp3 files available for downloading. Broadly speaking, there are two types of mp3 files on the Net: official and unofficial.

The official sources of mp3 files include the Web sites of record companies and music groups. For example, a record company may release one or two songs from a new album in mp3 format, in order to promote that album. Similarly, many music groups use the Internet to release their own music, without the help of a record company. In fact, the rise of mp3 technology is making significant changes in the recording industry, because musicians can now publicize and distribute their songs without depending on record companies.

For the most part, the songs on these Web sites can be downloaded using your browser in the same way that you would download anything. You click on a link, the download process starts, and you specify where you want to save the file on your hard disk. Some songs are available in a streaming format, which means you can listen to them directly, without having to save them to your disk.

Most of the music you probably want, however, will not come from official Web sites. It will come from other people who are willing to share their mp3 files. There are a huge number of such files available on the Net. To get them, you need to use a file-sharing program. (See the Internet Resources below.)

The first extremely popular Internet file sharing program was Napster. Napster used a central server to connect people who had files to share. In May 1999, people around the world began to use Napster to share mp3 files. Over the next two years, millions of mp3 files were downloaded using Napster. Unfortunately, at the beginning of March 2001, Napster was shut down by the major music companies for copyright infringement. This was all too easy to do: all the music companies had to do was get a court order to shut down the Napster server. Once this was done, the entire Napster file sharing system collapsed.

Still, music sharing is alive and well on the Net. There are a number of newer, more sophisticated programs that allow people to share files. These programs work without a central server. Instead they use a decentralized PEER-TO-PEER technology, in which the individual computers join into a large, connected system. Such programs can be used to share any type of file, not only music, but video, text, games, programs, and so on. Moreover, because they do not use a central server, such systems cannot be shut down—ever.

To start sharing music, all you need to do is install one of these programs on your computer and join the crowd. There are a variety of such systems available, so I suggest you take a bit of time to experiment and choose the one you like best. Once you are all set up, and you are familiar with the system, you will find that sharing files is easy.

Internet Resources **Music File Sharing**

```
http://www.kazaa.com/
http://www.winmx.com/
http://www.aimster.com/
http://www.limewire.com/
http://www.zeropaid.com/
http://gnutella.wego.com/
http://www.bearshare.com/
http://www.musiccity.com/
http://www.jawed.com/mp3voyeur/
http://www.filetopia.org/home.htm
```

Listening to Mp3 Files

Once you have a collection of mp3 files, there are several ways you can listen to them. First, you can listen to the files on your computer by using an audio player.

Second, if you have a CD-RW drive, you can use your mp3 files to create your own custom CDs. Since these are ordinary music CDs, you can listen to them with a regular CD player, or you can play them on your computer.

Finally, you can use a small, portable device called a DIGITAL MUSIC PLAYER that is designed to store and play mp3 files. To use such a device, you connect it to your computer and upload mp3 files. You can then disconnect the music player, and take it wherever you go. To change the music, all you need to do is upload new files.

hint

To help you organize your files, most mp3 players allow you to create PLAYLISTS.

A playlist holds the names of a group of mp3 files. Once you create a playlist, you can use it to load a whole group of mp3 files at once.

The Issue of Copyright

Any time you produce a creative work, such as music, art or writing, you automatically own the copyright to that work. Owning the copyright means that you can do what you want with the work, such as publish it or sell the rights to someone else. In addition, you have control over what others can do with the work. Legally, copyrighted material cannot be uploaded or downloaded without the permission of the copyright holder.

There is a lot of music available on the Internet that is perfectly legal to download and share with others. Some of this music is in the public domain; some of it is specifically designated by the copyright holder as being freely accessible.

However, many of the mp3 files that are traded on the Net are copies that were made from CDs. Strictly speaking, it is illegal to make such copies, and it is illegal to share them with other people. Still, countless people do so, and as you might expect, the recording industry is very upset about this.

Within the world of mp3 files, many, many files are passed around illegally. As you enter this world, you are going to notice a huge amount of hypocrisy, so let's take a moment to cut through it all with the butter knife of truth.

Sharing mp3 files of copyrighted songs is illegal. However, lots of things in life are illegal, and you have to decide for yourself what you are willing to do. Realistically, unless you get caught trying to use someone else's music to make a significant amount of money, nothing is going to happen to you.

As a general rule, whenever people are faced with a system in which common activities are illegal, the resulting conflict leads to a great deal of denial and deception, so let's be realistic. If you feel comfortable with copying and sharing mp3 files, go ahead. Just don't do anything dumb, like setting yourself up in the bootleg CD business. And, for goodness sake, if you work for a politically correct organization like the government or a major corporation, don't download megabytes of music files at work. Save your questionable activities for the privacy of your own home.

CD-RW Drives

To create your own CDs, you need a CD-RW DRIVE, sometimes called a REWRITABLE CD DRIVE, a special type of drive that can read and write to CDs. This type of drive can write on two types of discs: CD-RWs and CD-Rs.

CD-RW DISCS behave like large floppy disks, in that they are reusable: you can read, write and delete data as often as you want. These discs have a storage capacity of 650 MB. However, before you can use a CD-RW disc for the first time, you must FORMAT it. (Formatting is the process that prepares a new disk to be used for the first time.) This process uses up some of the space, and after formatting, the disc can hold only 530 MB of data. Still, this is nothing to sneeze at. You can put a *lot* of data in 530 MB. This makes CD-RWs perfect for backing up important data.

CD-R DISCS are similar to CD-RWs, except you can only write data once to each part of the disc. If you delete files on a CD-R disc, you cannot reclaim the space and use it again. CD-R discs are cheaper than CD-RWs, which makes them perfect for applications in which you don't need to change the data once it is written. In particular, CD-Rs are the ones to use when you make your own music CDs. In fact, CD-R discs are so inexpensive that, if you make a mistake creating a CD, you can throw it away and start again.

Aside from being able to use CD-RWs and CD-Rs, CD-RW drives can also read regular music CDs and CD-ROMs (computer software CDs). Thus, you can use a CD-RW drive in several ways:

- to listen to music CDs
- to create music CDs
- to use CD-RWs to store files
- to read CD-ROMs
- to copy CD-ROMs

hint

If you plan on upgrading your computer by buying a CD-RW drive, and you don't like working with the internals of a computer, have someone install the drive for you.

Even if this means you must pay a service charge, do so. It is money well spent.

Many computers come with CD-RW drives. If your computer doesn't have one, and you don't plan on buying a new machine soon, I strongly suggest that you think about getting a CD-RW drive. One reason is that CD-RWs are perfect for backups, as well as archiving data for long-term storage.

Creating Your Own Music CDs

When you use a CD-RW drive to create your own music CD, we say that you BURN it (although nothing really burns). Most CD-RW drives come with a CD BURNER program that allows you to create your own CDs. If you don't like the program that came with your CD drive, you can download another one from the Net.

In most cases, your music files will be stored in mp3 format. Some CD burning programs will work directly with mp3 files. Other programs, however, require wav files.

If this is the case with your program, you must create wav files from your mp3 files before you can burn a CD. To do so, you use a program called a DECODER. To create mp3 files from wav files, you use an ENCODER. Many CD decoders will encode as well, so you can use the same program to convert audio data back and forth between mp3 and wav formats.

In general, here are the steps you use to make your own music CDs:

1. Get a whole bunch of mp3 files. You can either rip them from CDs or download them from the Internet.

2. Use a CD decoder to convert the mp3 files to wav files. (Remember, wav files are much larger.)

3. Use a CD burner program to burn the CD. Within this program, you will be able to organize the songs in whatever order you want. Some programs have a tool to let you design and print a cover for the plastic CD case (which is called a JEWEL CASE).

4. Once the CD is finished, delete the wav files, as they take up a lot of space. If you need them again, you can always recreate them from the mp3 files.

hint

Making your own CDs can be a lot of fun. However, it is a time-consuming process. It can take hours to gather the mp3 files, encode them, organize the CD to be just the way you want it, and burn it. However, once you know what you are doing, you can let the ripping, encoding and burning run by itself in the background as you work on other things.

Internet Resources   **CD Burners**

```
http://www.musicmatch.com/
http://www.liquidaudio.com/player/
http://www.sonicspot.com/cdwriters.html
http://www.musicex.com/mediajukebox/
http://www.hitsquad.com/smm/win95/CD_BURNERS/
```

Internet Resources   **CD Decoders/Encoders**

```
http://www.musicmatch.com/

http://www.dors.de/RazorBlade/

http://www.fmjsoft.com/awframe.html

http://www.sonicspot.com/encoders.html

http://www.acoustica.com/mp3converter/features.htm
```

11

Finding Stuff on the Net

*The Internet has a rhythm,
and once you tune into this
rhythm, you will be able to
find whatever you want.*

The Internet is one of the best sources of information in the world. There are hundreds of millions of Web pages and tens of thousands of Usenet discussion groups: the products of people all over the world who contribute and share.

However, information is only useful if you can find it, and the Internet has no central directory. Moreover, since no one is in charge, there is no one to organize everything. Nevertheless, once you understand what is out there and how to access it, there are ways to find what you want when you want it.

In this chapter, I am going to show you how it all works by answering one of the most common questions people ask me: How do I find stuff on the Net?

Starting a Search

Searching the Net requires more than skill and knowledge. It requires time to develop your skills. I was once at an Internet conference when a young man came up to me and asked, "How do I find information about Carnegie Hall?" My answer was, "Practice, practice, practice."

I spend a lot of time finding stuff on the Net. For almost a decade, I have published a book called *Harley Hahn's Internet Yellow Pages* (the original Internet Yellow Pages). Every year, I revise the book and spend many, many hours looking for information on the Internet.

I published the first edition of the book in 1992, and, since then, I have watched the Internet grow and change. Although the Internet is much larger than it was in 1992, it is, in my opinion, easier to search than ever before. The main reason is that millions of people are compiling information and creating resources and putting it all on Web sites to share with everyone else.

For example, say you are looking for information about ancient Roman coins. Somewhere on the Net, other people with the same interest have created Web sites devoted to this topic. When you visit these sites, you will find more than information and pictures, you will also find links to other Web sites about ancient Roman coins.

When I am searching for something, I often start by looking at the Web pages of people who are fanatics about that particular topic. Such people almost always collect links to related resources.

Search Engines

A SEARCH ENGINE is a program that can search a large database for specific information. On the Web, there are a number of search engines devoted to keeping track of everything on the Web, and you can use them for free. (The companies that maintain them make their money by selling advertising.) Each search engine is different, and you must learn to use it in its own way. As an example, let me talk about two of my favorite search engines, Yahoo and Google. Both of these search engines keep track of a great deal of the content on the Web, but they do so in different ways.

The YAHOO search engine seeks to categorize everything on the Web. When you use Yahoo to search for something, the results are given as a list of categories related to that something. If you select a category, you will be shown links to Web pages in that category.

The GOOGLE search engine has a different emphasis. Google does its best to maintain a copy of all the information on the Web. You use Google to look for specific words, and it responds by showing you a list of links to Web pages that contain those words.

The following example illustrates the differences. If you search Yahoo for my name, `Harley Hahn`, the results look something like this:

```
Business and Economy >

        Shopping and Services >
        Books >
        Booksellers >
        Computers >
        Authors

• Hahn, Harley
```

The first six lines show a sequence of categories and subcategories. Following these lines are a list of all the resources in the rightmost sub-category. (In this case, there is only one resource, a link to my Web site.) As you can see, Yahoo has classified my Web site as belonging to the category of computer book authors.

In our example, the results of the search consisted of a single item within a single subcategory (perhaps because there is only one Harley Hahn).

More often, the results of a Yahoo search will be a list of subcategories, each of which contains multiple items.

Now let's compare this to a Google search. If you search Goggle for my name, the results will consist of a long list of links to all the Web pages in the database that contain the words `Harley Hahn`. When I performed this search, Google found several thousand Web pages. The Google database is huge, and within that database, there are a lot of Web pages on the Net that contain the words `Harley Hahn`. However, the results are organized with the most relevant links first. In this case, the very first item was:

```
Harley Hahn Web Site
... Welcome to a place to think, learn, and
have fun -- the Web site of Harley Hahn,
the best-selling Internet author of all time
and the creator of... ...
www.harley.com/ - 24k - Cached - Similar pages
```

The first five lines of information (the title and some text) are taken from the beginning of the actual Web page. They are included to help you decide whether or not you want to look at that page. If so, you have several choices.

First, you can click on the title, which is a link to the URL shown in the second to last line. This will take you directly to the Web page.

Second, you can click on the word `Cached`. This will take you to the *copy* of the Web page that is stored in the Google database. This is a fast way to see the Web page, because the Google Web server is designed to respond very quickly. However, since you are looking at a copy of the page, it may be out of date.

Your third choice is to click on `Similar pages`. The meaning of "similar" is difficult to pin down. Just try it, and see what you get.

I chose these examples because they were simple. Yahoo, Google, and all the other search engines have far more complex capabilities than what you see here. Every search engine has built-in help documentation, and you should take the time to read it. Knowing even the basic ideas will make a big difference in the type of results you get and, ultimately, in your ability to find stuff on the Net.

As computer programs go, search engines are complex. However, they are only tools. Your success in searching the Internet depends more on your skill than on which particular search engine you use. In order to hunt down specific information, you will often have to examine various Web pages, following links from one page to another.

In general, search engines can only show you places to begin a search. It is not realistic to depend on them to do all the work, because they do not have the intelligence and discrimination of a human mind. Moreover, when you are looking for something, only you know what you really want.

My advice is to experiment with various search engines. Then choose the *two* you like best, and learn how to use them well by reading the help information and by practicing.

There are a great many search engines on the Internet. For reference, here are some of the best ones. If you have a copy of my Yellow Pages book, look in the section called "Finding Stuff on the Net", where you will find a more comprehensive collection of resources.

Internet Resources   **Search Engines**

```
http://www.lycos.com/
http://www.yahoo.com/
http://search.aol.com/
http://search.msn.com/
http://www.excite.com/
http://www.google.com/
http://hotbot.lycos.com/
http://www.alltheweb.com/
http://www.altavista.com/
http://www.webcrawler.com/
```

Techniques for Using a Search Engine

The best way to learn how to use a search engine is to read the help documentation and then practice. To get you started, I will show you a few techniques that should work with most search engines.

First, if you want to search for words that must be together, you can put them within quotation marks. For example, let's say you use Google to search for:

```
Harley Hahn
```

This tells Google to search for all Web pages that contain either of the words `Harley` and `Hahn` anywhere on the page. When I did this, Google found 17,100 such pages. It would be more expedient to search for pages that contain the two words `Harley Hahn` together. To do so, put the words in quotation marks in the order you want to see them:

`"Harley Hahn"`

The better the search criteria, the more exact the results. In this case, Google found 4070 pages. However, you have to be careful. If you search for this pattern with Google, you will get good results. If you use the same pattern with Yahoo, it won't work as well, because Yahoo classifies author names with the first name last:

`Hahn, Harley`

Thus, if your first search doesn't find what you want, it is a good idea to try different combinations (especially with Yahoo).

One nice thing about using Yahoo is that, if it can't find what it wants in its own database, it will automatically search the Google database. For example, as I mentioned, if you search for `"Harley Hahn"`, Yahoo won't be able to find the entry in the Yahoo database. But, it will check the Google database and come up with something.

Sometimes the best way to use a search engine is to specify a list of words that are related to what you want. For example, one day, I wanted to make a pizza for someone who is a vegetarian. To find a suitable recipe, I said to myself, "What words are related to what I need?" I then used Google to search for:

`recipe vegetarian pizza`

The results contained over 40,000 items. Why? Because I asked for all the Web pages that contain any of these three words in any order. To narrow it down, I specified that the words `vegetarian` and `pizza` must be together:

`recipe "vegetarian pizza"`

This still yielded way too many items, because I was picking up all the Web pages with the word `recipe` regardless of the context.

When this happens, there are two easy ways to narrow the search.

- Use a plus sign (+) to indicate you only want Web pages that contain a specific word

● Use a minus sign (-) to indicate you only want Web pages that do not contain a specific word

So, to narrow down the pizza search, I searched for pages that contained both of my search terms:

```
+recipe +"vegetarian pizza"
```

Now the search was more successful: there were 729 items. However, as it happens, the person I was going to cook for does not like olives, so I needed to eliminate all the recipes with olives. To do so, I searched for:

```
+"vegetarian pizza" +recipe -olives
```

I was now down to 367 items. Then I remembered that my friend *does* like artichokes, so I changed the search to:

```
+"vegetarian pizza" +recipe -olives +artichoke
```

This yielded a nice, manageable set of results: 28 items. Within these items, I was able to find several suitable recipes for vegetarian pizza with artichoke but no olives. Thus, thanks to the Web (and a search engine), I was able to cook the pizza I wanted, and a good time was had by all.

Use the plus or minus sign when you suspect in advance that a particular set of words is going to yield a lot of spurious results. For example, say I was looking for information about the movie *Rocky* made by Sylvester Stallone. I could search for Web pages that contain either `stallone` or `rocky`:

```
stallone rocky
```

However, since I know I want to eliminate as many irrelevant pages as I can, I would start with a more specific search:

```
+stallone +rocky -mountain -bullwinkle
```

In this case, by specifying `-mountain -bullwinkle` I am able to eliminate a great many unwanted items.

Usenet Search Engines

In my experience, searching the Web allows you to find what you need almost all of the time. The Web is mature enough that virtually everything you might want is out there somewhere. Sometimes, however, you need more than information. There will be times when what you really

hint

If you want to get good at using a search engine, take some time to read the online help, and teach yourself how to use the advanced features.

need are people's opinions, particularly those having to deal with personal experience and preferences. At such times, you can often get better results by searching Usenet.

Usenet is a global system of thousands of different discussion groups. I described Usenet generally in Chapter 2, and will talk about it in detail in Chapter 13. For our discussion here, there are only a few important points you need to know.

To access Usenet, you use a program called a newsreader. (For historical reasons, Usenet discussion groups are often called "newsgroups", although they don't really contain news.) Anyone with an Internet connection can participate, and millions of people around the world have been doing so for years. There is a Usenet newsgroup for every topic you can imagine, including current events of all types. In fact, I would be inclined to say there is not much that happens in the world that isn't discussed somewhere on Usenet.

Within a specific newsgroup, people from all over the Net post (send in) articles that are seen by everyone who reads that group. Thus, one of the best ways to find help is to post a message to the appropriate Usenet newsgroup, especially if what you need is unusual or timely. Of course, you will have to wait for people to read and respond to your article.

hint

No matter what you need to know, there are people on the Net who already know it and would be glad to help you. You can use Usenet to help you find those people.

For example, I have a friend who wanted to buy a certain type of camera, but she wasn't sure exactly what to choose or where to buy it. She posted a message asking for help to one of the Usenet photography groups, and a half dozen people sent replies. Over the next few days, she was able to correspond with some of these people by email, and ask more questions as she narrowed down her search. The people who wrote her gave a lot of good advice, and, as a result, she was able to find exactly what she needed at a good price. Moreover, she made a few friends who know a lot about photography, people who would be glad to help her if she has a problem in the future.

Earlier in the chapter, I described how I used a Web search engine to look for a recipe for a particular type of vegetarian pizza. Probably, at some time, someone on Usenet discussed a similar recipe. However, the conversation on Usenet is always changing, and the articles are kept for only a short time. Nevertheless, there is a way to search through old articles.

There are a number of Usenet repositories on the Net which are maintained as archives. To search an archive, you use a USENET SEARCH ENGINE. These search engines allow you to access the vast number of articles that have been posted to all the newsgroups around the world. Like the Web search engines, Usenet search engines are free to use. (They are run by companies who make money by selling advertising.)

As with the Web search engines, it can take a bit of time to learn how to use these tools well, so be sure to read the help information. Moreover, your searching will be a lot more rewarding if you understand what Usenet is and how it works, so do take some time to read Chapter 13, where I discuss these topics in detail.

Internet Resources   **Usenet Search Engines**

`http://groups.google.com/`

Accessing Your Favorite Search Engines Quickly

There are two ways you can customize your browser in order to be able to access your favorite search engines quickly.

First, with Internet Explorer, you can put their addresses in your Favorites list. (I explain how to do this in Chapter 7.) My suggestion is to create a folder named **Search Engines**. If you are not sure which ones you like best, start with all the ones I mention in this chapter. Put them all in one folder, and experiment. Over time, you will develop your own favorites.

Accessing a search engine (or any Web site) from your Favorites list is easy, but for sites you visit a lot, you can make things even faster by creating customized buttons. (Again, this is something I discuss in more detail in Chapter 7.) Figure 11-1 shows custom buttons with Internet Explorer.

With Internet Explorer, you can create custom buttons on the Links toolbar. All you need to do is place items in the Links folder of your Favorites list. Internet Explorer will automatically create a custom button for each item in this folder.

FIGURE 11-1

Custom buttons for
accessing search engines

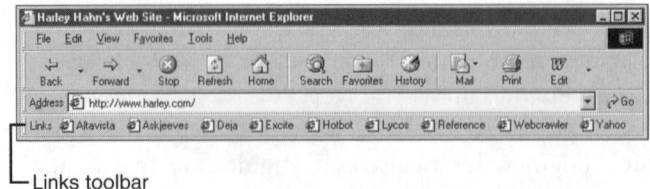

└─Links toolbar

The Internet Explorer Search Facility

Internet Explorer has a built-in search facility. To use it, click on the **Search** button or press **Ctrl-E**. When you do, Internet Explorer will open a special area called the EXPLORER BAR. (See Figure 11-2.) You can use the Explorer bar to make multiple searches, one after the other.

When you are finished, you can close the Explorer bar by clicking on the **Search** button or pressing **Ctrl-E** once again. Alternatively, you can click on the **X** in the top right-hand corner of the Explorer bar, to the right of the word **Search**. (Don't click on the **X** in the top right-hand corner of the browser window, or you will shut down Internet Explorer.)

As you are working with the Explorer bar, you can make it narrower or wider by dragging the rightmost edge to the left or right. (That is, move your mouse pointer to the line that separates the Explorer bar from the right side of the window. Then, while holding down the left button, move the mouse to the left or right.)

What's in a Name?

Explorer Bar

Within Internet Explorer, whenever you click on the Search, Favorites or History buttons, the browser opens up a special area called the Explorer bar.

Don't be confused by the word "bar". The name is just one of those meaningless Microsoft terms you can either ignore or memorize.

There are two ways to make use of the Explorer bar. First, you can use the SEARCH ASSISTANT. This allows you to enter words to search for, and then use more than one search engine, one after the other. The other choice is to specify only one search engine and use it for everything.

To use the Search Assistant:

1. Click on the **Search** button to open the Explorer bar.

2. Within the Explorer bar, make sure that **Find a Web page** is selected from the list of categories.

3. In the box below the list of categories, type the words for which you want to search.

4. Click on the small **Search** button at the right side of the box. Internet Explorer will submit your query to a search engine and display the results for you.

5. To repeat the search with another search engine, click on the **Next** button near the top of the Explorer bar.

6. To start a brand new search, click on the **New** button near the top of the Explorer bar.

(Once you get used to using the Search Assistant, it's a lot easier than it sounds.)

Learn how to...

Customize the Search Facility

You can customize the Search Assistant by choosing which search engines it should use. Alternatively, you can turn off the Search Assistant and use only one search engine.

See Chapter 17, *How to Do Stuff*, page 375 (Internet Explorer).

Search button

Explorer bar close button

Explorer bar

FIGURE 11-2
The Internet Explorer search facility

So, should you use the Internet Explorer search facility? My feeling is that, for several reasons, it is better to ignore the search facility and use your favorite search engines directly.

First, it is easy to create a few custom buttons on the Links toolbar to access the search engines of your choice. (I explain how to create custom buttons earlier in the chapter.)

Second, when you use the search facility, the results of your search are condensed (because they have to fit within the Explorer bar). You will only see a portion of the results, with many of the details omitted. If you use a search engine in the regular manner, you will see a lot more information.

Finally, as I discussed earlier in the chapter, it is a fallacy to assume you can get good results by using multiple search engines. The best way to find things on the Internet is to learn how to use one or two good search engines well, and to develop your own skills by reading the documentation and by practicing.

Cool Browser Tricks

Since searching the Web is such a common activity, your browser has a special feature to make the job easier. Wherever you can type a URL, you can also enter a **?** (question mark) character followed by a list of search words. When you press **Enter**, your browser will automatically submit the words to a search engine and then display the results. For example, to search for information about cats, you can click on the address bar and type:

```
? cats
```

This is shown in Figure 11-3. (Be sure to put a space after the question mark.)

FIGURE 11-3

Entering a search request into the address bar

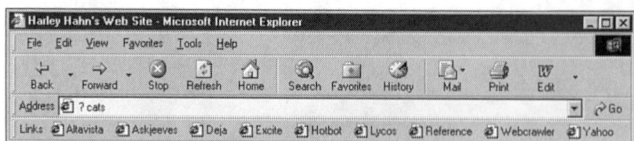

If you like, you can search for multiple words. For example:

```
? travel cruise bahamas
```

However, you can't, as a general rule, use more complex searches like the ones we discussed earlier in the chapter. If you want to use special characters (such as **+** and **-**), you need to use a search engine directly.

When you enter a query directly to your browser, how do you know which search engine will be used? The choice of search engine depends on the current marketing agreements the browser company has with the various search engine companies. As you probably will have guessed, making deals to send your queries to this or that search engine is another opportunity for browser companies to make money. Are you starting to get a feeling why both Microsoft and AOL (which owns Netscape) want to control the browser market?

When typing a search request, you can use either a `?` (question mark), the word `find`, or the word `go`. For example, the following search requests are equivalent:

```
? cats
find cats
go cats
```

If you are searching for more than one word at a time, you can even leave out the `?` character. For example:

```
travel cruise bahamas
? travel cruise bahamas
find travel cruise bahamas
go travel cruise bahamas
```

As I mentioned in Chapter 7, you can press **Ctrl-O** to display a window into which you can type an address. Well, you can also type a search request into this same window.

Thus, a quick way to perform a simple search is to press **Ctrl-O**, type `?`, followed by one or more search words, and then press **Enter**. For example, try this:

1. Press **Ctrl-O**
2. Type `? cats`
3. Press **Enter**

If you are entering more than one word, you can leave out the `?` character. Try this:

1. Press **Ctrl-O**
2. Type `travel cruise bahamas`
3. Press **Enter**

You can see such a search being initiated in Figure 11-4.

Learn how to...

Specify Which Search Engine to Use for Address Bar Searches

Within Internet Explorer, you can choose which search engine is used for address bar searches.

See Chapter 17, *How to Do Stuff*, page 376 (Internet Explorer).

FIGURE 11-4
Entering a search request
into an address window

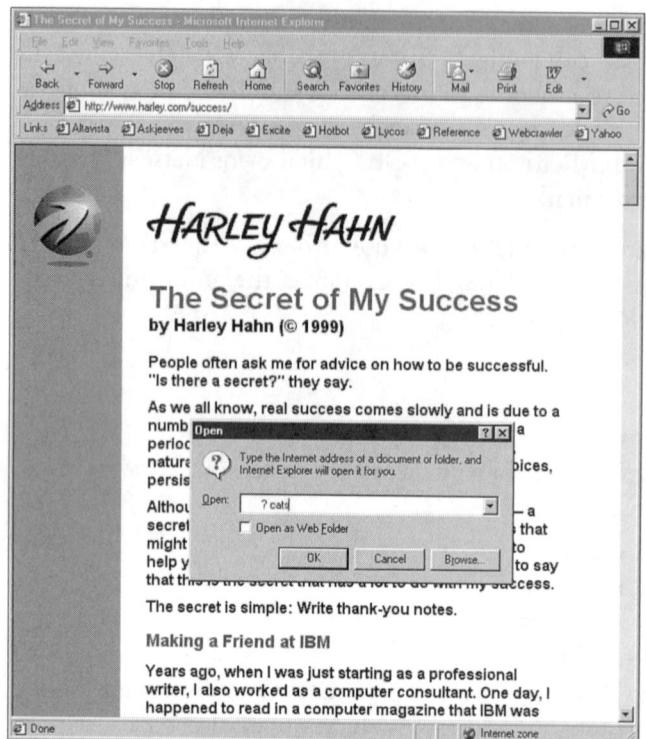

FAQs (Frequently Asked Question Lists)

It was a beautiful, sunny Southern California day. I was sitting on my beachfront patio, watching the intricate patterns of the waves as they lapped lazily on the sand. In the distance, a school of dolphins frolicked playfully, while the pelicans flew in tight formation, skimming down low, barely a foot above the tips of the whitecaps.

I had just finished an early morning surfing session and was relaxing in a comfortable chair, sipping a tall, cool fruit smoothie. I listened to the distant cry of the seagulls as they foraged for their breakfast. I closed my eyes and listened to the rhythmic sound of the waves and the gentle stirring of the wind as it rustled the leaves of the nearby palm trees.

It hadn't been more than five minutes when I felt a shadow cross my chair, and without even opening my eyes, I could tell who it was. Only a cop would walk with that heavy, thumping, flat-footed gait, even on the sand.

"Go away, Lieutenant," I said. "I told you never to bother me before noon. Why aren't you off catching criminals somewhere?"

"Aw… why do you have to be like that? You know we always cooperate with you. Why can't you help us out once in a while?"

"Because I don't like cops, especially dumb cops, and especially in the morning. What do you want? I assume you didn't come all the way to the beach just to get a suntan."

"They told me that someone named the Colonel has the whatcha-ma-hoosers."

"The what?"

He pulled a small, beat-up notebook out of his pocket, and flipped through a couple of pages. "The FAQs," he said.

I sat bolt upright in my chair and took off my lime-green sunglasses. "The Colonel's got the FAQs? If that's true it means trouble for you. Lots of trouble. How did it happen?"

The Lieutenant produced a stained white handkerchief and wiped his brow. He was sweating profusely. "I don't know, but if Superintendent Babin finds out, I'll be back pounding the street within a week. What are these FAQ things anyway?"

"How much do you know about finding information on the Internet?" I asked.

"The regular stuff, what they teach in the Academy. But I never heard of FAQs."

I lay back in my chair and closed my eyes. "A FAQ," I began, "is a frequently asked question list. Years ago, people who used Usenet noticed that newcomers always seemed to ask the same questions. For example, whenever people join, say, the cat discussion group, they ask the same basic questions about cats.

"So, in many Usenet groups, someone would prepare a list of all the frequently asked questions along with the answers. This list, a FAQ, would be posted to the group regularly, as well as to one or two special groups used for periodic postings. Over time, a great many FAQs were written dealing with many, many topics.

"Today, there are several thousand different FAQs, just from Usenet alone. As a matter of fact, when I am looking for information, I often search for a FAQ from a related Usenet group. For example, if you wanted some information about cats, you could check to see if the cat discussion group had a FAQ. If so, there is a good chance that what you need would be in the FAQ."

The Lieutenant thought about it. It took him a few minutes. Thinking was not his strong point. "So how do you find a FAQ when you need one?"

I laughed. "Don't you learn any of this at the Academy? What do you do, ride horses all day long?"

He snorted like a bulldog choking on a bone.

"There are several ways to find a FAQ," I continued. "First, there are Web sites that act as FAQ repositories. You can check those, or you can use a search engine to look for a FAQ related to the topic you want. For example, to find FAQs about cats, you could search for:

`+cats +FAQ`

"Alternatively, you can use your Usenet newsreader and look in the appropriate discussion group. As I told you, FAQs are posted regularly to the related groups. If you know the name of a discussion group, that's always a good place to look for a FAQ. For cats, that would be `rec.pets.cats`.

"Another group to check is `news.answers`. This is a special Usenet group to which people post copies of all the FAQs and other periodic Usenet postings. When you look in `news.answers`, you'll see all kinds of FAQs. Sometimes I look just for fun, to see what's there.

"And, of course, you can use one of the Usenet search engines. That's often the fastest way to find a FAQ and get the information you need."

The Lieutenant nodded. "I see. But what does that have to do with the Colonel?"

"The idea of a FAQ," I answered, "has proven to be very popular. People make up FAQs on all different topics, not just those associated with Usenet groups. For example, I have a FAQ on my Web site to answer the most common questions people ask me.

"Now, I happen to know that for the last six months, Inspector Babin has been working on a set of FAQs about police procedures and tracking down criminals on the Internet. These FAQs are highly confidential and were never supposed to leave your internal computer network. Just before he left for Guatemala, he encoded everything. Evidently, the Colonel has found a way to break into your system and decode the files."

"So, can I find the Colonel?" The Lieutenant was really beginning to sweat now. "Can you help me get back the FAQs before it's too late?"

"The Colonel is a very talented hacker in the pay of a foreign power. Fortunately for you, we are dealing with a highly secretive person who moves slowly and deliberately. Chances are, yes, if we find the Colonel quickly, we can get the FAQs back before it is too late."

"So what should we do?"

"Hold on." I went inside and used my high-speed connection to make a few fast searches on the Net. "You're in luck," I told the Lieutenant. "I think I know where we can find the Colonel. Let's take my car."

We jumped into the red BMW 328i, and in twenty minutes, we pulled up outside a nondescript gray building. Fifteen seconds later, we were knocking on the door of #127.

"Better call for a patrol car. Then get your handcuffs out, " I said.

We heard the sound of gentle footsteps and, a moment later, the door was opened by a ravishing ash blond woman with a set of curves that could cause a traffic jam in the Gobi Desert. She was wearing a black and gray skin-tight outfit that accentuated every natural resource in her collection. Her eyes were a chilled blue, the color of the ocean on a winter afternoon, and her plump crimson-lined lips were twisted upward, in a shallow half-smirking smile. If she was surprised, she didn't show it.

"Lieutenant," I said, "may I present Colonel Valerie Babushka." I walked into the room and picked up a CD from the table. "And here, if I am not mistaken, are the missing FAQs."

She tried to run, but the Lieutenant had his own ideas. It was the work of a moment for him to produce the handcuffs, clamp them over the Colonel's slender, feminine wrists (from which I caught just a hint of fragrance of *chypre*) and hustle her out the door.

I threw the CD to the Lieutenant. He looked at me gratefully. "The entire department," he said, "is in your debt."

The Colonel looked up at me, pouting. "You're a good guy," she said.

"Can't you help me? Without your expert testimony they haven't got a case. Couldn't we make a deal?"

"Sorry, sister, but you play too rough for me. You used Sammy to get the FAQs, but when he wanted more than you agreed on, you hired Starkwell to bump him off. And when Starkwell wouldn't play along, you took care of him yourself that night with the dwarf and the one-eyed harmonica player. You thought you could get away with it then, and you think you can play me for a sap now. Well, you can't. You were just about to skip town, to sell the CD to The Little Nipper and stiff your own people, weren't you?"

At the mention of The Little Nipper, her blue eyes grew wide with fear and her mouth quivered. "I don't know what you're talking about," she said.

I motioned to the Lieutenant and pointed at the police car which had just driven up. "Take her in," I said. "I'll catch up with you later. "

As the car started, she began to panic. "Look," she said, "it isn't too late. We can still make a deal. What do you need? I'll give you anything you want."

The color of her eyes changed to a deeper, more magnetic blue, and her pupils widened. Her mouth took on a wry, vulnerable smile as she raised her carefully manicured eyebrows like two question marks. As I watched the car pull slowly away from the curb, the nearby jacaranda trees cast a pattern of bar-like shadows over her face, and her expression changed to a silent and fearful plea for help.

She twisted her body toward me and leaned out the window. "Surely, there must be something I can give you. Isn't there anything you want? Anything at all?"

"Just the FAQs, ma'am," I said, as I pulled down my lime-green sunglasses, slipped into the red BMW 328i and drove off into the warm, California sun.

Internet Resources **FAQs (Frequently Asked Question Lists)**

```
http://www.faqs.org/faqs/
http://www.landfield.com/faqs/
http://www.cs.ruu.nl/cgi-bin/faqwais/
```

Web Rings

A WEB RING is a collection of Web sites organized into a loop. From any Web site in the ring, you can follow a link to move forward to the next site, or a different link to move backward to the previous site. If you keep moving in one direction, you will eventually transverse the entire ring and end up where you started.

The idea behind Web rings is to make it easy to visit a group of related Web sites. There are literally tens of thousands of Web rings devoted to a variety of subjects: movies, computers, sports, health, hobbies, pets, and so on. A popular topic will have many different rings; a more esoteric topic will have only a single ring. A typical Web ring might have 10 or 20 Web sites, although many rings are larger, some with well over a hundred sites.

The Web ring system is organized by a group of people who manage a central Web site containing a catalog of the various rings. They also maintain the software that makes the whole thing operate. The content of the rings, however, consists of hundreds of thousands of regular Web sites created by individuals around the Net.

If you have a Web site, it is free to have it become part of an existing Web ring. Similarly, anyone is allowed to start a new ring, which is also free. Each Web ring is administered by a volunteer known as a RINGMASTER, usually the person who started the ring. He or she will maintain a master list of the Web sites in the ring and ensure that the links stay intact as various sites join and drop out. The ringmaster will also build up the ring by inviting people to add new sites.

hint

If you have your own Web site devoted to a particular topic, you can attract people to the site by joining a Web ring.

I like Web rings because they are useful for finding information. The best way to do so is to start at the main Web ring site (see below), where you can search for rings devoted to a particular topic. Once you find such rings, you can check the individual Web sites for what you need.

Internet Resources   **Web Rings**

http://webring.yahoo.com/

An Approach to Searching the Net

In this chapter, I have discussed a variety of different tools and techniques you can use to find information on the Net. However, tools and techniques only take you so far. In my experience, the best Internet researchers develop a feeling for the Net and an innate sense of how to approach a problem. To help you develop a style of your own, I have a few final hints for you.

1. **If you have a copy of my book *Harley Hahn's Internet Yellow Pages*, use it as a starting place.**

   Every year, as I revise the book, I look for the best items I can find in each category. I particularly look for resources that will lead you to other resources. I often use the book myself as a shortcut when I need to find something fast.

2. **Pick at least two different search engines and learn how to use them well.**

   Search engines are complex tools that can help you in many ways if you know how to ask for that help. Each search engine is different and has its own strengths and weaknesses. The more you use them, the better they will work for you. Take time to read the help information and experiment with different types of searches.

3. **Become familiar with Usenet and how it works.** (See Chapter 13.)

   The strength of Usenet lies in the millions of people who participate in the discussion groups. There will be times when you will find the help of other people invaluable, so it is a good idea to learn about Usenet now. Once you are familiar with Usenet, spend a little time with the Usenet search engines. They are valuable tools that will often help you find what you need when all else fails.

4. **The more you know about your topic, the easier it is to find what you want.**

   If you are looking for information about which you are not particularly knowledgeable, it is often a good idea to start by looking up some of the basic facts and terminology. This helps you in two ways. First, you will be able to think of better search words.

Second, when you do find information, you will more likely be able to make sense out of it. The Net covers a lot of topics, but in many areas, there is a significant paucity of introductory material.

Preparing for a search is especially important if you are a student. The Internet is a great place for research, but it is not a substitute for the library. I can tell you that, although I search the Internet for a living, I have more than seventy different reference books on my bookshelf, and generally speaking, the information in these books is more reliable than what I find on the Net.

5. **Ask other people for help.**

If you find a Web site that is close to what you want, you can send a polite note to the person who maintains the site asking for help. Most people who create Web sites are willing to help people with similar interests.

However, don't be disappointed if you do not get an answer. Some popular Web sites take a lot of work to maintain, and there isn't always time to answer every message, especially when someone receives a lot of mail.

6. **Learn to search creatively.**

The best researchers learn to be creative in how they look for something. If your first search doesn't return what you want, change the search words and try again. You will often find that you need to slowly close in on your target. However, with practice, you will become faster. Some of my researchers are so fast that just watching them is an awe-inspiring experience. You would not believe how quickly they can break an idea into parts, and try various combinations, one after the other, until they get what they want.

My goal is to teach you more than how to use search engines, FAQs and Web rings. What I want is for you to begin to think in a new way. There is no central Internet administration, but that does not mean there is no order. The information on the Internet (and the Web in particular) tends to organize itself in certain ways that you can teach yourself to understand. The Internet has a rhythm, and once you tune into this rhythm, you will almost always be able to find whatever you want, whenever you want it.

hint

Give a man information about a fish, and he will be satisfied for a day. Teach a man how to find information about fish on the Internet, and he can satisfy his needs for a lifetime.

12

Safety, Security and Privacy

*As long as you follow a few
common sense guidelines,
there isn't all that much
for you to worry about
on the Net.*

There are millions of people on the Net —and millions of computers which you might access —and you and I have no control over any of them. Using the Internet connects your personal computer to the outside world, and that brings up several important concerns: safety, security and privacy. In this chapter, I will talk about all of these issues, and show you how to make your time on the Net pleasant and comfortable.

(In addition to what we discuss in this chapter, you may also want to take a look at Chapter 6, where I discuss privacy as it relates to email.)

Before we start, let me assure you that, regardless of what you might hear, safety, security and privacy on the Internet are not big problems for individual users. It is true, that if you are running a computer network at a company, a school or some type of organization, you do need to pay a lot of attention to security issues. The same is true if you have your own Web server or mail server. Indeed, many organizations have full-time network administrators whose job is to make sure the networks and servers are secure.

However, when you use the Internet at home, even if you have a small home network and a high-speed connection, you don't need to worry — not as long as you follow a few simple guidelines. We will talk about these guidelines later in the chapter. In the meantime, don't worry.

Is It Safe to Send Personal Information Over the Web?

SECURITY on the Internet refers to protecting yourself against problems that might arise as you interact with the outside world. In the broadest terms, there are two types of situations in which you might encounter a security problem:

- When data is going out of your computer
- When data is coming into your computer

In this chapter, I will discuss the various possibilities, along with potential problems and how you should think about them. Let's start with a real-life example of what happens when information leaves your computer.

Imagine you are using the Web, and you happen upon the Web site of the Acme Internet Shopping Company. As you peruse the site, you see

hint

For a fascinating discussion of privacy, safety and security issues, see my book *Harley Hahn's Internet Insecurity*, published by Prentice Hall PTR.

a stuffed Bill Gates doll on sale for only $29.95. You immediately recognize this as an ideal Mother's Day gift and decide to order one right away. To do so, you need to fill out a form on the Web site. You do so, typing your name, address and credit card information. Let's pretend that you have just finished filling out the form, and are about to click on the **Send** button. What is going to happen when you click that button?

So far, everything you have typed is still on your computer. However, once you click the **Send** button, the information on the form is going to be sent to a remote Web server run by the Acme Internet Shopping Company. At that point, the data will be processed by a program which, presumably, will do whatever is necessary to initiate your order for the stuffed Bill Gates doll.

As long as everything works perfectly, it seems like a good system. After all, it might take you months to find a nearby store with stuffed Bill Gates dolls, and it is certainly more convenient to buy one over the Web. However, before you press that button, you need to ask yourself, "Is it safe to send my personal information over the Web to the Acme Internet Shopping Company?"

This question really has two parts. First, is your personal information secure as it travels from your computer to the remote Web site? Second, do you trust the Acme Internet Shopping Company to use the information responsibly?

The answer to the first question is easy: your personal information is secure as long as no one intercepts it along the way. In theory, a gang of bad guys with sophisticated equipment, exceptional skills, a lot of time, and enormous motivation might find a way to intercept your data as it travels from your computer to the remote Web site. These guys could make a copy of all the data, analyze it so as to extract your credit card number, and then use the information for nefarious purposes. However, the chances of all this happening are about the same as you being hit by a meteor right now as you read this. In other words, don't worry —the Internet is secure.

Let's put this in perspective. Suppose the Acme Internet Shopping Company takes orders over the phone, and instead of using their Web site, you decide to call them to place an order. Is that really safe? After all, someone could be tapping your phone illegally, listening day and night on the off-chance that, eventually, he might overhear some valuable information. Since such a scenario is technically possible, shouldn't you be afraid to say your credit card number out loud over the telephone?

Of course not. Although it is possible for someone to tap your phone line, it's not likely to happen, so you don't worry about it. I can tell you it's a lot harder to intercept data on the Internet than to tap a phone line, and no one is going to do either one just to steal your credit card number. People who steal such numbers have ways to get them that are far easier and much less risky.

So, the answer to our first question —is your personal information secure as it travels from your computer to the remote Web site? —is yes, so don't worry about it.

But what about the second question: Do you trust the Acme Internet Shopping Company? After all, you *are* sending them your credit card number. This is the same question you need to answer before you place an order with any company you don't know, whether the order is over the phone, by regular mail, or on the Internet. You need to ask yourself if you feel comfortable doing business with that company.

The nature of the Web is such that you can't judge a company by the quality of its Web site. On the Net, it is easy for a small, one-person business to look like a large, well-established firm. Questionable companies will often design a great-looking Web site that very carefully gives no information about how to reach a real person. So here is my advice.

hint

When it comes to sending personal information on the Web, you can assume that the Net itself is safe.

However, you do need to confirm that the people who will be receiving the information are trustworthy.

Never do business with a company or person over the Web unless their Web site gives their phone number and postal address. Before you send an order to a company for the first time, call them on the phone and check things out. At the very least, ask if the item you want is in stock, confirm the price, and have them explain their refund policy. If you can't get a real person on the phone, or if you get a funny feeling about the company, do not do business with them.

If you want to be extra careful, order over the phone the first time you buy something from a new company. If everything works out well and you like the customer service, you can start ordering over the Net.

Spending Money on the Net

The most common way to spend money on the Internet is by using your credit card number. I suggest you keep a record, on paper, of everything you order: the date, the amount, and the name of the company. This information will come in handy if you have a problem. If you buy many things over the Net, you may find that some of the charges don't appear on your credit card account right away. Thus, it is important for you to keep track of what you are spending.

Buying things over the Internet is so easy that the money will add up faster than you might expect. For example (and this is a true story), I have a friend who bought a lot of stuff over the Internet and didn't keep track of what she was spending. When the credit card statement came, it was so costly, she didn't have money left to pay her phone bill.

Unnecessary Security Warnings

From time to time, you may see a warning telling you that you are about to send data from your computer to the Internet. Typically, this will happen when you have filled out a form of some type and have just pressed a button to send the information. Figure 12-1 shows a typical warning you might see with Internet Explorer. When you see such a warning, you must choose whether or not you want to continue with the data transmission.

hint

As you buy things over the Internet, keep a running total of all the money you are spending.

Before you use your credit card to buy something, take a moment to calculate how many hours of work it will take you to pay for the purchase.

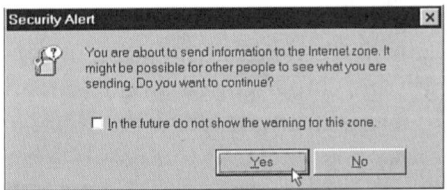

FIGURE 12-1
Security warning when sending data

These warnings are useless, and you can always ignore them. In fact, you should select the option within the warning box to indicate that you never want to see these warnings again.

So why are these warnings used in the first place? After much thought, the only reason I can come up with is to limit the legal liability of the browser company. Once Microsoft or Netscape shows such a warning to you, you cannot sue the company and say their browser sent information to the Internet without your knowledge. This is why, if you don't want to see the warnings all the time, you must turn them off explicitly.

Surely no one at Microsoft or Netscape actually believes you need a reminder that information is being sent to the Internet —not after you have just used your browser to fill out a form and have clicked on a **Send** button.

Secure Connections

When electronic commerce started on the Internet in the mid-1990s, the Web was still new, and many people were reluctant to use it for sending personal information, such as credit card numbers. This, of course, was an obstacle to business on the Net, and a number of companies, realizing that a lot of money was at stake, decided to do something about it.

Their goal was to make people feel comfortable about online transactions. To do so, they popularized the idea that what was holding back commerce on the Net was the lack of a completely secure means of data transmission. So, having invented a nonexistent problem, they proceeded to create a solution: a way to encrypt (scramble) data as it is sent over the Web. At the other end, the remote Web site that receives the data automatically decrypts it. When data is transmitted in this way, we say that it is sent over a SECURE CONNECTION.

Once secure connections were available, the Internet industry announced that electronic commerce was now "safe". As long as data is encrypted, they declared, you have nothing to worry about, because even if some bad guys do intercept a data transmission, they will not be able to read it.

Actually, as I explained earlier in the chapter, there is nothing inherently insecure about sending information over the Net, and, in real life, secure connections are never necessary. What you need to worry about is *what* you send and to *whom* you are sending it, not the safety of the actual transmission.

The reason I mention all this is because your browser has a lot of unnecessary security features. I won't go into them in detail, but I do want to mention them so you won't waste time worrying about silly ideas. Moreover, I do not want you to get a false sense of security. A secure connection will not protect you if you send valuable information to dishonest people.

There are a number of systems and protocols used on the Web to provide secure connections. The most common protocol is SSL which stands for Secure Sockets Layer. (A "sockets layer" is a facility used by programs to pass data back and forth.)

On occasion, you may see Web pages whose URLs begin with `https` (as opposed to `http`). The extra letter, `s`, indicates that the page uses a

hint

Technology, no matter how sophisticated, is not a substitute for common sense.

secure connection to transmit data. However, if you would like to know when you are using a secure connection, there is an easier way to tell. Just look on the status bar (the bottom line of your browser window).

Within Internet Explorer, a secure connection is indicated by a small picture of a locked padlock on the right half of the status bar. When you don't see a padlock (most of the time), it indicates a normal connection.

Cookies

As you wander around the Web, have you ever asked yourself, "Can a remote Web server track what I am doing?" The answer is, yes it can, to a limited extent. Such tracking is done by using what are called cookies.

A COOKIE is data sent by a remote Web server and stored in a file on your computer by your browser. At any time, a Web server (either the same one or a different one) can request a particular cookie, at which time the browser will look in the file, get the cookie and send it to the server. In other words, cookies are a way for any Web server in the world to store information on *your* computer for later retrieval.

What's in a Name?

cookie

The term "cookie" dates back to systems that are much older than Windows. In technical terms, a cookie is a small token of data that is passed between two programs in order to relate the current transaction to a later one. Consider the following analogy.

In many parking lots, you get a ticket as you enter, and on the ticket is the time and date. Later, when you leave the lot, you give the ticket to an attendant, who uses the information to tell you how much you need to pay. The parking lot ticket is a cookie.

Nobody knows the exact origin of the word "cookie", but clearly, it reflects a spirit of whimsy —neatly capturing the idea of a small object that is passed from one program to another. In the Unix operating system, cookies are often referred to as "magic cookies", and it is from Unix that the word "cookie" was appropriated for use on the Web.

In principle, cookies can be used to store just about any type of textual data. In practice, they are usually used to track your identity, your preferences, and your actions as you navigate the Web.

Obviously, this is a gross invasion of your privacy. Why, you might ask, would the browser companies build a cookie facility into their products? The answer to this question lies in understanding who are Microsoft's and Netscape's real customers. You and I are not their customers. We got our browsers for free, and no one makes money giving away free software. The real customers are the companies that pay for the server software and the programming tools used to build commercial Web sites. These companies want a way to track what you do on the Web, and that's why Microsoft and Netscape put a cookie facility into their browsers.

This is not to say that cookies are always bad. They are often used to keep track of information in a way that makes your life a bit easier. For example, there is a movie information site I sometimes use to find the names and times of movies playing in my town. The first time I used this Web site, I entered my zip code, which the Web server stored as a cookie on my computer. Now, each time I visit the site, the server retrieves my zip code (from my computer), and shows me information about the movies in my area.

Here is another example. Say you visit an online shopping site in which you move from one Web page to another, putting various items into your "shopping basket". When you are ready to "check out", the Web server sends you an order form containing a list of all the items you have chosen to buy. How does the server keep track of what you want? By storing cookies on your computer.

In such cases, cookies serve the legitimate needs of commerce. All too often, however, cookies are used to track your movements and your decisions as you use the Web. For example, many companies program their Web servers to store cookies on your computer documenting what you did when you visited their site. Later, as you visit various Web pages, those cookies are retrieved by servers that run sophisticated programs. These programs can control what you see, based on your previous movements. The programs also accumulate statistics and other information which is used for commercial purposes.

Similarly, a marketing company can put up attractive advertisements around the Web in order to induce you to click on them. Once you do, the server to which you connect might show you various types of information in order to gather data about your preferences and habits. This data can be stored on *your* computer, to be picked up later by the Web site of any company that subscribes to that particular marketing service.

So what can you do about cookies? You have several choices:

- You can look upon cookies as a necessary evil and forget about them.

- You can change certain settings in your browser. With Internet Explorer version 6, you get a lot of control over cookies. If you care about cookies, this is the browser for you. With older versions of Internet Explorer, you get a lot less control.

- You can use a special program to give you control over cookies. Some of the ad blocking programs I mentioned in Chapter 7 will block cookies as well as advertisements. As I write this, my ad blocking program has blocked 111,689 cookies and 98,923 ads for me in the last 48 days. (I use my computer a lot.)

Try the different choices, and see what you prefer —you can't harm anything by experimenting. If you want, you can look at your cookies, or even delete them.

Learn how to...

Control and Delete Cookies

If you want some control over how your browser handles cookies, there are various settings you can control.

See Chapter 17, *How to Do Stuff*, page 372 (Internet Explorer).

Internet Resources   **Programs that Control Cookies**

```
http://www.adsubtract.com/
http://www.cookiecentral.com/
http://www.kburra.com/cpal.html
http://www.webroot.com/washie.htm
http://www.thelimitsoft.com/cookie.html
http://www.webveil.com/cookietools.html
```

Java and ActiveX

Earlier in the chapter, I said there are two types of situations in which you might encounter a security problem:

- When data is going out of your computer

- When data is coming into your computer

We have already discussed what can happen when data leaves your computer. I would now like to talk about the possible risks of data from the outside world entering your computer and causing a problem.

The term "data" is a general one. It encompasses anything that can be stored on a computer. However, it is important to realize that the only type of data that can damage your computer is data that actively does something (such as a program). Data that just sits there (such as text or pictures) can't hurt you.

A program running amuck on your computer can cause a lot of damage. Such a program might freeze the entire system, modify important settings, or delete a lot of files. A cookie file, on the other hand, might contain information that invades your privacy, but the file itself won't damage your computer. Only a program that is running can damage your computer.

So, when we look at risks from the outside world, we have to ask the question: Is it possible for a program to enter your computer without your knowledge, and to start running automatically? If so, such a program poses a possible security risk.

Before I can answer this question, I need to digress for a moment and talk about two systems, called Java and ActiveX.

The Web was originally developed as a system to display various types of information. Information is sent from a Web server to your browser. The browser receives the information, and does whatever is necessary to process it for you.

Some years ago, programmers realized that the power of the Web could be increased significantly if Web servers could send more than information to be displayed. If there were a way for a Web server to send a program that would be run on your computer automatically, such a facility could open the door to a lot of cool and useful stuff.

Of course, a system that downloads programs from the Net and starts them running on your computer also opens the door to a massive amount of potential problems. For example, imagine you are using the Web, and you see an advertisement for free money. You click on the ad, and it takes you to a Web site where the server automatically sends a program to your computer that wipes out all the files on your hard disk.

Such catastrophes do not necessarily need to be the work of an evil mind. Even a legitimate program can have a bug that causes damage accidentally. The point is, if you are going to design a system in which programs can be run automatically on someone else's computer, you have to be very careful.

The programmers who wanted to develop such systems were well aware of these considerations. The first such system, JAVA, was developed by

Sun Microsystems. From the very beginning, Java was designed with safeguards. (By the way, the name Java doesn't mean anything in particular.)

Java was based on a system that Sun had originally designed for controlling consumer electronic devices such as microwave ovens and telephones. The basic idea is to create small programs, called APPLETS, that are embedded within a larger system. (On the Web, Java applets are embedded within Web pages.) To maintain security, applets can only run within a special operating environment. This environment —called the JAVA VIRTUAL MACHINE —is provided by your browser. The Java system is designed very carefully to ensure that no applet can ever cause a problem on your computer, either on purpose or by accident. Moreover, Java is portable, so that an applet created for one type of computer (say, a PC) can run on another type of computer (such as a Macintosh).

The design of Java draws a clear line between your computer and the outside world. There is a basic assumption that programs that arrive from the outside world cannot be trusted. Thus, they are only allowed to run in a restricted environment (the Java virtual machine) that sets limits on what the program may do.

At Microsoft, they have a different philosophy. Microsoft (and especially Bill Gates) feels that there should not be a well-defined line between your computer and the rest of the world. You should be able to look at data and programs anywhere, and use them without caring where they are. Within this vision, a program that resides on a computer down the hall, or on the other side of the world, should be as accessible as a program on your own computer.

Thus, when Microsoft wanted their own Web-based facility to download and run programs automatically, they developed two completely different solutions.

First, they licensed Java from Sun Microsystems and created a Java system of their own. Thus, Internet Explorer (as well as Netscape) will run Java applets.

Second, they created a brand new system called ACTIVEX. ActiveX is based on Microsoft's family of programming tools, and is promoted as a richer, more powerful alternative to Java.

Unlike Java, ActiveX programs (which aren't really applets) are not constrained to run within a restricted environment. Thus, they have no limitations and, as such, are the cornerstone of Microsoft's vision that there is no real line between your computer and the outside world. Of course, having no limitations also means that it is possible for an ActiveX program to cause damage to your computer.

Obviously, there is a security problem here. If you can't guarantee that a program is safe, how can you feel comfortable running it on your computer? The answer is, you can't, so there is a clear tradeoff:

- Java keeps its programs safe, but by doing so, limits their usefulness.

- ActiveX is not safe, but it allows more powerful and more useful programs.

So what did Microsoft do about this? After all, customers —especially corporate customers —are uneasy knowing that every time a person clicks on a link, he might be downloading and running a potentially damaging program.

To reconcile all these considerations, Microsoft created a system of security settings within Internet Explorer that gives you the *illusion* of safety without limiting the power of ActiveX. To me, this is a remarkable achievement —a triumph of marketing and double-talk over rational thought.

Are you intrigued? Read on.

Security Settings in Your Browser

One day, a total stranger walks over to where you are sitting, hands you a cup containing an unknown liquid, and says, "Drink this." He then walks away. Would you drink the liquid or would you be too suspicious?

Suppose your mother were to offer you a similar-looking drink. Would you be more likely to try it?

As far as Microsoft is concerned, the answer is yes, because you trust your mother more than you trust a total stranger. This is the idea behind the Internet Explorer security settings.

As I explained in the previous section, Java applets are inherently safe, but limited in what they can do for you. ActiveX programs can be much more powerful, but pose a definite security risk. ActiveX, however, is Microsoft's first choice, so to deal with the uncertainty, they have devised a complex scheme that is implemented within Internet Explorer by a system of security settings.

There is no way to guarantee that any particular ActiveX program is safe. However, you can ask yourself, "Who created the program, and do I trust that person or organization?" For example, if an ActiveX program comes from the Web site of an unknown college student, you might think twice before allowing the program to run on your computer. On the other hand, if a program comes from, say, Microsoft's Web site, you would feel more comfortable about letting the program run on your computer. At least, that's the theory.

To put this theory into practice, Internet Explorer requires you to classify all Web sites as being in one of four different categories, called ZONES. You can then assign a particular SECURITY LEVEL to each zone. Whenever you visit a Web site, Internet Explorer checks to see what zone it is in. Then, based on what security level you have assigned to that zone, the browser knows what to do if the Web site sends an ActiveX program to your computer.

The details, as you might imagine, are appalling, and the whole system is pretty much useless. However, as I said earlier, the system does give the *illusion* of safety, which is not to be sneezed at. In real life, very few programs on the Web actually cause trouble, and realistically, there isn't all that much to worry about. As such, there is a lot to be said for making people feel more secure.

In case you want to investigate the Internet Explorer security system for yourself, I'll give you a quick summary, and then tell where to find the actual settings.

The four different zones are as follows:

- **Internet Zone**: All the Web sites that are not part of another zone.

- **Local Intranet Zone**: This zone contains all the Web sites within your organization's internal network (which doesn't mean much unless you have an organization with an internal network).

- **Trusted Sites Zone**: This zone contains all the Web sites you believe will *not* cause damage to your computer.

- **Restricted Sites Zone:** All the Web sites you believe *might* cause damage to your computer.

Your job is to assign a specific security level to each zone. You have several choices:

- **High Security:** Never do anything that could potentially cause trouble.

- **Medium Security:** Warn the user and ask for permission before doing anything that could potentially cause trouble.

- **Medium-low Security** (Internet Explorer version 6): Allow a few actions that could cause trouble but are highly unlikely to do so.

- **Low Security:** No warnings, no protection. (Just do it!)

- **Custom Security:** A customized security level, based on selections you make from a large list of confusing choices.

Of course, all of this begs the question, how do you know whether or not a Web site has the potential to cause a problem? Microsoft's solution is to recommend that Web sites use a SECURITY CERTIFICATE, an electronic confirmation that a particular Web site is "secure and genuine".

For example, let's say you are willing to put a particular IBM Web site into your trusted sites zone, as long as you are sure that the site really does belong to IBM. The way IBM convinces you the site is really theirs (and hence, can be trusted) is by obtaining a security certificate for that site. Whenever you go to the site, the IBM Web server sends your browser the security certificate, which your browser can verify automatically.

Are you confused? So is everyone else. My advice is to ignore the whole thing and hope for the best. The chances of your ever running into a damaging ActiveX program are very low. In fact, I have never met anyone who has had trouble —it's mostly a psychological problem.

If you are curious, and you would like to look at the Internet Explorer security settings:

1. Pull down the **Tools** menu and select **Internet Options**.
2. Click on the **Security** tab.

hint

When I was in medical school, I had a good friend named Tim Rutledge who once made a philosophical observation I will never forget. The reason I mention it here is that Tim's comment is the very best advice I can give you about the Internet Explorer security settings:

"When you get serious about bullshit, you're getting into serious bullshit."

—Tim Rutledge

Computer Viruses

You have probably heard about computer viruses, but you may not understand exactly what they are. Is a computer virus like a real virus? Computers don't really get sick —or do they?

The answer is, a computer virus is not a real virus. The idea is a metaphor. A computer VIRUS is a small program that is designed to insert itself into a file containing another program. When the second program runs, the virus becomes active. Depending on how the virus is designed, it may or may not cause a problem. Thus, computer viruses are *not* biological organisms. They are small, carefully crafted programs deliberately designed by bad people to do bad things.

Your computer cannot be "infected" by a virus, the way you and I can catch a cold. The only way you can get a virus on your computer is to run a program that already contains the virus. Now, the Internet is the largest repository of software in the world. (See Chapter 9.) It is natural to wonder whether or not it is dangerous to download software from the Net.

The answer is no. There is virtually no chance that you will encounter a virus by downloading software. Personally, I have downloaded more software than I can remember, and I have never even seen a virus.

The reason that downloading is safe is because the people who run software repositories scan programs for viruses before making the programs available to the general public.

There are only two situations in which you need to be concerned about viruses: when you use a floppy disk to copy programs from another computer, and when you open email attachments. Let's deal with each one in turn.

If you copy a program from someone else's computer to your own, that program might have a virus. This can happen when you use a floppy disk that was in a public computer, such as the ones you find in a library or in a school. Because so many people bring their own disks to use with public machines, it sometimes happens that such computers have a program containing a virus.

Here is an example. Your son is working at school and he finds a program he wants to use at home. So he puts a floppy disk into the school computer, and copies the program to the disk. Later, your son brings home

hint

To prevent a virus from spreading to your computer:

- Never use a floppy disk to transfer a program from someone else's computer.
- Never allow your children to bring home floppy disks from school.

the disk, and copies the program to your home computer. Unfortunately, if the program had a virus, it has now spread to your computer.

The easiest way to avoid this problem is to make a rule that no one is allowed to put a floppy disk in your computer, if the disk has ever been in a computer that is outside your control.

Email Attachments and Viruses

As I explained in the previous section, a virus will only become active when you run a program in which the virus is embedded. Is it possible for a virus to get to your machine via an email message? The answer is, yes, it is possible, but only if someone mails you an attachment that contains a program *and* you run that program.

An attachment is a file that is sent along with an email message (see Chapter 5). To access an attachment, you must open it.

In Chapter 9, we discussed what happens when Windows "opens" a file. There are two possibilities. First, if the file contains data, Windows will start a program that knows how to deal with that type of data. For example, if you open an attachment that contains a picture, Windows will start a program to display the picture for you. If you open an attachment that contains a word processing document, Windows will start your word processor.

The second possibility is that the file contains a program. In that case, Windows will run the program, and herein lies the problem. Most of the viruses on the Net are embedded in programs that are passed, as attachments, from one person to another. A typical scenario is that someone receives a message from a friend. The message contains an attachment and, without thinking, the person clicks on the attachment, which tells Windows to open it. Windows then starts running the program, and the virus becomes active.

How can this happen? There are two main reasons.

First, the malevolent people who write email viruses disguise them to look safe. (I'll give you an example in a moment.) Unless you know what to look for, it is easy to be fooled into opening an unsafe attachment. When you do, you activate the virus.

Second, there is a serious security flaw in the way Microsoft has designed its email programs, Outlook and Outlook Express. This security flaw allows a virus to email a copy of itself to everyone in your address book. This means that everyone whose address is in your address book will get a message that looks as if it came from you and, within the message, will be an attachment containing a copy of the virus.

When this happens, the virus does its work silently. You won't even know what happened until you start to get complaints from your friends. Fortunately, this can't happen unless you use Outlook or Outlook Express. However, since these mail programs are widely used, the problem is a significant one.

How to Guard Against Email Viruses

How do you guard against email viruses? It's easy; all you have to do is make sure that you never open an attachment that contains a program. Unless you are 100 percent sure that an attachment is safe, don't click on it. Just delete it.

At attachment is just a file. As we discussed in Chapter 9, you can tell what is contained in a file by looking at its name. In particular, you need to look at the last part of the name, called the extension.

For example, let's say someone sends you a file named `cat.jpg`. In this case, the extension is `jpg`, which indicates that the file contains a picture in JPEG format. This file is safe to open.

However, let's say you get another file named `freestuff.exe`. In this case, the extension is `exe`, which indicates that the file contains a program. This file is *not* safe to open.

So how can you tell whether or not an attachment is safe to open? Easy, just look at the file name and determine the extension by checking with the lists in Figure 12-2 and 12-3. The extensions listed in Figure 12-2 indicate that the file contains some type of program. These files are not safe to open.

Unless you are sure that the attachment is safe to open, delete it. That's all you have to do, and you will never have problems with an email virus.

hint

If a message containing an attachment comes from someone you trust, can you assume that the attachment is safe to open?

No. It may be that the message was sent by a virus running on your friend's computer.

Figure 12-2: File extensions of attachments that are unsafe to open

Extension	Meaning
bat	Batch file
chm	Compiled HTML file
com	Program
eml	Outlook Express mail message
exe	Program
htm	HTML file
html	HTML file
js	JScript program
jse	Encoded JScript program
lnk	Windows shortcut [link]
nws	Outlook Express news message
pif	Program information file
vbs	VBScript program
vbe	Encoded VBScript program
wsf	Windows Script File program
wsh	Windows Scripting Host Settings File

Figure 12-3: File extensions of attachments that are safe to open

Extension	Meaning
gif	Picture in gif format
jpg	Picture in jpg format
mp3	Music
txt	Plain text
wav	Sound

There is one trick virus programmers use of which you should be aware. They try to disguise the file extension of the virus file in order to fool you.

Suppose you receive an attachment with the name:

`sexpicture.vbs`

You would know not to open it because the file extension is **vbs**, which indicates a type of program. However, what if you receive a file named:

`sexpicture.jpg.vbs`

You must look carefully. Ignore the fact that this looks like a `jpg` file. It isn't. It's really a `vbs` file. A file can only have one extension. In this case, the `jpg` is thrown in to be misleading.

The problem is that, in some cases, your mail program may not show you the full file name. It may omit the extension, thinking it is doing you a favor. If this happens, all you will see is:

`sexpicture.jpg`

You will then think that the attachment is safe, when it isn't. Fortunately, this only happens with Microsoft mail programs. To keep this from happening, you must tell Windows that, at all times, you want to see full file names. You do so by setting an option in Windows Explorer. Take a moment and do it right now.

1. Start Windows Explorer. (Click on the **Start** button. Select **Programs**, and then click on Windows Explorer.)

2. Pull down the **View** menu and select **Folder Options**. (With some versions of Windows, you pull down the **Tools** menu and select **Folder Options**.)

3. Click on the **View** tab.

4. In the **Advanced settings** area, look in the **Files and Folders** section. Look for the option **Hide file extensions for known file types**. Make sure this option is turned *off*.

5. Click on the **OK** button to close the window.

6. Close Windows Explorer.

Protecting Against Email Viruses with Outlook Express

If you have Outlook Express version 6 (it comes free with Internet Explorer version 6), there are some settings you can use that go a long way toward protecting your system against email viruses.

Here is how to use them:

1. Start Outlook Express.

2. Pull down the **Tools** menu and select **Options**.

3. Click on the **Security** tab.

4. Under **Virus Protection**, make sure that the following two options are turned *on*:

- **Warn me when other applications try to send mail as me.**

- **Do not allow attachments to be saved or opened that could potentially be a virus.**

5. Click on the **OK** button.

Antivirus Programs

To help detect and protect against viruses, there are a variety of ANTIVIRUS PROGRAMS available. Such programs will scan all the files on your hard disk, looking for telltale signs of known viruses. Antivirus programs may also run in the background, continuously checking for viruses as you work.

Do you need an antivirus program? Under certain circumstances, the answer is yes:

- If your computer is on a network that you do not control, say, at work.

- If people can access your computer and you cannot guarantee that they will follow the rules we have discussed in this chapter.

- If you are running some type of server, such as a Web server or mail server.

In general, if you have a computer at home, or at a small office without a network, you do not need an antivirus program. I know that you have probably heard a lot about viruses. I also know that many people say that, to be safe, you need to have an antivirus program. This is not true. As long as you follow the guidelines I have outlined in this chapter, you will be okay.

But why not use an antivirus program anyway? The answer is that antivirus programs are not completely benign. Because they are so intrusive, they can slow down your system, and they can cause other programs to fail in mysterious ways.

When you use an antivirus program, you must keep it up to date, and updates cost money. (That is how antivirus companies make money.)

Here is the whole thing in a nutshell. If you use an antivirus program, you won't be absolutely safe unless you follow the rules we have discussed. But if you follow the rules, you don't need an antivirus program.

In case you do need an antivirus program — for example, if you can't keep your kids from bringing home floppy disks from school — here are some resources to help you.

Internet Resources   **Antivirus Programs**

```
http://cws.internet.com/virus.html
http://www.davecentral.com/virus.html
http://networkone.tucows.com/system/virus95.html
```

Macro Viruses

Some programs, such as word processors, have a facility called MACROS. A macro is a list of instructions that you create in order to automate a specific task. Once you create a macro, you can attach it to a document.

It is possible to make a macro that, if attached to a document, will act like a virus when that document is opened by a program. Sometimes, such MACRO VIRUSES are attached to files that are then shared among a number of people. Thus, if someone sends you a word processing file by mail, it behooves you not to run any macros that may be attached to the file.

If you use Microsoft Word or Excel (a spreadsheet program that also offers macros), there is an option you can set to help guard against macro viruses. With Word 97 or Excel 97:

1. Pull down the **Tools** menu and select **Options**.
2. Click on the **General** tab.
3. Make sure **Macro Virus Protection** is turned on. If not, click on it.
4. Click on the **OK** button.

With Word 2000 or Excel 2000:

1. Pull down the **Tools** menu and select **Options**.
2. Click on the **General** tab.

hint

To protect yourself against viruses, all you have to do is follow these three precautions:

- Delete all email attachments except those with a file extension of `gif`, `jpg`, `mp3`, `txt` or `wav`.
- Never use a program that has been on someone else's computer.
- Never put a floppy disk into your computer if it has been in another computer.

3. Make sure **Macro Virus Protection** is turned on. If not, click on it.

4. Click on the **OK** button.

Once you set this option, the program will warn you whenever you open a file that might contain a macro virus. You can then choose to disable the macros attached to that file. As long as you always disable such macros, you will never have a problem with macro viruses. Thus, the only way to have trouble is to open a document that has a macro virus and then choose not to disable the macros.

Since macros run within a specialized environment (such as a word processing program), macro viruses are not as harmful as regular viruses. Still, a macro virus can be troublesome if you get one. This might happen if you work with people who mail you documents that contain macros that you do not want to disable.

If you work in such an environment, you may want to get an antivirus program that is capable of checking for macro viruses. Such a program will scan every document as you open it and tell you if it contains a macro virus. If so, the antivirus program will neutralize the virus. This allows you to use macros sent to you by other people.

For most people, macro viruses are not a problem. Just set the option I mentioned above, and make sure you disable any macros that come from an outside source.

Virus Hoaxes

Far more troublesome than actual viruses are virus hoaxes. Information spreads rapidly on the Internet, and rumors and myths spread fastest of all. A VIRUS HOAX is an erroneous belief that a particular virus (which may or may not exist) is a potential source of trouble. Virus hoaxes spread by mail and on Usenet discussion groups when well-meaning people warn other people about nonexistent problems.

If you ever receive such a message, couched in terms of breathless panic and warning you of an impending virus, I can tell you right now the message is wrong. Perhaps it is human nature, but many people are all too eager to believe that forces beyond their control (such as computer viruses) are lurking nearby, ready to swoop down and cause a catastrophe. Unfortunately, too many people are willing to accept such a warning, no matter how unfounded it may be, simply because they don't understand the details.

One of the most common types of virus hoaxes purports to describe a deadly email virus. Such a hoax comes in the form of a message warning you not to read messages with specific words in the subject line. The warning declares that even the mere act of opening such a message may trigger a virus that will damage your computer. The virus hoax spreads because well-meaning people, who don't know any better, send copies of the warning to all their friends, thus perpetuating the hoax.

In real life, virus hoaxes are far more common (and far more disconcerting) than actual viruses. In fact, some people feel that the real viruses are the hoaxes themselves.

If you ever do receive a virus warning via email, take a moment and check with the Web sites mentioned below. It may be that the virus is real, in which case you can share the information with your friends. Most likely, however, the warning will be a hoax. For this reason, *do not forward any type of virus warning to anyone until you have checked it out.*

hint

The only way to activate a virus on your computer is by running a program in which the virus is embedded.

It is impossible to activate a virus by reading a mail message, as long as you never open an attachment that contains a program.

Internet Resources   **Virus Hoaxes and Myths**

```
http://www.vmyths.com/
http://hoaxbusters.ciac.org/
http://www.sophos.com/virusinfo/hoaxes/
http://www.icsalabs.com/html/communities/antivirus/ hoaxes.shtml
```

Spyware

Spyware refers to a program that runs on your computer, without your knowledge, and secretly uses your Internet connection. How does spyware get on your system? A number of programs — in particular, some freeware and shareware programs — secretly put a spyware program on your computer as part of their installation process. Of course, the companies that offer these programs don't tell you that, when you install them, you will be getting an unexpected visitor.

The purpose of the spyware is to monitor what you are doing and to send information about your computer and your activities to a remote computer. In most cases, this information is used for marketing purposes.

However, spyware is not always benign. Some spyware programs will actually make changes in your system.

To make things worse, in many cases, when you uninstall the original program, the spyware still stays on your system! If you think about it, you can see that, in many ways, spyware is like a virus. The main difference is that spyware does not spread by itself.

How do you detect spyware? Easy. Just use one of these free anti-spyware programs."

Internet Resources   **Anti-spyware Programs**

```
http://www.spychecker.com/

http://www.grc.com/optout.htm

http://www.alphalink.com.au/~johnf/dspypdf.html

http://www.camtech2000.net/pages/spychaser.html

http://www.infoforce.qc.ca/spyware/enknownlistfrm.html
```

Children and the Internet

There is an interesting paradox with respect to how we think about children. On the one hand, we know children need supervision and guidance. No matter how grown up they may act, they are not adults. On the other hand, we sometimes treat children as if they are fragile, worrying about them more than we need to.

There is an irony here, because we were all children ourselves at one time. Think back, and I bet you can remember how silly the adults seemed when they worried so much about things that were perfectly harmless. However, as we grow up, our memories fade, and one day we find ourselves having the same types of worries as our parents. Of course, now it is different, because these are *our* children.

So how should you think about the Internet when it comes to your children? Different children have different needs, and you have to do what you think is appropriate. My intention is to give you a few guidelines to consider and then talk a bit about the nature of the Internet, so you can figure out what's best for you and your kids.

In general, the Internet is a safe place. After all, when your kids use the Net, they are indoors, not wandering around the outside world. Because of the nature of the Net, you do need to show your children how to evaluate information and how to maintain their privacy. However, you do not need to worry about physical danger.

But what about those stories you read in the newspaper? Isn't it true that there was a kid who met an adult on the Internet, who then lured the kid to a real-life meeting in which something bad happened?

Perhaps somewhere in the world, at some time, something like this actually happened, but let me assure you that it's not going to happen to your kids. Millions of children around the world use the Internet every day in perfect safety. The scary stories you see in the newspaper are exaggerated and *extremely rare*.

Actually, what your kids already know about talking to strangers is most of what they need to know about the Internet. Tell them there are certain things they should not talk about (make up your own list) and certain types of people they should avoid.

Just as important, help your children understand that they must protect their privacy. Young children should know they cannot give out a mail address, phone number or street address without asking you first. Some parents do not let their kids fill out any form that requests information until they have shown it to a parent. For example, you may not want your children to fill out surveys that ask for marketing information about your family. Similarly, you might make a rule that your children are not allowed to download any files or programs without your permission.

Explain to your children that the Internet is a place where you really don't know whom you are talking to unless you already know the person in real life. For example, just because someone in a Web chat room says she is a 15-year-old girl, it doesn't mean she really is a 15-year-old girl. It is common, and perfectly acceptable, for people to use an alias (pretend name) when they talk to people on the Net.

What really helps is to find time to explore the Internet *with* your kids. As you use the Net, explain to them that they can't believe something just because they see it on the computer. Young children especially may not understand that anyone can create a Web site with whatever content they want.

Show your children that you expect them to make active judgments about the quality of the information they see. Teach them how to decide whether or not to believe what they read. At the same time, you may also want to talk to them about the massive amount of advertising they are going to encounter, and how they should think about it. (I strongly suggest you use one of the ad blocking programs I discussed in Chapter 7.)

A great way to help your children is to steer them toward Web sites that are suitable for their age level. There are several ways to do so. First, you can spend some time searching for Web sites you like and build your kids a customized Favorites or Bookmarks list (see Chapter 7). You can also trade URLs (Web addresses) with other parents.

With young children, it is best to start with a Web site that has lots of activities for kids their age. When you let them play on their own, take a look from time to time to make sure they haven't accidentally wandered off track.

Similarly, you can introduce your little ones to electronic mail in a gradual fashion. Have them send mail to friends you know, and read the replies together. As your kids get older, you can give them more freedom. Eventually, you can let them send and receive mail on their own, but they should know that you control the computer, and you have the right to look at any mail whenever you want.

If you would like some ideas about Web sites for your kids, I have a few suggestions. First, take a look at my book *Harley Hahn's Internet Yellow Pages* (published by Osborne McGraw-Hill), where you will find lots of Internet resources. In particular, there are sections for younger children, teenagers, families and parents.

Aside from books, another good way to find Web sites for your kids is on the Internet itself. Here are some places to get you started:

Internet Resources **Collections of Web Sites for Children**

```
http://www.yahooligans.com/
http://www.cochran.com/theodore/beritsbest
http://www.netmom.com/ikyp/samples/hotlist.htm
http://www.ala.org/parentspage/greatsites/amazing.html
```

Harley Hahn's 5 Guidelines for Happy Family Internet Usage

1. Learn about the Internet yourself. In particular, learn how to send and receive mail and how to use the Web.

2. Develop a *realistic* sense of what might hurt your children.

3. Spend some time with your children using the Internet together.

4. As your children get older and more responsible, give them time alone so they can enjoy the Internet by themselves.

5. Set a *few* basic rules to let your children know what you expect from them, and then enforce those rules.

Filtering Software and Rating Systems

The very best guardian for a young child is the eye of a parent. However, you can't be everywhere all the time. For this reason, there are various programs you can buy to restrict your children's use of the Internet. These programs are known as FILTERING SOFTWARE or CENSORWARE, depending on your point of view. (You will also see a lot of other euphemisms, such as "parental control software", "content filters", "blocking software", and so on.)

There are two basic approaches to such programs. Some operate with a list of forbidden sites called a BLACKLIST. The program works with your browser to make sure your child cannot go to any of the Web sites on the blacklist. Other programs use a WHITELIST of approved sites. In this case, the program allows access to only those Web sites that are *on* the list.

Such programs usually have a number of options that can be changed, but only by someone who knows the password (which you set). Thus, you can turn the various features off and on as you see fit.

The big question, of course, is how does a particular Web site get on a blacklist or a whitelist? Usually, these lists are maintained by the companies that sell the filtering programs, and as you might imagine, there is a lot of controversy. Although filtering software seems like a noble idea, in practice, such programs are restrictive and highly arbitrary. In my experience, parents who understand the Net well do not use these programs.

What works best is to tell your children what is acceptable and what is not, and then enforce the rules. With young kids, it is a good idea to use the Net together. With older kids, you can talk about their Internet activities around the dinner table. In this way, you can keep a careful eye on what your kids are doing, while having the same type of sparkling conversation that you already enjoy about their school activities:

Parent: So, what did you learn on the Net today?

Child: Nothing.

Parent: And what did you do?

Child: Nothing.

Parent: Well, who did you talk to?

Child: No one.

(You get the idea.)

Another approach to parental control is to use Web site ratings. The idea is to have many Web sites rated in some manner, and to use a browser that looks at the rating for each Web site before loading it. By changing various settings within the browser, you can control access to Web sites based on their ratings.

Toward this end, a set of standards called PICS has been developed for creating rating systems. (PICS stands for Platform for Internet Content Selection.) Internet Explorer has a built-in facility, known as the CONTENT ADVISOR, that lets you control access to Web sites, based on ratings from any PICS-compliant rating service. To access the content advisor:

1. Pull down the **Tools** menu and select **Internet Options**.
2. Click on the **Content** tab.
3. Under **Content Advisor**, click on the **Enable** button.

For more information about the Web site rating systems, you can check out the following resources:

Internet Resources   **Web Site Rating Systems**

http://www.rsac.org/

http://www.safesurf.com/

http://www.peacefire.org/

However, before you rush into any of this, I want to say a few more words.

The Internet is a public arena used by millions of people all over the world. Some of those people are bad, and some of the ideas on the Net are bad, and it is possible that your children could get hurt in some way by using the Net. However, the chances of anything bad happening are slight, and there is no reason why you can't feel comfortable letting your kids use the Internet.

Filtering software and rating systems may seem like worthwhile ideas, but my advice is to avoid them. Why? With any filtering system, you always have to ask, who is the censor? Who gets to decide for *your* kids what is okay and what is not okay? In my opinion, many (but not all) of the people involved in these schemes are fanatics, who see the world as a scary place and are doing their very best to scare as many other people as they can.

Moreover, filtering software and rating systems are far from foolproof, and using them can give you a false sense of security. In spite of what children may think, they do need our guidance — the child who doesn't need rules has yet to be born. However, it is also true that youngsters are far more resilient than we sometimes realize. (Just remember back to when you were a kid.)

Realistically, there is no such thing as a computer program or a ratings system that is going to protect your children. On the Internet, as in other aspects of life, the children who do best are the children who have the help of the people who love them more than anyone else in the world: their parents.

hint

As your children use the Internet, their safety and security are guaranteed by their behavior, your good judgment, and the innate goodness of the Net itself.

13

Usenet

Usenet is the largest global forum for uncontrolled freedom of expression, with discussion groups covering every topic a human being might care about.

We hear people talk a lot about the Web, but the Web is only *part* of the Internet. There are other parts of the Net I want you to learn how to use, the most important of which is Usenet, the worldwide system of discussion groups.

Usenet is not only a lot older than the Web, it is far more important as a vehicle for communicating with other people. Usenet is where millions of people from many different countries and cultures come together to talk, argue, pose questions, share information and help one another.

The Basic Ideas

In Chapter 2, I discussed the basic ideas related to Usenet. Before we talk about Usenet in detail, let's take a moment to go over those ideas.

USENET is a system of discussion groups. There are thousands of different groups and millions of participants all over the world. Usenet was started in 1979 by two graduate students at Duke University, Jim Ellis and Tom Truscott. Usenet was conceived as a way to send news and announcements between two universities in North Carolina (University of North Carolina and Duke University). Within a short time, however, the system had spread to other schools, and it soon developed into a system of discussion groups.

Because of its origin, Usenet is still referred to as the NEWS (or sometimes, NETNEWS), even though it is not a news service. Similarly, the discussion groups are referred to as NEWSGROUPS.

Like other Internet services, Usenet uses a client/server system. To access the newsgroups, you need a Usenet client program called a NEWSREADER. (A newsreader enables you to access Usenet in the same way that a browser allows you to access the Web.)

Usenet works as follows. People send messages, called ARTICLES or POSTINGS, to the various newsgroups. (When you send an article, we say that you POST it.) Most articles consist of text, but some also have pictures. The articles are propagated around the world (I'll explain how later) and stored on special servers called NEWS SERVERS. To look at the articles within a particular newsgroup, you use your newsreader to contact a news server. Your newsreader downloads the articles for that newsgroup and shows you a summary. You choose whichever articles you want to read, and your newsreader displays them for you.

How Does Usenet Work?

Usenet has no central authority, so there is no one to manage the system and no one to make any rules (and even if there were rules, there would be no way to enforce them). Usenet functions well because it is put together in a clever way, and because there is a lot of cooperation among the people who manage the news servers.

How are Usenet articles distributed? There is no central system to broadcast each new article to all the news servers in the world. Instead, each news server connects to other news servers at regular intervals. When the servers connect, they pass articles back and forth.

For example, let's say you compose an article for a particular newsgroup. When the article is finished, your newsreader will send it to your news server. Some time later, from a few minutes to a few hours, your news server will connect to another news server. At that time, your server will send a copy of your article to the other server. At the same time, the other server will pass on articles to your server. Eventually, the other server will connect to a third server and send it a copy of your article. Most news servers connect to only one or two other computers. But some news servers act as switching points by connecting to many other servers. When your article hits one of these major servers, it will fan out quickly to many different locations.

In this way, new articles are passed from one server to another, until they are propagated around the world. (Each article has a unique identification number so a server doesn't get more than one copy of the same article.) The system is designed so well that — although there is no central server and no one in charge — a new article will be distributed throughout most of the Internet within a day or two (and often much faster).

As you can see, Usenet does not require central management. Instead, each news server is managed by its own organization. In this way, the administration of Usenet is distributed in the same way as the administration of the Internet itself. So, although there is somebody in charge of each particular news server, there is no one in charge of the system as a whole.

Web-Based Discussion Groups

In a moment, we'll start talking about Usenet in detail. Before we do, I want to mention an alternative type of discussion facility: Web-based discussion groups.

Usenet is a vast, well-organized system with millions of participants, long-standing traditions, and thousands of discussion groups. However, it does take time and effort to learn how to use Usenet well. You need to learn how to use a newsreader program, and you need to understand how the system works.

One of the most common questions people ask me is, how does Usenet work? Since Usenet is so complex, there is no short answer to this question. All I can do is tell them to get this book and read this chapter.

There is an alternative to Usenet. There are a great many Web-based discussion groups, sometimes referred to as forums or message boards, that you can use for free. These discussion groups exist on Web sites, so they are easy to access. Instead of using a newsreader, you can simply use your browser.

Compared to Usenet groups, however, Web-based discussion groups, are less permanent, with a much smaller audience and a lot less variety. Moreover, the quality of the discussion is not nearly as good. For serious discussion, Usenet is the way to go.

Still, Web-based discussion groups do provide an easy way to share thoughts, ideas and opinions with other people, without having to spend a lot of time learning how to use new tools. If you'd like to try these types of groups, here are some Web sites to explore.

hint

Starting a Web-based discussion group is a great way to have your own private forum. For example, you could start a discussion group specifically for your family, or for a group of your friends.

Internet Resources **Web-based Discussion Groups**

```
http://www.delphi.com/
http://www.ezboard.com/
http://www.msnbc.com/bbs/
http://messages.yahoo.com/
http://communities.msn.com/
http://www.forumone.com/index/
```

The Usenet Tradition of Freedom

Since Usenet has no central authority and no rules, people who use Usenet have wide latitude as to what they write in their articles, what pictures they choose to send, and, generally, how they behave. Usenet has a long tradition of being completely without censorship. This is important, as Usenet is the largest global forum for uncontrolled freedom of expression, with tens of thousands of discussion groups covering just about every topic a human being might care about.

The reason that the whole system does not degenerate into mindless anarchy is that, over the years, various conventions and traditions have been adopted by the people who participate in Usenet. For the most part, these traditions are followed voluntarily.

If you have never participated in a completely open discussion, it may take you a while to get used to the freedom in Usenet. Since there is total freedom, you are bound to encounter articles — and people — that you find offensive in some way. It may be because a particular article is truly tasteless, or it may be because you are not used to someone from another culture or someone who holds opinions that are extremely different from yours.

Whatever the case, I promise you, there will be times when you will be offended. When this happens, you have only two choices: you can either argue with the offensive person, or you can ignore him. (It doesn't do much good to complain because there is no one to complain to.)

I won't go on and on about what you are supposed to do and what you are not supposed to do. As you gain experience, you will learn from other people and from your own observations (and, as one of my readers, I know you are intelligent, sensitive and considerate). So, to help you get started, I will condense the entire body of Usenet etiquette into two simple rules.

Harley Hahn's Rules for Using Usenet Successfully

1. Be a nice person.
2. Ignore people who do not follow rule #1.

What Newsreader Should You Use?

To use Usenet, you need a newsreader to act as your client, and you need a news server to use as a source of articles. Let's talk about the newsreader first.

Internet Explorer comes with a free newsreader, OUTLOOK EXPRESS. (This is the same program that acts as a mail client; see Chapter 5.) Outlook Express is okay, but if you get serious about Usenet, you should get yourself a better newsreader. There are a variety of such programs you can download for free. (For a discussion on how to download and install programs, see Chapter 9.)

As you will see in this chapter, Usenet involves a lot of details. Moreover, newsreaders have a large number of options and features. As a result, newsreader programs are complex, and take more time to master than browsers and mail programs. My goal in this chapter is to teach you the basic ideas you need to understand Usenet. Then I want you to find a newsreader you like and learn how to use it well.

If you are not sure which newsreader to use, start with the one that comes with your browser. To begin, read through the built-in help information, then start practicing. Once you have some experience using Usenet, move on to another newsreader. Each newsreader has its own quirks, so you may have to experiment to find the one you like best.

There is an alternative to using a newsreader that you may want to try. A number of Web sites offer a free service (supported by advertising) that allows you to read the News with your browser. That is, the various newsgroups and their articles are made available as ordinary Web pages. These Web-based Usenet services are handy and easy to use. However, in the long run, you will be better off using a newsreader of your own to connect to a real news server.

Once you learn how to use a newsreader, you will have a lot more flexibility and power than a Web site can give you. Moreover, you will find that accessing Usenet with your own client program is faster than reading articles over the Web, and you won't have to look at advertising. Finally, some (but not all) of the Web-based Usenet services will only show you text, not pictures. This is a major disadvantage if you like to look at pictures. (See the discussion on pictures later in the chapter.)

Internet Resources **Usenet Newsreaders**

```
http://www.tin.org/
http://xnews.3dnews.net/
http://www.usenetopia.com/
http://cws.internet.com/news.html
http://www.microplanet.com/gravity/
http://www.pure-mac.com/usenet.html
```

News Servers

In order to use Usenet, you must arrange to have access to a news server for two basic reasons. First, a news server acts as a repository for Usenet articles. When you want to read the articles in a particular newsgroup, your newsreader contacts your news server to get the articles. Second, when you post an article, your newsreader sends it to your news server, which distributes it to other servers.

Almost all ISPs (Internet service providers) maintain a news server for the benefit of their users. When you register with an ISP (see Chapter 3), they will tell you the hostname of the computer that acts as their news server. (If they don't, be sure to ask.) Typically, the hostname will start with the word **news**. For instance, the news server for the Undependable Internet Company might be **news.undependable.com**.

The protocol (see Chapter 1) used to distribute news articles is called NNTP (Network News Transfer Protocol). For this reason, news servers are sometimes called NNTP SERVERS. You will also see the term NEWSFEED used to describe the service offered by a news server. For example, a friend who is looking for a better news server might ask you, "Where do you get your newsfeed?"

Although most people use the news server supplied by their ISP, there are a number of companies that offer newsfeeds to anybody on the Net. This service costs money, but some people choose to pay a bit extra for several reasons.

First, commercial newsfeeds provide a high-quality service that may be better than the one offered by your ISP. For example, the commercial services carry a very large variety of newsgroups. In addition, they use fast, powerful computers that minimize the time you spend waiting.

Another point has to do with how long articles are kept on a news server. There are so many articles sent over Usenet that it takes a large amount of disk space on a server just to keep the new articles that arrive each day. For this reason, news servers keep each article for a limited time, after which it is deleted automatically. When this happens, we say that the article EXPIRES. The longer a news server keeps its articles, the more there is for you to read.

A commercial news server will devote more disk space to their newsfeed than will most ISPs. A commercial server might keep articles for several weeks before letting them expire, while an ISP might keep articles for only a few days.

Another important point is that, as a general rule, commercial news servers connect to many other news servers and, thus, have better Usenet connections than most ISPs. For this reason, if you use a commercial server, you will have a larger number of newsgroups from which to choose and, within those groups, more articles to read. Moreover, when you post articles of your own, they will propagate throughout the Internet faster than if they were sent via your ISP.

The final issue has to do with spam. As we discussed in Chapter 2, SPAM consists of advertisements and other irrelevant articles that are posted to newsgroups. (Most of the ads, by the way, are for schemes to make money or for pornography.) Spam is a huge problem on Usenet, to the point where it has overwhelmed many existing groups.

There do exist special programs to ferret out and cancel spam before it can propagate too far. There is also software to allow a news server to identify and delete spam automatically as it arrives. Most commercial services and some ISPs use these programs to offer spam-free newsfeeds. If the newsfeed you get from your ISP is full of unwanted advertisements, you may want to subscribe to a commercial newsfeed, just to get rid of the spam.

Internet Resources   **Usenet News Servers (free)**

`http://www.findolin.de/`

`http://www.newzbot.com/`

`http://www.newsservers.net/`

`http://freenews.maxbaud.net/`

`http://newssearch.pilum.net/`

`http://www.netwu.com/newswolf/`

`http://www.arcwebserv.com/jumpsite/usenet.html`

Internet Resources   **Usenet News Servers (commercial)**

`http://www.airnews.net/`

`http://www.altopia.com/`

`http://www.newscene.com/`

`http://www.newsfeeds.com/`

`http://www.supernews.com/`

`http://www.mammothnews.net/`

`http://www.news-service.com/`

`http://www.usenetplanet.com/`

`http://www.usenetserver.com/`

`http://www.triton.net/tritonnews/`

Newsgroups and Hierarchies

How many different Usenet newsgroups are there? There are two answers to this question:

- There are between 30,000 and 60,000 different Usenet newsgroups, depending on who is doing the counting and how they are counting.

- There are only about 8,000 newsgroups you need to care about.

How can this be? I'll explain in a minute, but first we need to talk about hierarchies and newsgroup names.

Usenet was started in 1979 and, for several years, growth (by today's standards) was slow. For example, by the end of 1986, Usenet was carrying an average of 500 articles a day. Today, there are hundreds of new articles posted *every minute*.

hint

Within a newsgroup name, the . (period) character is pronounced "dot". For instance, the name rec.humor is pronounced "rec dot humor".

(Note: In the U.K. and Canada, it is pronounced "rec dot humour".)

Within the first few years, the newsgroups were loosely organized into a few general categories, but it soon became evident that a better system was needed. Such a system was devised and implemented between the summer of 1986 and March of 1987. This system established seven categories, called HIERARCHIES (shown in Figure 13-1), and each newsgroup was placed in a specific hierarchy. Six of the hierarchies had specific descriptions, while a seventh (`misc`) was used for all the groups that did not fit anywhere else.

Figure 13-1: The seven original Usenet hierarchies

Hierarchy	Contents
comp	Computers
misc	Miscellaneous
news	Usenet itself
rec	Recreation, hobbies, arts
sci	Science and technology
soc	Social and cultural issues
talk	Debate, controversial topics

As part of the reorganization of Usenet, a system was adopted for naming newsgroups. This system worked so well that we still use it today. Each newsgroup name consists of two or more parts, separated by a . (period) character. The first part of the name shows the hierarchy in which the group resides. The following parts describe the topic of the group. For example, within the `rec` hierarchy, there is a group named `rec.humor` that is devoted to jokes and humor.

Within the seven hierarchies, a new group could be established only by certain procedures: a discussion followed by a referendum in which anyone who was interested could cast a vote. In 1986, a new hierarchy named `alt` was established to offer more freedom. Within the `alt` hierarchy, anyone could create a new group without a formal vote, and it wasn't long before a variety of new, and often strange, newsgroups sprung up. At the same time, other hierarchies were established to serve various regions, schools and organizations. For example, there was a `can` hierarchy for Canadian newsgroups.

Now, as I mentioned earlier in the chapter, Usenet is controlled at a local level, by the people and organizations that administer the computers that provide the services. Each administrator chooses which newsgroups his or her computer will carry. The mere act of creating a new group in itself does not guarantee that the group will be propagated around the world. In order to become established, a new group must be accepted by a large number of Usenet administrators.

Most Usenet administrators accept all new groups that are established according to the traditional discussion/voting procedure. However, other groups are not accepted as widely, especially where resources (such as disk space) are limited. For this reason, a group in the `rec` hierarchy, for example, will be carried by many more computer systems around the world than will a group in the `alt` hierarchy.

For this reason, the original hierarchies (including **humanities**, which was added in 1995) are called MAINSTREAM HIERARCHIES. All new groups in the mainstream hierarchies are created using a well-established, traditional procedure and, thus, receive the widest distribution. The eight mainstream hierarchies are shown in Figure 13-2.

Throughout the years, hundreds of other hierarchies have been established, most of which have few restrictions on creating new groups. However, only five of these hierarchies (including `alt`) are widely distributed. These are the ALTERNATIVE HIERARCHIES and are shown in Figure 13-2 along with the mainstream hierarchies.

Figure 13-2: Mainstream and alternative Usenet hierarchies

Mainstream	Alternative
comp	alt
humanities	bionet
misc	bit
news	biz
rec	k12
sci	
soc	
talk	

Together, the mainstream and alternative hierarchies comprise the most important part of Usenet, and contain virtually all the newsgroups most people care about. Figure 13-3 shows these hierarchies along with short descriptions. (Note: The `bit` hierarchy carries articles from a system of mailing lists called Bitnet, which we will talk about in Chapter 14.)

Figure 13-3: The most important Usenet hierarchies

Hierarchy	Contents
alt	Wide variety of miscellaneous topics
bionet	Biology
bit	Miscellaneous (from Bitnet mailing lists)
biz	Business, marketing, advertising
comp	Computers
humanities	Literature, fine arts
k12	Kindergarten through high school
misc	Miscellaneous
news	Usenet itself
rec	Recreation, hobbies, arts
sci	Science and technology
soc	Social and cultural issues
talk	Debate, controversial topics

As I mentioned, Usenet has several hundred hierarchies. Most of these, however, were established to serve a particular region of the world (such as a city or country) or a particular organization (such as a university or company). We call these REGIONAL and ORGANIZATIONAL HIERARCHIES, and you can see some examples in Figure 13-4. (For a full list, take a look at the Internet Resources at the end of this section.)

As you might imagine, the regional and organizational hierarchies are less important than the mainstream and alternative hierarchies and are not carried as widely. For the most part, you can ignore them unless you have an interest in a specific region or organization.

Now that you understand the idea of Usenet hierarchies, the system of naming newsgroups should make sense to you. Figure 13-5 shows some examples of typical newsgroup names. (I have chosen one from each of the mainstream and alternative hierarchies.) Notice that each news-group name starts with the name of its hierarchy.

There are literally tens of thousands of newsgroups, with more being created all the time. However, for various reasons, a large number of the newsgroups are not functional. We call these BOGUS groups.

Figure 13-4: Examples of regional and organizational hierarchies

Hierarchy	Description
ba	San Francisco Bay area
ca	California
can	Canada
fr	France, French language
hepnet	High Energy Physics Network
japan	Japan, Japanese language
microsoft	Microsoft
nyc	New York City
ox	Oxford University
ut	University of Toronto

Figure 13-5: Sample Usenet newsgroups

Newsgroup	Description
alt.celebrities	Celebrities
bionet.biology.deepsea	Deep-sea marine biology (moderated)
bit.listserv.travel-1	Travel
biz.marketplace.international	International business, import and export
comp.lang.java.help	Java programming, questions and answers
humanities.classics	Culture of ancient Greece and Rome
k12.news	News for teachers
misc.creativity	Creativity in all human endeavors
news.newusers.questions	Questions and answers for new Usenet users
rec.parks.theme	Theme parks
sci.chem	Chemistry
soc.feminism	Feminism and women's issues
talk.environment	Debate about the environment

The largest number of bogus newsgroups lie within the `alt` hierarchy, where, over the years, many new groups have been created but not widely propagated. For example, a good number of the `alt` groups were started as jokes, often with foolish names. Other bogus newsgroups used to be legitimate, but have outgrown their usefulness, and have since been abandoned or replaced. Still other groups have been deserted because of too much spam that choked out the legitimate discussions. (As I mentioned, spam has hurt Usenet significantly.)

So now let us return to the question I posed at the beginning of this section. How many Usenet newsgroups are there?

If you were to collect a list of every possible newsgroup name, from every hierarchy that ever existed, you would find between 30,000 and 60,000 names (depending on how selective you chose to be). Many of these newsgroups would be bogus, and many more would belong to regional and organizational hierarchies that have only a limited distribution.

Suppose, however, that you started with this huge list, selected only the newsgroups that belonged to the thirteen mainstream and alternative hierarchies, and then eliminated the large number of bogus groups. How many groups would you have left?

The answer is, you would be left with about 8,000 legitimate groups that enjoy a global circulation. I know this because I maintain just such a master list. (I will talk about it later in the chapter.)

In other words, although there may be 30,000 different Usenet newsgroups, realistically, there are only about 8,000 groups you need to care about. However, don't feel deprived. These 8,000 newsgroups encompass a *huge* variety of topics. I can assure you that no matter what you are interested in, people are talking about it on Usenet.

Internet Resources   **List of Organizational and Regional Hierarchies**

`http://www.magma.ca/~leisen/mlnh/mlnhtables.html`

Configuring Your Newsreader

Before you can use your newsreader for the first time, you must configure it by giving it certain information. In particular, you need to specify the name of your news server. (This is the computer from which your newsreader will download articles.) For help in choosing a news server, see the discussion earlier in the chapter.

Your newsreader may also want you to specify your name and email address. This information is put at the beginning of every article you post to Usenet. Such information is important, because when people read your articles, they will want to know who wrote them. Moreover, it is handy to have a mail address, in case people want to send private replies.

Against these needs, however, you must balance two considerations. First, you may want to maintain your privacy by being able to post articles without having people know who you are. You should understand that there are companies that archive every article posted to every newsgroup and store the information in publicly accessible databases. (See the discussion on Usenet search engines in Chapter 11.) Using one of these services, a person could read your article long after it has expired. It is also easy for someone to search for all the articles you have ever posted under your name.

The second consideration also relates to privacy: you may want to avoid getting on the lists of mail addresses used by spammers. (I talk about this problem in detail in Chapter 6.) Spammers use automated programs to scan every Usenet article in every newsgroup looking for new email addresses to add to their lists. This is done continually, and, if you ever post an article to Usenet with your real email address — even once — there is a good chance you will end up on spam lists. Before long, you will start to receive unsolicited advertising in your mailbox, and there will be nothing you can do about it.

So, when you configure your newsreader, you have several choices. You can specify your real name and your real address, and just not worry about the lack of privacy and the spam. Alternatively, you can specify a fake name and address, to protect your privacy. However, this will also make it impossible for the people who read your articles to send you private replies.

A good compromise is to use your real name, but to disguise your mail address. Change it in such a way that a person will know how to use it, but an automated spam program will not. For example, let's say your name is Ben Dover and your mail address is:

`bendover@undependable.com`

You can configure your newsreader to use an address similar to:

`bendover@undependableREMOVE-ME.com`

When a person replies to one of your articles, he will know to delete the characters **REMOVE-ME** from the address. The automated spam programs, however, will be fooled into adding the bogus address to their lists.

Learn how to...

Configure Your Newsreader

If you have not yet configured your newsreader, you must do so before you can use it. You may be prompted to enter the configuration information automatically. If not, you can do it manually.

See Chapter 17, *How to Do Stuff*, page 380 (Outlook Express).

Reading Usenet Articles

As I mentioned earlier in the chapter, newsreader programs are complex, and the details vary widely from one program to another. In this section, I am going to help you get started reading the News. I will explain the basic ideas you need to understand and show you how they work with Outlook Express. If you use a different newsreader, it won't be hard to figure out what to do.

To begin, start your newsreader:

Internet Explorer:

- Pull down the **Tools** menu, select **Mail and News**, and then click on Read News. This will start Outlook Express.

Once your newsreader is configured, you need to tell it which newsgroups you want to look at. Your newsreader will download a list of all the available newsgroups from your news server, so you can see what is available.

Since there are so many newsgroups, the master list is huge, and it would be too much trouble to select your favorite ones each time you want to look at them. Instead, you designate certain groups as being the ones you normally want to read, and your newsreader keeps track of them for you.

When you choose a group in this way, we say you SUBSCRIBE to it. If you get tired of reading a particular group, you can UNSUBSCRIBE. (Actually, the term "subscribe" is a misnomer. All you are really doing is telling your newsreader to remember that you want to read a particular newsgroup.)

Subscribing to a newsgroup is easy:

Outlook Express:

1. Click on the **Newsgroups** button.
2. Choose a group and click on the **Subscribe** button.

You can build up your subscription list to be as long as you want. (To practice, start with some of the newsgroups I listed in Figure 13-5.)

Once you have subscribed to some newsgroups, you are ready to read them. The details are as follows. (Warning: The details may look complicated at first, but once you figure out how it all works, it's easy.)

Click the **OK** button and close the subscription window. Within the main window, you will see the name of your news server. To the left of the name will be a + (plus sign) character. Click on the + character and you will see the list of all your subscribed newsgroups.

To read a group, click on it. Your newsreader will now contact the news server and download a summary of the available articles. To read an article, just click on it in the summary list. Your newsreader will download the article and display it for you.

Within your browser, it is possible to specify a Usenet newsgroup as a URL. Simply type `news:` followed by the name of the newsgroup. For example:

```
news:alt.celebrities
news:rec.parks.theme
```

Whenever your browser encounters such a URL, it passes the name of the newsgroup to your newsreader, which then displays the group. (This is also what happens when you click on a `news:` URL on a Web page.)

Figures 13-6 and 13-7 show what it looks like to read an article with Outlook Express and Messenger, respectively. If you want, you can customize the appearance by changing the size and location of the various windows.

hint

When you are using your browser, the quickest way to display a Usenet group is to enter `news:` followed by the name of the group.

FIGURE 13-6

Reading a Usenet article with Outlook Express (Internet Explorer)

The Format of a Usenet Article

A Usenet article has three parts: a header, a body and an (optional) signature. If this sounds familiar, it is because it is the same format as a mail message. In fact, the description of a Usenet article is pretty much the same as for a mail message. The main difference is that Usenet articles have slightly different headers.

At the beginning of every article is a HEADER consisting of a number of specific HEADER LINES. These header lines contain technical information used by news servers and newsreaders. The most important header lines are as follows. For more information, please see the discussion about header lines in Chapter 5 and Appendix B.

Header Line	Description
From:	Name, mail address of person who posted article
Newsgroups:	Groups to which the message was posted
Subject:	The subject of the article
Date:	The time and date the message was posted
Organization:	The organization from which the article was sent
Lines:	Number of lines in the message (not counting header)

hint

All newsreaders will show you the most important header lines by default. If you want to see the other header lines, you must tell your newsreader to show you more.

With Outlook Express, display the article. Then right-click on the `Subject :` line within the **Subject** box. Choose **Properties** and click on the **Details** tab.

After the header comes the BODY of the article, the main content. Most of the time, the body will be simple text. However, it is possible to use HTML in an article. Articles can also include pictures, similar to the attachments that can be sent along with a mail message. If the body of an article contains a URL, most newsreaders will recognize it as such, and turn it into a link you can click on.

A SIGNATURE is a small amount of personalized information included at the end of an article. Having a signature is optional, though many people use one. A typical signature might contain your name, mail address, and a link to your Web site (if you have one). Here is an example:

```
===================================================
Harley Hahn               http://www.harley.com/
(202) 456-1414            hhahn@little-nipper.com
===================================================
```

To use a signature, you create a small file, called a SIGNATURE FILE, and put whatever you want in it. Then you tell your newsreader that you want to use a signature and give it the location of the file. From then on, every time you post an article, your newsreader will automatically append the contents of your signature file to the end of the article.

Moderated Newsgroups

Usenet has been around for a long time, and throughout the years, people have developed a large number of customs and traditions. Some of these customs have to do with how Usenet is organized and maintained. Other customs involve how people talk, behave and use certain words. The overall effect is to keep Usenet running smoothly, and to allow people to communicate well without face-to-face contact. In the next few sections, I am going to explain a number of important ideas and traditions you will encounter as you start to use Usenet.

In general, Usenet groups are available for everyone to read. However, some newsgroups are MODERATED, which means that posting articles to the group is controlled by a person called the MODERATOR. All articles that are posted to a moderated newsgroup are first sent to the moderator. He or she looks at each article and decides whether or not to send it to the group.

Moderators do not censor. Rather, they discard articles that do not properly belong in the newsgroup. For these reasons, many people prefer moderated groups because the discussion is more focused, and there is no spam.

In most cases, you can't tell if a newsgroup is moderated just by looking at the name. You will have to look at the articles within the group. If you use my master Usenet newsgroup list (discussed later in the chapter), it will tell you if a group is moderated.

FAQs (Frequently Asked Question Lists)

An important Usenet tradition is the FAQ, or frequently asked question list. Over the years, it has been noticed that most newcomers to a newsgroup seem to ask the same questions. In the computer newsgroups, beginners always ask the same computer questions; in the cat-related newsgroups, beginners ask the same cat-related questions; and so on. In general, people on Usenet like to help one another and answer ques-

Learn how to...

Create a Signature

When you post Usenet articles, using a signature allows you to insert a few lines of personalized information at the end of each article.

See Chapter 17, *How to Do Stuff*, page 299 (Outlook Express).

tions, but answering the same questions over and over (for years) gets tiresome.

As a solution, many of the newsgroups have a volunteer who produces a FAQ containing the frequently asked questions along with their answers. Usenet has hundreds of FAQs on a large number of topics. Most FAQs are posted regularly (usually once a month) to the appropriate newsgroup. In addition, there are special newsgroups to which a copy of the FAQs are posted. These groups are shown in Figure 13-7.

Figure 13-7: Newsgroups to which FAQs are posted

Newsgroup	Description
`news.answers`	All the FAQs from every newsgroup
`alt.answers`	FAQs from the `alt` newsgroups
`comp.answers`	FAQs from the `comp` newsgroups
`humanities.answers`	FAQs from the `humanities` newsgroups
`misc.answers`	FAQs from the `misc` newsgroups
`rec.answers`	FAQs from the `rec` newsgroups
`sci.answers`	FAQs from the `sci` newsgroups
`soc.answers`	FAQs from the `soc` newsgroups
`talk.answers`	FAQs from the talk newsgroups

hint

On Usenet, it is considered good manners to look in the appropriate FAQ before you ask questions.

When you start to read a newsgroup that has a FAQ, you must read the FAQ *before* you post your first article to that group.

Whenever you start reading a newsgroup for the first time, it is a good idea to begin by checking out the FAQ. It will contain wisdom and knowledge that has been distilled from the newsgroup over a long period of time. Personally, I find the various FAQs fascinating, and I like to browse through them every now and then. For more information, including the addresses of Web sites that act as FAQ repositories, see the section on FAQs in Chapter 11.

Usenet Slang

People have been talking on Usenet for a long time, and over the years, certain words and expressions have evolved. Once you spend enough time reading newsgroups, you will begin to pick up the nuances. However, to help you get a head start, let's talk about a few of the words now.

To begin, people on Usenet use a great many abbreviations and acronyms. Such expressions are handy, and I want you to know what they mean. Figure 13-8 shows some of them, but when you get a moment, take a look at Appendix C, where I have put a larger and more comprehensive list.

Figure 13-8: Some of the abbreviations commonly used on Usenet

Abbreviation	Meaning
`:-)`	Smiley
`:)`	Smiley
`;-)`	Winking smiley
`BTW`	By the way
`F2F`	Face to face (that is, in person)
`FAQ`	Frequently asked question list
`FWIW`	For what it's worth
`FYI`	For your information
`<G>`	Grin (same as a smiley)
`IMHO`	In my humble opinion
`MOTAS`	Member of the appropriate sex
`MOTOS`	Member of the opposite sex
`MOTSS`	Member of the same sex
`Ob-`	(as a prefix) obligatory
`Objoke`	Obligatory joke
`ROFL`	Rolling on the floor laughing
`SO`	Significant other

The meaning of most of these abbreviations is obvious, once you know what they mean, but I do want to discuss a few of them. Let's start with the smileys.

There are many different types of people on Usenet, and it is not hard to make a remark that might be misinterpreted. Usenet is used around the world, and your articles will be read by people from another countries, many of whom speak English as a second language and come from an entirely different culture.

For this reason, whenever you suspect that what you are saying might be wrongly interpreted as being insulting, it is customary to use a SMILEY: a short sequence of characters that, when looked at sideways, looks like a small smiley face.

The purpose of a smiley is to show a sense of irony, as if you mean to say, "Just kidding." For example, say you are taking part in a discussion about the best way to make pizza. You might write:

```
I can't understand why you don't like to put macaroni and
tuna fish on your pizza. But then not everyone has good
taste like me :-)
```

(To see the smiling face, tilt your head sideways to the left.)

Smileys are important, and I want you to learn how to use them properly, so, when you get a moment, take a look at the section in Chapter 6 where I talk about them at length.

The next abbreviation I want to explain is the prefix `Ob-`. In some newsgroups, the participants make an effort to ensure that all the articles are relevant. For example, the group `rec.humor` is devoted to jokes and humor, and people do not like it when someone posts an article that does not have a joke. Of course, from time to time, someone does want to make a non-humorous comment, so, when they do, they always put at least one joke within the article. The tradition is to refer to this as an `Objoke` (obligatory joke). In other groups, you will sometimes see the `Ob-` prefix used in a similar way.

Sometimes the discussion of particular items does not belong in the same group as the items themselves. In such cases, there may be a separate newsgroup just for discussion. This group is often designated by a name ending with the characters `.d` (discussion). For example, the `rec.humor` newsgroup is supposed to be for jokes only. The group `rec.humor.d` is for related articles, such as the discussion of particular jokes or requests for jokes.

Here is another example. The newsgroup `alt.sex.stories` — an extremely popular group, by the way — is for people to post erotic stories (and only stories). Discussion about such stories must go to the group `alt.sex.stories.d`.

When you look at newsgroup names, another important suffix you will see is `.misc`. This indicates that there are several related groups, each devoted to a specific topic. The group whose name ends in `.misc` is for all the articles that don't belong in one of the other groups.

As an example, Figure 13-9 contains the names of newsgroups in which people discuss bicycles. Notice that most of the groups are for specific bicycle-related topics, while the `.misc` group is for everything else. In such cases, it is important to use the `.misc` group when appropriate. If you post miscellaneous articles to another, more specific group, it will dilute the focus of that group (and people will get mad at you).

Figure 13-9: Related Usenet newsgroups, including a .misc group

Newsgroup	Description
`rec.bicycles.marketplace`	Bicycles: buying and selling
`rec.bicycles.misc`	Bicycles: miscellaneous topics
`rec.bicycles.off-road`	Bicycles: mountain bikes
`rec.bicycles.racing`	Bicycles: racing
`rec.bicycles.rides`	Bicycles: tours and routes
`rec.bicycles.soc`	Bicycles: societal issues
`rec.bicycles.tech`	Bicycles: technical aspects

Returning to our discussion of Usenet slang, there are a few more words I want to mention. First, it is common for people on Usenet to disagree and to argue, and sometimes the discussion turns nasty. When this happens, someone will post a real stinker in which he criticizes another person or complains vociferously. We call such an article a FLAME. If an argument gets out of hand, with a lot of arguing back and forth, we call it a FLAME WAR. We also use the word as a verb, for example, "Sam got flamed by a lot of people because he didn't bother to read the FAQ before he started asking questions."

Another important word you will see is SPOILER. This refers to a statement about a book, movie or play that gives away the ending or reveals a surprise.

For example, let's say you are thinking about going to a particular movie. To make up your mind, you look in the newsgroup devoted to movie reviews (`rec.arts.movies.reviews`) to see if anyone has posted a review of that movie. If, while you are looking, you see an article that says it contains a spoiler, you would know not to read that review as it gives away the ending of the movie.

The last few words I want to discuss have to do with posting articles. It is common for someone to read an article and post a reply. This is called a FOLLOW-UP article. When people start to post replies to the reply, the sequence of related articles is called a THREAD. You can tell your newsreader to arrange articles into threads, to make it easy to follow the various separate discussions within a newsgroup.

Finally, when you post an article, you specify the newsgroups to which the article should be sent. If you send an article to more than one group, we say that you CROSS-POST it.

Pictures (Binaries)

There are a huge number of pictures posted to Usenet groups, so if you like to look at pictures, you are in the right place. However, I do need to tell you that, by far, most of the pictures on Usenet are erotic (or pornographic, depending on your point of view). Even a cursory inspection of the pictures people post to Usenet is enough to illustrate that, regardless of what anyone might say in public, looking at erotic pictures in private is an extremely popular pastime for human beings.

Still, I don't want to mislead you. You will find more than naked men and women on Usenet. There are all kinds of pictures, such as flowers, landscapes, cartoons and some absolutely wonderful images of paintings. You just need to know where to look.

Most of the pictures are posted to special newsgroups that are designated as being just for pictures. These groups are in the **alt** hierarchy and have the word **binaries** as part of their name. (I'll explain why in a moment.) Figure 13-10 shows a list of some of these newsgroups.

Looking at pictures is easy. Just read the articles in these newsgroups. If an article contains a picture, your newsreader will show it to you when you display the article.

If you decide you really like looking at pictures, there are a number of programs you can use to search through Usenet groups and automatically download all the pictures. (See the Internet Resources.)

What's in a Name?

binaries

In general, there are two types of data. TEXT consists of characters such as the letters of the alphabet, numbers, punctuation, and so on. Anything else is called BINARY DATA. The distinction is obviously a technical one, and I won't get into the details, except to say binary data is processed as bits (which I mentioned in Chapter 3) rather than as characters.

A file that contains binary data is called a BINARY FILE or, in the argot of Usenet, a BINARY. For this reason, the newsgroups devoted to non-text postings (such as pictures and sounds) all have the word **binaries** in their name.

Figure 13-10: Examples of Usenet newsgroups that contain pictures

Newsgroup	Contents
`alt.binaries.clip-art`	Clip art
`alt.binaries.erotica`	Erotic pictures
`alt.binaries.pictures.erotica.brunette`	Erotic pictures of brunettes
`alt.binaries.nude.celebrities`	Nude celebrities
`alt.binaries.pictures.autos`	Automobiles
`alt.binaries.pictures.cartoons`	Cartoons
`alt.binaries.pictures.celebrities`	Celebrities
`alt.binaries.pictures.fine-art`	Fine art
`alt.binaries.pictures.gardens`	Gardens
`alt.binaries.pictures.grotesque`	Grotesque images
`alt.binaries.pictures.horses`	Horses
`alt.binaries.pictures.motorcycles`	Motorcycles
`alt.binaries.pictures.movie-posters`	Movie posters

Internet Resources **Programs to Download Usenet Binaries**

```
http://www.tifny.com/
http://www.nijico.com/
http://www.a2asoft.com/
http://www.newsbin.com/
http://www.zeonews.com/
http://www.binarium.net/
http://www.binaryboy.com/
http://www.kbrowning.com/
http://www.allpicturez.com/
http://www.co.jyu.fi/~ap/bnr.html
http://www.techsono.com/pixnewsfree/
http://www.daansystems.com/newsreactor/
http://www.newsrobot.com/sbnews/frsbnews.html
```

Posting an Article

You can post a Usenet article either in reply to someone else's article (that is, a follow-up) or as a brand new article of your own. The details vary from one newsreader to another. I'll show you how to get started with Outlook Express (Internet Explorer), but generally speaking, posting an article is simple with all newsreaders.

Let's start with a follow-up. You are reading an article, and you decide to post a reply. You have a choice of either replying to the newsgroup (in which case everyone reads your reply) or replying directly to the author of the article (in which case your reply is private). Most of the time you will reply to the newsgroup, so your article will become part of the discussion.

Within Outlook Express, click on the **Reply Group** button. Within Messenger, click on the **Reply** button. The newsreader will set up an article for you in a separate window. All you need to do is type your reply.

When your newsreader sets up your reply, the `Subject:` line will be filled in for you. To show that your article is a reply, the letters `Re:` will be inserted at the beginning of this line. For example, say you reply to an article with a subject of:

`I need a Tuna and Grapefruit Recipe`

The subject of your article will be:

`Re: I need a Tuna and Grapefruit Recipe`

Creating a brand new article is just as easy. The simplest way to do it is to open the newsgroup to which you want to post. Then tell your newsreader you want to compose a new article. (Within Outlook Express, click on the **New Post** button.)

Your newsreader will set up a new article for you in a separate window. All you need to do is type the subject and the body of the article. When you are finished, click on the **Send** button.

When you reply to an article, it is customary to include part of the article in your reply, so people will know what you are talking about (just like when you reply to an email message). Your newsreader makes this easy by including the previous article within your reply.

When you include part of an article in this way, we say that you QUOTE it. To indicate which part of your message is quoted, your newsreader will insert a special character at the beginning of each line that is quoted. Traditionally, this character is a > (greater-than) sign.

If you have never posted an article before, or if you are using a new newsreader, you may want to run a test. If so, it is considered bad manners to post a test article to a regular newsgroup. Instead, there are several

---

hint

To send a picture as part of your article, you simply attach a file that contains the picture, just as you do with a mail message. (See Chapter 5.)

To do so, start composing an article, then (with Outlook Express), click on the **Attach** button.

groups just for test messages. You can post a message to one of these groups, and then take a look to see if your message came through successfully.

The test groups are shown in Figure 13-11. It is okay to send anything you want to these groups — that's what they are for. If you want to test posting a message to a moderated group, use `misc.test.moderated`.

Figure 13-11:	Usenet groups to which you can send test messages

```
alt.test
bit.test
biz.test
comp.test
k12.test
misc.test
misc.test.moderated
news.test
```

hint

When you reply to a Usenet article, it is considered polite to keep the reply short by quoting only the relevant parts of the original article.

As you compose your reply, take a moment to delete all the unnecessary lines. As a general rule, the parts you quote should be shorter than the new lines you add. This makes your reply easier to read, which increases the chances that people will read it.

To conclude this section, I would like to mention a few ideas for you to think about as you post articles to Usenet. Following these guidelines will help smooth your way in the Usenet community.

- **Don't bother flaming**. Most people on Usenet are nice, but there are some idiots. If someone writes something that makes you mad, ignore him. Flaming someone is generally a waste of time, and all it does is put you in a bad mood. (As you get older, one of the great lessons you learn about life is that it is okay to ignore people you don't like.)

- **Read the FAQ**. If a newsgroup has a FAQ, read it before you post an article to that group.

- **Use a short signature**. If you include a signature, keep it short.

- **Don't use HTML**. Some newsreaders allow you to include HTML within your articles. Do not do so. HTML belongs on Web pages, not in Usenet articles. There are many different newsreaders in use, and what looks good on your screen will probably not look good to other people. For a longer discussion of why you should avoid using HTML in messages, see Chapter 6.

- **Don't use all caps**. Do not type using all capital letters. Within a Usenet article, using all capital letters means YOU ARE SHOUTING.

- **Think before you post**. Once you post an article, there is no effective way to cancel it. Your article will remain on news servers around the world for several days to several weeks. In addition, it will be archived by the Usenet search engines (discussed in Chapter 11) and will be available to people indefinitely. So, as you compose an article, do your best to use good judgment, especially if you are angry or upset.

- **Avoid cross-posting**. As a general rule, you should post an article to one group only. If the article is relevant to more than one group, think carefully and pick the best one. On rare occasions, you might cross-post to two or three groups, but do not do so as a habit. The people you really want to read your article probably look at all the groups related to that topic, so cross-posting is almost always unnecessary. Some people do it, but they are not as intelligent and well-mannered as you and I.

Finding What You Want on Usenet

People often ask me for advice about how to use the Internet to find some information. If I think what they need will be on a Web page, I tell them to use a search engine (see Chapter 11). However, much of the time, I find myself telling people that the best way to get what they want is to send a question to the appropriate Usenet newsgroup and wait for someone to post an answer. This is especially true when you are looking for advice. Millions of people use Usenet, and many of them will be glad to help you.

The trick is, how do you find the right newsgroup? For example, say your baby has colic. Which newsgroup is the one to send a request for ideas and help? Suppose you want to buy a camera. Where do the photography buffs hang out? What if you want to talk about your favorite music group or writer or television show. Which group is the best one to read?

Sometimes you can guess what a group is for just by looking at its name. (For example, look at the newsgroups in Figure 13-5.) However, there are a huge number of newsgroups, and it is not an easy task to look through the entire list. Moreover, many of the names are obscure and won't make sense to you anyhow.

There is no easy answer to the question of how to find the newsgroup you want, but I can give you some good ideas. The best place to start is my Yellow Pages book, if you have it (*Harley Hahn's Internet Yellow Pages*). In the book, I have thousands of items, organized into categories, and a lot of these items have Usenet newsgroups as well as Web sites. In many cases, the quickest way to find the newsgroup you want is to look up a related topic in the book.

Another way to find a group is to search for it on the Web. There are a number of resources available. The best one I know of is the master list of Usenet groups that I maintain on my Web site. This list contains the names of all the non-bogus groups in the thirteen important hierarchies, about 8,000 groups in all. (See the discussion about hierarchies earlier in the chapter.)

For each group, I have written a short one-line description and placed the group in a category, so it is easy to search for what you want. Conversely, if you see the name of a newsgroup somewhere and you are not sure what it means, you can use my master list to look up the description. This is the same list I use when I need to find a newsgroup quickly, so I am sure you will find it helpful.

Internet Resources **Harley Hahn's Master List of Usenet Newsgroups**

`http://www.harley.com/usenet/`

Aside from my master list, there are a number of other Web sites you can use. First, there is the Usenet search engine I described in Chapter 11. At this site, you can not only look for newsgroups, you can search the archives of expired Usenet articles. Second, you can visit the Web sites that offer Web-based Usenet access (described earlier in this chapter). These sites allow various types of searches, and one of them may help you find what you need.

Internet Resources **Usenet Search Engine**

`http://groups.google.com/`

How Are Newsgroups Created?

Through the years, various procedures have been developed to create new Usenet groups. These procedures ensure that the process is handled in a thoughtful and practical manner. As I explained earlier, there are hundreds of Usenet hierarchies, the most important ones being the eight mainstream hierarchies and the five alternative hierarchies. The mainstream hierarchies have the most well-defined procedures for creating new groups, so let's start with those.

Within the **news** hierarchy, two groups are used specifically for newsgroup creation. These groups are: **news.announce.newgroups** and **news.groups**. **news.announce.newgroups** is a moderated group, and is used only for announcements relating to the creation of new groups. **news.groups** is an unmoderated group and is used for general discussion about new groups. Here is how it all works.

When the need arises for a new newsgroup, somebody will post an article to **news.announce.newgroups** proposing the creation of the group. This type of proposal is called an RFD ("request for discussion"). The moderator of **news.announce.newgroups** posts the RFD, at which time discussion begins in **news.groups**.

In most cases, the RFD will be discussed in other groups as well. For example, if the RFD proposes the creation of a new group related to bicycles, the discussion will take place not only in **news.groups**, but also in the various bicycle newsgroups. In this way, the people who would be most interested in the creation of a new group are the ones who discuss it. During the discussion, the people involved settle on a name for the group and create a CHARTER: a statement explaining the purpose of the group.

If, after several weeks of discussion, it is determined that there is a real need for the proposed group, someone posts another article to **news.announce.newgroups** calling for a vote. This announcement specifies a voting period, which must be between 21 and 31 days. During this time, people vote by email for or against the creation of the new group. Anyone is allowed to vote, and each person may vote only once.

At the end of the voting period, the results are announced. For a new group to be created, it must receive at least two-thirds "yes" votes, and there must be at least 100 more "yes" votes than "no" votes. If this criteria is not met, the group is not created. If the criteria is met, the moderator of **news.announce.newgroups** will create the group.

The moderator creates a new group by using a special directive called a CONTROL MESSAGE. This is a short message that is transported throughout Usenet in the same way as a regular article. However, a control message has special header lines that are recognized by all news servers, and within these header lines are instructions to the news server telling it to perform a specific task.

To create a newsgroup, the moderator sends out a control message instructing all news servers to add the new group to their master list. (If it becomes necessary to delete a newsgroup, it is possible to send a different type of control message telling news servers to remove a specific group from their master list.)

As I mentioned earlier in the chapter, Usenet administration is distributed, not centralized, and each individual news administrator decides which newsgroups will be carried on his or her system. In order to create a new newsgroup, you not only have to send an appropriate control message to news servers throughout the world, you also have to get the news administrators to agree to accept the newsgroup on their systems.

Because all mainstream groups go through a careful and deliberate creation process, news administrators throughout the world will always honor a control message that is sent from the moderator of **news.announce.newgroups** requesting the creation of a new group.

In the other hierarchies, however, newsgroup creation is handled differently. Some hierarchies are controlled by one person, some by a group of people, and others by nobody. The most important of these other hierarchies is **alt**, which is, by far, the largest hierarchy in all of Usenet, so let's talk about how an **alt** group is created.

The **alt** hierarchy was established as an alternative to the original mainstream hierarchies. As such, the rules for establishing new **alt** groups are far more liberal than in the mainstream hierarchies. In particular, there is no formal voting procedure. Anybody who knows how to send a control message can create a new **alt** group.

Within the **alt** hierarchy, there is a special newsgroup, **alt.config**, that is used for discussion of new **alt** groups. Before someone creates a new **alt** group, it is considered proper to post an article to **alt.config** describing the new group and asking for comments. Before actually creating the group, a person should wait at least a week to see how other people respond to the suggestion.

Remember, in order to successfully create a new group, it is necessary for the news administrators around the world to agree to create the group. If the group has not been previously discussed in `alt.config`, many news administrators will not create it. In fact, in such situations, it is common to see other people send out control messages canceling the group.

Some news administrators, however, will honor all newsgroup creation requests, and, as a result, you will see many frivolous `alt` groups with silly names. Still, the `alt` hierarchy does have a huge number of useful and active newsgroups, and the freedom that it offers is important to Usenet as a whole.

You will probably never need to create a new Usenet group, but if you ever decide to do so, make sure to wait until you have a fair amount of experience with Usenet. Wait until you understand how Usenet works and how groups are named and organized, and, before you move forward with your idea, discuss it in the related groups to see what other people have to say. Within the mainstream hierarchies, new groups usually arise as a consensus among a number of people. This is not necessary for `alt` groups, but having a discussion beforehand does make for better results. For more detailed information about newsgroup creation, check out the following resources.

(In the list below, you will notice that I have specified the names of several newsgroups as URLs. The format is `news:` followed by the name of the group. I discuss this type of URL earlier in the chapter.)

Internet Resources   **Creating a Newsgroup**

```
news:alt.config

news:news.groups

news:news.announce.newgroups

http://www.alt-config.org/justification.htm

http://www.faqs.org/faqs/usenet/creating-newsgroups/

http://www.gweep.bc.ca/~edmonds/usenet/good-newgroup.html

http://www.cis.ohio-state.edu/~barr/alt-creation-guide.html
```

Mailing Lists

*It is common to find
mailing lists in which the
participants have been
talking together for months
or even years. As such,
these lists develop a
community spirit.*

For many years — even before Usenet, and long before there was a Web — people have been using mailing lists to hold discussions. In fact, mailing lists are almost as old as the Internet itself.

Today, there are a vast number of mailing lists, even more than the number of Usenet groups. Many of these lists are open to anyone, and it is easy to participate: if you know how to use mail, you already know most of what you need to know. In this chapter, I will explain how mailing lists work, how to join them, and how to find the ones that interest you.

The Basic Ideas

A MAILING LIST is a facility that allows people to participate in an ongoing discussion via email. There are tens of thousands of mailing lists on the Internet. Many of them are private (and probably of no interest to you or me), but a large number of the mailing lists are — like Usenet discussion groups — open to anyone. When you join a mailing list (which is free), we say you SUBSCRIBE to the list. When you quit the list, we say you UNSUBSCRIBE.

Within a mailing list, messages are circulated by mail. The idea is simple: each time someone sends a message, a copy of that message is sent to everyone who has subscribed to that list. Thus, to participate in a discussion about a particular topic, all you have to do is subscribe to a mailing list devoted to that topic. From then on, a copy of every message that anyone sends to the list will be sent to your mailbox automatically. When you unsubscribe from the list, you will stop receiving messages.

Each mailing list is controlled by a person referred to as the LIST OWNER. In most cases, the owner is the person who started the list or, perhaps, inherited the job from someone else. The duties of the owner of the mailing list are minimal, because, as I will explain in a moment, most of the work is done by an automated program.

The basic job of the list owner is to monitor the messages and sort out any problems that may arise. The owner also creates a document, called a WELCOME MESSAGE, that is sent to each person who subscribes to the list. The welcome message contains general information about the list, including its purpose, any rules regarding the discussion, and a description of any special features. The welcome message also contains instructions on how to unsubscribe from the list.

Some mailing lists are MODERATED, which means that a person, called the MODERATOR, decides which messages are sent out. In most cases, the moderator is the list owner, although it can be a different person.

Most lists are not moderated, and when you send a message, everyone sees it. With a moderated list, the message is first sent to the moderator. The moderator reads all the incoming messages and decides which ones should be sent to the list.

The main advantage of a moderated list is that the discussion stays more focused than with an unmoderated list. However, with a busy list, moderating can require a lot of time, and it is necessary to find someone willing to volunteer the hours.

We use the terms TRAFFIC or VOLUME to refer to the average number of messages sent to a particular list. Some mailing lists have low traffic, and you may not see more than a few messages a week, or even in a month. Other mailing lists, however, have a lot of traffic, and a busy list can fill up your mailbox quickly. It is not uncommon, for example, to go away for a week's vacation and come back to find your mailbox overflowing with messages from your favorite mailing list. For this reason, some mailing lists provide a way to stop the messages temporarily when you know you are going to be away for a while. (I will show you how later in the chapter.)

When a list has a lot of traffic, it can be inconvenient to receive a lot of separate messages. Some mailing lists offer an alternative. Instead of receiving separate messages, you can choose to have all the messages for each day collected and sent to you as one large message, called a DIGEST.

How Are Mailing Lists Different From Usenet Newsgroups?

In some respects, mailing lists are similar to Usenet newsgroups (which I discuss in Chapter 13). They both cover a large variety of topics discussed by people all over the world. There are, however, important differences.

The articles in a Usenet newsgroup are stored on news servers around the Internet. When you post an article to a newsgroup, the article starts from your news server, and makes its way around the world by being copied from one server to another. Mailing lists are different. Each mailing list is managed by a MAILING LIST PROGRAM (sometimes called a LIST SERVER) running on a specific computer. When you send a message to a list, the mailing list program receives the message and sends a copy to everyone who is subscribed to the list.

To read the articles in a Usenet newsgroup, you have to use a special program, called a newsreader, to connect to a news server. To participate in a mailing list, all you need is a regular mail program.

This means that, when you subscribe to a mailing list, all the messages from that list are sent to your mailbox automatically. You do not pick and choose what you want to read. (Although you can always delete messages without reading them.) With Usenet, you need only look at a newsgroup when you feel like it, and it is easy to browse from one group to another.

Thus, Usenet lends itself to exploring and skimming. Once you learn how to use your newsreader, it is simple to take a peek at any newsgroup you want, whenever you want. With a mailing list, you must subscribe and then wait for new messages to arrive in your mailbox.

For this reason, people are more selective about which mailing lists they subscribe to, compared to which newsgroups they read. This leads to a mailing list culture in which you see more serious, and longer, discussions than on Usenet. For example, many mailing lists are used by researchers and students for scholarly collaboration, something that is more difficult to maintain on Usenet. In fact, it is common to find mailing lists in which the participants have been talking together for months or even years. As such, these lists develop a community spirit. Although some Usenet newsgroups do develop this type of spirit, most groups are more like open forums, with people tending to drift in and out.

Like Usenet, mailing lists offer a lot of variety. There are lists for just about any topic you can imagine, and, in fact, there are a lot more mailing lists than Usenet newsgroups. However, mailing lists tend to have more wheat and less chaff. In particular, there is virtually no spam — the unsolicited advertising that plagues Usenet.

The final difference I want to mention relates to names. Usenet newsgroups have names that consist of more than one part, such as:

```
alt.celebrities
biz.marketplace.international
rec.parks.theme
```

The first part of each name shows the hierarchy (in this case, `alt`, `biz` and `rec`).

Since every mailing list is run from a particular computer, there is no need for a standardized naming system. All that is needed is a name that uniquely identifies the list on its own computer. Thus, mailing lists use simple, one-word names. I will show you how the system works in the next section. For now, here are a few examples:

Mailing List	Description
`abstract-art-l`	Abstract art
`cinema-l`	Movies
`dinosaur`	Dinosaurs
`eat-l`	Food and drink
`humor`	Humor and jokes

What's in a Name?

listname-l

One of the oldest networks to support a large number of mailing lists was called Bitnet. (I will talk about Bitnet later in the chapter.) Within Bitnet, it was necessary to differentiate between a user name and a mailing list name. For this reason, people used the convention that all mailing list names would end with the characters -l (a hyphen followed by a lowercase "L"). For example, the Bitnet mailing list devoted to travel was called `travel-l`.

Today, Bitnet has been replaced by the Internet, but many of the Bitnet mailing lists still exist. Moreover, some people still use the -l naming convention. For these reasons, you will see many mailing lists with this type of name.

When you talk about such names, there are several ways to pronounce the -l characters. Many people pronounce the "el" but not the - character, so you might hear someone say, "I subscribed to the 'travel el' list."

Technical Unix people are more likely to pronounce the - character as "minus", because that is the custom with Unix. So a Unix person would talk about subscribing to the "travel minus el" list.

Mailing List Programs: Listserv, Listproc and Majordomo

As I mentioned earlier, every mailing list is managed automatically by a mailing list program. This program handles the details associated with running a list: processing subscription requests, making sure that messages are distributed to everyone on the list, creating digests, and so on. There are three common mailing list programs you will encounter on the Internet: LISTSERV, LISTPROC and MAJORDOMO.

A mailing list program has two jobs. First, there is the basic job of distributing the messages. The mailing list program receives every message sent to the list and sends a copy of the message to each person who has subscribed to the list. (If the list is moderated, every message is first sent to the moderator. The moderator then tells the program which messages to distribute.)

The second job performed by a mailing list program is to carry out various administrative commands. Anyone can issue such commands to a mailing list program by sending it a message with a particular format (which I will explain later in the chapter). When your message arrives, the program reads it and carries out your commands.

For example, to join a mailing list, you send a message to the mailing list program which administers that list. Within the message, you put a `subscribe` command. To quit a list, you send a message containing an `unsubscribe` command. Although there are a number of different commands you can send to any mailing list program, you really only need to know a few of them.

Thus, a mailing list program receives two types of mail: administrative messages that contain commands to be carried out, and regular messages that are to be distributed to everyone on the list. To keep things straight, each mailing list has two different addresses. The SUBSCRIPTION ADDRESS is the one to which you send commands. The LIST ADDRESS is the one to which you send messages. Here is an example.

In the last section, I mentioned a mailing list called `cinema-1`. The list address is:

`cinema-1@american.edu`

This is the address to which you would send regular messages. Anything sent to this address will be distributed to everyone on the list.

The subscription address is:

`listserv@american.edu`

This is the address to which you would send administrative commands, for example, to subscribe or unsubscribe to the list.

In most cases, a single mailing list program handles all of the mailing lists on a particular computer. For example, the Listserv program on `american.edu` manages all the mailing lists on `american.edu`. Thus, the subscription address will be the same for every mailing list on the same computer.

Figure 14-1 contains a few more examples, showing the subscription addresses and list addresses of the mailing lists I mentioned in the previous section.

Figure 14-1: Examples of mailing lists

Mailing List	Subscription Address	List Address
abstract-art-l	majordomo@itg.uiuc.edu.com	abstract-art-l@itg.uiuc.edu
cinema-l	listserv@american.edu	cinema-l@american.edu
dinosaur	listproc@usc.edu	dinosaur@ usc.edu
eat-l	listserv@listserv.vt.edu	eat-l@listserv.vt.edu
humor	listserv@listserv.uga.edu	humor@listserv.uga.edu

What's in a Name?

Listserv

Listproc

Majordomo

Listserv, Listproc and Majordomo are all mailing list programs. Listserv is the oldest. It was originally developed by Eric Thomas in 1986 for IBM mainframe computers on the Bitnet network (which I discuss later in the chapter). Later, Listserv was converted to run on other Bitnet computers, particularly DEC's VMS systems. The name Listserv stands for "list server".

As the Internet became popular, Listproc was created to be the equivalent of Listserv for Unix computers on the Internet. Listproc was developed by an organization called CREN (Corporation for Research and Educational Networking), the successor to Bitnet. The name Listproc stands for "list processor".

Majordomo was developed in 1992 by Brent Chapman, also to run under Unix. Majordomo is written in Perl (don't worry if that doesn't mean anything to you). Although it can do the basic job, Majordomo does not have as many features as Listserv and Listproc. The name Majordomo is taken from the term "majordomo", used to describe the chief steward in a large household, such as a palace. Within such a household, the majordomo is the servant with the most responsibility, the one who performs the most important jobs, while coordinating the activities of the other servants.

Subscribing and Unsubscribing to a Mailing List

Subscribing to a mailing list is easy. All you need to do is mail a short message to the subscription address. The subject of the message can be anything you want (it is ignored). In the body of the message, put a single line containing a `subscribe` command. The format is as follows.

Listproc and Listserv:

- the word `subscribe`
- the name of the mailing list
- your first and last names

Majordomo:

- the word `subscribe`
- the name of the mailing list

(The only difference for Majordomo is that you do not need to specify your first and last names.)

Here is an example that illustrates how to subscribe to a Listserv or Listproc mailing list. Let's say your name is Warren Peese, and you want to subscribe to the `humor` mailing list I mentioned in Figure 14-1. To do so, send the following message:

```
To: listserv@american.edu
Subject: subscribe cinema-l

subscribe cinema-l Warren Peese
```

The next example shows a subscription command sent to a Majordomo list. The main difference is you do not put your first and last names:

```
To: majordomo@itg.uiuc.edu.com
Subject: subscribe abstract-art-l

subscribe abstract-art-l
```

Notice that, in both cases, you do not have to specify your mail address. The mailing list program will pick up your address automatically from the header of your message.

To unsubscribe from a mailing list, send a message to the subscription address. In the body of the message, put a single line containing an **unsubscribe** command. The format is as follows:

- the word **unsubscribe**
- the name of the mailing list

Here is an example:

```
To: listserv@american.edu
Subject: unsubscribe cinema-l

unsubscribe cinema-l
```

When you send commands to a mailing list program, it doesn't matter what you put in the **Subject** line. I always put something descriptive (such as **subscribe to humor list**) to make it easier to recognize the message when I see it in my outbox.

As a summary, Figure 14-2 shows the general format for subscribing and unsubscribing to a mailing list.

Figure 14-2: Subscribing and unsubscribing to a mailing list

Subscribing: Listserv or Listproc

> `To:` *subscription-address*<u>w</u>
> `Subject:` *anything*
> `subscribe` *list-name your-first-name your-last-name*

Subscribing: Majordomo

> `To:` *subscription-address*
> `Subject:` *anything*
> `subscribe` *list-name*

Unsubscribing: Listserv, Listproc or Majordomo

> `To:` *subscription-address*
> `Subject:` *anything*
> `unsubscribe` *list-name*

Note: With Listserv, you will sometimes see a signoff *command used as a synonym for unsubscribe. The word "signoff" comes from the days of the old IBM mainframe computers, which were the original home of the Listserv mailing lists.*

When you subscribe to a mailing list, the mailing list program will send you a copy of the welcome message for that list. Save this message, as it will have information that may come in handy later. In particular, the welcome message will contain instructions for unsubscribing to the list.

If you subscribe to more than one list, an easy way to store the welcome messages is to create a folder (directory) called `Mailing-lists`. Each time you get a welcome message, save it in this folder. In this way, you can find any welcome message just by looking in your `Mailing-lists` folder.

Once you start reading mailing lists, you may end up with a lot of messages in your inbox. If so, here are two hints that can help. First, you can get an extra email address just to use for mailing lists. That way, the mailing list messages won't get mixed in with your regular mail. Alternatively, if your mail program has a filtering feature, you can use it to process your mailing list messages automatically as they arrive and put them in a special folder.

Keeping the Addresses Straight

As you know, a mail address has the following format:

name@hostname

where *hostname* is the name of a computer. Mailing lists use two different addresses:

- Subscription address (to which you send commands)
- List address (to which you send messages for the list)

The *name* in a subscription address will be the same as the name of the mailing list program: either `listserv`, `listproc` or `majordomo`. The *name* in a list address will be the name of the mailing list itself.

For an example, consider a Majordomo mailing list `abstract-art-1` on the computer `itg.uiuc.edu.com`. The two addresses are as follows:

- Subscription address: `majordomo@itg.uiuc.edu.com`
- List address: `abstract-art-1@itg.uiuc.edu.com`

It is important to keep these addresses straight. You should use the list address only to send regular messages. For everything else, use the subscription address.

Mailing List Commands

One of the jobs of a mailing list program is to carry out commands. To send such commands, you mail a message to the subscription address for a list. Within the body of the message, you can put as many commands as you want, one per line. The subject of the message can be anything you want (it is ignored).

hint

If you are new to mailing lists, you may be tempted to subscribe to several at the same time. My advice is to start with only one list. Wait a week and see how much traffic the list generates before you subscribe to another list.

If you subscribe to several high-traffic mailing lists at the same time, you will receive a lot of mail within a short time, and you may find it difficult to sort out the various messages.

hint

It is common for beginners to send an unsubscribe request to the list address, rather than to the subscription address. Not only will this not work, but a copy of the message will go to all the people on the list, annoying everyone.

When it is time to unsubscribe, send the request to the subscription address.

When your message is received, the mailing list program will process it, one line at a time. So far, I have described only two basic commands (`subscribe` and `unsubscribe`). However, there are others, the exact details of which vary depending on what type of mailing list program is being used.

In Figures 14-3, 14-4 and 14-5, I have summarized the basic commands for the three main mailing list programs: Listserv, Listproc and Majordomo. Most of the time, you will only have to use the `subscribe` and `unsubscribe` commands, but the others are there if you need them. My suggestion is to send for general help information to get a full list of commands. You can then ask for more specific instructions if you need them.

For example, to request general information from a Listserv program, you would use the `help` command. Here is a message that does just that:

```
To: listserv@uga.cc.uga.edu
Subject: help information request

help
```

When the Listserv program receives this request, it will send you the help information by return mail.

If you want to send more than one command, remember to put each one on a separate line. (The `info ?` command requests a list of all the help topics. See Figure 14-3.)

```
To: listserv@uga.cc.uga.edu
Subject: help information request

help
info ?
```

When you mail these types of messages, there is a potential problem I want you to be aware of. The mailing list program reads your message and processes it one line at a time. If the message happens to have any lines after the last command, the program will try to interpret them as commands, which will result in error messages.

This will happen if you have set your mail program to append a signature to the end of each message (see Chapter 5). It will also happen if you are using a free email facility that puts an advertisement at the end of each message.

To avoid such problems, put a single line with the word **end** after the last command. This tells the mailing list program to stop processing commands. Here is an example:

```
To: listserv@uga.cc.uga.edu
Subject: help information request

help
info ?
end

These lines will be ignored by the
mailing list program.
```

Figure 14-3: Summary of important Listserv commands

Subscribing and Unsubscribing

    subscribe *list-name your-first-name your-last-name*
    unsubscribe *list-name*
    signoff *list-name*　[same as unsubscribe]

Information About Lists

    lists global/*keyword* [send list names containing the specified keyword]
    info *list-name*　[send information about the specified list]

Help Information

    help　[send general help information]
    info ?　[send a list of help topics]
    info *topic*　[send information about the specified topic]

Temporarily Turn Off Mail From the List

    set *list-name* **nomail**

Turn Mail From the List Back On

    set *list-name* **mail**

Request Messages to Be Sent in Digest Format

    set *list-name* **digests**

Change Back to Normal (Non-digest) Format

    set *list-name* **mail**

Figure 14-4: Summary of important Listproc commands

Subscribing and Unsubscribing
> `subscribe` *list-name your-first-name your-last-name*
> `unsubscribe` *list-name*

Information About Lists
> `info` *list-name* [send information about the specified list]

Help Information
> `help` [send general help information]
> `help` *topic* [send information about the specified topic]

Temporarily Turn Off Mail From the List
> `set` *list-name* `mail postpone`

Turn Mail From the List Back On
> `set` *list-name* `mail`

Request Messages to Be Sent in Digest Format
> `set` *list-name* `mail digest`

Change Back to Normal (Non-digest) Format
> `set` *list-name* `mail`

Figure 14-5: Summary of important Majordomo commands

Subscribing and Unsubscribing
> `subscribe` *list-name*
> `unsubscribe` *list-name*

Information About Lists
> `info` *list-name* [send information about the specified list]
> `lists` [send summary of all lists on that computer]

Help Information
> `help` [send summary of commands]

Finding Mailing Lists

There is no central directory of mailing lists, so when you are searching for a list devoted to a particular topic, there is no single place to look. I do, however, have four suggestions.

First, my Yellow Pages book (*Harley Hahn's Internet Yellow Pages*) is an excellent place to start. In the book, I have thousands of different items, and many of them have mailing list information (along with Web sites and Usenet groups). Just look up the topic you want, and there is a good chance you will find an appropriate mailing list.

The second place to look for mailing lists is on the Web, where there are a number of well-maintained Web sites devoted to collecting and categorizing mailing list information. These sites contain information on a huge number of lists, so, with a little work, you will probably be able to find what you want. These Web sites are independent of one another, so my suggestion is to search them all before you make a final selection.

Third, check Web sites devoted to the topic in which you are interested. Many such Web sites support their own mailing lists, or have links to lists. For example, if you are looking for a mailing list for model railway discussion, spend some time visiting model railway Web sites, and you'll probably find a mailing list or two.

Finally, there are a number of services that allow you to start your own Web-based mailing list for free. We will discuss such services in the next section. These services make it easy to search through their public mailing lists, which makes them good resources for finding what you want. (The Web addressees are at the end of the next section.)

Internet Resources   **Lists of Mailing Lists**

```
http://www.paml.net/
http://www.sparklist.net/
http://www.tile.net/lists/
http://www.webscoutlists.com/
http://www.lsoft.com/lists/listref.html
```

Starting Your Own Mailing List

There are two ways to start your own mailing list. First, you can find a place that runs a mailing list program (Listserv, Listproc or Majordomo) and see if someone will agree to create a list for you.

The best place to start is with your ISP. Many ISPs will set up mailing lists for their customers, either for free or for a fee. If you work or study at a university, you can probably get one of the system administrators to start a mailing list for you. Ask around to see what the local policy is.

As an alternative, there are a number of companies on the Web that provide "free" Web-based mailing lists. These services allow you to send and receive messages via your Web browser, as well as by regular mail. The interface for these lists is also designed to be used over the Web, and it is usually easy to subscribe and unsubscribe.

Of course, such services are not really free. Everyone who subscribes to your mailing list will have to look at advertisements, either at the Web site or inserted into the actual messages. Moreover, reading messages via a Web browser is a lot slower (and a lot more frustrating) than using your own mail program.

For this reason, these services are not my first choice. However, they do provide a practical alternative if you do not want to pay a fee, and you can't get your ISP or anyone else to set up your list for free. This is especially true if you want a small mailing list for a very specific purpose. For example, many people set up a free Web-based mailing list to keep in touch with the members of their family. What could be more cool than having your own family mailing list?

Internet Resources   **Free Web-based Mailing Lists**

```
http://www.topica.com/
http://groups.yahoo.com/
http://communities.msn.com/
```

Mailing List Gateways

Although there are important differences between mailing lists and Usenet newsgroups, they both contain a similar type of information: messages (or articles) sent in by various people. Because of this similarity, it is possible to arrange for a mailing list to have a corresponding Usenet newsgroup. This means that every message sent to the mailing list is automatically posted to the newsgroup, and every article posted to the newsgroup is automatically sent to the mailing list. In such cases, you can participate by subscribing to the list or by reading the newsgroup. Either way, the content will be the same.

This type of facility requires a special program called a GATEWAY. The job of a gateway is to provide an automatic connection between two different types of information systems. In this case, we are talking about a Usenet/mailing list gateway. (We sometimes use the word "gateway" as a verb. For example, I might say that a mailing list is gatewayed to a particular Usenet group.)

The reason I mention all of this is because there is a well-known set of mailing lists that are gatewayed to an entire Usenet hierarchy. These mailing lists used to belong to a network called BITNET, and, some years ago, it was felt that some of them should be available via Usenet as well. To make this happen, a Usenet/mailing list gateway was created along with a set of newsgroups, one for each mailing list. All of these newsgroups are in the `bit` hierarchy.

Bitnet was started as an academic network in 1981 and grew so much that, by 1992, it connected about 1,400 organizations (mostly universities and research institutions) in 49 countries and supported several thousand mailing lists. Since then, however, the Internet has become the global network of choice. By the end of 1996, the Internet had absorbed most of what used to be Bitnet. Still, a large number of the mailing lists exist to this day, and some of them are gatewayed to Usenet newsgroups within the `bit` hierarchy.

The Listserv mailing list program was originally developed to run on Bitnet, and it is this program that supported the Bitnet mailing lists for so many years. For this reason, many of the `bit` Usenet groups have the word `listserv` in their name. You can see this in Figure 14-6, which shows a few examples of Bitnet mailing lists along with their corresponding Usenet newsgroups.

Figure 14-6: Examples of gatewayed Bitnet mailing lists

Mailing List	Newsgroup	Description
`blues-1`	`bit.listserv.blues-1`	Blues music
`games-1`	`bit.listserv.games-1`	Computer games
`railroad`	`bit.listserv.railroad`	Railroads and trains
`museum-1`	`bit.listserv.museum-1`	Museums
`scuba-1`	`bit.listserv.scuba-1`	Scuba diving
`travel-1`	`bit.listserv.travel-1`	Travel

What's in a Name?

Bitnet

Bitnet was started in the days when many universities had large IBM mainframe computers. In 1981, two researchers, Ira Fuchs at City University of New York and Greydon Freeman at Yale University, were discussing the Network Job Entry (NJE) protocol that was available for IBM mainframes. They decided that NJE could be used to connect computers over a leased telephone line, and they figured out a way to do so. Although they didn't know it at the time, this tiny two-computer network became the nucleus for what was to become the largest academic network in the world.

In other words, Fuchs and Freeman created the connection because they happened to have NJE. So, for this reason, they named their network BITNET, meaning "Because It's There Network". Later, this evolved to "Because It's Time Network".

15

Creating Your Own Web Site

*Devote your Web site to an
area of life you find
fascinating. Share your
passion with the world.*

There is a lot involved in making your own Web site. Creating even a simple Web site can require you to understand a fair amount of detail. However, with the right tools and a bit of practice, the job becomes a lot easier.

In this chapter, I will explain the important ideas relating to creating your own Web site and show you where to find the resources you need. Before we start, I want to make sure you are familiar with the following sections from previous chapters. Please take a few minutes now to review this material, as it will make our job much easier.

Chapter 4 [Internet Addresses]

- URLs
- File Names and Extensions
- Directories and Subdirectories
- Pathnames

Chapter 7 [The Web]

- The Basic Ideas
- Entering a URL

Before you start to build your Web site, I want you to give some thought as to what you are going to put on it.

My suggestion is to devote your Web site to an area of life you find fascinating. Do you like to collect trading cards? Do you enjoy knitting or needlework? Are you a history buff? Do you write stories or draw cartoons?

Look within yourself and ask, "What do I love to do or make or collect or think about so much that I would do it all day long if I didn't have to work?"

That should be the theme of your Web page. Share your passion with the world.

HTML

When you look at a Web page, you see text, pictures and other objects. It is important to understand how these components are put together into a single page.

hint

Look within yourself and ask, "What do I love to do or make or collect or think about so much that I would do it all day long if I didn't have to work?"

That should be the theme of your Web site. Share your passion with the world.

Each Web page is stored as a file on a Web server. This file contains the text that will be on the page, along with special instructions called TAGS. When your browser reads the file, it uses the tags as guidelines. The tags specify which components are to be used and how they should be displayed on the page.

The tags are written according to a set of specifications called HTML (Hypertext Markup Language). To create a Web page, you need to make a file containing the text of the page along with the appropriate HTML tags. You can put in the tags yourself, or you can have a program do it for you. When you create such a file, it will be stored with a name that ends with the extension `html` or `htm`, for example, `harley.html` or `harley.htm`.

HTML tags have a special format, so they won't be confused with regular text. Each tag starts with a < (less-than) character and ends with a > (greater-than) character. To explain what I mean, I will show you a few examples. You don't have to memorize the details. I just want you to get a feeling for what HTML tags look like.

Let's start with one of the tags used for text formatting, the `<br>` tag. When a browser displays text, it ignores extra spaces and blank lines. All the words are formatted as a continuous stream. The browser breaks the lines in such a way as to make them fit within the width of the page.

However, there may be times when you want to force your browser to break a line at a particular place. To do so, you put a `<br>` tag at that place. For instance, when the following text is displayed, the browser will jump to a new line after the word `lamb`:

`Mary had a little lamb <br> Its fleece was white as snow.`

Here is another example of an HTML tag. The `<img>` (image) tag tells the browser to display a picture:

`<img src="cat.gif">`

In this case, the picture to be displayed is stored in the file `cat.gif`. (The term `src` means "source".)

Many HTML tags work in pairs. For instance, to display words in italics, you use a "start-italics" tag `<i>` and an "end-italics" tag `</i>`. As an example, the tags in the following line tell the browser to display the word `best` in italics:

hint

We use the term HTML in two ways. First, it is the name of the system used to define the appearance and structure of Web pages. So we might say, "Every Web page has an HTML file that contains the text of the page along with the tags that describe that page."

Informally, we often use the term HTML to refer to the contents of such a file. For example, you might hear someone say, "Don't get rid of that file. It contains the HTML for the main page of my Web site."

```
This is the <i>best</i> Web site in the world.
```

Here is another example of tags used in a pair. To create a link to another page, you use:

`<a>` to indicate the beginning of the link
`</a>` to indicate the end of the link

(The letter **a** stands for "anchor", an HTML technical term.)

Let's say you are designing a Web page containing the following sentence:

`Visit my cat's Web page.`

Within this sentence, you want the words **my cat's** to be a link. When someone clicks on this link, you want their browser to jump to the file `little-nipper.html`. To do so, you use the `<a>` and `</a>` tags to define the link as follows:

`Visit <a href="little-nipper.html"> my cat's </a> Web page.`

(The term **href** means "hypertext reference".)

What's in a Name?

HTML

When you embed tags within text, we say that you MARK UP the text. Thus, we can explain the name HTML —Hypertext Markup Language —as follows:

- "Hypertext" refers to text that contains links.
- "Markup" shows that there are tags embedded in the text.
- "Language" sounds cool even though HTML isn't really a language.

As you might imagine, the HTML system has a *lot* of details. There are many tags, and it can take a long time to learn how to use them well. However, it is not necessary to understand HTML to create Web pages. Instead, you can use a program called a Web page editor to handle all the details. All you need to do is lay out the page the way you want, and the editor will create the HTML file for you. (We will talk about Web page editors later in the chapter.)

Does this mean you do not have to learn HTML? For most people, the answer is yes, you do not need to learn HTML. However, if you are the type of person who likes to control every little detail of your work, having an understanding of HTML allows you to read and modify the file generated by your Web page editor.

Figure 15-1: HTML for a simple Web page

```
<!-- Sample Web Page: Copyright 2001, The Little Nipper -->
<!-- Start of the page -->
  <html>

<!-- Head -->
  <head>
    <title>The Little Nipper's Web Page</title>
  </head>

<!-- Start of the body -->
  <body>

<!-- Picture of The Little Nipper   -->
  <center>
    <img src="nipper.jpg">
    <p>
    <font size="5" face="Arial">
      I am The Little Nipper
    </font>
  </center>
  <p>

<!-- A Message from The Little Nipper -->
  <font size="4" face="Arial">
    I was born in Southern California, on April 6, 1991.
    Since then, I've lived a life made up of one part
    hard work (chasing things and being a good companion)
    and two parts leisure (eating, sleeping and sitting
    in the sun).
    <p>
    <center>
      Check out this cool Web site:
      <a href="http://www.harley.com/">
        Harley Hahn's Web Site</a>
    </center>
  </font>

<!-- End of the body -->
  </body>

<!-- End of the page -->
  </html>
```

If you know enough HTML, you can create a Web page from scratch, writing all the tags yourself without the help of a program. I do this myself. In fact, this is how all Web pages used to be created in the olden days (the mid-1990s).

To show you what HTML looks like, Figure 15-1 contains the specifications for a small Web page. The Web page itself is shown in Figure 15-2. This is a simple example, but it does give you the flavor of HTML. (Note: All the lines that begin with <!-- are descriptive comments that are ignored by the browser. The purpose of comments is to help people read the HTML.)

FIGURE 15-2

A simple Web page

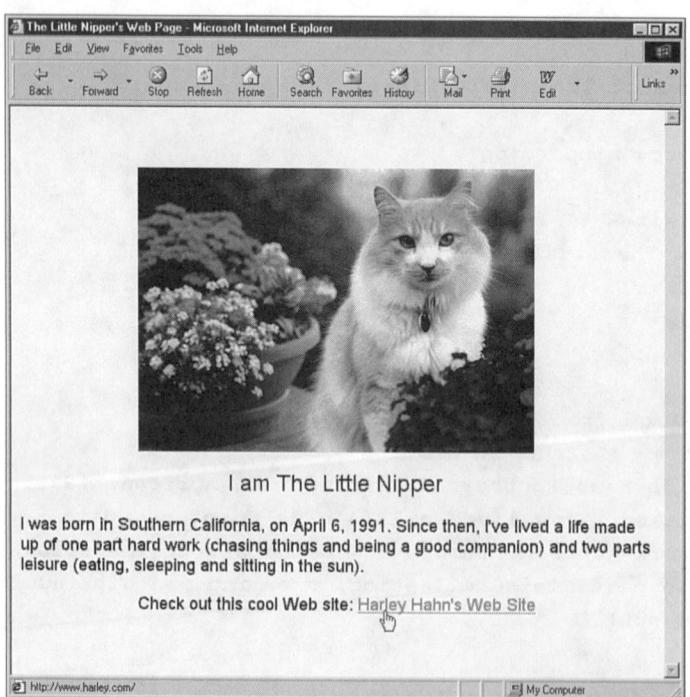

If you want to look at more complex examples, your browser can help you. With Internet Explorer, go to any Web page, pull down the **View** menu and select **Source**. Your browser will open a new window and show you the HTML for the page you are looking at. For some good examples, visit the pages on my Web site:

`http://www.harley.com/`

You will find it interesting to compare the HTML tags with what you see on your screen.

If the time comes that you want to learn more about HTML, the following resources will help you. For reference, Figure 15-3 contains a list of the most important HTML tags and what they do.

Figure 15–3: The most important HTML tags

HTML Tag	Purpose
`<!--`*text*`-->`	a comment (ignored by browser)
`<a href="`*URL*`">` *text* `</a>`	define a link *text* to specified *URL*
`<b>` *text* `</b>`	display *text* in boldface
`<body>...</body>`	define the body of the Web page
` `	break text onto a new line
`<center>` *text* `</center>`	center *text*
`<font>...</font>`	change the color, style or size of the typeface
`<form>...</form>`	create a form
`<frame>...</frame>`	define an individual frame
`<frameset>...</frameset>`	define a set of frames
`<head>...</head>`	define the head of the Web page
`<h1>` *text* `</h1>`	display text in heading 1 style
`<hr>`	display a straight line (horizontal rule)
`<html>...</html>`	define beginning and end of Web page
`<i>` *text* `</i>`	display *text* as italics
`<img...>`	display a picture (image)
`<map>...</map>`	create an image map
`<meta>`	information for the Web server or a search engine
`<ol>...</ol>`	create an ordered (numbered) list
`<p>`	start a new paragraph
`<table>...</table>`	create a table
`<title>` *text* `</title>`	specify the title of the Web page
`<u>` *text* `</u>`	underline *text*
`<ul>...</ul>`	create a non-numbered list

Internet Resources **HTML Tutorials for Beginners**

http://www.x86central.com/

http://www.december.com/html/

http://www.w3schools.com/html/

http://www.werbach.com/barebones/

http://www.davesite.com/webstation/html/

http://wdvl.internet.com/Authoring/HTML/

http://www.htmlgoodies.com/primers/basics.html

The Components of a Web Page

Web pages are built out of eight different types of components. They are:

- Text
- Links
- Pictures
- Sounds
- Tables
- Forms
- Frames
- Programs

Let's take a moment and discuss each of these building blocks in turn.

Text: A Web page can contain any text you want. The text is stored in the HTML file along with the tags for that page. You have some degree of control over how the text is to be displayed. For instance, you can use italics or boldface, and you can specify that the text should be a particular font (typeface). You can also make text wrap around pictures, line up in columns, or be formatted into a list.

Most of the time, it is best to use plain, ordinary text broken into paragraphs. When a browser displays the page, it will automatically format the paragraphs to fit within the size of the browser window.

Links: The links on your page are what turns the text into hypertext. A link points to a specific Internet resource such as a Web page, a picture, a sound, a mail address, or a Usenet group. When you click on a link, your browser does whatever is necessary to follow that link. In most cases, this means fetching and displaying another Web page.

You can attach links to either words or pictures. One special type of picture is an image map. Within an image map, various parts of the picture correspond to different links. Image maps are often used as navigation aids.

Pictures: You can use various types of pictures on your Web pages: drawings, icons, photographs, and so on. Each picture is stored in a separate file. As a general rule, photographs are stored using a format called JPG or JPEG (Joint Photographic Experts Group), while all other pictures are stored using a format called GIF (Graphics Interchange Format). You can tell the format of a picture by looking at the extension of the file name. For example, a file containing a photograph of a car might be called `car.jpg`; a file containing a drawing of a box might be called `box.gif`.

What's in a Name?

jpg

gif

The jpg format is used to store photographs. The name comes from the organization that developed the standard: the Joint Photographic Experts Group.

The gif format is used to store all other types of images, especially drawings, cartoons and icons. The gif format was developed by a company named Compuserve, which used to run an online service. (The service was bought by AOL.) The original gif format was developed so Compuserve's users would have a way to store and exchange pictures. The name gif stands for "Graphics Interchange Format".

You will often see people use the terms jpg and gif to refer to pictures that use these formats. For example, let's say you are at a Web page party, and you overhear two people talking in the hallway:

Person 1: I'm almost finished building my new Web site. I already put in a bunch of jpgs of my family. Now all I need is some small drawings to fill in the empty spaces.

Person 2: I have some drawings of space aliens talking to Elvis that will look great on your page. I'll send you the gifs in the morning.

Person 1: Thank you, Person 2. You sure are a good friend.

One particular type of gif you will see is an ANIMATED GIF. This type of gif consists of one file that contains a sequence of pictures. When a browser encounters an animated gif, it displays the pictures one after another, creating a simple animation. To make an animated gif, you must first create the separate pictures. You then use a special tool that puts the pictures together into a gif file using the animated gif format.

Sounds: It is possible to put sounds on a Web page. Like pictures, each sound is stored in its own file. The most common way to use sounds is to create a link to a sound file. When you click on the link, your browser retrieves the sound file and plays its contents.

There are a number of different file formats used to store sounds and music. The most common sound format is wav. For instance, you might put a file named `moo.wav`, that contains the sound of a cow, on one of your Web pages. The most common music formats are mid (MIDI) and mp3. For more details about sound and music files, see Chapter 10.

Tables: A TABLE is a structure that contains information in rows and columns. When you create a table, your Web page editor generates HTML tags that describe the size of the table and its contents. Figure 15-4 shows a Web page that contains a table.

Forms: A FORM contains specific areas into which you can type information as you are reading a Web page. Once a form is filled out, you click on a button. The browser then sends the information to the Web server, where it is processed by a separate program. Figure 15-5 shows a Web page that contains a form.

Using forms on a Web page requires special facilities. First, you need to write (or find) a program to process the information that will come from the form. Next, you need to place the program in the appropriate directory on the Web server. I won't go into the details, as they are too complicated. I will, however, mention a common technical term associated with forms, so you will recognize it when you see it.

When you write a form-handling program, the information is passed between the server and the program using a system called the Common Gateway Interface, or CGI. The term "CGI programming" refers to creating a program that processes data from a Web page form. CGI programs are often programmed in a computer language named Perl.

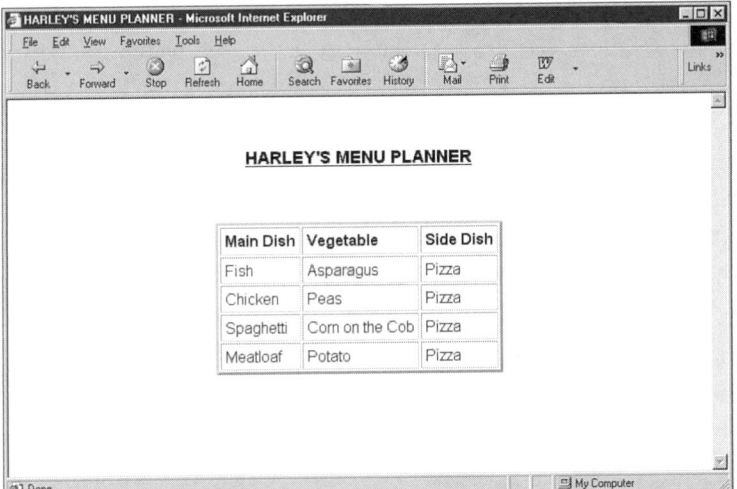

FIGURE 15-4
A Web page containing a table

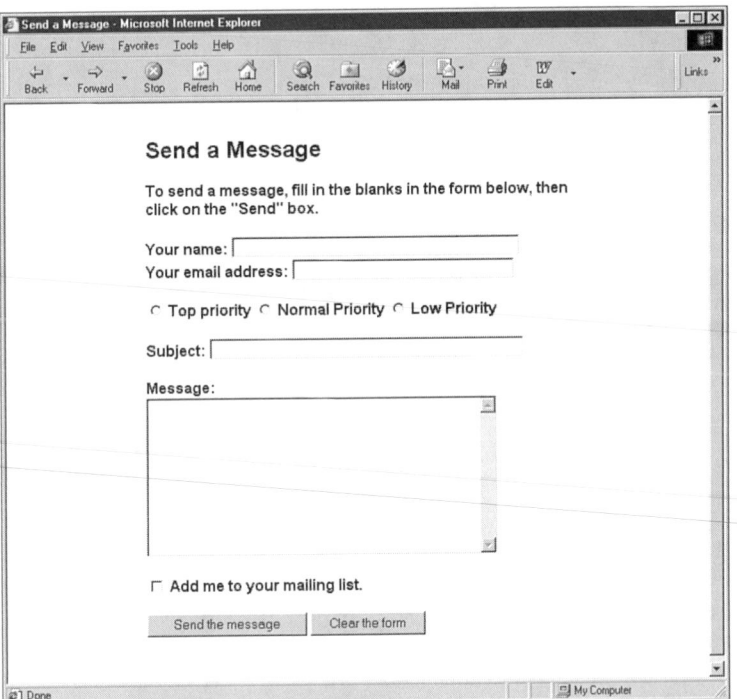

FIGURE 15-5
A Web page containing a form

Frames: It is sometimes convenient to design a Web page that contains other, smaller Web pages. This is done by using a facility called FRAMES. A frame is a specific area of a Web page that can contain data from another page.

When you create frames with your Web page editor, it generates the appropriate HTML tags to specify the size and contents of each frame. When your browser encounters such tags, it creates the frames and fills them with the appropriate content.

Frames are useful when you wish to have a Web page that consists of several independent components. For example, let's say you are designing a picture gallery. You might use one frame to display the names of all the pictures that are available for viewing. When someone clicks on a name, the actual picture is displayed in a second frame. Figure 15-6 shows a Web page that contains frames.

FIGURE 15-6
A Web page containing frames

Programs: Using a program as part of a Web page enables you to utilize many different types of features on your Web site. There are a variety of tools and programming languages available for working with Web pages. However, they are all complex, and the details are well beyond the scope of this book.

If you can't program, don't worry. Programming is not necessary for building most types of Web pages. In fact, HTML was designed so that people would be able to create Web pages *without* programming.

For reference, here are the names of the most common Web programming tools, so if you see them, you will at least know what they are. (For a discussion of Java and ActiveX, see Chapter 12.)

- Java
- ActiveX
- Javascript
- JScript
- VBScript
- Visual Basic
- Perl
- C++
- C

By the way, although the names Java and Javascript look similar, they have nothing to do with one another. The Javascript tool was created by Netscape, and for marketing reasons, they chose a name that sounded like Java.

Web Page Editors

A WEB PAGE EDITOR is a program used to create, modify and maintain Web pages. Some Web page editors also have tools that make it easy to send your files to the Web server and to manage large Web sites consisting of many pages.

There are two basic types of Web page editors. The first type is called a WYSIWYG EDITOR. The name "wysiwyg" (pronounced "whiz-ee-whig") stands for "what you see is what you get". With a

hint

Some wysiwyg editors offer dual functionality, as they can also function as HTML editors.

wysiwyg editor, you work directly with the elements on your Web page: text, pictures, tables, and so on. You create and arrange them however you want. Behind the scenes, the editor generates the HTML for you and saves it in a file. Wysiwyg editors are easy to use because you never need to look at the actual HTML.

Some people would rather write the HTML themselves. These people use an HTML EDITOR. This type of editor allows you to work directly with the HTML tags. You can immerse yourself in as much detail as you want, with complete control over the final product. (I often use an HTML editor myself.)

Once you have created a Web page, all you have to do is copy it to a Web server and the page is on the Internet. (I will discuss how to find a Web server later in the chapter.) When you copy a Web page to a server, we say that you PUBLISH the page. More formally, you upload the page from your computer to the Web server. (Remember, "upload" means to copy data from your computer to the Internet; "download" means to copy data from the Internet to your computer.)

Wysiwyg editors have a built-in feature that makes it easy to publish your Web pages. Some HTML editors do not have such a feature, and you have to upload the pages yourself using FTP (which I discuss in Chapter 2 and Chapter 9). If you use such an editor, you will need an FTP client program to do the uploading for you.

All Web page editors are complex programs that take time to master. My suggestion is to start with a wysiwyg editor and spend some time learning how to use it well. As you become more advanced, you can try an HTML editor if you want.

Internet Resources **Web Page Editors: For Beginners**

```
http://www.sitebud.com/
http://easy-web-editor.net/
http://www.faico.net/dida/
http://www.coolpage.com/cpg.html
http://www.avantrix.com/koalahtm.htm
http://www.webpage-teacher.com/webteach.htm
http://www.pysoft.com/ActualDrawingMainPage.html
```

Internet Resources   **Web Page Editors: For Advanced Users**

```
http://www.evrsoft.com/
http://www.40tude.com/html/
http://www.html-helper.com/
http://www.kevingunn.com/weborama.htm
http://www.arachnoid.com/arachnophilia/
http://www.virtualmechanics.com/imsdwarf.htm
http://www.xoology.com/concertox/xool/home/products/
  coda.html
```

Internet Resources   **FTP Client Programs**

```
http://www.3dftp.com/
http://www.wsftp.com/products/ws_ftp/
http://www.cuteftp.com/products/cuteftp/
http://sourceforge.net/projects/filezilla
```

Pictures and Sounds

For variety, you may want to use some non-textual components to enhance your Web pages. For example, you can put photographs on your Web site as well as decorate the pages by using drawings, icons, buttons and other types of graphics. You can even set the background to be a color or a particular design. Finally, you might want to put some sounds on your page (although this is a resource that should be used sparingly).

So where do you get such components? You can either make them yourself or find them for free on the Net. Let's start with photographs.

To use a photograph, it must be stored in a file, usually a jpg file. There are several ways you can turn your own photos into jpgs.

First, you can use a digital camera. A digital camera stores photographs as computer files, rather than using regular negatives. Such a camera will come with an interface to connect to a PC, along with whatever software you need to transfer the files to your computer. If you have a video camcorder, you can buy an adapter called a VIDEO CAPTURE BOARD, which you install in your computer. Once you connect your camcorder to the board, you can create copies of individual video frames and store them as image files on your computer.

Alternatively, you can take regular pictures and use them to create jpgs. The best way to do this is to use a SCANNER, a device that you connect to your computer. A scanner processes an image on paper and creates a computer file containing that image. (We say that the scanner DIGITIZES or SCANS the image.) Scanners, of course, cost money. If you want to digitize a lot of photos, you may want to buy your own scanner. Otherwise, you may be able to find a place —such as a copy shop — where you can pay to use a scanner whenever you need one.

There is another way to get jpgs from regular photos. Some film processing companies will develop regular film and create not only prints or slides, but also computer files. The computer files will be stored on a floppy disk or CD. Some companies have a service where you can send in your film and download the finished files from the company's Web site.

hint

Once you have photos stored as computer files, it is easy to share them with your friends. To share a photo stored as a jpg, all you need to do is attach it to a mail message (see Chapter 5).

In addition to your own photographs, you can also make use of photos that are available for public use. There are many such photos on the Internet. If you are looking for a particular type of image, the following Internet Resources will help you find what you need.

Internet Resources   **Web Page Images: Photographs**

```
http://www.freefoto.com/
http://gallery.yahoo.com/
http://www.freeimages.co.uk/
http://www.yahooligans.com/downloader/pictures/
```

You may or may not want to use photographs on your Web site, but you will probably want to use other types of pictures. For example, you can use buttons to act as links, or drawings to illustrate the text. As with photographs, you can either make your own pictures or use ones that are ready-made.

If you want to make your own pictures, you can use a GRAPHICS PROGRAM. There are lots of different programs, ranging from easy-to-use utilities to complex, sophisticated tools used by graphic artists. Using such programs, you can create your own pictures, modify existing pictures, make image maps, animated gifs, and so on.

However, you do not need to be an artist to use pictures on your Web site. There are a huge number of pictures available for free on the Internet. There are also a lot of backgrounds available for free.

When you are using the Web and you see an image you like, it is easy to save a copy to a file. Simply right-click on the image. Then select **Save Picture As** (with Internet Explorer). Obviously, it is easy to steal pictures on the Web. However, if you are going to use a picture on your Web site, be sure to ask for permission first. (Send mail to the person who runs the site.)

Internet Resources **Web Page Images: Graphics, Backgrounds, Clip Art**

```
http://www.animfactory.com/
http://www.barrysclipart.com/
http://www.backgroundcity.com/
http://www.graphicsfreebies.com/
http://www.grapholina.com/Graphics/
http://www.coolarchive.com/index.cfm
http://www.webplaces.com/html/clipart.htm
http://www.thefreesite.com/freegraphics.htm
```

Aside from pictures, you may also want to use sound on your Web site. If so, there are many sounds available for free on the Web. In addition, if your computer has a microphone, you can record your own sounds and save them as **wav** files. To do so, you can use the Sound Recorder program that comes free with Windows.

To start the Sound Recorder program:

1. Click on the **Start** button.
2. Select **Programs**, then **Accessories**, then **Entertainment** (with older versions of Windows, **Multimedia**).
3. To start the program, click on **Sound Recorder**.

Internet Resources **Sounds**

```
http://wav.homez.net/
http://www.dailywav.com/
http://www.slonet.org/~rloomis/
http://wav-emporium.forsite.net/
http://www.cyberspy.com/~visual/sound.html
http://www.yahooligans.com/downloader/sounds/
```

Web Page Design Tips

To help you develop your Web page design skills, here are a few tips.

When you finish your Web pages, look them over carefully before you upload them to your Web server. As you do, it is important to realize that not everyone uses the same browser. What you see on your computer, with your monitor and your browser, will not be the same as what other people see.

Professional Web designers always look at their designs on a variety of systems, using a number of different browsers and monitors. They strive for a design that will look good and behave correctly with a variety of configurations. You don't have to be that picky, but at the very least, I want you to look at your Web pages with both major browsers: Internet Explorer and Netscape. You probably already use one of these, but you will need to install the other one for testing purposes.

Let's move on now to some specific design points. As you explore the Web, you will see many sites —especially corporate sites —that use elaborate graphics. In my opinion, such graphics are not that important. In fact, a graphics-laden site will irritate many people, because the pictures can take a long time to download over a slow connection.

Remember, most people who use the Web are looking for *information*, not pictures. Strive to make your Web site easy to read, well-organized, and pleasant to look at. There is no need to make your Web pages look like an avant-garde magazine (unless you are an avant-garde magazine).

Here are some practical guidelines. First, follow your heart and your passions. Use your Web site to develop and share information about the areas of life that are important and interesting to you. Your goal should be to attract the *right* people to your site: the people who care about the same things as you.

There are too many Web sites out there that have nothing to say. How much time do *you* spend looking at other peoples' family photos and personal information?

As one of my readers, I know you are a melting pot of intelligence, creativity, imagination and good taste. Let your Web site celebrate what is special about you: share your interests and your expertise with the world.

The next guideline has to do with how you organize your Web site. Build a home page that acts as a central gateway for the whole site. This home page will often be the first thing people see when they visit your site, so choose a simple title that shows the theme of your site. Make sure this page has links to all the major features of your site, to make it easy for people to find what they want.

Remember, though, there is no way to force people to use the home page to enter your site. For example, someone might find your site via a search engine, and there is no guarantee that the search engine will point to your home page. It is altogether possible that people will jump right into the middle of the site.

For this reason, you should design your pages so that people can navigate through the entire site from any one of the pages. To do so, put some navigation aids on every page. For example, you might use a set of links at the top or bottom of the page. The links should point to the home page, as well as the other major features of your site. The goal is that, no matter where someone starts, he or she should be able to get to your home page with a single click.

I won't go on and on about Web page design. I have faith that, with a bit of practice, you will be able to create an interesting, well-organized Web site. However, I do want to offer one last piece of advice. There are a number of design techniques I want you to avoid —things that do not work well on the Web:

- It is possible to make words blink off and on. Do not do so.

- Anything that blinks, flashes or changes will keep catching the eye of your reader and irritate him.

- Avoid bright or complex backgrounds for your pages. Use a simple, low-contrast background. Otherwise, your pages will be too hard to read, and people will just skip them.

- Never make your Web site play music automatically: it is too annoying. If you want to put music on your pages, set it up so the visitor must click on a button to start the music.

- Do not design your page so that clicking on a link creates a new browser window. When you create a new window automatically, it forces your visitor to close the window later, which is a bother. If someone wants a new browser window, he can create one himself whenever he wants by pressing the **Ctrl-N** key.

- If you use frames on your Web site, make sure that a visitor who follows a link to another Web site will not find himself trapped in one of your frames. You do not need to make it convenient for people to return after leaving your site. If someone wants to return, he can click on the **Back** button.

- Test your Web pages after you upload them to the Web server. Do not assume they work properly just because they worked on your computer.

- If you link to other sites from your Web pages, test the links regularly (at least every month) to make sure they still work.

- Finally, never, ever use a notice that says your Web site is "under construction". All good Web sites are *always* under construction. The metaphor was cute for a short time in 1994, and that time has long since passed. If your Web site is not ready, do not show it to people. If your Web site is ready, it is not necessary to advertise that you will be improving the pages from time to time.

Finding a Server to Host Your Web Site

In order to have a Web site, you need to arrange for the use of a Web server that is connected to the Internet. Once you upload your Web pages to such a server, they will be available to anyone on the Net. When someone provides this service for you, we say that they HOST your Web site.

When you look for a Web site host, you want a server that runs 24 hours a day and has a high-speed Internet connection. However, there is no reason why your Web site needs to be on a computer near you. A Web site can be hosted anywhere on the Internet, even in another country.

There are a great many Web site hosting services on the Internet, so you have a lot of choice. Start your search by checking with your ISP (Internet service provider). Many ISPs offer free or low-cost Web hosting to their customers.

If your ISP does not provide this service —or you want more choice — you can turn to one of the commercial providers. Some commercial providers charge money, others offer Web hosting for free.

Now, free sounds like a good deal, but I want you to think twice before you sign up. These services are free because they subject your visitors to a lot of advertising. Most likely, the Web hosting service will put ads on your Web pages, and there is nothing you can do about it. In many cases, there will be animated ads and pop-up ads, which are particularly obnoxious.

(A POP-UP AD is an advertisement that appears in a window of its own. In order to get rid of a pop-up ad, you have to stop what you are doing and close the window manually.)

Some people say, "Well, what's so bad about a few advertisements? Isn't it worth it if I can have my Web site hosted for free?" My opinion is, no. Remember, *you* are not the one who has to look at the ads. The people who visit your Web site are the ones being imposed upon. If you want to attract people to your site, you should make it as pleasant as possible.

Suppose some company were to offer you free telephone service with the condition that every time someone called you, that person would have to listen to a short commercial before they could connect to your phone. Would you agree to such a service? I hope not. All it would do is irritate everyone who called you. So, think twice before you subject your Web visitors to a similar imposition.

Moreover, there is another potential consideration. Before you are allowed to create a free Web site, you must agree to certain limitations. These limitations are buried in legal fine print, and many people don't bother to read them. However, they are important. Some of the companies that provide "free" Web hosting assert that they own the rights to whatever you put on your Web site, including all the content. In other words, after spending many hours creating your own Web site, you may discover that it does not belong to you.

Finally, you need to ask yourself, how can a company stay in business if it is giving away Web hosting services for free? One answer is that the company can make money on ads. However, in many cases, this is not enough. The sad truth is that many free Web hosting companies have gone out of business, often without warning. When this happens, all the "customers" lose their Web sites. This is why, in all of my books, I don't use any Internet resources that are hosted on free Web servers. Such sites just aren't stable enough (and there are too many ads).

The Web hosting business is extremely competitive, and it is not hard to find such services at a reasonable price. However, like many other services on the Internet, you get what you pay for. If you are creating a Web site for a business, don't even think about using a free service. You need the support (and the ad-free environment) of a regular commercial provider.

When you investigate Web hosting services, look for the following:

- **Price**: Get a flat rate, so you know what you will be paying. Many Web hosting services have different plans. Check how the prices will change if you need to move from one plan to another.

- **Disk space**: How much disk space will you get to store your files? How much does it cost for extra space should you need it?

- **Connectivity**: Does the provider have reliable high-speed access? To find out for yourself, connect to several Web sites hosted by the same provider and see how fast they load. Be sure to try this experiment at different times of the day, as the demand can vary: almost everything looks fast in the middle of the night.

- **Technical support**: When you have a problem, it is important to be able to reach a live person. Is such support available? What are the hours? Realistically, you can't expect anyone to spend a lot of time helping you design a Web page. However, you should be able to get assistance if you have a logistical problem, such as trouble sending files to their Web server.

- **Frontpage support**: One of the most popular Web page editors is Microsoft's Frontpage. (See the discussion on Web page editors earlier in the chapter.) Some Web hosting services use Web servers that have special built-in support for Frontpage. These services are referred to as "Frontpage Extensions". If you use Frontpage for your Web page editor, find a hosting service that offers such support.

If you have a business (or if you are an extra-cool person), you may want to get your own domain name to use with your Web site. For example, here is a typical Web site address you might have with an ISP:

```
http://www.undependable.com/users/harley
```

With your own domain name, you can use an address like:

`http://www.harley.com/`

If this is important to you, you need to find a Web hosting company that supports personalized domain names. (This service may cost extra.) For more information about getting your own domain name, see Chapter 16.

To investigate free Web hosting services, check out the Internet Resources below. To find regular pay-for-service companies, use a search engine to look for "Web hosting". You will find a lot of choices. (I discuss search engines in Chapter 11.)

Internet Resources   **Free Web Site Hosting**

`http://tripod.lycos.com/`

`http://www.freeyellow.com/`

`http://geocities.yahoo.com`

`http://www.freeservers.com/`

`http://angelfire.lycos.com/`

`http://www.freewebspace.net/`

`http://www.firststepsite.com/`

Promoting Your Web Site

Once your Web site is ready, it is only natural to want to share it with other people. Indeed, one of the most common questions people ask me is, "How can I promote my Web site."

The answer is, there is no simple way to draw large amounts of people to your Web site. One suggestion is to get your site listed with various search engines (see Chapter 11). Many search engines have a form you can fill out to submit your Web site for inclusion in their database. Another idea is to register your Web site as part of a Web ring (also described in Chapter 11).

In addition, here are some tools that can help you find good ways to promote your Web site.

Internet Resources **Promoting Your Web Site**

http://www.uswebsites.com/submit/

http://www.addme.com/

http://www.accusubmit.com/promote.html

http://www.the-vault.com/easy-submit/

http://websiteawards.xe.net/dvworksheet.htm

http://www.promotionworld.com/

http://www.stars.com/Search/Promotion/

http://www.jimworld.com/

16

Getting Your Own Domain Name

If you use the Net just for fun, the time may come when you want to have your own domain name just because it seems like a cool thing to do (which it is).

The time may come when you want to have your own domain name. For example, if you run a business, you may want an address that is easy to remember, such as `important-stuff.com`. Or, if you use the Net just for fun, you may want to have a personal domain like `coolgal.info`, just because it seems like a cool thing to do (which it is).

In this section, I will explain what you need to do to acquire and use your own domain name.

How to Get Your Own Domain Name

A domain name only works if the rest of the world has a way to translate your hostnames into IP addresses (see Chapter 4). This means you need to arrange for your domain to be serviced by DNS (the domain name system).

The easiest way to do this is to find an ISP (Internet service provider) to help you. The ISP will arrange two things. First, they will register your domain name with the appropriate authority. Second, the ISP will provide DNS service for your name by adding it to their name server. In addition, the ISP can also arrange to handle mail for your new address, and host a Web site for you.

Let's consider an example.

Say that your name is Elmo and you want to use the domain name `important-stuff.com`. To start, you find an ISP and arrange for them to register the name `important-stuff.com` for you. At the same time, they put this domain name in their name server. Your domain is now accessible to anyone on the Net.

Next, your ISP arranges to accept mail on your behalf. This allows people to send mail to an address like:

`elmo@important-stuff.com`

When messages are sent to this address, they are received by your ISP's mail server and stored until you are ready to read them. If necessary, your ISP can also set up other mail addresses within the same domain, such as:

`suzanne@important-stuff.com`

`angel@important-stuff.com`

`pesky@important-stuff.com`

`sales@important-stuff.com`

Finally, you might have your ISP set up a Web site for you under the name `www.important-stuff.com`. Once this is done, anyone on the Net can access this site by using the URL:

`http://www.important-stuff.com/`

Thus, having your own domain name means arranging for four separate services:

- Registering your domain name with the appropriate authority
- Setting up DNS service for your domain name
- Arranging for mail service using your domain name
- Hosting a Web site using your domain name

As you saw in our example, it is common for ISPs to provide all four of these services. Be advised, however, that each of these services costs money, so it is a good idea to shop around for a good price. You do not need to buy all four of these services from the same ISP, although it is certainly more convenient to do so.

Registering a Domain Name

In Chapter 4, we discussed how there are two types of top-level domains: organizational domains (`biz`, `com`, `edu`, `gov`, `info`, `int`, `mil`, `org` and `net`) used mostly—but not exclusively—within the United States, and geographical domains (such as `au`, `ca`, `fr`, `jp` and `uk`) used widely outside the U.S. Top-level domains are administered by organizations called REGISTRARS.

For geographical domains, each country has a registrar charged with the responsibility of managing the top-level domain for that country. For example, the `ca` (Canadian) domain is managed by a Canadian registrar, the `fr` (French) domain is managed by a French registrar, and so on. In some parts of the world, a regional registrar handles the domains for a group of countries.

The organizational domains, which are more generic, are handled differently. A large number of registrars are authorized to register the public domain names: `biz`, `com`, `info`, `org` and `net`. Any one of these registrars can register a name in the `biz`, `com`, `info`, `org` and `net` domains. Since these domains are so popular, the idea is to create competition by having many different registrars.

hint

The yearly domain name registration fee only covers the fee for establishing and maintaining the domain name. There are other costs to consider.

You will still have to pay your ISP for DNS service, mail service and Web site hosting. In addition, most ISPs charge an extra fee if they send in the domain name registration for you (on top of the money you must pay the registrar).

Thus, it is a good idea to shop around and compare ISP fees. They can vary significantly.

If you want your own domain name, either you or your ISP must register that name with the appropriate registrar. This is done by submitting a form via email. If you are technically knowledgeable, you can do this yourself.If you don't want to bother with the technical details, have your ISP do it for you. For a geographical domain, you must work with the appropriate organization in your country. For one of the public organizational domains (`biz`, `com`, `info`, `org` or `net`), you must register the name with one of the authorized registrars.

Depending on the domain name you want, there may or may not be a cost for registering it. Some countries register geographical-based names for free, while others charge for the service. With the organizational domain names discussed above, there is always a fee: the most common fee is $35 U.S. per year, with the first two years being paid in advance. Thus, it costs about $70 up front to register a new name. However, the fee can vary depending on which registrar you use, so do shop around. Be sure to find out the *total cost*.

Internet Resources   **Registrars for Organizational Domain Names**

```
http://www.internic.net/regist.html
http://www.afilias.info/cgi-bin/registrar-list.cgi
http://www.icann.org/registrars/
  accreditation-qualified-list.html
```

Internet Resources   **Registrars for Geographical Domain Names**

```
http://www.corenic.org/find.htm
http://www.uninett.no/navn/domreg.html
http://www.iana.org/cctld/cctld-whois.htm
```

Choosing a Domain Name

The first step in choosing a domain name is to decide which top-level domain you want to use. If you are in the U.S., you probably want to use one of the `biz`, `com`, `info`, `org` or `net` domains. If you are outside the U.S., you can choose either a geographical domain or an organizational domain. However, unless you have a good reason to do otherwise, you should probably use the geographical domain for your country.

Next, you need to decide what domain name you want. With an organizational domain, the format will be:

name.domain

If you want a domain name for a business, your first choices would be `biz` or `com`. For example, if you have a company named The Important Stuff Company, you might choose the name:

`important-stuff.com`

If you want a miscellaneous name for a personal project, try the `info` domain. For example, if you want to create a fun, irreverent Web site that will contain cool stuff for young women, you might choose:

`coolgal.info`

If you are using a geographical domain, visit the Web site of the registrar and look for their rules. These will vary from country to country. As an example, here is a typical name you might use for a company in England:

`important-stuff.co.uk`

(The `co` means "commercial".)

When it comes to picking a name, there are only a few simple rules you must follow. A name must:

- Contain no more than 67 characters overall.
- Contain only letters, numbers and hyphens.
- Start and end with a letter or number.
- Cannot have two hyphens in a row.

Using Whois to Check a Domain Name

Once you know what domain name you want, you must check to see if it is available. To do so, you use a service called WHOIS (pronounced "who is").

There are a number of whois servers on the Net serving the different domains. You can use a whois server to check if a domain name is already in use. If the name is available, you can register it for yourself. Otherwise, you will have to choose a different name.

If a domain name is in use, the whois server will display a summary of the registration information for that name. This is a good way to find out information about who controls a particular domain name. For fun, I have shown the whois information for a typical domain name in Figure 16-1.

Internet Resources   **General Whois Servers**

```
http://www.swhois.net/
http://www.dwizard.net/
http://www.allwhois.com/
http://www.nsiregistry.com/cgi-bin/whois
```

Figure 16-1:   Whois information for a typical domain name

```
Microsoft Corporation (MICROSOFT-DOM)
1 Microsoft Way
Redmond, WA 98052
US


Domain Name: MICROSOFT.COM

Administrative Contact:
    MSN Hostmaster  (MH37-ORG)   msnhst@MICROSOFT.COM
    425 882 8080   fax: 206 703 2641

Technical Contact, Zone Contact:
    MSN NOC   (MN5-ORG)   msnnoc@MICROSOFT.COM
    425 882 8080

Billing Contact:
    Microsoft-Internic Billing Issues (MDB-ORG)
    msnbill@MICROSOFT.COM
    425 882 8080

Record last updated on 11-Dec-98.
Record created on 02-May-91.
Database last updated on 16-Jun-99 08:12:31 EDT.

Domain servers in listed order:
ATBD.MICROSOFT.COM              131.107.1.7
DNS1.MICROSOFT.COM              131.107.1.240
DNS4.CP.MSFT.NET                207.46.138.11
DNS5.CP.MSFT.NET                207.46.138.12
```

Specifying Contact Names When You Register a Domain Name

You register a domain name by filling out a form and emailing it to a registrar. When you fill out the form, you will have to specify certain information. The forms may differ a bit from one registrar to another. Typically, you will have to specify the name, address and phone number of the person or organization that will own the domain name. You will need to specify the names of three people: a technical contact, an administrative contact, and a billing contact.

The technical contact is the person who will be contacted if a technical problem arises with the domain name. Normally, this contact would be your ISP. The administrative contact is the person who administers the domain name, and the billing contact is the person to whom the invoices will be sent.

My advice is to make sure that *you* are named as both the administrative and billing contact. In addition, make sure that you, not the ISP, are listed as the owner of the name. Here is why.

Once a domain name is established, the registrar will not let just anyone make changes. After all, you don't want some malevolent person to be able to send in a form by email and steal other people's domains. The only people allowed to make changes are the technical and administrative contacts. When you first register, you specify email addresses for these contacts, and only mail that comes from one of these addresses will be accepted when a change is requested.

It is common for ISPs to put their address down for all three contacts. However, if you ever decide to move your domain name to a different ISP, you will have to get the old ISP to send in the change for you.

Don't let this happen. If your ISP sends in the form for you, insist that *you* be the administrative contact. That way, no matter what happens, you will have control over your own domain name. (After all, you are paying for it.) Take my word for it: this small precaution can save you a lot of trouble.

Also, when it comes to paying the bills, you want to make sure you are the billing contact to ensure that the invoices go directly to you. If your ISP is the billing contact, they may neglect to forward the bill, and if you don't pay it, you will lose your domain name.

Remember, it's your domain name, so stay in control.

hint

When the going gets tough, the tough get their own domain names.

17

How to do Stuff

I want you to understand

how things work.

In this chapter, I will show you how to perform a number of procedures that are necessary from time to time as you use the Internet. I explain each procedure as a series of steps for you to follow in sequence. As you do, go slowly and take a moment to think about the steps. I want you to know more than simply how to do stuff; I want you to understand how things work.

Throughout the book, I have referenced this chapter in various places. At the beginning of each procedure, I will show you the places in the book that reference that procedure. This will allow you to refer to the text if you need more information.

It is possible that the instructions in this chapter may differ slightly from what you should use with your computer. This may be the case if you are using an old version of Windows or an old browser.

If you are using an old browser, I suggest that you upgrade to the latest version. The Internet Resources below will help you.

Windows is different. There is no need to upgrade. Wait until you get a new computer, which will come with the latest version of Windows pre-installed.

Internet Resources

Browsers

```
http://www.netscape.com/download/
http://www.microsoft.com/windows/ie/
```

Windows

Internet Explorer

Outlook Express

Windows

How to Set the Date and Time on Your Computer

(See Chapter 5, page 103.)

1. Click on the **Start** button.
2. Point to **Settings**, and click on **Control Panel**.
3. Within the Control Panel, double-click on **Date/Time**. Windows will display a window showing you the date and time. To display the time zone, click on the **Time Zone** tab.
4. Make any necessary adjustments.
5. Click on the **OK** button.

See Appendix B for:

- Information on how time zones are used on the Internet
- How to find a program to maintain the correct time and date on your computer automatically

How to Use the Windows Clipboard

(See Chapter 6, page 131.)

The CLIPBOARD is an invisible storage area maintained by Windows to allow you to copy or move information from one place to another, even between windows. You can use the clipboard to copy almost any type of data that can be displayed on your screen, including text and pictures.

In general terms, here is how it works. You select some information and then copy it to the clipboard. You then move to a new location (which can be in another window), and copy the information from the clipboard to that location.

Here are the details:

1. Go to the window that contains the information you wish to copy.
2. Click your mouse at the beginning of the information you want to copy.

3. Select (highlight) all the information you want to go into the clipboard. To do so, you can use either your mouse or your keyboard. To use your mouse, hold down the left button and move the mouse pointer over the data you want to select. To use your keyboard, hold down the **Shift** key and use another key (**Left, Right, Up, Down, PageUp, PageDown**) to move the cursor over the data you want to select.

Once the information is selected, you can either copy or cut it to the clipboard. If you COPY, it does not change the selected information; if you CUT, it removes the selected information as it is copied to the clipboard.

4. To copy, pull down the **Edit** menu and choose **Copy**. To cut, pull down the **Edit** menu and choose **Cut**. The data is now in your clipboard.

Now that the information is in the clipboard, you can PASTE it into a new location.

5. Move to where you want to paste the contents of the clipboard. This location can be in the same window or in a different window.

6. Click your mouse at the exact position where you want to insert the data.

7. Pull down the **Edit** menu and choose **Paste**.

From time to time, you may make a mistake while using the clipboard. For example, you might choose **Cut** when you meant to choose **Copy**. In some cases, you can fix such a mistake. When you do, we say you UNDO the mistake.

To do so, pull down the **Edit** menu and choose **Undo**. In most cases, this will reverse the last change you made. For example, if you cut the wrong information from a file, undo will get the information back. However, be sure to undo the mistake right away, before you perform another operation.

If you like shortcuts, there are two fast ways to copy, cut and paste without using the **Edit** menu.

First, when you are ready to copy or cut, you can right-click on the selected data (click the right mouse button). This will display a menu

hint

Many programs allow
you to undo mistakes
that go beyond simple
cutting and pasting, and
some programs even
allow you to undo multi-
ple changes, one after
the other.

For example, word pro-
cessing programs usually
allow you to reverse a
whole stream of changes.
This is handy when you
realize you want to undo
the last ten things you
have done. Just press
Ctrl-Z repeatedly. Each
time you do, one more
change will be reversed.

from which you can choose **Copy** or **Cut**. After you move to the place where you want to paste, you can right-click again. This will display a menu from which you can choose **Paste**.

The second set of shortcuts is to use the keyboard as follows:

Operation	Shortcut Key
Copy	Ctrl-C
Cut	Ctrl-X
Paste	Ctrl-V
Undo	Ctrl-Z

Personally, I always use these shortcuts, as they are a lot faster than using the mouse to pull down the **Edit** menu. Be sure to remember **Ctrl-Z**, as it is a particularly easy way to undo a mistake.

Once you copy or cut something, it stays in the clipboard until you replace it with new data (or until you turn off the computer). This means you can paste the same data over and over.

However, you must be careful. The clipboard is meant to be a *temporary* storage area, and it can only hold one thing at a time. As soon as you put new information into the clipboard — even a single character —it replaces all the previous information. For this reason, it is safer to copy, not cut. That way, if you make a mistake, you still have the original.

Cutting is faster when you want to *move* data, and you know you do not need to preserve the original. However, if you are working with large amounts of data, especially in different windows, it is better to copy. Then, after you have verified that the data is safely pasted, you can return to the original location and delete what you don't need.

If you want to see what is in the clipboard, you can use a program called the CLIPBOARD VIEWER. When you run Clipboard Viewer, it creates a new window that will show you the information currently in the clipboard. Whenever you copy or cut new information, you will see the contents of the window change.

Here is how to run the Clipboard Viewer:

1. Click on the **Start** button.
2. Point to **Programs**, then **Accessories**, then click on **Clipboard Viewer**.

Using the Clipboard Viewer is an excellent way to teach yourself what happens when you copy, cut and paste. Just start the program, run a few experiments and see what happens.

Once you understand the clipboard, there is really no need to use the Clipboard Viewer. In general, you only need the contents of the clipboard for a short time —usually a few seconds —and it is just not practical to check the Clipboard Viewer every time you copy or cut.

Remember, however, since the clipboard can hold only one thing at a time, even a simple mistake will wipe out the entire contents. So do be careful.

hint

Once data becomes invisible, it is easy to lose.

How to Change Your Mouse to Be Left-handed

(See Chapter 7, page 154.)

1. Click on the **Start** button.
2. Point to **Settings**, and click on **Control Panel**.
3. Within the Control Panel, double-click on **Mouse**. You will see the mouse settings panel.
4. On the **Buttons** page, under **Button configuration**, click on **left-handed**.
5. Click on the **OK** button.

Internet Explorer

How to Control the Appearance of Your Browser

(See Chapter 7, page 143 and Chapter 10, page 220.)

There are two different ways to control which toolbars are visible:

- Pull down the **View** menu and point to **Toolbars.**

or:

- Right-click on an empty area of one of the toolbars.

In either case, you will see a list of toolbars. Select the name of a toolbar. Doing this acts as an off/on switch.

You can also choose which buttons appear on the Standard toolbar and control how they look:

- Pull down the **View** menu, point to **Toolbars,** and select **Customize.**

or:

- Right-click on an empty area of one of the toolbars and select **Customize.**

Finally, you can turn the status bar (at the bottom of the browser window) off and on:

- Pull down the **View** menu and select **Status Bar.** This acts as an off/on switch.

In most cases, Internet Explorer will remember the settings and maintain them the next time you start the program. This is not the case, however, for the Radio toolbar (with Internet Explorer version 5). If you want to always have it visible when you start your browser, you need to turn it on (with **View**) *and* set an option. To set the option:

1. Pull down the **Tools** menu and select **Internet Options.**
2. Click on the **Advanced** tab.
3. Under the **Multimedia** section, turn on the option **Always show Internet Explorer Radio bar.**
4. Click on the **OK** button.

Why do you need to set an option for this particular toolbar? When you show the Radio toolbar, it causes Internet Explorer to pre-load the program used to listen to radio stations (Windows Media Player). On some systems, this may slow down the starting of Internet Explorer. For this reason, the browser will not show the Radio toolbar automatically unless you deliberately set the option.

How to Tell Your Browser to Not Underline Links

(See Chapter 7, page 150.)

1. Pull down the **Tools** menu and select **Internet Options**.
2. Click on the **Advanced** tab.
3. Look under the **Browsing** section for **Underline Links**.
4. Click on **Never** or **Hover**. (If you click on **Hover**, a link will be underlined only when you point to it.)
5. Click on the **OK** button.

Note: If the current page does not change, you may need to reload it.

How to Change the Cache Settings

(See Chapter 7, page 160.)

1. Pull down the **Tools** menu and select **Internet Options**.
2. Click on the **General** tab.
3. Under **Temporary Internet Files**, click on the **Settings** button.
4. Make whatever changes you want. (If you are not sure what you are doing, write down the original settings, so you can restore them if necessary.)
5. Click on the **OK** button.
6. To close the **Internet Options** window, click on the **OK** button.

How to Control and Delete Cookies, Internet Explorer 6

(*See Chapter 12, page 259.*)

To change the cookie settings:

1. Pull down the **Tools** menu and select **Internet Options**.

2. Click on the **Privacy** tab.

3. On the left side of the **Settings** section, you will see a small bar that can slide up and down. To move the bar, point to it, hold down the left-mouse button, and move your mouse up and down. As you move the bar, you will see the privacy setting change. Choose the one you want.

4. If you want to override the automatic settings, click on the **Advanced** button. Make your choices and then click on the **OK** button. You will see reference to two types of cookies. "First-party cookies" are those that are sent to your computer by the Web site you are visiting. "Third-party cookies" are sent from a different source, for example, a computer run by a third-party advertising company.

5. To close the **Internet Options** window, click on the **OK** button.

To look at your cookies within the cache:

1. Pull down the **Tools** menu and select **Internet Options**.

2. Click on the **General** tab.

3. Under **Temporary Internet Files**, click on the **Settings** button. Internet Explorer will create a new window named **Settings**.

4. Within this window, click on the **View Files** tab. Internet Explorer will create a new window showing you the contents of your cache directory.

5. Within this window, look for your cookies. (Most cookies have names that begin with `Cookie:`.)

6. When you are finished, close the cache directory window. (Click on the close button in the top right-hand corner of the window or press **Alt-F4**.)

7. To close the **Settings** window, click on the **Cancel** button (so you don't accidentally change a setting).

8. To close the **Internet Options** window, click on the **OK** button.

To delete your cookies:

1. Pull down the **Tools** menu and select **Internet Options**.
2. Click on the **General** tab.
3. Under **Temporary Internet Files**, click on the **Delete Cookies** button.
4. Within this window, click on the **View Files** tab. Internet Explorer will create a new window showing you the contents of your cache directory.
5. Within this window, look for your cookies. (Most cookies have names that begin with `Cookie:`.)
6. When you are finished, close the cache directory window. (Click on the close button in the top right-hand corner of the window or press **Alt-F4**.)
7. To close the **Settings** window, click on the **Cancel** button (so you don't accidentally change a setting).
8. To close the **Internet Options** window, click on the **OK** button.

How to Control and Delete Cookies, Internet Explorer 5.5 or older

(See Chapter 12, page 259.)

To change the cookie settings:

1. Pull down the **Tools** menu and select **Internet Options**.
2. Click on the **Security** tab.
3. In the content zone window near the top, click on **Internet**.
4. Click on the **Custom Level** tab. Internet Explorer will display a new window named **Security Settings**.
5. Within this window, scroll down until you see the **Cookies** heading. You will see various cookie-related settings. (If there are no settings visible, double-click on **Cookies**.)
6. Make whatever changes you want. (If you are not sure what you are doing, write down the original settings, so you can restore them if necessary.)

7. Click on the **OK** button.

8. Internet Explorer will display a dialog box, asking you to confirm that you want to change the security settings. Click on the **Yes** box.

Internet Explorer keeps two copies of each cookie. The first copy is in your cache (see Chapter 7). The cache consists of a collection of files stored in a directory named `Temporary` Internet Files. This directory lies in the `Windows` directory. That is:

`C:\Windows\Temporary Internet Files`

A duplicate of each cookie is kept in a directory called `Cookies`, also within the `Windows` directory:

`C:\Windows\Cookies`

To look at your cookies within the cache:

1. Pull down the **Tools** menu and select **Internet Options**.

2. Click on the **General** tab.

3. Under **Temporary Internet Files**, click on the **Settings** button. Internet Explorer will create a new window named **Settings**.

4. Within this window, click on the **View Files** tab. Internet Explorer will create a new window showing you the contents of your cache directory.

5. Within this window, look for your cookies. (All cookies have names that begin with `Cookie:`.)

6. When you are finished, close the cache directory window. (Click on the close button in the top right-hand corner of the window or press **Alt-F4**.)

7. To close the **Settings** window, click on the **Cancel** button (so you don't accidentally change a setting).

8. To close the **Internet Options** window, click on the **OK** button.

To get rid of your cookies, you must use Windows Explorer to delete the cookie files from *both* directories.

`C:\Windows\Temporary Internet Files`
`C:\Windows\Cookies`

It is not enough to delete the files in the `Cookies` directory.

Note: It is possible to tell Internet Explorer to clean out the cache for you. (Look on the `General` *tab in the* `Internet Options`*.) However, doing so will delete only regular files, not cookies. You must delete the cookies yourself.*

How to Customize the Search Facility

(See Chapter 11, page 239.)

You can customize the Search Assistant by choosing which search engines it uses. To do so:

1. Click on the **Search** button to open the Explorer bar.

2. Within the Explorer bar, click on the **Customize** button. Internet Explorer will open a new window named **Customize Search Settings**.

3. At the top of the window, select the first choice: **Use the Search Assistant for smart searching**.

4. Just below, make sure that **Find a Web page** is selected.

5. Under **Find a Web Page**, choose the search engines you want to use, by clicking on boxes so that a checkmark appears next to the ones you want. When you choose a search engine, its name will appear in the list within the little window to the left.

6. The Search Assistant will access the search engines in the order they appear in this list. To change the position of a search engine within the list, click on the name and then click one of the small up or down arrows below the list.

7. When you are finished, click the **OK** button.

Question: Can you tell the Search Assistant to use a search engine that is not one of the choices?

Answer: No, because that company didn't make a marketing deal with Microsoft.

The second way to customize the search facility is to skip the Search Assistant and use only one search engine. To do so:

1. Click on the **Search** button to open the Explorer bar.

2. Within the Explorer bar, click on the **Customize** button. Internet Explorer will open a new window named **Customize Search Settings**.

hint

If you are outside the United States, you may find that you don't have much choice in the list of search engines. If so, change your country to the United States temporarily. (Click on the Start button, select Settings, then Control Panel. Then double-click on Regional Options or Regional Settings.)

Once you reboot, Windows will think you are in the U.S., and you will have a lot more search engines from which to choose. After you finish customizing your search settings, you can reset your computer back to your home country. Don't worry, you won't lose your search settings.

3. At the top of the window, select the second choice: **Use one search service for all searches**. Internet Explorer will display a small window with a list of search engines.

4. Within that window, click on the search engine you want to use.

5. Click on the **OK** button.

How to Specify Which Search Engine to Use for Address Bar Searches

(See Chapter 11, page 241.)

You can perform simple searches by typing a search request directly into the address bar. In its simplest form, such a request consists of a **?** (question mark) character followed by a list of search words. When you press **Enter**, your browser will automatically submit the words to a search engine and then display the results.

To specify which search engine will be used for such requests:

1. Click on the **Search** button to open the Explorer bar.

2. Within the Explorer bar, click on the **Customize** button. Internet Explorer will open a new window named **Customize Search Settings**.

3. At the bottom of this window, click on the **Autosearch settings** button. Internet Explorer will open a new window named **Customize Autosearch Settings**.

4. In the top part of this window, click on the small down arrow, just below **Choose a search provider for address bar searches**.

5. Click on the name of the search engine you want to use.

6. Click on the **OK** button to close the **Customize Autosearch Settings** window.

7. Click on the **OK** button to close the **Customize Search Settings** window.

Outlook Express

Outlook Express is the program that serves as the mail client and Usenet news-reader for Internet Explorer.

How to Display the Full Header of a Mail Message

(See Chapter 5, page 101.)

1. Right-click on the message and then select **Properties**.
2. Click on the **Details** tab.

How to Turn Off HTML in Mail Messages

(See Chapter 5, page 107, and Chapter 6, page 130.)

1. Pull down the **Tools** menu and select **Options**.
2. Click on the **Send** tab.
3. Under **Mail Sending Format**, click on **Plain Text**.
4. Click on the **OK** button.

How to Attach a File to a Mail Message

(See Chapter 5, page 108.)

1. Start Outlook Express and prepare a message to send.
2. Pull down the **Insert** menu and select **File Attachment**. Outlook Express will display a new window named **Insert Attachment**.
3. Navigate to the file you want to attach.
4. Click on the name of the file, then click on the **Attach** button. You will be returned to your message composition window. Below the **Subject** line, you will see an **Attach** line with the name of your file.
5. Complete the message in the regular way. When you are ready to send the message, click on the **Send** button. The file will be attached to your message.

How to Create a Signature

(See Chapter 5, page 109, and Chapter 13, page 299.)

There are two ways to create a signature with Outlook Express. Once you create a signature, Outlook Express will append it to the end of all your mail messages as well as any Usenet articles you may post.

The first way to create a signature is to type the signature directly into a particular Outlook Express window. Outlook Express will store the signature for you and let you change it whenever you want.

The second way to create a signature is to store it in a file and tell Outlook Express the location of the signature file. If you like, you can prepare more than one signature file and switch from one to another whenever you want.

To type your signature directly:

1. Pull down the **Tools** menu and select **Options**.
2. Click on the **Signatures** tab. Outlook Express will show you a new window with three sections: **Signature settings, Signatures** and **Edit Signature**.
3. To the right of the **Signatures** section, click on the **New** button.
4. In the **Edit Signature** section, select **Text**, then type the signature you want in the small window to the right.
5. Click on the **OK** button.

To create a signature file:

You must use either a text editor or a word processing program. Windows has a built-in text editor, called Notepad, that is perfect for small editing jobs like this. To start Notepad:

1. Click on the **Start** button.
2. Point to **Programs**, then point to **Accessories**, then click on **Notepad**.

If you use a word processor (such as Microsoft Word), be sure to save the data as a text file, not as a document.

To use a signature file once you have created it:

1. Pull down the **Tools** menu and select **Options**.

2. Click on the **Signatures** tab. Outlook Express will show you a new window with three sections: **Signature settings**, **Signatures** and **Edit Signature**.

3. To the right of the **Signatures** section, click on the **New** button.

4. In the **Edit Signature** section, select **File**, then specify the name of your file in the small window to the right. (If you would like to navigate to the file, click on the **Browse** button.)

5. Once you have specified the name of your signature file, click on the **OK** button.

How to Resend a Mail Message

(See Chapter 6, page 124.)

Outlook Express has no easy way to resend a message. You can forward it, but that makes changes in the body of the message. The only way to resend a message is to create a new message, copy the body of the old message to the new one, and then send the new message.

1. Open the message you want to resend. (Let's call it the old message.)

2. Create a brand new message. Either click on the **New Mail** button, or pull down the **File** menu, select **New**, then **Mail Message**. Outlook Express will open a new window called **New Message**. Within that window:

3. If you want to pass on an interesting message, such as a joke or news article, to a group of people, put your own address in the **To** line and put all the recipient addresses in the **Bcc** line. (If you do not see the **Bcc** line, pull down the **View** menu and select **All Headers**.)

4. If you want to resend the message to only one person, put his or her address in the **To** line.

5. In the **Subject** line, type the subject of the message.

6. Move to the window that contains the old message.

7. Click on the body of the message, then select the entire message. (Pull down the **Edit** menu and select **Select All**. As a shortcut, you can press **Ctrl-A**.)

8. Copy the message to the Windows clipboard. (Pull down the **Edit** menu and select **Copy**. As a shortcut, you can press **Ctrl-C**.)

9. Move to the window that contains the new message.

10. Click on the empty area that will hold the body of the new message.

11. Paste in the old message from the Windows clipboard. (Pull down the **Edit** menu and select **Paste**. As a shortcut, you can press **Ctrl-V**.)

12. Edit the new message to make it as easy to read as possible. In particular, delete all the superfluous lines.

13. To send the new message, click on the **Send** button.

How to Search for a Mail Address

(See Chapter 6, page 134.)

1. Look for the small arrow to the right of the **Find** button. (The **Find** button is to the right of the **Addresses** button.) Click on this arrow and then select **People**. Outlook Express will display a new window.

2. Within this window, if the **People** tab is not on top, click on it.

3. Select a directory from the list to the right of **Look in**.

4. Type a name to the right of the word **Name**.

5. To perform the search, click on the **Find Now** button.

hint

Outlook Express offers a number of address directories. Each directory is different, so do not give up until you have searched them all.

How to Configure Your Newsreader

(See Chapter 13, page 295.)

1. Pull down the **Tools** menu and click on **Accounts**. Outlook Express will create a new window named **Internet Accounts**.

2. Click on the **News** tab.

3. Click on the **Add** button and select **News**.

At this point, you will be led through the configuration procedure.

Top-Level Internet Domains

*Organizational domains
represent a particular
category; geographical
domains represent
a particular country
or region.*

In Chapter 4, I discuss Internet addresses in detail. All Internet addresses end with a domain name, which consists of a number of sub-domain names, separated by . (period) characters. The rightmost sub-domain is called a top-level domain. For example, in the following URL (Web address), the domain is `www.royal.gov.uk`, and the top-level domain is `uk`.

`http://www.royal.gov.uk/`

In the following mail address, the domain is `harley.com`, and the top-level domain is `com`.

`little-nipper@harley.com`

The period is pronounced "dot". For example, `harley.com` is pronounced "harley-dot-com".

There are two types of top-level domains. Organizational domains represent a particular category; geographical domains represent a particular country or region.

This appendix contains a full list of all the organizational and geographical top-level domains in current use. In a few places, where it is not obvious how the domain name was derived, I have included a short explanatory note in square brackets.

Organizational Top-Level Domains

Domain	Description
biz	businesses
com	miscellaneous [commercial]
edu	United States universities [educational]
gov	United States federal government
info	miscellaneous [information]
int	international organizations
mil	United States military
net	miscellaneous [network providers]
org	miscellaneous [organizations]

Geographical Top-Level Domains

Domain	Description
ac	Ascension Island
ad	Andorra
ae	United Arab Emirates
af	Afghanistan
ag	Antigua and Barbuda
ai	Anguilla
al	Albania
am	Armenia
an	Netherlands Antilles
ao	Angola
aq	Antarctica
ar	Argentina
as	American Samoa
at	Austria
au	Australia
aw	Aruba
az	Azerbaijan
ba	Bosnia-Herzegovina
bb	Barbados
bd	Bangladesh
be	Belgium
bf	Burkina Faso
bg	Bulgaria
bh	Bahrain
bi	Burundi
bj	Benin
bm	Bermuda
bn	Brunei Darussalam
bo	Bolivia
br	Brazil
bs	Bahamas
bt	Bhutan
bv	Bouvet Island
bw	Botswana
by	Belarus
bz	Belize

Domain	Description
ca	Canada
cc	Cocos Islands [Keeling Islands]
cd	Congo [Democratic People's Republic]
cf	Central African Republic
cg	Congo [Republic of]
ch	Switzerland [*Confoederatio Helvetica*]
ci	Ivory Coast [*Cote D'Ivoire*]
ck	Cook Islands
cl	Chile
cm	Cameroon
cn	China
co	Colombia
cr	Costa Rica
cu	Cuba
cv	Cape Verde
cx	Christmas Island
cy	Cyprus
cz	Czech Republic
de	Germany [*Deutschland*]
dj	Djibouti
dk	Denmark
dm	Dominica
do	Dominican Republic
dz	Algeria [*Al Djazair*]
ec	Ecuador
ee	Estonia [*Eesti*]
eg	Egypt
eh	Western Sahara
er	Eritrea
es	Spain [*España*]
et	Ethiopia
fi	Finland
fj	Fiji
fk	Falkland Islands [Malvinas Islands]
fm	Micronesia [Federated States of]
fo	Faroe Islands
fr	France
ga	Gabon

Domain	Description
gd	Grenada
ge	Georgia
gf	French Guiana
gg	Guernsey
gh	Ghana
gi	Gibraltar
gl	Greenland
gm	Gambia
gn	Guinea
gp	Guadeloupe
gq	Equatorial Guinea
gr	Greece
gs	South Georgia and South Sandwich Islands
gt	Guatemala
gu	Guam
gw	Guinea-Bissau
gy	Guyana
hk	Hong Kong
hm	Heard and McDonald Islands
hn	Honduras
hr	Croatia [*Hrvatska*]
ht	Haiti
hu	Hungary
id	Indonesia
ie	Ireland
il	Israel
im	Isle of Man
in	India
io	British Indian Ocean Territory
iq	Iraq
ir	Iran
is	Iceland
it	Italy
je	Jersey
jm	Jamaica
jo	Jordan
jp	Japan
ke	Kenya

Domain	Description
kg	Kyrgyzstan
kh	Cambodia [formerly Khmer Republic]
ki	Kiribati
km	Comoros
kn	Saint Kitts and Nevis
kp	North Korea [Democratic People's Republic of Korea]
kr	South Korea [Republic of Korea]
kw	Kuwait
ky	Cayman Islands
kz	Kazakhstan
la	Laos
lb	Lebanon
lc	Saint Lucia
li	Liechtenstein
lk	Sri Lanka
lr	Liberia
ls	Lesotho
lt	Lithuania
lu	Luxembourg
lv	Latvia
ly	Libya
ma	Morocco
mc	Monaco
md	Moldova
mg	Madagascar
mh	Marshall Islands
mk	Macedonia [*Makedoniya*]
ml	Mali
mm	Myanmar
mn	Mongolia
mo	Macau
mp	Northern Mariana Islands
mq	Martinique
mr	Mauritania
ms	Montserrat
mt	Malta
mu	Mauritius
mv	Maldives

Domain	Description
mw	Malawi
mx	Mexico
my	Malaysia
mz	Mozambique
na	Namibia
nc	New Caledonia
ne	Niger
nf	Norfolk Island
ng	Nigeria
ni	Nicaragua
nl	Netherlands
no	Norway
np	Nepal
nr	Nauru
nu	Niue
nz	New Zealand
om	Oman
pa	Panama
pe	Peru
pf	French Polynesia
pg	Papua New Guinea
ph	Philippines
pk	Pakistan
pl	Poland
pm	St. Pierre and Miquelon
pn	Pitcairn Island
pr	Puerto Rico
ps	Palestinian Territory
pt	Portugal
pw	Palau
py	Paraguay
qa	Qatar
re	Réunion
ro	Romania
ru	Russia
rw	Rwanda
sa	Saudi Arabia
sb	Solomon Islands [formerly British Solomon Islands]

Domain	Description
sc	Seychelles
sd	Sudan
se	Sweden
sg	Singapore
sh	St. Helena
si	Slovenia
sj	Svalbard and Jan Mayen Islands
sk	Slovakia
sl	Sierra Leone
sm	San Marino
sn	Senegal
so	Somalia
sr	Suriname
st	Sao Tome and Principe
sv	El Salvador
sy	Syria
sz	Swaziland
tc	Turks and Ciacos Islands
td	Chad [*Tchad*]
tf	French Southern Territories
tg	Togo
th	Thailand
tj	Tajikistan
tk	Tokelau
tm	Turkmenistan
tn	Tunisia
to	Tonga
tp	East Timor [formerly Portuguese Timor]
tr	Turkey
tt	Trinidad and Tobago
tv	Tuvalu
tw	Taiwan
tz	Tanzania
ua	Ukraine [*Ukraina*]
ug	Uganda
uk	United Kingdom: England, Scotland, Wales, N. Ireland
um	U.S. Minor Outlying Islands
us	United States

Domain	Description
uy	Uruguay
uz	Uzbekistan
va	Vatican City State
vc	St. Vincent and the Grenadines
ve	Venezuela
vg	British Virgin Islands
vi	U.S. Virgin Islands
vn	Vietnam
vu	Vanuatu
wf	Wallis and Futuna
ws	Western Samoa
ye	Yemen
yt	Mayotte
yu	Yugoslavia
za	South Africa
zm	Zambia
zw	Zimbabwe

Times Zones on the Internet

*The Internet is used around
the world, and times must
be expressed carefully.*

The Internet is used around the world, and times must be expressed carefully, especially within the headers of mail messages and Usenet articles. In general, the Internet uses a 24-hour clock. For example, within a header, you will see `20:50` instead of 8:50 PM. (If you are not used to a 24-hour clock, use the conversion information in Figure B-1.)

Aside from the actual time, it is also important to know the time zone. This information is usually expressed in one of three ways.

First, you might see a specific time along with the local time zone. For example, the following header line specifies a time of 8:50 PM, Pacific Daylight Time (PDT):

`Date: Tue, 18 Sep 2001 20:01:17 PDT`

Another way you might see this same information is with the time converted to GMT (Greenwich Mean Time), also referred to as UT (Universal Time) or UTC (Coordinated Universal Time). You will see GMT/UT/UTC times even when a mail message or Usenet article did not originate in that time zone. The conversion is done automatically by the software. Here is the same time as above specified as GMT:

`Date: Wed, 18 Sep 2001 03:01:17 GMT`

Notice how, in this example, the GMT time is 3:50 AM one day later. This is because GMT is 7 hours ahead of PDT. For reference, Figure B-2 summarizes the time zones used in the U.S. and how they compare to GMT.

One last way in which you may see time specified within a header is a local time followed by the number of hours difference from GMT:

`Date: Tue, 18 Sep 2001 20:01:17 -0700`

Learn how to...

Set the Time and Date on Your Computer

It is up to you to make sure the time and date settings are correct on your computer.

See Chapter 17, *How to Do Stuff*, page 366 (Windows).

This header line shows the same time, 8:50 PM, and indicates that the local time zone is -7 hours different from GMT.

Whenever your programs need to know the time, date, or time zone, they get the information from settings that are maintained by Windows. For example, when you send a mail message, your mail program puts the date, time, and time zone on the message.

To ensure that your time and date are always correct, you can use a program that will synchronize your computer's clock with an exact time source on the Internet. Once you install one of these programs, it will run on its own in the background, checking the time and date automatically at regular intervals, and making corrections as necessary. However, you do need to make sure your time zone is set correctly.

Internet Resources **Time and Date Synchronization
Programs**

```
http://www.kaska.demon.co.uk/
http://www.arachnoid.com/abouttime/
http://www.dillobits.com/products.html
http://www.locutuscodeware.com/swatch.htm
```

What's in a Name?

GMT, UT, UTC

Greenwich (pronounced "Gren-itch"), a borough of London, was the home of the Royal Observatory from 1675-1985. It was at this observatory that our modern system of timekeeping and longitude was developed. For this reason, the imaginary north-south line that runs through the observatory is designated as 0 degrees longitude.

In 1884, the time at Greenwich was adopted as the global standard used to determine all the time zones around the world. This global standard time is called Greenwich Mean Time or GMT. (In this context, the word "mean" refers to "average".) GMT is used widely on the Internet, and is sometimes referred to by the newer, more official name of UT (Universal Time).

In addition to UT, you may see another name, UTC (Coordinated Universal Time). UTC is the official value of Universal Time as calculated by the U.S. National Bureau of Standards and the U.S. Naval Observatory.

By the way, you might wonder why the abbreviation for Coordinated Universal Time is UTC, not CUT. Here is why:

UTC was adopted as an official international standard in 1970. The work was done by a group of experts within the International Telecommunication Union. When it came time to name the new standard, the group had a problem. In English, the abbreviation for Coordinated Universal Time would be CUT. But in French, the name is Temps Universel Coordonné and the abbreviation would be TUC. The group wanted the same abbreviation to be used everywhere, but they couldn't agree on whether it should be CUT or TUC. The compromise was to use UTC. Although the abbreviation is inexact in both English and French, it had the enormous advantage of keeping the peace.

(Not too many people know this, but now you do.)

Figure B-1: The 24-hour time system compared to the AM/PM system

On the Internet, time is often specified using a 24-hour clock. The following table shows the 24-hour values and their equivalent AM/PM times.

```
12 midnight = 00:00      12 noon = 12:00
    1:00 AM = 01:00      1:00 PM = 13:00
    2:00 AM = 02:00      2:00 PM = 14:00
    3:00 AM = 03:00      3:00 PM = 15:00
    4:00 AM = 04:00      4:00 PM = 16:00
    5:00 AM = 05:00      5:00 PM = 17:00
    6:00 AM = 06:00      6:00 PM = 18:00
    7:00 AM = 07:00      7:00 PM = 19:00
    8:00 AM = 08:00      8:00 PM = 20:00
    9:00 AM = 09:00      9:00 PM = 21:00
   10:00 AM = 10:00     10:00 PM = 22:00
   11:00 AM = 11:00     11:00 PM = 23:00
```

Figure B-2: U.S. time zones compared to GMT

Abbreviation	Time Zone	Difference from GMT
GMT	Greenwich Mean Time	0
UT	Universal Time	same as GMT
UTC	Coordinated Universal Time	same as GMT
EST	Eastern Standard Time	-5 hours
EDT	Eastern Daylight Time	-4 hours
CST	Central Standard Time	-6 hours
CDT	Central Daylight Time	-5 hours
MST	Mountain Standard Time	-7 hours
MDT	Mountain Daylight Time	-6 hours
PST	Pacific Standard Time	-8 hours
PDT	Pacific Daylight Time	-7 hours

Abbreviations Used When Talking on the Net

People really do talk like this on the Net.

A great deal of communication on the Internet consists of people typing text to one another — in mail messages and Usenet articles, and while talking to other people using IRC, chat rooms, talk facilities and muds.

To save time and effort, there are a number of common abbreviations and acronyms used while communicating on the Net. I have collected the most important ones in Figure C-1.

Some of the abbreviations are used only in certain contexts. For example, you will generally see `Objoke` only in Usenet humor groups (where a person posting a message has included an "obligatory joke"), while `BRB` would be used when two people are chatting and one tells the other he must leave for a moment, but will "be right back".

Aside from abbreviations and acronyms, you will commonly see people use a smiley. This indicates that what the person is saying should not be taken as offensive. Here are the three most common smileys:

```
:-)     :)     ;-)
```

(To see the smiling faces, tilt your head sideways to the left. Notice that the rightmost smiley is winking.)

You will sometimes see `<grin>` or `<g>` used instead of a smiley. Thus, all of the following examples have the same meaning:

```
We can't all be smart and good-looking :-)
We can't all be smart and good-looking :)
We can't all be smart and good-looking ;-)
We can't all be smart and good-looking <grin>
We can't all be smart and good-looking <g>
```

There is a convention that, while talking on the Net, you put words that describe an emotion within angled brackets, < >, in order to set the words off from regular text. For example, say you are in a Web chat room talking with someone at work about the new artichoke crop in Venezuela. All of a sudden, the boss walks into your friend's office, so your friend types:

```
BRB, boss <grumble>
```

You may also see asterisk characters * * used instead of < >. For instance, when your friend gets back to the keyboard, he types:

```
Gotta leave *sigh*. I have to collate
1000 copies of the company's "Employee
Guidelines for Proper Internet Usage".
```

To which you reply:

```
ROFL!
```

Note to parents and teachers: You will notice that a few of the words in Figure C-1 are swear words. I have included them for two reasons. First, people really do talk like this on the Net, so don't get excited; second, I want you to know what your kids mean when they use these abbreviations.

Figure C-1: Abbreviations used while talking on the Net

Abbreviation	Meaning
:-)	smiley
:)	smiley
;-)	winking smiley
:-O	surprised smiley
:-P	disgusted smiley (with tongue sticking out)
:-P	excited smiley (with tongue sticking out)
ADDY	address
AFAIK	as far as I know
AFK	away from keyboard
A/S/L	what is your age, sex, and location?
BBL	be back later
BF	boyfriend
BFD	big fuckin' deal
BG	big grin
BRB	be right back
BTW	by the way
CU	see you
CUL	see you later
CUL8R	see you later
CYA	see ya (good-bye)
F2F	face to face (in person)
FAQ	frequently asked question list
FOFLMAO	falling on the floor laughing my ass off

Figure C-1: continued

Abbreviation	Meaning
FRP	fantasy role playing
FUBAR	fucked up beyond all recognition
FWIW	for what it's worth
FYI	for your information
<G>	grin (same as a smiley)
GAL	get a life
GD&R	grinning, ducking and running
GF	girlfriend
GG	good game (if playing an online game)
GRIN	grin (same as a smiley)
HB	hurry back
HTH	I hope this helps
IANAL	I am not a lawyer
IC	I see
IC	in character (while role playing)
ICWUM	I see what you mean
IM	instant message (can be a verb)
IMHO	in my humble opinion
IMNSHO	in my not so humble opinion
IMO	in my opinion
IOW	in other words
IRL	in real life
J/K	just kidding
L8R	(see you) later
LMAO	laughing my ass off
LDR	long distance relationship
LOL	laughing out loud
MOTAS	member of the appropriate sex
MOTOS	member of the opposite sex
MOTSS	member of the same sex
NM	never mind
NP	no problem
Ob-	(as a prefix) obligatory
Objoke	obligatory joke
OIC	oh, I see
OMG	oh, my God!

Figure C-1: continued

Abbreviation	Meaning
OOC	out of character (while role playing)
OS	operating system
OTOH	on the other hand
PAW	parents are watching
PDA	public display of affection
POV	point of view
PM	private message
PUTER	computer
RL	real life
ROFL	rolling on the floor laughing
ROTFL	rolling on the floor laughing
ROTFLMAO	rolling on the floor laughing my ass off
RPG	role playing game
RTFM	read the fuckin' manual (before asking a question)
SO	significant other
THX	thanks
TTFN	ta-ta for now (good-bye)
TTYL	talk to you later
TTYS	talk to you soon
TY	thank you
TYVM	thank you very much
WTF	who the fuck?/what the fuck?/why the fuck?
WU?	what's up?
WUF?	where are you from?

Internet Resources **Lists of Smileys**

http://www.smilies.cz/

http://www.pop.at/smileys/

http://paul.merton.ox.ac.uk/ascii/smileys.html

GLOSSARY

ActiveX: A programming system, developed by Microsoft and promoted as a richer and more powerful alternative to Java. Unlike Java applets, ActiveX programs do not run within a controlled environment. [12]

address:
1. A specification describing the exact name of a computer, person or resource on the Internet. [2]
2. Informally, a synonym for either a mail address or a URL (Web address). [4, 5]

address bar: Within a browser, an area in the browser window that displays the URL of the current Web page, and into which you can type a specific URL when you wish to load a different page. [7]

address book: Within a mail program, a facility for storing names and addresses along with other related information. [5]

ADSL: (Asymmetric Digital Subscriber Line) A technology that allows high-speed Internet connections over a telephone line. See also **DSL**. [3]

alias: A name, within a mail address book, that represents a list of addresses. [6]

all caps: Describes words that are typed in uppercase (that is all capital letters). [6]

alternative hierarchy: Within Usenet, one of five hierarchies, distributed around the world, which do not use standardized procedures for creating new groups. The alternative hierarchies are `alt`, `bionet`, `bit`, `biz` and `k12`. [13]

analog: Describes a quantity that can vary continuously from one value to another. **Compare to digital**. [3]

animated gif: A type of gif file that, when displayed, creates a simple animation. [15]

anonymous FTP: An Internet service that allows people to download files without having an account on the computer on which the files are stored. [2, 9]

[X] indicates the chapter or appendix in which the term is defined.

antivirus program: A program used to search out, identify, and, when possible, neutralize such viruses as may be present in the memory or the file system of a computer. [12]

AOL: A large ISP that offers extra content and services along with Internet access. In the U.S., the name AOL stands for America Online. [3]

applet: A small program, designed to be embedded within a larger system and run within a controlled environment. [12]

application sharing: Within a talk facility, a feature that allows people to collaborate by having joint control over a program running on one person's computer. [8]

archive: A single file that contains a collection of one or more compressed files. Programs to be downloaded are stored as archives to make the downloading process faster and simpler. After an archive is downloaded, it must be unpacked. [9]

ARPA: (Advanced Research Projects Agency) An agency that used to be part of the U.S. Department of Defense. [1]

Arpanet: An early computer network, the ancestor of the Internet. The Arpanet was funded by ARPA. [1]

article: Within Usenet, a message sent to a discussion group. Same as a **posting**. [2, 13]

asymmetric: Describes an Internet connection in which the available bandwidth is allotted unevenly between downstream and upstream transmissions, usually with more bandwidth for downstream. [3]

attach: To combine a file with a mail message such that the file is sent to the recipient along with the message. [2, 5]

attachment: A file that is combined with a mail message such that the file is sent to the recipient along with the message. [2, 5]

AutoComplete: In a browser, as you are typing a URL, a facility that guesses which URL you want by looking at what you have already typed and comparing it to URLs you have used previously. [7]

avatar: Within a talk facility, a small picture or figure that moves and talks on your behalf. [8]

backup: A copy of a file or a set of files, maintained as a safeguard in case the original data is damaged or lost and needs to be restored. [3, 7]

bandwidth: The capacity to transmit data. On the Internet, bandwidth is measured in bits per second (bps). [3]

B-channel: In an ISDN system, one of two channels that carry computer and voice data with a bandwidth of up to 64K bps (a total of 128K bps for both B-channels). The designation "B" stands for "bearer", because B-channels bear (transport) the data. Compare to **D-channel**. [3]

binary: Within Usenet, slang for a binary file. [13]

binary data: Any data that is not text. [13]

binary file: A file that contains binary data. [13]

binary system: A mathematical system, based on powers of 2 (such as 1, 2, 4, 8, 16, 32, and so on), used by computer scientists and programmers to work with computer memory. [3]

bit: The smallest unit of data storage; there are 8 bits in 1 byte. Mathematically, bits are represented by quantities that can have a value of either 0 or 1. The name "bit" stands for "binary digit". [3]

Bitnet: A large, defunct academic network, now absorbed by the Internet, that at one time supported several thousand mailing lists. [14]

bits per second: The unit of measurement used to describe the speed of an Internet connection. Abbreviated as bps. [3]

blacklist: As used by filtering software, a list of Web sites to which the software will block access. [12]

blind copy: A secret copy of a mail message sent to one or more recipients. Within the header of the message, the recipients who are to receive a blind copy are specified on the Bcc line. [5]

body: The main part of a mail message or Usenet article, containing the text of the message/article. [5, 13]

bogus: Describes a newsgroup that does not really exist or is not used in a meaningful way. [13]

[X] indicates the chapter or appendix in which the term is defined.

bot: Within IRC, a program that, within a channel, performs certain actions automatically. (The name comes from the word "robot".) [8]

bounce: After sending a mail message, to have that message returned as undeliverable. [5]

bps: Abbreviation for "bits per second". The unit of measurement used to describe the speed of an Internet connection. [3]

browser: A client program, such as Internet Explorer or Netscape, used to access the Web as well as other Internet facilities, such as mail, Usenet and anonymous FTP. For most people, a browser acts as the primary interface to the Internet. [2, 7]

buddy list: With respect to a talk facility, a personal list containing the names and addresses of people to whom you may want to talk. Same as a **contact list** or **friend list**. [8]

buffer:
1. [verb] With respect to an audio player or multimedia player, to accumulate a reservoir of data before starting to play an audio or video stream. [10]
2. Within a computer program, a temporary storage area used for input or output. [10]

bundled: Describes a product that is included, for no extra cost, when you purchase another product. For example, most new PCs come bundled with a variety of software. [3]

burn [a CD]: To create a CD using a CD-RW drive. [10]

byte: Within a computer, a unit of data storage consisting of 8 bits. Each byte can store a single character. [3]

cache: Within a browser, a temporary storage area used to hold the contents of recently viewed Web pages. [7]

carbon copy: A paper copy produced on a typewriter by using carbon paper on top of a second piece of paper. [5]

case sensitive: Describes a name in which the difference between lower- and uppercase letters is significant. [4]

CD: (compact disc) A thin, portable, disc-shaped storage device. CDs can be used to hold computer data, music, sound and video. [3]

CD burner: A program used to burn (create) a CD using a CD-RW drive. [10]

CD-R disc: A type of CD to which data can be written and deleted, but not rewritten. [10]

CD-ROM: A type of CD that holds computer data that can be read but not changed. CD-ROMs are often used to distribute software. The name CD-ROM stands for "compact disc, read-only memory", and indicates that the data can only be read. [3]

CD-RW disc: A type of CD to which data can be written, deleted and rewritten. [10]

CD-RW drive: A CD drive that can both read from and write to CD-RW discs. If you have a rewritable CD drive, you can create your own CDs. Same as **rewritable CD drive**. [3, 10]

censorware: A pejorative term for filtering software, used by people who believe that such software is unnecessarily restrictive. [12]

CGI: (Common Gateway Interface) A system used to pass data between a Web server and a program designed to process the data. [15]

channel:
1. On IRC, a facility supporting a single multiuser conversation. [2, 8]
2. Within an ISDN system, one of three separate parts, each of which furnishes a specific amount of bandwidth. ISDN uses two B-channels and one D-channel. [3]

channel operator: Within an IRC channel, a person who has certain privileges allowing him or her to control the channel in various ways. Same as **op**. [8]

charter: With respect to a Usenet newsgroup, the description and purpose of the group as written by the people who created the group. [13]

chat: To talk by typing messages back and forth in real time. [8]

chat room: On the Web, a facility allowing a group of people to talk by typing messages. Same as **Web chat room**. [2, 8]

[X] indicates the chapter or appendix in which the term is defined.

click: To press a mouse button; unless otherwise stated, to press the left mouse button. [7]

client: A program that requests a service. On the Internet, you use client programs to access various services from servers. [1]

clipboard: An invisible storage area maintained by Windows to allow you to copy or move data from one place to another, even between windows. [17]

close button: On a window, a small button with a picture of an "X" in the top right-hand corner of the window that, when pressed, closes the window permanently. [7]

coaxial cable: The type of cable used for cable TV services and for cable Internet access. [3]

compression utility: Any program that provides the service of creating and unpacking archives, in particular, zip file programs. [9]

contact list: With respect to a talk facility, a personal list containing the names and addresses of people to whom you may want to talk. Same as a **buddy list** or **friend list**. [8]

content advisor: Within Internet Explorer, a facility that allows you to control access to Web sites based on a rating system. [12]

context menu: Within Windows, when you right-click on an object, the menu that is displayed containing selections relevant to that object. [7]

control: A self-contained program, created within Microsoft's ActiveX system, designed to provide a specific function. Controls can be used as components within other programs or to enhance the functionality of Web pages. [9]

control message: Within Usenet, a short message with special header lines that act as instructions to a news server, telling the sever to perform a specific task. [13]

cookie: Data sent by a Web server and stored in a file on your computer by your browser. [12]

copy [to the clipboard]: To copy selected data to the clipboard without changing the original data. [17]

cross-post: On Usenet, to post an article to more than one newsgroup at the same time. [13]

cut [to the clipboard]: To move selected data to the clipboard while deleting the original data. [17]

cyber: To participate in Net Sex. [8]

cyberspace: A deprecated term used to refer to the Internet. Note: Use of this word will instantly mark you as a person who does not know what he is talking about. [1]

DALnet: One of the large IRC networks. The others are EFnet, Undernet and IRCnet. [8]

data: Information that is stored on a computer. [1]

DCC: (Direct Client to Client connection) Within IRC, a facility that allows you to establish a direct connection with another person, either for chatting or for transferring files. [8]

D-channel: In an ISDN system, a channel that carries internal control information with a bandwidth of up to 16K bps. The designation "D" stands for "data", although it is the B-channels that carry the actual computer and voice data. Compare to **B-channel**. [3]

decoder: A program that converts mp3 files to wav format. [10]

demodulation: The process used by a modem to convert analog data to digital data. [3]

desktop: Within Windows, the background of your display area; what you see when you have no open windows. [7]

dialog box: A window, displayed by a program, in which you are asked to enter information or choose from a selection of choices. [7]

dialup connection: A means of connecting to the Internet using a modem and a regular phone line. [3]

digest: With respect to a mailing list, a format in which individual messages are collected and sent out in the form of a single large message. [14]

digital: Describes a quantity that can take on only specific, discrete values. **Compare to analog.** [3]

[X] indicates the chapter or appendix in which the term is defined.

digital music player: A small, portable hardware device designed to store and play music in the form of mp3 files. [10]

digitize: With respect to a scanner, to process an image on paper and create a computer file containing a digital copy of that image. Same as **scan**. [15]

directory: Within a file system, an entity that contains files and other directories. Same as **folder**. [4]

disc: An informal term for a CD. [3]

disk: An informal term for a hard disk or a floppy disk. [3]

disk drive: A long-term storage device in which data is stored on disc-shaped plates. [3]

diskette drive: A long-term storage device that reads and writes data on a removable floppy disk. Same as **floppy disk drive**. [3]

DNS: (domain name system) The system used to organize all the hostnames on the Internet, and to translate a hostname into an IP address. [4]

DNS server: A server, maintained by an ISP for the use of its customers, that handles DNS requests (such as the translation of a hostname into an IP address). [4]

domain: A set of hostnames that have the rightmost part of their names in common. For example, all the hostnames that end in `edu` belong to the `edu` domain. [4]

domain name system: Same as **DNS**. [4]

double-click: To press a mouse button twice in a row quickly. [7]

down: Describes a computer or communication link that is currently not working. [1]

download: To copy a file from another computer to your computer. [2, 9]

downstream: Describes the transmission of data from the Internet to your computer. [3]

drag: To use a mouse to move an object from one location to another by pointing to the object, pressing a mouse button, and moving the mouse while holding down the button. [7]

DSL: (Digital Subscriber Line)
1. A family of technologies that allows high-speed Internet connections over a telephone line. The DSL family includes ADSL (Asymmetric DSL), HDSL (High-bit-rate DSL), RADSL (Rate Adaptive Asymmetric DSL), SDSL (Symmetric DSL), and VDSL (Very high-bit-rate DSL). [3]
2. In common parlance, DSL is often used as a synonym for the term ADSL. [3]

DVD: A type of CD that can store computer data, sound and video. DVDs store a lot more data than CD-ROMs and music CDs, and are used to distribute movies. Originally, the name DVD meant "Digital Video Disc". However, for marketing reasons, the DVD industry has changed the meaning to "Digital Versatile Disc". [3]

EFnet: One of the large IRC networks. The others are Undernet, DALnet and IRCnet. [8]

electronic mail: Same as **mail, email**. [2, 5]

email:
1. A system for sending and receiving messages from one Internet address to another. [2, 5]
2. Messages that have been sent via this system. [2]
3. [verb] To send a message. Same as mail. [2]

email virus: A type of virus that, supposedly, can cause damage to a computer merely by the act of opening or reading a mail message. There are no email viruses — the belief that they exist is a virus hoax. [12]

embedded system: A small specialized computer, used within a larger machine, such as a car, microwave oven or VCR. [3]

emulate: The action of a program that makes a computer act like a different type of device. For example, a telnet client is a program that emulates a terminal. [2]

encoder: A program that converts wav files to mp3 format. [10]

Ethernet: A particular technology used to connect computers to a local network. [3]

Ethernet port: In a PC, a socket you can use to connect your PC to a network. [3]

[X] indicates the chapter or appendix in which the term is defined.

execute [a program]: To have a computer follow the instructions in a program. Same as **run** (a program). [1, 9]

expire: With respect to a Usenet article, to delete the article after it has been stored on a news server for a particular amount of time. [13]

extension: Within a file name, the last part of the name, indicating the type of data contained in the file. For example, in the file name `index.html`, the extension `html` indicates that the file contains a Web page (hypertext). [4]

faceplate: Same as a **skin**. [10]

FAQ: (frequently asked question list) A list of questions and answers about a particular topic, written for people who are new to that topic. [9, 13]

Favorites list: Within Internet Explorer, a list of items used to store URLs for later recall. [7]

file: A collection of data stored under a specific name. [2, 4]

File Manager: The program used to manage files and directories within Windows 3.x. [4]

filter: Within a mail program, a facility that scans incoming mail and performs a particular action whenever an incoming message meets specified criteria. [6]

filtering software: Programs used to control access to Web sites based on specific criteria, such as blacklists and whitelists. [12]

flame:
1. Within Usenet, an article in which someone criticizes another person or complains vociferously (that is, a real stinker). [13]
2. [verb] To post such an article. [13]

flame war: A situation in which a group of people flame one another repeatedly. [13]

floppy: Same as **floppy disk**. [3]

floppy disk: A small, plastic-encased, portable data storage device. The most common type of floppy disk can store up to 1.44 MB of data. [3]

floppy disk drive: A long-term storage device that reads and writes data on removable floppy disks. Same as **diskette drive**. [3]

focus: The attribute of a window that makes it the active window, the one currently controlled by the keyboard. [7]

folder:
1. Within a file system, an entity that contains files and other directories. Same as **directory**. [4]
2. Within a mail system, one of several containers for messages stored on your computer. [5]
3. Within a list, a collection of items and/or other folders. [7]

follow: While looking at a Web page, to use a link by clicking on it with your mouse. [2, 7]

follow-up: Within Usenet, an article that is written in reply to a previous article. [13]

form: Within a Web page, a component that contains specific areas into which the user can type information. This information is then sent to a Web server to be processed. [15]

format: To prepare a new disk to be used for the first time. [10]

forward: After receiving a mail message from someone, to send a copy of that message to a third person. [5]

frame: Within a Web page, a specific area that can contain data from another page. [7, 15]

freeware: Software that can be distributed and used for free. [9]

friend list: With respect to a talk facility, a personal list containing the names and addresses of people to whom you may want to talk. Same as a **buddy list** or **contact list**. [8]

FTP:
1. An Internet service that allows you to copy files from one computer to another. [2, 9]
2. [verb] To copy files using the FTP service. [2]

FTP client: A program used to copy files to or from an FTP server. [2]

FTP server: A server to which (or from which) you can copy files using FTP. [2]

gateway: A program that provides an automatic connection between two different types of information systems, such as between a mailing list and a Usenet newsgroup. [14]

[X] indicates the chapter or appendix in which the term is defined.

GB: Abbreviation for **gigabyte**. [3]

geek: A nerd who is cool. [1]

geographical domain: A two-letter top-level domain that is assigned to a particular country or region. See Appendix A for a list of all the geographical domains. [4]

gif: (Graphics Interchange Format)
1. A file type commonly used to store non-photo pictures, such as drawings, cartoons and icons. Compare to **jpeg**. [15]
2. Informally, a file containing a picture in gif format. For example, "My friend sent me a gif of Mickey Mouse." [15]

gigabyte: A unit of measurement used for computer memory and data storage, 1,073,741,824 (2^{30}) bytes. Informally, a gigabyte is about 1,000,000,000 (a billion) bytes. Abbreviated as GB. [3]

GMT: (Greenwich Mean Time) The time zone based on the location of the Royal Observatory in Greenwich (a borough of London), used as an international standard. Equivalent to UT and UTC. [B]

Google: A particular search engine having an emphasis on archiving the content of the Web, which can then be referenced by searching for all the Web sites that contain specific words. [11]

graphics: Data consisting of pictures (such as drawings, photographs and illustrations) or other visual elements. [2]

graphics program: A program used to create, manipulate and modify pictures. [15]

hard disk: A long-term storage device in which data is stored on several hard disc-shaped plates. [3]

hardware: The physical components of a computer. [1]

header: Within a mail message or Usenet article, a standard section at the beginning of every message that contains technical information such as the `From`, `To`, `Date` and `Subject` lines. [5, 13]

header line: A single line within the header of a mail message or Usenet article. [5, 13]

hierarchy: Within Usenet, one of the top-level categories into which newsgroups are organized. The first part of a newsgroup name shows the hierarchy to which the newsgroup belongs. For example, the newsgroup `rec.humor` is in the `rec` hierarchy. [13]

history list: Within a browser, a list of the URLs of Web pages you have visited recently. [7]

home directory: In Unix, a directory that is assigned to a particular user for his exclusive use, within which he can create files and subdirectories as he sees fit. [4]

home page:
1. Within a browser, the Web page that is loaded automatically each time the browser starts. [7]
2. On a Web site, the main Web page, designed as the starting place for users of that site. [7]

horizontal scroll bar: A scroll bar at the bottom of a window, used to scroll the contents of the window to the left and right. [7]

host:
1. Any computer connected to the Internet. [4]
2. When using telnet, the computer to which you log in. [2]
3. [verb] To provide the service of maintaining a Web server used by people to make their Web sites available to the public. [15]

hostname: The unique name given to an Internet computer. [4]

HTML: (Hypertext Markup Language)
1. The system of specifications used to define the appearance and structure of Web pages. [7, 15]
2. Informally, the contents of an HTML file. For example, "Be sure to keep that file. It contains the HTML for the main page of the Web site." [15]

HTML editor: A Web page editor designed to help people create Web pages by composing HTML. Compare to **wysiwyg editor**. [15]

HTTP: (Hypertext Transfer Protocol) The protocol used to transfer data between Web servers and Web clients (browsers). [7]

hypertext: Data that contains links to other data or to resources. On the Web, hypertext is displayed on Web pages. [2, 7]

icon: A small picture that represents a file or a specific resource of some type. [7]

IETF: (Internet Engineering Task Force) An organization that forms working groups to study problems and to create solutions related to the technology used to run the Internet, particularly the various Internet protocols. [1]

[X] indicates the chapter or appendix in which the term is defined.

IM: (Instant Messaging)
>**1.** A talk facility that makes it easy to establish a direct connection with another person. [8]
>**2.** [verb] To talk with another person by using an IM facility. [2, 8]

image map: Within a Web page, a picture in which various parts correspond to different links. [7]

IMAP: (Internet Message Access Protocol) A protocol used by a mail client program to receive incoming messages from a mail server. With IMAP, messages remain on the server until they are deliberately deleted by the user. Compare to the **POP** protocol. [5]

IMAP server: A server to which a mail client program can connect to receive incoming mail via the IMAP protocol. [5]

installation program: A program that, when run on a particular computer, performs all the tasks that are necessary to make specific software ready to run on that computer. [9]

instant messaging: (same as **IM**)
>**1.** A talk facility that makes it easy to establish a direct connection with another person. [8]
>**2.** [verb] To talk with another person by using an IM facility. [2, 8]

[the] **Internet**: The worldwide, general-purpose, communication and information system. Same as the **Net**. [1]

Internet Engineering Task Force: Same as **IETF**. [1]

Internet Explorer: A browser, developed by Microsoft. [2, 7]

Internet phone system: A type of voice chat that allows you to use your computer to call a telephone. When the person at the other end answers, you talk to him using your microphone and speakers (or headset). [8]

Internet Relay Chat: An Internet service that allows people all over the Net to have multiple, multiuser conversations, each one on a separate "channel". Same as **IRC**. [2, 8]

Internet service provider: A company that provides Internet access to the public. Same as **ISP**. [2, 3]

IP: (Internet Protocol) The protocol, used along with TCP, to send data over the Internet. IP sends the data packets. TCP manages the flow and ensures that the data arrives intact without errors. [1]

IP address: A unique, four-part number, identifying a specific Internet computer. For example, the IP address of **www.harley.com** is **207.155.37.136**. Same as **IP number**. [4]

IP number: Same as **IP address**. [4]

IRC: (Internet Relay Chat) An Internet service that allows people all over the Net to have multiple, multiuser conversations, each one in a separate "channel". [2, 8]

IRC client: A client used to access IRC. [2, 8]

IRC network: A system in which various IRC servers are connected so as to allow anyone connected to one server to talk to anyone connected to any of the other servers. The four largest IRC networks are EFnet, Undernet, DALnet and IRCnet. [8]

IRC server: A server used to provide IRC services. [2, 8]

IRCnet: One of the large IRC networks. The others are EFnet, Undernet and DALnet. [8]

ISDN: (Integrated Services Digital Network) A service, offered by a telephone company, that allows you to connect to an ISP using all-digital technology. [3]

ISP: (Internet service provider) A company that provides Internet access to the public. [2, 3]

item: Within a Favorites list, an object with a name and other properties, used to store a particular URL. [7]

Java: A set of specifications developed by Sun Microsystems, used to create programs (called applets) that can be embedded within Web pages and run within a controlled environment (the Java virtual machine), thereby ensuring a measure of safety and security to the computer on which the applet is running. [12]

Java virtual machine: A controlled environment, designed for safety, within which Java applets must run. [12]

jewel case: A plastic case used for storing CDs. [10]

join: Within IRC, to become a participant in a channel. [8]

jpeg: Same as **jpg**. [15]

[X] indicates the chapter or appendix in which the term is defined.

jpg: (Joint Photographic Experts Group)
   1. A file format commonly used to store photographs. Compare to **gif**. [15]
   2. Informally, a file containing a photograph in jpg format. For example, "My friend sent me a jpg of his cat playing the piano." [15]

KB: Abbreviation for **kilobyte**. [3]

kilobyte: A unit of measurement used for computer memory and data storage, 1024 (2^{10}) bytes. Informally, a kilobyte is about 1000 bytes. Abbreviated as KB. [3]

lag: While talking on the Internet, a noticeable delay. [8]

LDAP: (Lightweight Directory Access Protocol) A protocol used by client programs to communicate with servers that provide access to directories containing names, mail addresses, and related information. [6]

leave: Within IRC, to stop being a participant in a channel. [8]

link: Within hypertext (on a Web page), an item that, when selected, causes a jump to either another Web page, more information, or another resource on the Net. [2, 7]

links bar: Within Internet Explorer, a bar that can be customized with buttons that point to whatever URLs you want. [7]

list address: With respect to a mailing list, the address to which you send messages that are to be distributed to all the people who have subscribed to the list. [14]

list owner: The person who is in charge of a mailing list. [14]

list server: Same as **mailing list program**. [14]

Listproc: A type of mailing list program. [14]

Listserv: A type of mailing list program. [14]

log in: To initiate a work session with a host computer by specifying a user name and password. [2]

lowercase: Describes the small letters of the alphabet (a, b, c, d…). Compare to **uppercase**. [4]

macro: Within an application program, such as word processor or spreadsheet program, a list of instructions that, when carried out by the program, automates a specific task. [12]

macro virus: A macro that, when attached to a file such as a document or spreadsheet, can act like a virus when that file is opened by a program. [12]

mail:
1. A system for sending and receiving messages from one Internet address to another. Same as **email**. [2, 5]
2. Messages that have been sent via this system. [2]
3. [verb] To send a message. [2]

mail address: A unique identifier used to send mail to someone. [4]

mail program: A client used to send and receive mail. [2, 5]

mail server: A server that receives and stores incoming mail. [2, 5]

mailing list program: A program that automatically performs the routine tasks needed to support a mailing list. [14]

mailing list: A facility used for group discussion in which the messages are sent by mail to the members of the group. [2, 14]

mainstream hierarchy: Within Usenet, one of eight hierarchies, distributed around the world, that are subject to well-defined procedures for the creation of new groups. The mainstream hierarchies are `comp`, `humanities`, `misc`, `news`, `rec`, `sci`, `soc` and `talk`. [13]

Majordomo: A type of mailing list program. [14]

mark up: To insert HTML tags into text. [15]

maximize: To change the size of a window to be as large as possible. [7]

maximize button: On a window, a small button near the top right-hand corner of the window. When the maximize button has a picture of a single square, clicking the button changes the size of the window to be as large as possible. When the button has a picture of two overlapping rectangles, clicking the button restores the window to its original size. [7]

MB: Abbreviation for **megabyte**. [3]

megabyte: A unit of measurement used for computer memory and data storage, 1,048,576 (2^{20}) bytes. Informally, a megabyte is about 1,000,000 (a million) bytes. Abbreviated as MB. [3]

[X] indicates the chapter or appendix in which the term is defined.

megahertz: The unit of measurement used to describe the speed of a processor. Megahertz means millions of cycles per second. Abbreviated as MHz. [3]

MHz: Abbreviation for "megahertz", the unit of measurement used to describe the speed of a processor. Megahertz means millions of cycles per second. [3]

mid: A file type used to store music in MIDI format. [10]

MIDI: (Musical Instrument Digital Interface) A file format used to store and manipulate music on computers, synthesizers, keyboards, and other electronic music devices. [10]

minimize: To make a window disappear without closing it permanently, and without stopping the program that is currently running in the window. [7]

minimize button: On a window, a small button with a picture of a single line, near the top right-hand corner of the window, that when clicked makes the window disappear without closing it permanently and without stopping the program that is currently running in the window. [7]

modem: A device that provides an interface between a computer and a communication line, such as a phone line or cable. The name "modem" stands for "modulator/demodulator". [3]

moderated: Describes a newsgroup (or mailing list) in which a person, called the moderator, controls which articles (messages) are allowed to be sent to the group (list). [13, 14]

moderator: A person who controls which articles or messages are allowed to be sent to a particular Usenet newsgroup or mailing list. Such a newsgroup or mailing list is said to be moderated. [13, 14]

modulation: The process used by a modem to convert digital data to analog data. [3]

motherboard: In a PC, the main circuit board. [3]

mp3: (Moving Picture Experts Group 1 audio layer 3)
1. A file type commonly used to store music. [10]
2. Informally, a file containing music in mp3 format. For example, "My friend sent me an mp3 of her favorite Beach Boys song." [10]

mpeg: Same as **mpg3**. [10]

mud: An elaborate, multiuser, text-based imaginary environment, used for talking and role-playing, often based on a fantasy, gothic or science fiction theme. [2, 8]

mud client: A client used to access a mud. [2, 8]

multimedia: Data consisting of sound, animation or video. [2]

name server: A computer that provides DNS information on behalf of all the hostnames in a particular domain. [4]

navigate: On the Web, changing from one Web page to another. [7]

nerd:
   1. A person who spends large amounts of time engaged in an activity in which he is particularly knowledgeable. [1]
   2. An expert who is knowledgeable about the Internet or computers. [1]

[the] **Net**: The worldwide, general-purpose, communication and information system. Same as the **Internet**. [1]

Net sex: An activity in which two people type erotic messages back and forth in order to achieve a state of sexual arousal leading to physical resolution. [8]

Netnews: Same as **Usenet**. [2, 13]

Netscape: An informal term for the browser Netscape Navigator, part of the Communicator collection of software, developed by the Netscape Communications company and now owned by AOL. [2, 7]

network: Two or more computers connected together in order to share resources or information. [1]

newbie: A person who is new to the Internet. Note: Don't use this word. It makes you look like a goofball. [1]

[the] **News**: Same as **Usenet**. [2, 13]

news server: A server that stores Usenet articles and makes them available via newsreaders (Usenet client programs). [2, 13]

newsfeed: The service offered by a news server. [13]

[X] indicates the chapter or appendix in which the term is defined.

newsgroup: A Usenet discussion group. [2, 13]

newsreader: A client program used to access the Usenet system of discussion groups. [2, 13]

nick: Within IRC, an anonymous name chosen by a person. Same as **nickname**. [8]

nickname: Within IRC, an anonymous name chosen by a person. Same as **nick**. [8]

NNTP: (Network News Transfer Protocol) The protocol used to distribute Usenet articles. [13]

NNTP server: Same as a **news server**. [13]

on (the Net): Being connected to the Internet. [1]

online:
1. Describes a person or computer currently connected to the Net. [1]
2. Describes a service on the Net that is currently available. [1]

op: Within an IRC channel, a person who has certain privileges allowing him or her to control the channel in various ways. Same as **channel operator**. [8]

open (a file):
1. Within Windows, to process a file in an appropriate manner. [9]
2. Informally, to cause Windows to process a file, say, by double-clicking on a the file's icon. [9]

operating system: The master control program that runs a computer. The most widely used operating systems for PCs are the various versions of Microsoft Windows. [3]

options: Within Internet Explorer, a setting that contains configuration information or that allows you to control some aspect of the operation of the browser. [7]

organizational domain: A top-level domain that represents a particular category. See Appendix A for a list of all the organizational domains. [4]

organizational hierarchy: Within Usenet, a hierarchy in which the newsgroups are of interest primarily to people with an interest in a particular organization, for example, a university or a company. [13]

Outlook Express: A mail program and Usenet newsreader, part of the Microsoft Internet Explorer suite of Internet software. [5, 13]

packet: On the Internet, a small amount of data, sent as an intact unit from one computer to another. When a computer needs to send data over the Internet, it divides the data into packets which are sent to the destination computer. The destination computer reassembles the packets into the original data. [1]

page icon: Within Internet Explorer, an icon, just to the left of the address bar, that represents the URL of the current Web page. [7]

parent directory: A directory that contains another directory. (A directory within a parent directory is referred to as a subdirectory.) [4]

paste [from the clipboard]: To copy the entire contents of the clipboard to a specified location within a window. [17]

path: Same as **pathname**. [4]

pathname: The specific description of the location of a file or directory, consisting of a series of directory names, separated by slash (/) characters, possibly ending with a file name. [4]

peer-to-peer: Describes a decentralized technology in which individual computers join into a large, connected system. [10]

PICS: (Platform for Internet Content Selection) A set of specifications used to create rating systems for Internet resources. [12]

playlist: A list of songs, used by a program that can play or process music files. [10]

point: With respect to a URL, to refer to a particular resource. [4]

POP:
1. (point of presence) An access point provided by an ISP (Internet service provider). A POP is usually accessed by dialing a telephone number. [3]
2. (Post Office Protocol) A protocol used by a mail client program to receive incoming messages from a mail server. With POP, messages are deleted from the server once they are sent to the client. Compare to the **IMAP** protocol. [5]

POP server: A server to which a mail client program can connect to receive incoming mail via the POP protocol. [5]

[X] indicates the chapter or appendix in which the term is defined.

pop-up ad: A Web page advertisement that appears in a window of its own. In order to get rid of a pop-up ad, you have to stop what you are doing and close the window manually. [15]

port number: A number, used by a client program, to indicate to a server exactly what type of service is being requested. [8]

post: To send an article to a Usenet newsgroup. [13]

posting: Within Usenet, a message sent to a discussion group. Same as an **article**. [2, 13]

processor: In a PC, the main chip that carries out the instructions within a program; informally, the "brain" of the computer. [3]

program: A list of instructions that, when carried out by a computer, makes the computer perform in a certain way. [1]

protocol: A specification (set of technical rules) used by client and server programs to communicate with one another. [1]

publish: With respect to a Web page, to upload the page from your computer to a Web server. [15]

quote: To include all or part of an original mail message or Usenet article within a reply. [5, 13]

RAM: The working memory inside a PC, measured in MB (megabytes). The name RAM stands for "random access memory", a term used for historical reasons. [3]

readme file: A file, included within an archive, containing important information about the other files in the archive. If the archive holds a program, the readme file will usually contain information about installing and using the program. [9]

real-time: Describes a process in which you sense and respond to something as it is happening. [8]

rebuffer: With respect to an audio or multimedia player, after a connection to a server has been broken and restored, to fill up the buffer once again in order to restart an audio or video stream. [10]

regional hierarchy: Within Usenet, a hierarchy in which the newsgroups are of interest primarily to people in a particular country, city or other region. [13]

registrar: An organization charged with the responsibility of managing the registration of domain names within one or more top-level domains. [16]

reply:
1. A mail message sent in response to a previous message. [5]
2. [verb] To send such a message. [5]

resize: To change the size of a window. Same as **size**. [7]

rewritable CD drive: A CD drive that can both read from and write to CD-RW discs. If you have a rewritable CD drive, you can create your own CDs. Same as **CD-RW drive**. [3, 10]

RFD: (Request for Discussion) Within Usenet, a proposal inviting discussion regarding the creation of a new newsgroup. [13]

right-click: To press the right button of a mouse. [7]

ringmaster: A person who administers a Web ring. [11]

ripper: A program that reads data from a music CD and converts the music to mp3 format. [10]

root name server: One of a number of special computers that maintain a list of those name servers that handle the various top-level domains. [4]

run (a program): To have a computer follow the instructions in a program. Same as **execute** (a program). [1, 9]

scan: With respect to a scanner, to process an image on paper and create a computer file containing a digital copy of that image. Same as **digitize**. [15]

scanner: A device, connected to a computer, that processes an image on paper and creates a computer file containing a digital copy of that image. [15]

scheme: Within a URL, the first part of the URL. The scheme describes the type of resource being identified. For example, in the URL `http://www.harley.com/`, the scheme is `http`. [4]

scroll: To move the contents of a window in a particular direction, either up, down, left or right. [7]

[X] indicates the chapter or appendix in which the term is defined.

scroll bar: Within a window, a bar at the far right or at the bottom of the window, used to scroll the contents of the window. [7]

Search Assistant: With Internet Explorer, a facility that lets you perform a search using multiple search engines, one after another. [11]

search engine: A program that can search a large database for specific information. More specifically, a facility that allows you to search a database containing information about the contents of the Web. [11]

second-level domain: The set of all hostnames that have the two rightmost parts of their names in common. For example, all the hostnames that end with `mit.edu` belong to the `mit.edu` second-level domain. [4]

secure connection: A facility, used to transmit data, in which the data is encrypted as it is sent and decrypted as it is received. [12]

security: Issues related to protecting yourself and your computer, as you use the Internet, against problems from the outside world. [12]

security certificate: An electronic confirmation, offered by a Web site and recognized by Internet Explorer, indicating that the Web site is "secure and genuine". [12]

security level: Within the Internet Explorer security system, a description of those security features that are to be applied to particular Web sites. [12]

server: A program or computer that provides a service. On the Internet, all services are accessed by client programs that communicate with servers. [1]

shareware: Software that can be distributed and evaluated for free, but which you must pay for if you want to use after the evaluation period. [9]

shortcut: An icon that points to a specific resource, such as a URL or file. [7]

signature: A small amount of information, stored in a signature file, that is automatically appended to the end of outgoing mail messages or Usenet articles. Typically, a signature will contain information such as a name, mail address, street address, phone number or Web site address. [5, 13]

signature file: A file, containing a signature, whose contents are automatically appended to the end of outgoing mail messages or Usenet articles. [13]

size: To change the size of a window. Same as **resize**. [7]

skin: An accessory that changes the appearance of a program without changing its functionality. [10]

smiley: A series of characters, such as `:-)` or `:)`, that looks like a sideways face, indicating that what you are saying should not be taken as being offensive. [6, 8, 13]

SMTP: (Simple Mail Transfer Protocol) The protocol used to send messages to a mail server. [5]

SMTP server: A server to which a mail client program can send outgoing mail via the SMTP protocol. [5]

snail mail: Regular post office mail. On the Net, the word "mail" always refers to email. [2]

software: Computer programs. [1]

spam: Unsolicited advertisements or inappropriate messages sent by email or posted to Usenet newsgroups. [2, 6, 13]

spammer: A person or company that sends spam. [2, 6]

spoiler: A statement about a book, movie or play that gives away the ending or reveals a surprise. [13]

spyware: A program that runs on your computer without your knowledge, and secretly uses your Internet connection, typically to send information about your activities to a marketing company.

SSL: (Secure Sockets Layer) A protocol used to provide secure connections over the Internet. [12]

status bar: Within a browser, an area at the bottom of the browser window in which URLs and various informative messages are displayed. [7]

streaming: Describes a system used to transmit audio or video, in which data is played in real time as it arrives. Streaming is what makes continuous broadcasting possible over the Internet. [10]

[X] indicates the chapter or appendix in which the term is defined.

subdirectory: A directory that is contained within another directory. (The other directory is referred to as the parent directory). [4]

sub-domain: A domain that belongs to a more specific domain. For example, `pacbell.net` is a sub-domain of the `net` domain; `mail.pacbell.net` is a sub-domain of the `pacbell.net` domain. [4]

subscribe:
1. Within Usenet, to indicate to your newsreader that it should put a specific newsgroup on the list of groups you read. [13]
2. With respect to a mailing list, to tell a mailing list program that your address should receive copies of all messages sent to the list. [14]

subscription address: With respect to a mailing list, the address to which you mail commands to the mailing list program. This is the address to which you send mail to subscribe or unsubscribe to the list. [14]

suite: A collection of related computer programs, sold as a unit. [3]

surf: A deprecated term meaning "to use the Internet". Note: Use of this word will instantly identify you as a person who does not know what he is talking about. [1]

table: Within a Web page, a component that presents information in rows and columns. [15]

tag: An HTML command. All tags are contained within < (less-than) and > (greater-than) characters, for example, `<br>`. [15]

talk:
1. To send data from one computer to another. [1]
2. To have a real-time conversation with someone over the Internet, either by typing messages back and forth or by voice. [2, 8]

talk client: A program used to talk on the Internet. [8]

talk server: A server used to maintain a talk connection. [8]

taskbar: Within Windows, a long bar, displayed at one edge of the desktop, that contains the **Start** button as well as other buttons, each of which represents a program that is currently running. [7]

TB: Abbreviation for **terabyte**. [3]

TCP: (Transmission Control Protocol) The protocol, used along with IP, to send data over the Internet. IP sends the data packets. TCP manages the flow and ensures that the data arrives intact without errors. [1]

TCP/IP: The family of protocols used to run the Internet. (TCP/IP is pronounced as five separate letters, "T-C-P-I-P".) [1]

telnet: A service that allows you to connect to a remote computer, log in and run programs on that computer. [2]

telnet client: A program that allows you to use telnet to access a remote host. The telnet client connects to the remote host and then begins to act like (emulate) a terminal. [2]

terabyte: A unit of measurement used for computer memory and data storage, 1,099,511,627,776 (2^{40}) bytes. Informally, a terabyte is about 1,000,000,000,000 (a trillion) bytes. Abbreviated as TB. [3]

terminal: The hardware used to access a remote host via telnet. In the olden days, people would use terminals that had a keyboard, a screen, and possibly a mouse. Today, we use a PC to run a program (called a telnet client) that makes the PC act like (emulate) an old-fashioned terminal. [2]

text: Data consisting of characters such as the letters of the alphabet, numbers, punctuation, and so on. [2, 13]

texture: Same as a **skin**. [10]

thread:
1. With respect to email, a sequence of mail messages relating to the same subject, each message (except the first) being a reply to one of the previous messages. [5]
2. On Usenet, a sequence of related articles consisting of an original article, replies to that article, and all subsequent replies. [13]

tilde: The ~ character (pronounced "til-duh"), used within a Unix pathname to indicate the home directory of a particular user. [4]

title bar: Within a window, a bar at the top of the window that contains descriptive information about the contents of the window. [7]

topic: Within an IRC channel, a short description of the purpose of that channel. [8]

[X] indicates the chapter or appendix in which the term is defined.

top-level domain: The most general domains—com, edu, au, ca, and so on—comprising the organizational domains and the geographical domains. [4]

traffic: A measure of the average number of messages sent to a mailing list. Same as **volume**. [14]

troll: To scan a large amount of ever-changing data, looking for a specific type of information. For example, spammers use programs that troll Web pages and Usenet newsgroups looking for mail addresses. [6]

Undernet: One of the large IRC networks. The others are EFnet, DALnet and IRCnet. [8]

undo: When using the clipboard, to reverse the action of the most recent copy, cut or paste operation. [17]

uniform resource locator: Same as **URL**. [4]

uninstall: To follow a specific procedure in order to remove an installed program from your computer. [9]

unpack: To process an archive so as to reconstruct the original files stored within the archive. [9]

unsubscribe:
1. Within Usenet, to indicate to your newsreader that it should remove a specific newsgroup from the list of groups you read. [13]
2. With respect to a mailing list, to tell a mailing list program that you no longer want to receive copies of messages sent to the list. [14]

unzip: To unpack a zip file. [9]

up: Describes a computer or communication link that is currently working. [1]

upload: To copy a file from your computer to another computer. [2]

uppercase: Describes the capital letters of the alphabet (A, B, C, D...). Compare to **lowercase**. [4]

upstream: Describes the transmission of data from your computer to the Internet. [3]

URL: (uniform resource locator) A formal specification used to identify specific Internet resources. In particular, URLs are used to identify Web pages. [4]

Usenet: A worldwide system of discussion groups. Same as **the News, Netnews**. [2, 13]

Usenet search engine: A search engine devoted to searching a database in which the contents of all the Usenet newsgroups are archived. [11]

UT: (Universal Time) One of the names for the principal time zone used as an international standard. Equivalent to UTC and GMT. [B]

UTC: (Coordinated Universal Time) One of the names for the principal time zone used as an international standard. Equivalent to UT and GMT. [B]

V.90: The standard used by 56K bps modems to send and receive data. V.90 replaced two older, obsolete standards: K56Flex and X2. Pronounced "vee-dot-90". [3]

vertical scroll bar: A scroll bar at the far right of a window, used to scroll the contents of the window up and down. [7]

video capture board: An adapter that, when installed in your computer and connected to a video camcorder, allows you to create copies of individual video frames and store them as image files on your computer. [15]

virtual: Describes objects and experiences that exist only on the Net or on your computer. [2, 9]

virus: A small program designed to insert itself into a file containing another program, becoming active when that program runs. [12]

virus hoax: An erroneous belief or rumor that a particular virus, perhaps nonexistent, is a potential source of trouble. Virus hoaxes spread by mail and in discussion groups when well-meaning people warn other people about nonexistent problems. [12]

voice chat: A talk facility that allows you to communicate with other people using voice (regular talking). [8]

volume: A measure of the average number of messages sent to a mailing list. Same as **traffic**. [14]

[X] indicates the chapter or appendix in which the term is defined.

wav: (waveform data) A file type used to store the basic sound files used by Windows. [10]

[the] **Web**: Part of the Internet, a global information delivery system used to display various types of data and to provide access to a variety of services. To access the Web, you use a client program called a browser. [2, 7]

Web chat room: On the Web, a facility allowing a group of people to talk to one another by typing messages. Same as **chat room**. [2, 8]

Web page: On the Web, the information that is displayed from a file containing hypertext. [2, 7]

Web page editor: A program used to create, modify and maintain Web pages. [15]

Web ring: A collection of Web sites organized into a loop such that, from any Web site in the ring, you can follow links to move forward or backward so as to traverse the entire ring. [11]

Web server: A computer that stores Web pages and makes them available to anyone with access to that computer. [2, 7]

Web site: A group of related Web pages, maintained by a person or organization. [2, 7]

webcam: A special video camera that, when connected to your computer, let's people watch you as you talk with them. [2, 7]

website: Same as **Web site**. [2, 7]

welcome message: A message that is sent automatically to new subscribers of a mailing list. [14]

whiteboard: Within a talk facility, a feature that allows people to collaborate by drawing within a shared window. [8]

whitelist: As used by filtering software, a list of Web sites to which the software will allow access. [12]

whois: A service, provided by a registrar, that allows you to look at some of the registration information related to a particular domain name. You can use whois to see if a specific domain name has already been registered. [16]

Windows:
> **1.** A family of operating systems (master control programs) used to run PCs. Windows was developed by Microsoft. [3]
> **2.** Informally, a member of the Windows family, such as Windows 98. [3]

Windows Explorer: The program used to manage files and directories within Windows 95 and Windows 98. [4]

[the] **World Wide Web**: An old system that was the predecessor of the Web. [2]

wysiwyg editor: A Web page editor that allows you to work directly with the elements of a Web page—text, pictures, tables, and so on— without having to concern yourself with the writing HTML. The name "wysiwyg" (pronounced "whiz-ee-whig") stands for "what you see is what you get". Compare to **HTML editor**. [15]

Yahoo: A particular search engine having an emphasis on organizing the content of the Web according to categories. [11]

zip drive: A disk drive that uses removable hard disk cartridges. The name comes from a particular brand of removable hard disk made by the Iomega company. [3]

zip file: An archive using the "zip" format. Zip files have an extension of `zip`, for example, `harley.zip`, and must be unpacked by a special program called a zip file program. [9]

zip file program: A program that provides the service of unpacking zip files. [9]

zone: Within the Internet Explorer security system, one of several categories into which you can classify Web sites. [12]

Index

H

J-K

S

S/MIME (Secure MIME), 9
safe call, 196
safety. *See* security
saving
 files when downloading programs, 207-208
 images from Web pages, 347
 URLs, 162-164
scanners, 346
scanning images, 346
schemes (URLs), 82-83
Schroeder, Sandra, xxiv, xxvi-xxvii
sci (Usenet hierarchy), 290, 292
scroll bars, 152
scrolling in windows, 152
Search Assistant (Internet Explorer), 238-239,
 375-376
search engines, 231-233. *See also* Search
 Assistant; searches
 accessing quickly, 237
 specifying for Internet Explorer address bar
 searches, 376
 tips for using, 233-235
 Usenet, 235-237
 Web sites, promoting, 353-354
searches. *See also* search engines
 directly from browsers, 240-242
 for mail addresses, 132-134, 380
 starting, 230
 tips for, 248-249
 Usenet, 308-309
 Web rings, 247
second-level domains, 74
secure connections, 256-257
Secure MIME (S/MIME), 9
Secure Sockets Layer (SSL), 256
security, 252. *See also* privacy; viruses
 ActiveX, 261-262
 children, safety precautions on Internet, 274-279
 cookies, 257-259
 DCC (Direct Client to Client connection), 188
 downloading data, 259-260
 filtering software, 277-279
 Internet connections, 256-257
 Internet Explorer security zones, 262-264
 Java, 260-261
 personal information, sending over the Web,
 252-254
 warning messages, 255
security certificates, 264
security levels, 263

selecting
 data in windows, 367
 domain names, 358-359
 mail programs, 99-100
 ISPs, 59-61
 theme of Web page, 332, 348
 Web site hosts, 350-353
self-control in Internet usage, 16
selling geographical top-level domains, 70-71
sending
 articles (Usenet), 305-308
 copies of Web pages, 165-166
 personal information over the Web, security of,
 252-254
 private messages on IRC, 186
 URLs in mail messages, 165
sending mail messages
 to groups, 131-132
 to yourself, 123-124
Sent Items folder (mail programs), 110
separate mail addresses, 120-121
servers, 6-7. *See also* mail servers; news servers
 DNS, 78-79
 FTP, 29
 hosting Web sites, 350-353
 instant messaging, 173
 IRC, 182
 list servers, 316
 name servers, 77-78
 NNTP servers, 287
 root name servers, 77
 talk facilities, 171
 types of, 36
 Web servers, 25, 141
 whois servers, 359-360
sex, Net sex, 197-198
shareware, 206
sharing
 mail addresses, 120-121
 music files, 223-224
 Web pages, 165-166
shortcuts to Web pages, creating, 160-161.
 See also keyboard shortcuts
shouting
 in mail messages, 126
 in talk facilities, 180
signatures, 101, 299
 articles (Usenet), 298-299
 mail messages, 101, 108-109
 Outlook Express, creating, 378-379
Simple Mail Transfer Protocol (SMTP), 9, 95-96
sites (Web). *See* Web sites

V

W